THE CHAIN OF THINGS

signale
modern german letters, cultures, and thought

Series editor: Peter Uwe Hohendahl, Cornell University

Signale: Modern German Letters, Cultures, and Thought publishes new English-language books in literary studies, criticism, cultural studies, and intellectual history pertaining to the German-speaking world, as well as translations of important German-language works. *Signale* construes "modern" in the broadest terms: the series covers topics ranging from the early modern period to the present. *Signale* books are published under a joint imprint of Cornell University Press and Cornell University Library in electronic and print formats. Please see http://signale.cornell.edu/.

THE CHAIN OF THINGS

*Divinatory Magic and the Practice
of Reading in German Literature
and Thought, 1850–1940*

ERIC DOWNING

A Signale Book

CORNELL UNIVERSITY PRESS AND CORNELL UNIVERSITY LIBRARY
ITHACA AND LONDON

Cornell University Press and Cornell University Library gratefully
acknowledge the College of Arts & Sciences, Cornell University,
for support of the Signale series.

First published 2018 by Cornell University Press and
Cornell University Library

Printed in the United States of America

Library of Congress Cataloging-in-Publication Data

Names: Downing, Eric, author.
Title: The chain of things : divinatory magic and the practice of reading
   in German literature and thought, 1850–1940 / Eric Downing.
Description: Ithaca : Cornell University Press, 2018. | Series:
   Signale : modern German letters, cultures, and thought | Includes
   bibliographical references and index.
Identifiers: LCCN 2017060430 (print) | LCCN 2017061791 (ebook) |
   ISBN 9781501715938 (pdf) | ISBN 9781501715921 (epub/mobi) |
   ISBN 9781501715907 | ISBN 9781501715907 (cloth ; alk. paper) |
   ISBN 9781501715914 (pbk. ; alk. paper)
Subjects: LCSH: German literature—19th century—History and
   criticism. | German literature—20th century—History and criticism. |
   Books and reading—Germany—History—19th century. | Books and
   reading—Germany—History—20th century. | Divination in literature.
   | Magic in literature. | Aesthetics, German—19th century. | Aesthetics,
   German—20th century.
Classification: LCC PT345 (ebook) | LCC PT345 .D69 2018 (print) |
   DDC 830.9/008—dc23
LC record available at https://lccn.loc.gov/2017060430

For Chris, magic reader

Was nie geschrieben wurde, lesen.

Hugo von Hofmannsthal

CONTENTS

Acknowledgments xi

Introduction 1

1. Painting Magic in Keller's *Green Henry* 36

2. Speaking Magic in Fontane's *The Stechlin* 121

3. Reading Magic in Walter Benjamin 202

Notes 271

Works Cited 327

Index 339

Acknowledgments

One of the several threads running throughout this study concerns the connective quality of reading at its most magical. That holds, too, for the writing of this book, whose most lasting joy has been the weave of relations that supported it. Such connecting influences shaping a text most often remain hidden. It is my pleasure to make them manifest here.

I owe special thanks to Christopher Wild. Almost all of the ideas and readings making up this text were worked through during walks and talks together among the trees and mountains of North Carolina, over dinner tables and conference tables, and over phone lines and email exchanges. His intellectual friendship meant that this project was never a solitary one, and always a happy one. I owe special thanks, too, to Derek Collins, whose scholarship, correspondence, and encouragement were crucial to launching the earliest stages of this project: it couldn't have begun without his guidance. And I owe most special thanks to Catriona MacLeod, who read drafts, early and late, of every chapter, gave invaluable feedback, and, most essentially, brought the magic of her friendship and support to bear on the undertaking as a whole. I've been very fortunate in my friends.

Many other colleagues and friends read or heard portions of this book and provided useful criticism. I would like especially to single out Leslie Adelson, Ruth von Bernuth, Rory Bradley, Lindsey Brandt, Paul Fleming, Mary Floyd-Wilson, Kata Gellen, Eva Geulen, Willi Goetschel, Jason Groves, John Hamilton, Martha Helfer, Jonathan Hess, Peter Hohendahl, Brook Holmes, Dania Hueckmann, David Jenkins, Andrea Krauß, Alice Kuzniar, Dick Langston, Michael Levine, Pablo Maurette, John McGowan, Helmut Müller-Sievers, Thomas Pfau, Inga Pollman, Jim Porter, Jaine Rice, Anette Schwarz, John H. Smith, Lauren Stone, Elisabeth Strowick, Christian Thomas, Jane Thrailkill, and Gabriel Trop. I need to thank, too, my students at both the University of North Carolina and in the Carolina-Duke Graduate Program in German Studies for listening patiently and responding so insightfully to many of the ideas behind this study in their most inchoate form.

Audiences at the University of Chicago, Cornell, Duke, and Johns Hopkins University all heard parts of this work and provided their encouragement and criticism. I am especially grateful to those whose invitations made those occasions possible. I thank, too, the Institute for the Arts and Humanities at the University of North Carolina for a semester's leave to help lay the groundwork of this project, and the members of the seminar at the Institute that accompanied that leave. Thanks are also due to the editors of the Signale series who helped steer this work to publication, Peter Hohendahl, Mahinder Kingra, Marian Rogers, and Kizer Walker, as well as to the anonymous readers who reviewed the manuscript for Cornell University Press. Their advice was very helpful, and this book is clearly better for it.

Finally, first and last, my thanks to my family. To my mother, to whom I dedicate this work, and to Nancy and Jessica, the binding magic in my world.

Portions of the introduction and of chapter 3 originally appeared in print, in different form, as "Magic Reading," in *Literary Studies and the Pursuits of Reading*, edited by Eric Downing, Jonathan M. Hess, and Richard Benson (Rochester, NY: Camden House, 2012), 189–215. Part of chapter 1 was published, in different form, as "Binding Magic in Keller's *Der Grüne Heinrich*," *Germanic Review* 90 (Fall 2015): 156–170; part of chapter 3 as "Divining Benjamin: Reading Fate, Graphology, Gambling," *MLN German Issue* 126, no. 3 (2011): 561–580, © 2011 Johns Hopkins University Press; and a German version of part of chapter 2 as "Sprachmagie, Stimmung, und Geselligkeit in Theodor Fontanes *Der Stechlin*," in *Herausforderungen des Realismus: Theodor Fontanes Gesellschaftsromanen*, edited by Peter Hohendahl and Ulrike Vedder (Breisgau: Rombach, forthcoming). I gratefully acknowledge these journals and presses and their editors for their permission to include these pieces in revised form in the present study.

THE CHAIN OF THINGS

Introduction

"Wie verketten sich die Dinge?"[1]

Near the end of his 1929 essay on surrealism, and in the context of serious discussions of the occult, Walter Benjamin declares that "the most passionate investigation of telepathic phenomenon will not teach us half as much about reading (which is an eminently telepathic phenomenon) as the profane illumination of reading will teach us about telepathic phenomena."[2] The suggested link here between practices of reading and the occult is a profound one, both historically and for Benjamin's own time and work, and not just in terms of telepathy. Some of the earliest practices of reading were not of letters, words, or books, but of stars, entrails, and birds, and these practices had a significant impact on the way literature was read and understood in the ancient world. And the relations between such ancient magic and the reading of literature were still (or again) of crucial importance to the modernists of the early twentieth century, including Benjamin; and perhaps more surprisingly, they were just as important to the realists of the mid- to late nineteenth century, precisely those artists usually imagined as most distant from such practices and concerns.

In this study I intend to explore some of the more salient connections between the practices of reading and magic during the realist and modernist periods in German literature and thought, with a particular focus on the magic most closely aligned with practices of divination. I concentrate on those aspects of magic most associated with divination for two reasons. First, because practices of divination seem historically most associated with the reading of literature, and this future- or fortune-telling dimension remains an underappreciated aspect of our own reading practice, one rarely considered in its impact on modern aesthetics, even of the most realist of works. But second, I focus on divination because it engages a closely related issue of particular importance to the period here addressed, namely, the issue of futurity itself, and primarily as it fared in the transition from realism to modernism during the long turn of the nineteenth to the twentieth century: both the different ways that the future figured in the reading of texts during this period, and the evident (or apparently evident) fading of its force as a narrative determinant or article of historical faith at the same moment. Posing the problem of the future during this time as one of reading—not just of texts but of the world—invites inquiry not only into traditions of divination but also into the model of the world that supported them. And as we'll see, this involves tracing out the genealogy and fate of a "sympathetic" world order that, in ancient and premodern times, allowed for future reading and that, in the realist and modernist periods, underwent significant transformations that accompanied the changing shape of reading, magic, and the future in German art and thought.

My investigation into these concerns proceeds in three basic stages. After this introduction, I engage in readings of three major authors situated at different critical moments along this time span: Gottfried Keller, writing near the beginning of so-called poetic realism as it emerges out of romanticism; Theodor Fontane, whose so-called social realism extends up to the late 1890s, and so to the very edge of modernism; and finally, Walter Benjamin, whose cultural studies fall firmly within the modernist period itself. Keller presents us with a midcentury *Bildungsroman*, firmly grounded in a fairly traditional faith in temporal progress and development, and working toward a transformation of a "romantic" conception of both the human subject and the world into a realist one; Fontane offers *Gesellschaftsromanen* that come increasingly to lose faith in temporal progress, both narratively and historically, and so, too, to question realist aesthetics; and Benjamin provides inquiries into contemporary German culture at a moment when time itself has become convoluted, speculation into the future all but banned, realist conceptions of both character and world abandoned, and an ancient, primitive world newly and problematically reascendant. Not coincidentally, these same works also show the transformation—rather unique to the German tradition—of so-called *Naturphilosophie* into *Lebensphilosophie*, with a crucial dislocation during the realist period. As we'll see, these changes to the understanding of human relations to the nonhuman world closely track the changing face of time and the future in both German literature and thought. But, as we'll also see, through all these changes and throughout this period, magic and magic reading, with a special emphasis on divination, remain absolutely central forces and practices, securing the most crucial links between the governing notions of time, world, the "real," and art.

This art itself will take different shapes in the different works, extending beyond just literature to encompass the art of realist painting in Keller, of social conversation in Fontane, and the art of reading per se in Benjamin. But in every case, magic and magic reading will remain center stage, both for characters within the texts and for us as readers of the texts.

This introduction also proceeds in three stages. After a few additional orienting points, it begins by drawing extensively on work by Derek Collins and Peter Struck to trace out some of the early history of magical and divinatory reading and how these come to inform—even determine—key aspects of reading literature in the Western tradition, from classical antiquity up through the early modern era and into the early nineteenth century. It then offers some general consideration of magic reading and the novel, with a focus on the mid- to late nineteenth-century tradition that eventually yields to modernism. And it closes with a brief look at the changing shape of the "sympathetic" world order during the period covered by this study, an order that, I claim, undergirds understandings of both the world and art, and with them, of both magic and divination.

Magic Reading

I do not begin with a definition of magic any more than with one of literature, but I will set down some of the basic features shared by magic and divination, particularly those that most suggest the connection with reading per se. Most obviously, both magic and divination represent ancient discourses, systems, even theories of representation and signification that run alongside—and not only alongside—those of both ordinary language and literature. More-over, their discourses of signification always share two related features: they are consistently conceived as ancillary, parasitic, or sim-ply attendant upon other more ordinary systems of signification, producing meanings in excess of those established by more normal semantic systems; and as part of this, both magic and divination point to or posit another hidden world beyond the apparent one, a world whose signs require special interpretation or manipulation in order to manifest themselves in this one.

While these two features overlap and complement each other, they also have different implications for my investigation. The fact that magic and divination present autonomous but never exclu-sive systems of meaning—such that, for example, even in primitive cultures magic readings of the world do not preclude other, more scientific or rational modes—this reminds us that, for all its inelim-inable uniqueness (it will never not be there), magic reading always takes place in the context of other, equally viable and active read-ing practices, and is even always in complex, interactive, dependent relation with them.

The second feature, the posited hidden other world in need of interpretation for access to its secrets, is one of the most tick-lish aspects of magic and divinatory readings. It is clearly one of the reasons for their perpetual status, even in ancient times, as suspect—for it must be said that, for all that magic is never not there and is impossible to dismiss, it is also always open to dismissal, just because it deals with what is not there. The source of its power is also that of its fragility. This feature is of course shared by other ancient discourses, including medicine, whose early diagnostic procedures were clearly allied with both magic and divination, and like them dealt with an often mystified world of hidden causes: coming out of the nineteenth century and into our own present day, both "alternative" medical practices such as homeopathy and psychoanalysis also posit such unseen causal worlds, and so, too, invite their questioning.[3] In the case of literature, even when approached not from a psychoanalytic perspective but from the driest of narratological vantages, the existence of this hidden other world and its agency (its well-nigh divine authority and intentions) is more readily, even universally granted. It is what in this study is called its metatextual dimension.

For all its general acceptance, considering this metatextual aspect of literary discourse in terms of both magic and divination casts its other world in a less familiar light, and helps account for why literature remains what Michel Foucault called one of the last retreats and occasions for magic in the modern world.[4] In the case of magic, this hidden world is regularly imagined to be peopled not only by divine (possibly demonic) authorities, but also by the dead, such as always to entail a certain commerce or communication with those dead. In the case of divination, this other world is imagined as always already prescribed, such as always to entail a certain traffic with a past that, in the reader's present, is still in the future tense.[5] In both cases, this hidden other world brings with it a temporal dimension that asserts itself more or less autonomously from the everyday objective realm and its time experience: the function of reading and interpretation is to access that other time experience and make it active in the present—which is to say, the otherness of this hidden world is in important ways a temporal one. Stephen Greenblatt is not alone in recognizing our own reading experience as still moved by a desire to speak with the dead, a temporal experience of pastness that accompanies independently our sequential reading practices: I wish to stress how reading the future, what Peter Brooks calls the promises and annunciations of reading, is equally part of this experience.[6]

Two additional features common to magic and divination with suggestive force for thinking about reading per se can be set out here at the outset. First, both begin in a sense by acting upon the wishes or responding to a demand of the audience or interpreter, who in turn expects to be affected, indeed benefited, by the response.[7] This could be called the hermeneutic dimension of magic (the posing of a question, the awaiting a reply), except that it is also something more, and that is what makes it magic. In every case, a self and its future are at stake, and are invested in the procedure in a way that exceeds the subject/object relation—not least because what is sought in or asked of the engaged object or event is intrinsic to the self. This is perhaps more obviously true of divination but also holds for magic: in both cases, reading is predicated on what the anthropologist Lucien Lévy-Bruhl and the psychologist C. G. Jung would call mystical participation, which includes an identification with the object and the hidden dimension that endows it with force and makes it a sign.[8] This feature is clearly allied with Walter Benjamin's notion of the mimetic faculty (his idea that we are dislocated [*entstellt*] by our participation in everything around us), as well as Roland Barthes's Lacanian model of fragmenting imaginary reading (his "That's me!").[9] But the main points for our beginning purposes are these: magic's signification is inseparable from identification, which in turn is deeply invested in divining the self; and magic reading is an *occasional* reading, responding to a particular, even if unformulated, initiating wish or demand on the part of its audience or interpreter. The first point requires that there always be a porous boundary between subjects and their object world, a dispersed sense of participation in their reading practices; the second that, as Benjamin always insisted, the future, fortune seeking of reading remain indissolubly bound to both a special moment and an idea of happiness (*Glück* in all its senses).[10]

The second additional feature of both magic and divination to be stressed here at the outset is how both are steeped in a reading logic based on analogy and similarity, a logic that is key to understanding their peculiar modes of both signification and identificatory participation. Adumbrated in E. B. Tylor's *The Origins of Culture*, James G. Frazer's *The Golden Bough* most famously identified this logic with what Frazer called *sympathetic* magic, and he distinguished between two types of its associational thought: homeopathic or imitative logic, based on the association of ideas through resemblance; and contagious logic, based on the association of ideas and objects through contact or contiguity.[11] Each of these terms will need elaboration: "sympathy" has quite specific connotations within the historical tradition I intend to trace out, connotations that ground both the significatory and the identificatory practices of Western magic reading. And "homeopathic" and "contagious" already suggested to Roman Jakobson his own Saussurian distinctions between the metaphorical and metonymical axes of language as well as Freud's between condensation and displacment, distinctions that have come deeply to inform both literary and psychoanalytical readings.[12]

As noted, more anon, but it is already worth mentioning how, when thinking about magic reading, these two types of magical thought—the imitative and the contiguous—are just as likely to be contrasted as combined, with the one suggesting the meaning created via mimesis (resemblance) and the other that more properly created via relation (*Beziehung* or *Verhältnis*). Max Horkheimer and Theodor Adorno focused on the magic of the former, that of mimesis; I will mostly be concentrating on the latter, on relation and what Samuel Coleridge called the connective powers of our understanding.[13] Tylor defined magic as "the mistaking of an ideal connexion for a real one, the confusion of ineffective analogy with effective cause": one of the implicit goals of this study is to question the distinction in his first clause, and to reimagine the non-causal effect in his second.[14]

One final preliminary point. One of the major distinctions between magic and divination is that while the latter purports only to read the presented signs, and so to anticipate the future in a more or less passive way, the former actively achieves its future effect (and fortune). As valid as this distinction sometimes is, it is also to be contested, especially in the specific context of reading: another goal of this study and its exploration of magic reading will in fact be to emphasize the active performative dimension and force of such divinatory reading, especially with respect to futurity.[15]

Divination in the Ancient World

In Aeschylus's *Prometheus Bound*, when Prometheus enumerates the many crafts he contrived for mortals, chief among these are the gifts of seercraft (*mantikē*), and chief among these are three arts of divinatory reading: of entrails, birds, and chance words and co-incidences (kledonomancy).[16] Of these, entrail reading (extispicy) seems to have been the most established in the ancient world, in terms of both its cultural standing and its interpretive procedures: unlike many other forms of divinatory reading, it seems always to have been practiced by a trained professional.[17] As Collins explains, this reader would have been guided by two factors: by fixed points of reference with "objective" meaning on the entrails themselves, such as we see on the many so-called model livers that survive from antiquity (but also including size, shape, color, and smoothness); and by tacit signals and contextual connections between these points and the moment of the interpretation itself that help to establish an overall meaning.[18] That is, entrail reading was both rule-bound by established, systematized norms and criteria, and open to association, individualized and responsive to the particular occasion and reader.

Although several internal organs were accepted sites for divinatory reading, Collins notes that the liver was the privileged one among the Greeks and Romans, primarily because it was considered the locus of emotions (especially desire, fear, anger, and anxiety), in complex relation to the faculties of reason. The primary such relation was that it was independent of intellect, the same reason animal livers were used, not human: liver reading was thought to concentrate on what we would call the nonrational, even animalistic realm, as the conveyor of a truth that could run counter to rational deliberation, such as the expert judgment of a military adviser to proceed with a campaign.[19] Its magic reading was aimed at what we could call the unconscious and its truth, its subtext—but an unconscious that was not so much (or only) part of the human as it was of the natural world, or rather, of the world humans shared with nature.

A closely related reason for the practice of extispicy was that it was through the liver, not the intellect, that the gods were thought to communicate with men—to some extent, precisely because, as the seat of the emotions, it was not subject to the interference of the intellect, of the registered intents and signified responses of human consciousness. This is the same reason why animal, not human, livers were employed: since animals themselves have no future consciousness—and especially no anticipatory response to impending death or danger—their own conscious expectations would not mark livers in ways that might be mistaken for divine signs.[20] This yields something of a double paradox for this form of reading, in which intellection interferes with the desired intelligence, and future knowing with knowing the future. In any case, the liver was chosen as the site for divinatory reading because it was the seat both of subrational emotions and of the superrational divine, which is to say, of signs produced not by the conscious subject but by some "other" authority—an authority or force both residual in natural things and capable of divinely communicating through things.

The principle by which the gods were thought to communicate through the signs of the liver was that of analogy, grounded in the ancient belief in the connections between the microcosmic and macrocosmic realms and mediated by the force that Frazer, and more importantly the Stoics and Neoplatonists, came to call *sympatheia*, a sense of participation in a common *logos* that connects all parts of nature by contact and likeness. For example, in the case of the so-called Piacenza model liver, its outer edge was divided into sixteen parts, each with the name of a divinity inscribed on it; these corresponded to the sixteen regions of the Etruscan sky, such that the liver mapped the heavens' astrology in microcosm.[21] The *mantis* would hold the liver up to the sky, properly oriented, and then read the intentions of the gods by matching up regions of the heavens (linked to the gods) and organ-text (joined to the sky), and then matching these in turn to the boding events of the human world—with this last step in particular opening space for improvisation and selection (as to what counts as similar to what).[22] In this way, the liver played a key role in bridging between cosmic and human affairs through a linked chain of analogies whose connections were secured by a hidden, unified world made manifest by corresponding likenesses. Crucially, this chain includes elements both seen and unseen in its drawing of the relations between the hidden divine realm and the realm of signs, whether astrologic or organic, and between the realm of signs and the hidden human future.

What we see in the example of extispicy, then, is that the most intimate connection to the other world, the most sure access to its secret truth and fate, is by reading the analogies that sign themselves in things (and I should add, animate things) below, beyond, or aside from ordinary perceptions and rational judgments, purposely bypassing the most exclusively human dimension of the world; but also that the primary guide for reading, and hence for drawing analogies, is the habit of making micro/macro connections, seeking the similarity between the present self and outside world. Both the exclusion and inclusion of the human are equally key components in the animation of the liver that transforms it into a sign (which is to say, text); both are equally key in charging the sign with its future—indeed, with the future that makes it a sign and underwrites its reading.

Collins shows that reading the birds, what Hesiod called *ornithas krinōn*, seems likewise to have operated according to a principle of analogy that linked together things (and again, animate things), the divine, and the human in a complex system of mutual mappings.[23] Unlike extispicy, it does not appear to have been limited to specially appointed practitioners—Odysseus or Helen is as qualified as Kalchas or Theoklymenos to make a reading—or to have had as established rules: augury seems to have brought divination more broadly into the everyday activity and experience of the shared world, no longer the exclusive practice of a marked-off expert. As a result, it was open to not only more readers but more readings as well, with a corresponding increase in the polysemy of its signs and possibly contested status of its conclusions, even apart from the contest with other deliberative modes.[24]

The procedure basically began with the projection of an aporetic occasion—one that stymied simple intellect or experience but with clear consequences for future fortune—out of the reader's human world onto the essentially chance activity of fowl. The projection would be grounded on conditions of analogy and coincidence that transformed the birds into signs or symbols: the assumption was that the projection (or dislocation) onto the unwilled, and so un-influenced, activity of the birds could reveal a clearer and more meaningful picture of the present human predicament than could be directly perceived; as with the detour through the animal liver, it was its nonhuman, indeed animal, identity that made it serve as a sign, indeed as an animate sign and of the human.[25] Again, there was also the belief that these animal signs, because free of human intention, were privileged conduits for the communication of another, invisible realm of divine will and authority, which is also what transformed them into signs: their double animation, by nature and the divine, would be conveyed by their movement. So as in the case of extispicy, the sign quality—which is to say, the reading—in augury proves a complex interaction between three realms: that of things (or texts); that of humans (or readers); and that of the divine (or authorial intent), with the animation of those signs derived from all three (inherent, projected, and communi-cated), but again in such a way that the distinctly human realm was both present and occluded from the equation (or perhaps better: dislocated and dispersed).[26]

Even more, the reading of signs in augury—and the same would hold for extispicy—was an equally complex interaction between three different times: between an event that had already happened and been recorded or experienced, that is, the omen to be read, always considered as a sui generis, particular occasion;[27] the un-decided present of the reader's condition, which every bit as much as the omen was a particular occasion in need of reading; and the future fortune, what was being augured forth by the past event to resolve the present one, and what was ostensibly actually being read.[28] It is, after all, this dimension that determines that significa-tion is a form not only of identification (through sympathy and analogy), but also of divination (and that divination is a reading of not only the divine but also what is to come), and as such intricately temporal—indeed that identification is itself a form of divination, and as such itself temporal. As Cicero insists in his *De divinatione* (our single most comprehensive ancient source), bird activity on its own and while it is happening is not a portent or sign, but only becomes so once it has happened and is made "like" some later (present) moment, a moment that transforms that past thing into a present sign, even as that sign (from the past) then functions to transform—which is to say, to read—the present in light of its signified future.[29] Magic, divinatory reading is thus staged at once between three realms and three times both in its production and reception of signs, and in its displacements and investments of the subject.[30]

The occasionality of divinatory reading, whether of birds or livers, is clearly conditioned by both these dimensions. In responding to a particular constellation of linked demands and sign-things, this form of reading depends on the successful and necessarily somewhat improvised alignment of both the different realms and the different times, and both in the one present instance of its immediate reading and then in the test of subsequent moments of future experience. In the first case, its magic is always to a large extent performative, its reading a mode of action and intimately bound to the immediate moment—but crucially a performance, action, and occasion heavy with, and kept empty by, a deferred futurity. In the second, that occasional reading exposes itself to the contingency of its own temporality, which can either fufill it or, even without negating the original reading, belatedly expose the omen to the consequences of its own polysemy.[31] In both cases, its reading takes place in a realm of exceptional power and peril, far beyond those of ordinary time- and place-bound experience, or for that matter far beyond that of ordinary deliberative or causal thought.

The inclusion of divinatory reading—and especially of augury—within ancient literature as a self-reflexive model for the reading of poetic texts themselves happens very early, and is already fully evident in Homer and the tragedians, as well as (a bit later) Virgil: we have the examples of Kalchas in the *Iliad*, Helen, Halitherses, and Theoklymenos in the *Odyssey*, Kalchas again in the *Agamemnon*, all reading bird signs; and then of dreams in the *Elektra*, oracles in *Oedipus Tyrannos*, and all manner of omens in the *Aeneid*, especially in Book 7—the list could easily be extended. On the one hand, this early inclusion emphasizes the parallel between the modes of reading in these two different realms: divination is from early on explicitly a part of the literary experience. On the other hand, the actual form of its inclusion also suggests that the parallel is never exclusive, that divinatory readings have to compete with other more "normal" and equally viable modes of reading; and also that they are not always successful. But in either case, the models of divinatory reading in the ancient texts do suggest to their audience particular modes of literary reading of the text itself. They suggest, for example, a mode of reading that is future driven, aimed at the predictive quality of present signs; one that looks elsewhere than at the intentions and expectations of the human characters for its most trusted clues; one that looks to similarity or analogy as a not quite causal but still transformative force that can override ordinary logic; one that is dependent on the coincidence of the occasion and the produced or recognized sign; and finally, a mode of reading that is always at risk, always open to dismissal or counter-readings, both concurrent and subsequent.[32] Even as the depiction of this mode of reading alerts its audience to the personal and projective dimension of all reading, it leads it to turn away from the purely (and fallible) human dimension of the text in its search for signs; even as it teaches readers to look for signs of future fortune in external things, to depend on those sign-things, it also leads them to recognize the unreliability of signs themselves.

The last form of ancient divinatory reading underscored by Aeschylus's Prometheus focuses on the reading of chance words and coincidences, so-called kledonomancy; and although it seems to have been the least rule-bound, the least requiring of specialized training, it seems also to have been the mode that ends up being the most productive as a model for reading literature—perhaps because it is also in many ways a model for divinatory reading itself. From earliest times, divination placed great weight on seemingly chance meetings, sounds, gestures, or utterances, either singly or in some kind of combination. Indeed, there was a special word for these things, words, or events happened upon: they were called *symbola*, the objects of a chance meeting.[33] The "symbolic" chance behind such instances was in a sense, and as we have come to expect from our previous examples, double. First, and I'll use the example of words, the word spoken or overheard needed to coincide with the particular occasion of the concerned subject, an occasion that introduced a new context for interpreting the word, a context that in some sense distorted, overlooked, or simply added to the ordinary meaning context of that word: and it was this coincidence—the joining of that with this—that made it a sign, or rather a particular kind of sign: a symbol.[34] Second, just because of the word's status as a coincidence, as occuring over and above the ordinary causality of its context, it was thought to be a vehicle for divine communication, for the manifestation of a super-rational, super-intentional meaning in the rational, intentional word: to be a sign, a symbol linking the divine and the everyday.

A famous example of this, cited by Struck from Pseudo-Plutarch in his *Life of Homer*, comes in Book 20 of the *Odyssey*, when Odysseus overhears the first servant he chanced to meet that morning uttering a general curse against the suitors, and he reads this as a sign of divine support, even guarantee, for his planned attack against them later that day.[35] It is, significantly, a sign that only he can read, one that is ancillary to or over and above the normal semantic meaning of the servant's words, whose ordinary meaning continues to function; and the reason Odysseus can read it is that it coincides with (is like, echoes, is in sympathy and contact with) his moment, his need, his occasion: the occasionality of this reading is an aspect of his participatory identification, which in turn makes the sign a divination (for him). It is this added occasion of Odysseus's personal need and fortune that dislodges the overheard word from its immediate embedded context and intent; and it is in turn this dislodging, the opening up of a nonintentional, nonimmediate space, that creates the room for divine communication. This mode of divinatory reading has its later descendants not only in the practice of Freudian slips, but also in *biblicae sortes*, the chance readings of biblical passages such as Augustine's conversion experience made famous—both forms of magic reading, the latter directly so.[36]

One consequence of this mode of divinatory reading that I want to call special attention to is how it comes to treat words as autonomous things, even animate things, like livers and birds. In availing itself of the "natural" sign, taking it out of its given context and adding to its inherent meaning, this magic form of reading turns language on the one hand into a surface for subject projection, and on the other into a vessel for divine projection, in both cases animating it with a life not strictly its own without depriving it of the life that is its own: a peculiarly oscillating process of thingification and animation that is inseparable from its magical status. This treating of utterances and words as autonomous, animate things exactly like livers or birds—which are themselves treated as utterances or words—is, we'll see, something that carries over into written language, where words can decompose into the materiality or activity of their letters, and where letters can become charged with autonomous significance in excess even of the words in which they find themselves. But more anon.

Interestingly, even as in Homer's poem Odysseus extracts (or extends) the words of the servant from their original context and applies them instead to his personal need, so in the ancient world there developed a tradition of extracting Homer's words from the poem itself and applying them to new "outside" contexts, new occasions, in ways that were likewise considered to have certain magic, divine effects. At its simplest, this practice could resemble that in the famous story of Empedokles, who chanted the lines from Book 4 of the *Odyssey* describing Helen's administration of *nepenthes* as a way of soothing (or more literally, charming) an enraged young man in his audience.[37] But as Collins has shown, the use of Homeric lines as magic charms extended far beyond this, loosening the words from their simple place and function in the poem to apply to some new extra-textual occasion (be it medicinal, erotic, or vengeful) through the same principles of analogy and coincidence operant for characters in the poem itself.[38] The sympathy or similarity of the Homeric verse with the "real-world" occasion

magically expanded the meaning and force of the verse far beyond
its represented realm—precisely because *sympatheia* was felt to be
an active organizing principle behind all things, poetic works and
world alike.

This truly magic tradition of reading Homer's (and not only
Homer's) verses outside of literature also became folded back
into literary reading itself. Readers accustomed to the extraliterary magic reading of Homeric verses would apply this same mode
of reading back into the poems themselves, imagining that certain
lines effective outside the poem had magical (esoteric) connotations in the poem as well, over and above their immediate meaning.[39] But traditions of magic and divination also came more directly and equally decisively to inform the reading of Homer (and
not only Homer) with the Neoplatonists and their allegorical or,
more properly, "symbolic" readings of ancient texts.

As Struck has shown, the Neoplatonists were critically instru-
mental in transforming the traditions of divinatory magic into formal strategies for the reading of literary texts, especially those of
Homer: and they did so in part by first formalizing the associational schemata of magical *sympatheia*. In the works of Iamblichus
and Proclus (echoing Greek magical papyri), specific chains or *seirai* of like things were identified by which the sympathetic force of
the divine emanated and communicated itself throughout nature,
linking, to give just one example, the divine One with the goddess
Athena, and then through her with the Platonic Form of the moon,
with the moon itself, with bulls, with vegetation, with silver, with
moonstones, and so on.[40] These celestial bodies, animals, plants,
minerals, and stones thus all became signs in an eminently readable
even if riddling world-text: all were considered *symbola* animated
with and joining up with the divine in ways that cut across ordinary classificatory systems, in ways largely hidden and only hinted
at by similarities. Crucially, these *seirai* linked not only visible material things but also, with them, invisible immaterial entities such
as Platonic Forms, souls, and, most importantly for us, words as
well, which were considered yet another and in some ways the last
link in the sympathetic chain, participant in the same ontology as
all things visible and invisible, and so, too, partaking of the same

associational play that linked things according to sympathetic resemblances quite apart from or alongside their normal representational or semantic function.

The Neoplatonic systematization of the associational schemata of magical *sympatheia* (adumbrated by the Stoics) also transformed the occasional, individual nature of such magic reading—transformed, but not eliminated. For although the formalized chains would seem to limit the free play of associational thought, these chains were also still hidden, open, and endless; they still required individual unriddling in the form of collection and decipherment by the inquiring reader (the double sense of both *legere* and *lesen*); and this reader still operated not on the basis of his strictly rational faculties, which were more or less useless in this context, nor on that of a codex that was perhaps posited but nonexistent, but rather on that of his own sympathetic participation, his own microcosmic self as a crucial link in the chain—or more accurately perhaps, on the basis of the active suggestiveness of the *symbola* themselves, to which the individual needed sympathetically to respond. But even more, the occasionality of the reading was preserved by the ritual context within which such symbolic magic took place, those rituals originally associated with the theurgy practiced by Neoplatonists. Although not perhaps motivated by the more narrow kinds of immediate needs or demands associated with extispicy, augury, or kledonomancy, theurgy still began with a demand on the part of the human inquirer, and still aimed at divining the future. As Struck describes it, the "reader" would approach a statue of the god—which was not just a representation of the god, but rather through the chain of sympathetic linkages via resemblances was actually animated, even inhabited, by the god—and insert into specified slots tokens, *symbola*, of a sympathetic material (e.g., moonstone for Athena) and inscribed with appropriate signs or "characters": the insertion would complete the "symbolic" sympathetic connection, and the divine would communicate the future to the human subject through the chain of signs.[41]

Neoplatonic readings of literature reproduced in their versions of texts the same basic conditions that were operant in their version of the natural world and their theurgic rituals.[42] Again, there were chains, *seirai*, that stretched from the divine One through various links, including the divine Homer, down through various realms of increasingly material signification, and eventually into the actual words of Homer's poems, and through those words connecting the reader back up the chain to that divine One—the model for this chain being that described by Plato himself in the *Ion*.[43] Crucially, the words or passages that were signed by this hidden order of meaning, the "seeds" scattered throughout the material and obvious world of the epic and its language, were precisely those that seemed to run counter to the normative logic of the rest of the poem. Without denying or negating the surface sense of such words and passages, the Neoplatonists identified them—exactly like specific plants, animals, or stones—as *symbola*, animated with and joining up with the divine in ways that defied the ordinary diegetic or mimetic dimension of the text, and signifying their meaning in mostly hidden ways only reached via sympathetic analogical thought that could follow up and along the chain of similarities. It is through the Neoplatonists that the more modern notion of the literary "symbol" comes down to us, as well as the practice of what becomes known not as symbolic but rather allegorical reading; a practice originally as fully steeped in magic and divination as extispicy and augury, and yielding much the same effect as the reinsertion of Homeric charms into the reading of the epics themselves.

Novel Divinations

According to Foucault in *The Order of Things*, this magic reading of the world and texts persists in the Western tradition up through the seventeenth century, when, he claims, a major epistemic shift occurs that henceforth dominates and displaces it.[44] The world he describes before that moment is, however, one instantly recognized as extending the genealogy we've traced, especially in its Neoplatonist configuration—something we see in Benjamin's writings on the baroque as well. Magic, Foucault says, was still a required *form* in the early modern era, inherent in the very way of knowing, prescribing a divinatory way of reading both the world and texts, organized by the principles of sympathy, analogy, likeness, and contiguity (Benjamin calls it allegory); with chains of similitude connecting both the visible and the invisible forms of the world, and linking the microcosm of the reader with the macrocosm of objects and the hidden world behind them, the world that gave them meaning. Foucault speaks of the secret "signatures" of things that pointed via similitudes—or rather, chains of similitudes—to a meaning beyond their immediate being, to the "something else" that made all the world and texts at once both readable and riddling, and made so by the very resemblances the world endlessly suggested. Most importantly for us, he describes this divinatory reading as still future driven, "wholly intent on what it will have said," as motivated by what he calls the "promise of reading": the promise that the desired revelation of the future (what Benjamin calls fate) will come *through* reading.[45]

Of course, Foucault also claims that magic reading eventually came to an end with this period, that there emerged soon after "a new arrangement in which we are still caught," which changed forever our understanding of both things in the world and their relation to language, such that there is now, for us, nothing that recalls that earlier way—nothing, says Foucault, except literature.[46] But that claim is easily contested, or at least qualified, and perhaps especially in the German context. As Pierre Hadot shows, the Neoplatonist worldview continued to exert a profound influence on the German romantics at the end of the eighteenth century, perhaps especially in the form of Novalis's "magic idealism" and Friedrich Schelling's *Naturphilosophie*, about which we'll have more to say in the following section.[47] And as Benjamin shows, drawing on his own Neoplatonist and romantic influences, magic and magic reading again played a major role a century later in the modernist period, and again in ways not restricted to literature. But as stated at the outset, magic reading and the world that supports it also persist in the intervening mid- to late nineteenth century, during the realist period, in which Foucault's "new arrangement" would seem most fully and incontestably to have arrived—and not yet departed.

In the next section of this introduction I will consider some of the extraliterary conditions supporting magic and divinatory reading during the realist period; but before that I'd like to sketch out some of the most general ways that magic reading figures specifically in its literature, the one area Foucault himself allows as still embedded in the older, magical mode of thinking and being. The paradox, of course, is that the literature at stake here is (and self-identifies as) "realist," in ways that would seem to exclude such magic. But it is just that assumption that needs questioning; and somewhat ironically, this requires questioning both some Foucauldian critics and Benjamin. For these two hugely influential scholars of early modern aesthetics also helped define realism in ways that exclude the earlier tradition they themselves helped make visible, and this in spite of Foucault's own caveat and Benjamin's studies of nineteenth-century allegory. I wish to show how it still persists.

Perhaps the most telling place for the continued functioning of magic reading in the new literary order is in the relations therein between objects and people—which is to say, in how objects can and should be read as signs of the human world and, even more, as signs communicating authorial truth about the human world and, as part of that, offering intimations, indeed promises, of future fortune.[48] Speaking of realist art in a slightly different context, Roland Barthes describes how "objects are accepted inducers of associations . . . or, in a more obscure way, are veritable symbols," adding, "Objects no longer perhaps possess a *power*, but they certainly possess meanings."[49] But of course, in literature at least, meaning can *be* a power, transforming things into signs, and signs into forces affecting human lives and future fates.

These relations and forces are, I believe, especially evident in novels, not least because of their temporal extensivity and usual depth of material settings; and they are even especially so in realist novels of the mid-nineteenth century, with their heavy investment in objects and collections, in hidden authors who communicate only from behind the represented world, and in causal, sequential, end-driven plots. In her seminal study, *How Novels Think*, Nancy Armstrong explores some of these relations, focusing on how objects function to convey meaning about the human in novels of this period.[50] Her claim, however—an exemplary one—is that realist fiction aims at *surmounting* the magical thinking that attributes excess meaning and mysterious power to things beyond ourselves, as an essential part of the novels' training the given subject to assume a self-contained individuality limited to the norms of rational bourgeois society. The argument clearly elaborates on Foucault's model for the "new arrangement" in which modern subjects are caught, extending it into the one area Foucault himself described as still exempt; and it just as clearly echoes a Benjaminian position that also opposes novel reading to earlier, more magical ones, and equates it instead with an ideal of bourgeois rationality.[51]

There is considerable truth to this argument, and it plays an important part in my own. But it also needs to be balanced by that of Roman Jakobson, who reminds us how realist novels produce their meaning by establishing metonymical chains that necessarily link the protagonist to the nonhuman world of objects, animals, and so on (and on). To paraphrase Jakobson's own example, the novel will link its protagonist's emotion to the impatience of his horse, the swaying of nearby trees, and the sudden flight of a bird on the occasion of his anxious approach to the closed door of his future fortune.[52] In large part, this is how realist novels teach us to read as part and parcel of their thingification of the world: they teach us to look for meaning in the signs of resemblance and sympathy between the human and the nonhuman world, and especially to regard the perceived coincidences and correspondences that cannot be attributed to human intention as privileged conduits for authorial communication. And this is especially the case in the absence of direct authorial communication that becomes ever more prevalent in nineteenth-century fiction. As Barthes says, the authorial meaning "somehow 'emerges' from all these signifying units [i.e., things] which are nonetheless 'captured' as though the scene were immediate and spontaneous, that is to say, without signification."[53] A hidden world of shaping forces manifests itself in the disparate objects of the narrative world: the reader's task is to divine the links binding them together and leading back to authorial intent. Realist novels might seem to militate against magic reading in their characters, and to advocate for more rational, purely "human" modes of reckoning. But the very nature of novel reading brings the magic back.

A few especially "magical" things happen in the process. First, despite any emphasis on the formation of individualized subjects as the core mission of the bourgeois novel, the very dependence of realist fiction on metonymical chains—which is to say, on the principle of contiguity—brings with it what Armstrong, following Adam Smith, calls "contagion" and Benjamin "mimetic blending," and what Collins, following Lévy-Bruhl, calls "distributed or fractal personhood," on which the very notion of contagious magic depends.[54] This latter is the notion that "a person's possessions or body parts can be distributed throughout his environment, and that in some sense these accoutrements and parts can be thought of as replicating him. Magic capitalizes upon the belief that acting on the distributed parts will still affect the whole. The sympathetic relation guarantees that the part of the person being acted upon magically stands for the whole person and that this connection holds true at a distance in time and space."[55] Just so, I'd say, the typical realist novel that can condemn the protagonist to the fate of his snuffbox, or better, that can allow the reader to anticipate the fate of the character by the sympathetic reading of his snuffbox, and far more accurately than characters can anticipate their own fate.[56] And crucially, the very process of reading the novel—which Foucault would call disciplining—requires the *reader* to participate in the distribution of his or her own person throughout the text, to experience the contiguous magic in his own practice: to become, as it were, part of the thingified fictional world, and not just its human dimension.[57] Insofar as the disciplining work of individuation is linked to the process of reading, it is linked to a practice that by its nature also dissolves such individuation and undoes such work.

The second magical dimension to the reading of even realist novels concerns the experience of time. The narrative arc of realist fiction is one often described as ineluctably aimed at the progressive development of an individual fitted to its social context, an arc familiar to the German world as the teleological trajectory of *Bildung*. Temporality becomes sequence, sequence consequence, and the causal chain one with a final, this-worldly goal. This rather Foucauldian position is closely linked with that of Benjamin in "The Storyteller," who adds the alignment of the novel with a specific notion of unfolding, progressive history: both echo the assumption that novels enforce a linear notion not only of character but also of reading, quite different from the selective excisions characteristic of Augustine's Bible reading or Foucault's—or Benjamin's—premodern world. The assumption is that this linearity (and its *durée*, its unbreachable continuum) reinforces a rationalized, disenchanted mode of charting both the world and personhood.

But these assumptions bear rethinking on several fronts. To begin, the very idea of human time as a causal chain of events leading to a prescribed end-point is every bit as magical as it is realist—and as always, the presence of a realist explanation of an event does not rule out a magical one. As Peter Brooks argues, this magic is accentuated by the particular way novelistic texts engage in "binding" actions and events, working to "allow us to bind one textual moment to another in terms of similarity or substitution rather than mere contiguity": one event is bound to another not so much (or not only) in terms of crude cause and effect, but in terms of successive likeness and repetition—and it is important to remember how "binding" is a magical term well before it becomes either a psychoanalytical or literary one.[58] Which is to say, realist texts temporalize the *seirai* of ancient magic, but do not eliminate them: and in so doing they accentuate rather than dispose of the magical dimension of the literary world, *especially* in their notion of sequence as consequence.

Second, the fact that realist fiction is as a rule always retrospective, and in a highly intentional way, reinforces the magic to its narrative world and reading—indeed, this might be its most basic inheritance from ancient epic. Like epic poems, novels invite us to read each always already past event, thing, or sign as an omen of an already scripted even if still unknown future; and in this way they radically enforce a practice of divinatory reading, of parsing each past or present moment for its excess future meaning, for its resemblance to the end point that, while unknown, is still known to be set. As again Brooks argues, this mode of reading radically disrupts the strictly linear temporality of the novel, and not least because it is always directed beyond the events themselves and toward a hidden world of authorial intention that, however guardedly, is always there, in silent excess of the real and rational.[59] Retrospection transforms intentionality into temporality, and in such a way that reading becomes at once a traffic with the dead (the voice from beyond the end) and the future (the voice that knows the end), a traffic that runs alongside but also above the simple following of the plot. The opening up of this other temporal dimension, in which readers are especially trained to look for significance, keeps reading magical, quite apart from the magical experience of bound sequence in the time world of the story itself. And that it is the reader's role to follow the prescribed rituals that bring that hidden world of the author down and to bear on the human world of the novel's characters—this keeps his own role thoroughly magical as well.

One last point regarding the magic reading of realist novels, on the occasionality of such reading. This is an aspect of magic reading that much traditional reader theory overlooks—systematically overlooks, as it constructs a model of reading that is reproducible, universalized, and normalized, very much in imitation of its model of realist poetics. But the occasion is there, along with its identificatory participation. Foucauldian readings hint at some of this in their insistence that realist fiction is targeted toward the disciplining of the reading subject and not just the represented one, that the reader's self is at stake, is indeed required to be at stake: in this, reading realist fiction still fulfills much the same role of spiritual exercise as Proclus or Augustine suggest. Benjamin pushes the point even further in "The Storyteller" by saying that novel readers are drawn to the certainty of significance that novels, via their certain endings, are able to give to a life, a subject: the novel reader is conceived as approaching the work with a present need or demand, projects that need onto the past signs of the given text, and tries to divine his own future fortune out of that of the work's protagonist. The divinatory practices that are established for reading the fortune of those within the text also model (or copy—either way) the divinatory practice in effect for reading the self's fortune through the text: the novel serves the reader as omen, with the temporal structure that adheres to all omens, and with all the possibilities for either confirmation or disappointment, ambiguity or even vacuousness, that have always held for divination.

But while both Foucauldian critics and Benjamin point to the reader's identificatory participation, and Benjamin in particular to its divinatory aspect (*Ahnung*), the primary focus of both on the end point tends to overlook another magic aspect of the practice and occasion of the reading itself. This is Roland Barthes's point about the very process of reading as grounded in a fragmenting imaginary identification: insofar as it is the reader's own individual fate, his own person that is being put in and out of the text, then the points of entry need to be those particular moments where the text coincidentally signs him, and just him: where the text links his (microcosmic) world and person via a chain of resemblances to its narrative cosmos, and even more, where this coincidental signing of the reader seems also to signal authorial intent, not least by the ability of the reader to find the sign confirmed in the future events of the text.[60] The reader's taking of such signs as signs, while rule bound, will nonethless be somewhat arbitrary and selective, which is to say, occasional, because inevitably based on the coincidence with his immediate situation: indeed, one might say such signs will only, magically, appear as signs to him. Moreover—and this is D. A. Miller's brilliant revision of Benjamin on novel reading— because this aspect of reading always involves a process of vertical participatory integration, linking the events of the novel's world with those of the reader's life, it will always fragment the text, draw it out of its immediate narrative context, and contemplate its (happy) coincidence with the present real world, in a revivified version of the aleatory excisions of the ancient tradition of *sortes*, or of the magical application of Homeric lines to extraliterary occasions and then back into the poems themselves.[61] All of which is to say that, even in the novel, reading remains a *practice*, a ritualized but deeply personal activity or occasion, and that the practice, activity, or occasion it resembles, indeed instantiates, is still magic.

Benjamin himself gives a wonderful figure for this, a figure that while it already points to the modernism that succeeds realism, also suggests how modernism itself emerges from realism and a deeper past. The figure or *Denkbild* is called "Pretzel, Feather, Pause, Lament, Clowning" (*Breze, Feder, Pause, Klage, Firlefanz*), and it describes a children's game popular in the mid-nineteenth century that would take such words, unbound and unconnected (*ohne Bindung und Zusammenhang*), and work to link them together meaningfully, without changing their order. He then asks us to imagine turning the game around, to think of reading any given sentence as if it had been constructed according to these rules; and he claims that "in reality, something of this perspective is contained in every act of reading," where the text's surface meaning becomes "merely the background on which rest the shadows cast" by one's arbitrarily imposed focus or desires, "like figures in relief."[62] As an isolated form of reading, he says, it closely mimics that connected with sacred works; as a form of writing, that connected to modernist surrealist prose; but as an integrated occasional practice, it is there in the most ordinary reading of novels—including realist ones.

Sympatheia and *Stimmung*

It is not just that magic and divination persist in mid-nineteenth- to early twentieth-century German literature because of intrinsic qualities of its prose fiction. These also endure because the world model that originally supports such reading—the sympathetic world of the ancients—persists as well. I mentioned how the Neoplatonic worldview elaborated in the first section continued to exert a profound influence on the German romantics, especially in the form of so-called *Naturphilosophie*. One of the chief forms in which *Naturphilosophie* exerted its own profound influence on the following period was through the again rather uniquely German tradition of *Stimmung*, a concept that began lexically to organize itself at about the same late eighteenth-century moment that the term *Sympathie* began to lose some of its ancient meaning. But as Leo Spitzer has shown, *Stimmung* itself has ancient roots in the Platonist past, and came to attract to itself much of the broader conceptual framework of classical *sympatheia*; and as a dominant concept in both science and art during the German nineteenth century it kept alive and active the world on which both magic and divination depend.[63] For this reason, this study of magic reading and the future is also one of the changing shape, and fate, of *Stimmung*, qua *sympatheia*, during the realist and into the modernist period.

I will elaborate in considerable detail the idea set represented by *Stimmung* in the chapters that follow. What I want to do here, in the last part of this introduction, is give the barest outlines of the concept itself and some of the transformations it undergoes over the course of the period engaged. *Stimmung* is a nearly untranslatable term that hovers somewhere between human mood, surrounding atmosphere, and the attunement between the two, and although originating in the sphere of music, it found some of its broadest applications in the newly privileged field of landscape painting in the nineteenth century—a field that combined aesthetic, natural-scientific, and religious concerns. One of its most important theorists was the scientist and painter Carl Gustav Carus (1789–1869). Carus was directly influenced by the *Naturphilosophie* of Schelling as well as by its variants in Goethe and Alexander von Humboldt; and in his *Nine Letters on Landscape Painting* (*Neun Briefe über Landschaftsmalerei*, 1824) and *Twelve Letters on Earth-Life* (*Zwölf Briefe über das Erdleben*, 1841), he worked to translate that philosophy into the rituals of landscape painting, or more broadly, into a model for the interaction of the human subject with the nonhuman natural world.

He did so in terms of *Stimmung*, defining the principal task of landscape painting as "representation of a certain *Stimmung* of affective life (sense) through reproduction of a corresponding *Stimmung* of natural life (truth)."[64] *Stimmung* is thus presented as both an "attunement" within the natural world itself—a kind of macrocosmic order—and an attunement between that natural life and the microcosmic observing (or representing) human subject, conceived in more affective than strictly rational terms. To characterize these relations he invokes an analogy found in many ancient texts, including Cicero's *De divinatione*, to describe *sympatheia*: "Even as a string struck on an instrument will set a second, corresponding string in a higher or lower octave to vibrate as well; similarly, related impulses respond to each other, both in nature and in the soul, and here again the individual human appears an inseparable part of a higher whole."[65]

Clearly, Carus's model of *Stimmung* engages the conditions of a momentary coinciding occasion, of a "mystical participation" that dissolves strict subject/object relations between the human and nonhuman world, and of a common *logos* that is felt to connect all parts of nature, man included, by means of contact and likeness. In all this, *Stimmung* reproduces *sympatheia*. Even more, and just as clearly: as a feature of man's relation to the natural world, *Stimmung* proposes a model for *reading* that world, a (magical) model delicately balanced between self-projection and a participatory engagement dissolving the strictures of discrete subjectivity. The model allows for a range of possible modes of reading, extending from a "romantic," subjective contagion of the external world to a keenly attentive, "objective" reception of its visible *and* invisible order and connections. For Carus, this yields an aesthetics that can become a new kind of scientific observation of the natural world, one that calls for the active engagement and identificatory occasion of the human subject. And as we'll see for Keller, it yields an aesthetics—and *Bildung*—that can potentially reconcile "romantic" magical thinking (in its most pejorative sense) and realist vision.

Carus's model of *Stimmung* posits connections between the subject-ive and object-ive worlds, based on a principle of (momentary) similarity. But it also posits connections between both these worlds and an invisible divine one that communicates itself to men through the visible objects of the natural world. Indeed, it is the reading and representation of this attendant divine order, and not of things alone, that ultimately ground his practice of landscape painting, whose purpose is to interpret the apparent objects of the natural world as signs that communicate and manifest an otherwise hidden one. That is, the reading model of *Stimmung* is never only a matter of certain linked (nonrational) communications between the human subject and natural world. It is also one of communications between the natural and the divine world in ways that keep its human reception, even at its most objective, a form of intimation or divination (*Ahnung*): an intimation of the divine providence (*Vor-sehung*) and forces in-forming the natural world, animating it with a sign-ificance beyond either its intrinsic nature or its momentary reflection of a human subject.

In landscape painting, then—and in the model of natural science and religion that support it—*Stimmung* becomes divination, a way of reading the correspondences, the likenesses and connections, between the human, natural, and divine realms that sees all three in the one order of visible things—but those things as both themselves and signs of a projected human and a communicated divine (or "metatextual") order. When translated into literature—as in the case of Keller's novel, which takes the education in landscape painting as the basis for its protagonist's *Bildung*—this same model of *Stimmung*, depending on the same correspondences, can, I'll argue, yield a "realism," for both the world and its representation, that excludes neither the subjective participation of the human agent nor a hidden divine (or metatextual) dimension to its represented world, but rather works to realize these in ways not distinct from things themselves, but always and only to be divined through such things. Moreover, since its represented world is narrative rather than just pictorial, in the novel the *Vor-sehung* and forces of its divine/metatextual dimension can and will acquire a more pronounced temporal and futural dimension. But in either case, for both Carus's "scientific" landscape painting and Keller's realist novel, the world made manifest through *Stimmung* emerges as a recognizably sympathetic and so still magical one, and its required mode of reading that world a form of divination.

Keller's novel takes us well into the mid-nineteenth century and the emergence of poetic realism as the dominant aesthetic in German literature. It is at about this same time that Ute Frevert, in her book *Emotions in History—Lost and Found*, records a beginning shift in the meaning of the term *Sympathie* in Germany and indeed throughout Europe.[66] While arguing that *Sympathie* comes to operate "on a new scale and with far greater urgency than before," she also notes that it starts to lose the primary meaning it had held up until then as "a natural concept of 'hidden correspondence[s]'" and "cosmic or magical connection"—the meaning we have followed—and to acquire a more "psychic" sense restricted to the human world: a sense of *Mitempfindung* or empathy with one's fellow man.[67] And it is also at about this same time that David Wellbery, in a seminal essay still to be discussed, implies a similar shift in the meaning and force of *Stimmung*, moving away from its sense as a property of or force in the external natural world to become more exclusively a property or force of the individual human psyche, more or less equivalent to mere mood: dissipating the sense of reciprocal, macro-micro interaction and becoming more simply a matter of psychological self-projection.[68] Each of these critics offers a variant of the argument we encountered earlier in Foucault for magic reading per se, while moving the timeline for the shift from the end of the seventeenth to the later nineteenth century: each sees the transition from a paradigm of magic—whether called *Sympathie* or *Stimmung*—as a force of the natural world to one of a human world alone.

As we see in Fontane's novels, there is considerable truth to both these arguments, and they mark a crucial shift between early and late realism, and between the role of *Stimmung* qua *sympatheia* in poetic and so-called social realism. But both also require qualification. So, for example, the lexical retreat of *Sympathie* from the natural world to a purely human one that Frevert identifies does seem confirmed by the aesthetic stance of Fontane's later texts, and with it a dimunition in man's identificatory relation to nature and so, too, of the magic in the world itself. But it is also the case that *Sympathie* in its more traditional form stubbornly persists in that same world in the guise of folk, pseudoscientific, alternative medical, or superstitious beliefs and practices, and in ways that prove intrinsic to both that world and its literary realist representation. Many characters in his novels, and by no means the least astute ones, continue to subscribe to a "sympathetic" view of nature, despite its high-cultural discrediting (a dismissal, we know, there since ancient times), and continue, too, to engage in related divinatory readings. And as noted in the previous section, objects in the external natural world continue to function as signifiers of a metatextual world for readers of the novels themselves, in ways that also still require divinatory or, if you will, sympathetic magic readings of the novel world.

Equally important, the retreat that Wellbery notes of *Stimmung* into the purely human world does not seem quite as individually restricted as his Foucauldian framework might suggest. That is, the concept of *Stimmung* seems not just to move from describing external binding or coercive forces in the cosmos to describing interiorized disciplinary ones, situated within a self-contained bourgeois subject, psychologically conceived. Rather, it seems also, as Frevert's model of sympathy suggests, to have moved into the cosmos of social interaction, with man—and life—"sociably" conceived. Even as psychology emerges at the end of the nineteenth century as a newly dominant discourse, so too sociology; and even as we saw key aspects of *sympatheia* migrate into the new idea of *Stimmung* (without ever having fully left *Sympathie*) in the midcentury, so, too, do key aspects of *Stimmung* qua *sympatheia* seem now to migrate into the equally new concept of *Geselligkeit* or sociability (without fully leaving *Stimmung* either). As we'll see in both the near-contemporary sociology of Georg Simmel and the *Gesellschaftsromanen* of Fontane, the idea of "sociability" reproduces the elements of a momentary occasion, of micro-macro relations, of a well nigh "mystical participation" that dissolves strict subject/object relations, and of a common *logos*—in this case, language itself—that connects its world via contact and likeness; and in the case of Fontane, this idea of "sociability" will still be cast in terms of *Stimmung* itself. For both Simmel and Fontane, *Stimmung* qua sociability (qua *sympatheia*) will still involve a hidden world of invisible, communicating forces attendant upon ordinary material signifying things (including words), a world that requires a special kind of divinatory reading to become manifest or realized through those things. And for both, that world and its reading will still be magical.

This is not to say that the dimunition in man's participatory identification with nature and the nonhuman world in general that is evident in Frevert's account of *Sympathie* and Wellbery's of *Stimmung*, and even in Simmel's notion of sociability, is without consequence. It certainly is, and in ways that endanger both the magical *and* the realist worlds, threatening their similar dependence on binding connections with forces of a more modernist dissociation. And a crucial corollary to this—not important to Frevert's or Wellbery's arguments, but very much so to mine—is that the seeming retreat of *Sympathie* and *Stimmung* from man's relation to the natural world is accompanied by a retreat from his relation to the future as well. This is the case for subjects in the historical world, whose faith in progress becomes notably diminished at the turn of the century; for characters in novels, whose lessened capacity to predict their future is conspicuous in Fontane's last works; and for novels and their readers, who can no longer always rely on consequential, linearly unfolding plots. *Sympathie* and *Stimmung*, magic and divination, novels and the future: the argument of this study is that all seem linked to a similar fate.

The sense of dissociation from both nature and the future that appears to emerge near the end of realism becomes, as Barbara Stafford argues, dominant in modernism, where it even comes increasingly to include a sense of broken connections to the social order and its recent past.[69] But the paradox is that, at the same time and under these very conditions, modernism also represents a new, and often problematic, resurgence of felt magic in both the world and art. In part, this is reflective of conditions more or less unique to the twentieth-century world: the rise of new technologies ("techno-magic"), the pervasiveness of newly manufactured things (commodity-magic), and the en-trancing spread of mass political movements (fascism). But in part it also reflects conditions extending out of the previous half century, including the elaboration of those somewhat debased forms of *Naturphilosophie* and *Sympathie* evident in the pseudo- or occult sciences of Fontane's time into what becomes the *Lebensphilosophie* or vitalism of Benjamin's; and including, too, a reckoning with the magical, binding, sympathetic powers that had come to inhere in bourgeois society (and realism) itself. But even beyond this, the magic that erupts in modernism reflects a direct turn back to more ancient traditions: as Benjamin says, "Precisely modernity is always citing primal history."[70] And in his own case that included invoking a Neoplatonist-inflected model of *sympatheia* for understanding both his own present world and its relation to the past, recent and ancient; and along with it, the practices of its divinatory reading—albeit now all but deprived of its future dimension.

This re-turn to a Neoplatonic world-model of *sympatheia* and its divination—what Benjamin calls "natural prophecy"—is perhaps most evident in his "Storyteller" essay on the mid- to late nineteenth-century author Nikolai Leskov, where he writes, "The hierarchy of the creaturely world, which has its apex in the righteous man, reaches down into the abyss of the inanimate through many gradations. In this connection, one particular circumstance must be noted. This whole creaturely world speaks not so much with the human voice as with what could be called 'the voice of Nature'"; and he adds, "The lower Leskov descends on the scale of created things, the more obviously his way of viewing things approaches the mystical. . . . The mineral is the lowest stratum of created things. For the storyteller, however, it is directly connected to the highest. He is able to see in it a natural prophecy."[71] To be sure, Benjamin posits a growing loss of connection to this world, one fading along with the storyteller, a figure at once epically archaic and of the recent nineteenth-century past. But the sympathetic world itself is imagined as still there: it is just a matter of divining and releasing its hidden powers anew.

The form that those sympathetic powers (and their reading) take in Benjamin's modern world is once again that of *Stimmung*; although, as in the cases discussed above, there is also a migration of some of its key aspects into new terms, even if themselves ancient. So, for example, in the penultimate sentence of the "Storyteller" essay, Benjamin refers to "the incomparable *Stimmung*" that surrounds and adheres to every true storyteller of the preceding century. And in his essay on surrealism, he writes, "Surrealism brings the immense forces of '*Stimmung*' concealed in past things to the point of explosion,"; and insofar as they do so, the surrealists are, he says, "visionaries and augurs": in this respect, very much the modernist descendants of storytellers.[72] But a good part of the idea set of *Stimmung* also comes to be absorbed by Benjamin's now more familiar notion of "aura," certainly one of his most explicitly magical terms and one with its own links to ancient *sympatheia*.

We see this shift already in his "Little History of Photography," which has one of the earliest mentions of aura, and where it and *Stimmung* are used as synonyms—and where we also have one of the earliest formulations of Benjamin's ambivalence toward it.[73] He defines aura as the "weave" or *Gespinst* of an object in space and time and as a mode of participation in the natural object world, and in a formulation he repeats across several essays, he writes, "What is aura, actually? A strange weave of space and time. . . . While at rest on a summer's noon, to trace a range of mountains on the horizon, or a branch that throws its shadow on the observer, until the moment or the hour become part of their appearance—that is what it means to breathe the aura of those mountains, that branch."[74] It is described as an invisible power that seems to both emanate out of a given object and encompass it; and as a perceptual experience that belongs only to objects that have successfully evaded our conscious mind. But most decisive for my present purpose is, first, how aura is presented as a quality of both the ancient world— Benjamin refers to it elsewhere as a "breath of prehistory"—and the nineteenth century, in the latter case explicitly linked to *Stimmung*; and second, how it is a quality that much of modernism works to disrupt, to disperse in favor of an alienated, dissociated *stimmunglos* ideal.[75] Every bit as much as realism, modernism is imagined as playing out in a dialectic of magic and disenchantment, with now one, now the other the privileged state—but (as in antiquity itself) with neither one ever really not there.

Despite—or perhaps because of—its centrality to so many takes on Benjamin's work, and despite, too, its emphatically magical quality, this study does not overly dwell on aura. Rather, even as it sees aura as a reformulation of *Stimmung*, so does it follow Miriam Hansen in regarding aura itself as a transitional formulation on the way to Benjamin's more encompassing notion of the mimetic faculty, or, more precisely, of his doctrine of the similar, a doctrine that more fully re-presents the world model of *sympatheia* and, with it, more directly the matter of divinatory reading.[76] Reflecting on the claim that "to experience the aura of an object we look at means to invest it with the ability to look back at us," Hansen writes, "The reflexivity of [such] a mode of perception, its reciprocity across [time], seems to both hinge upon and bring to fleeting consciousness an archaic element in our present senses, a forgotten trace of our material bond with nonhuman nature."[77] That archaic element is the mimetic faculty, that material bond one that, like both nineteenth-century *Stimmung* and ancient *sympatheia*, unites through similitude the human and nonhuman worlds, and, also like them, determines the conditions of their necessarily divinatory reading. It is on the consequences for the practices of reading that this arrangement entails that Benjamin chooses to focus, and we along with him: practices heavily inflected by a modernist questioning of its value and futurity, but nonetheless still divinatory, and still magic.

1

Painting Magic in Keller's
Green Henry

Gottfried Keller's *Green Henry* (*Der Grüne Heinrich*, 1854–55) is a *Bildungsroman* and, like Adalbert Stifter's *Indian Summer* (*Der Nachsommer*, 1857), one representative of the realist period. As a *Bildungsroman*, the narrative focuses on the subject formation of the protagonist, Heinrich Lee, and his integration into social norms and expectations; and, as is typical of the genre, it does so in large part by following both his erotic and his aesthetic educations. As reflective of a particularly realist program, the latter education focuses especially on Heinrich's engagement with an external object world, both social and natural; and with the problem of the representation of that world, in this case through painting—and especially, landscape painting.

The various elements of these two sets of concerns—*Bildung* and realism, subject formation and the relation to objects, Heinrich Lee as both lover and painter—are clearly deeply implicated with each other: and they are often especially considered as jointly implicated in the overarching project of *disenchantment*, of gradually divesting both Heinrich's inner world and the text's external world of all traces of magical thinking and being, in ways that directly impact both his erotic and his aesthetic educations. It is this latter assumption that I wish to contest, and there is one particular if minor moment in the early part of this novel—in the so-called "Story of My Youth" (*Jugendgeschichte*)—that brings the play of these various elements and the way I want to address them into sharp focus.

Heinrich Lee has just left the city, where he has been pursuing his training as a painter, and returned to the country setting where he had previously met Anna, the first and primary object of his erotic attentions. He is surprised to learn that her father has sent Anna away to be educated (*gebildet*) for a year in a different city. In her absence, Heinrich is often invited to stay in her room, and one day, remembering a spot in the woods where he and Anna had once sat together, he tells us:

> I couldn't keep myself from drawing a neat square on the snow-white wall of the little room and painting the picture of the Heathen Chamber in it, as best I could. This was to be a silent greeting for her, to show her later how constantly I thought of her.

> Ich konnte mich nun nicht enthalten, auf der schneeweißen Wand des Kämmerchens ein sauberes Viereck zu ziehen und das Bild mit der Heidenstube so gut ich konnte hineinzumalen. Dies sollte ein stiller Gruß für sie sein und ihr später bezeugen, wie beständig ich an sie gedacht.[1]

The "Heathen Chamber" that is the subject of this painting is in many ways a variant of the topos of the *locus amoenus*, a usually idealized natural setting removed from the social world and suggestive of erotic play; and Heinrich's depiction of it here on the wall of Anna's room is often taken as an endearingly naïve and innocent expression of both his struggling after a painterly ideal of realism ("as best I could") and his still rather romantic erotic imagination ("how constantly I thought of her"). But while it is both these things, it is also something more—or rather, in being these also entails something more: this picture is painted on Anna's wall as a kind of magical charm with the covert intent of binding and, eventually, killing her with it; and Heinrich will succeed in realizing this intent, and by this means, and will do so concurrently with the realization of the work's *Bildung* and realist programs.

This at least is my claim, and in what follows I will not so much be concerned with *why* Heinrich Lee should want his beloved Anna dead, although the analysis will inevitably touch on this. Rather, my primary interest will be in *how* he goes about making it happen, that is, realizing this intent, and what this tells us about the realism, and enchantment, at stake in the novel. I want to know, what are the conditions pertaining to both the narrated world and representation in that world that allow for such an *actio in distans* and, as part of that, to such a future force to things? What relations must obtain between the painter and his subject, that is, his landscape, between the landscape and his beloved victim, Anna, between his painting and both these things (the landscape and Anna) in order for these effects to come about and be realized—which is to say, for the *reader* to realize them, draw them out, and as it were activate them beneath the level of the overtly represented, since in fact these relations and their forces will remain essentially invisible? And even more, what do these invisible forces and their visible effects reveal to us about realism itself, about the nature of its things, its temporalities and causalities?

In pursuing these questions, I want to identify but also delimit two approaches that are often applied to related issues in *Bildung* and realism, both of which prove productive but also betray a kind of suspect temporal reasoning in their causal explanations.[2] Shorthand for these approaches would be the Foucauldian and Freudian. The first is a sophisticated variant on the position that any magical properties in realism are residues of a romantic—or more extensively, an early modern—sensibility, and that one of the primary tasks of a realist program is to overcome and banish such discounted, antiquated beliefs from its operant world: from its understanding of things, of time, and of relations of cause and effect.[3] This is more or less the approach elaborated by Nancy Armstrong in her important book, *How Novels Think*, which, moreover, extends this agenda to include the nineteenth-century novel genre as a whole and bourgeois *Bildung* with it.[4] As we'll see, the general assumptions of her argument can go a long way—though by no means the whole way—toward accounting for the seeming surplus of forces, of the superrational and perhaps even supernatural forces, evident in Keller's novel. But the drawbacks to this approach are easy to see: it assumes such "magic" to belong only to some prior extrinsic realm, and not as intrinsic to realism itself; and it assumes the continued presence of such forces in the realist world to be symptoms of a failure fully to achieve its agenda, rather than necessary, constituent elements both producing and produced by that realist world.

If a Foucauldian approach banishes the magical to a romantic or early modern past and sees only its afterlife in realism, the Freudian, while proving equally rich, exiles it to a modernist, psychological future and sees only its own adumbrations in the literature that immediately precedes it. In this approach, magical effects are recast as exclusively unconscious projections, functioning along lines laid out by various Freudian models, the most relevant of which are probably his theories of displacement and the omnipotence of thought. This approach, too, is seductive in its explanatory force, and has been productively applied to the realm of the seemingly fantastic in *Green Henry*, sometimes even in sophisticated conjunction with a Foucauldian approach.[5] But the reservations to be registered are obvious on this front, too: it converts the magic in the realist world into a mere (and not fully understood) expression of a later modernist mind-set rather than, again, something already recognized and singularly appropriate to realism itself: whereas from the one approach the presence of magic represents the failure to let go of residual falsities, from the other it represents a failure fully to grasp an emergent truth—in other words, once again as somehow not quite proper to realism itself. In any case, an added pitfall to both this Freudian and the more Foucauldian approach is the shared, initial, unquestioned assumption that magic in realism is centered only in the (human) subject and not in the world itself or in its representations: in their own materiality, temporality, and causality.[6] And yet perhaps it is just this assumption that needs first to be questioned—and not least when we include in our field of inquiry realism as, finally, a reading experience.

What I would therefore like to propose instead, or in addition, as theoretical background for this study is a discourse recently fore-grounded in the work of David Wellbery, Hans Ulrich Gumbrecht, Thomas Pfau, and others that focuses on the properly German concept of *Stimmung*, a notion with notable affinities with the earlier traditions of sympathetic magic we traced from the ancient world through the early modern period.[7] These affinities are not accidental: as Leo Spitzer shows, the idea set of *Stimmung* emerges out of a strain of Western thought stretching back to Greek antiquity.[8] But as Wellbery shows, in the semantic field of *Stimmung* such affinities become central to German aesthetic discourse beginning in the early nineteenth century and, while originating in music, find particular application within both the literary sphere and that of landscape painting. Wellbery skips from the very beginning of the century to its end in his own historical account of *Stimmung*, but the idea itself is clearly relevant to works in the realist period in between—perhaps most readily applicable to the novellas of Theodor Storm, but also, I hope, to Keller's *Green Henry*, with its own essential merging of literature and landscape painting.[9]

Stimmung

There is no need to give a detailed, specific account of Wellbery's exposition, especially since I do not intend, as he does, to focus only on uses of the word itself (although doing so would certainly reveal the relation of *Stimmung* in Keller's novel to magic, music, art, eros, and death).[10] Rather, I want only to sketch out the set of defining features encompassed by the idea as it unfolds in the areas of aesthetic experience, literature, and painting in this period. Focusing on *Stimmung* in this way, in this period, and in this novel will, I believe, accomplish two things. On the one hand, it will allow us to complicate the notably Foucauldian historical trajectory of Wellbery's own analysis, which posits a fairly relentless move toward the radical interiorization of *Stimmung* over the course of the nineteenth century; our complication will come not least by showing how the literature of this period skipped by Wellbery reengages some of the dimensions implicit in *Stimmung's* classical history. On the other hand, it will allow us to show how the basic terms of *Stimmung* can encompass and extend the reach of both Freudian and Foucauldian approaches to Keller's novel in more satisfactory and comprehensive ways that admit consideration of otherwise overlooked elements—elements that are intrinsic to realism and not at all reducible to a program of disenchantment.

The first characteristic of *Stimmung*, and the one that makes it as difficult to pin down as most aspects of magic thinking, is that it is basically *preconceptual*, or not quite present at an explicit level of representation. *Stimmung* is grounded in a sensible experience that suggests but does not fully attain cognitive articulation or clarity: in this way, it is an aesthetic experience par excellence.[11] As such, *Stimmung* remains something "dark," diffuse, and spectral, attached neither to a particular object nor to a particular thought. Still, key to its preconceptual nature is also the essential impulse to move from the merely sensed to the grasped: there is almost by definition something premonitory about *Stimmung*, something awaiting expression, understanding, and affective response. In this way, it parallels the parasitic, hidden quality we have ascribed to most magical experience, a hidden quality that needs to be overcome and brought into the world, by means of what Burkhard Meyer-Sickendiek calls *Gespür*: "the capacity to grasp affectively a hidden, not actually visible circumstance" (*die Fähigkeit, einen verborgenen, nicht wirklich sichtbaren Sachverhalt gefühlsmäßig zu erfassen*).[12]

The second characteristic of *Stimmung* is that it is *relational*, what Wellbery calls a "setting-into-relation of parts," a "uniformly colored weave of relations (*Beziehungsgeflecht*)," an "interplay of echoing tone variations." Crucially, this relationality pertains at once and in turn to an objective sphere, a subjective one, and to the micro-macro connections between them. It is in the first place a relation of objects and events *in and of themselves*, a property of the external world quite apart from the individual subject: what in earlier times (and in the popular literature of the day) would have been called the sympathetic relations of the natural world, and in more modern times the atmosphere, it is in any case decisively

nonpsychological, indeed nonhuman.[13] But as part of this relational weave, *Stimmung* also posits a similarly sympathetic relation between those objective relations and the observing human
("aesthetic") subject—even between those objective relations and
the subjective relations of parts (memory, imagination, desire, understanding) of the observing subject.[14] In Wellbery's terms, the objective harmony requires a "subjective correlative" in the aesthetic
subject in order to be perceived and expressed, even as, conversely,
that subject must find in the natural order the objective correlative
for his inner state.[15] In more traditional terms, we would say that
Stimmung implies an active back-and-forth movement and connection between the macro- and microcosmic orders.[16] In any case,
like ancient magic, *Stimmung* depends upon a porous boundary
between the subject and object world: it is a matter of mutual projection, a "mystical participation" or open identification in which
the world of things injects itself into the human every bit as much
as the human projects itself onto things.[17]

An additional aspect of the relational character of *Stimmung*
is that it presents itself as a *unity*, a harmony (a *kosmos*).[18] Three
things can be said about this. First, while aiming at, even defined
by, a unity, a oneness between things themselves—clouds, trees,
rocks, water, light, and so on—and also between those things and
the apprehending aesthetic subject, that unity cannot necessarily
be said to reside in the particular things themselves, but only in
diffuse form between or behind them (nor, as mentioned, can it
be said simply to emanate from the human subject). In this sense,
too, *Stimmung* represents something spectral, invisible, manifest
without being present, a supplementary reality that is both there
and not there, something both tied to the world of things and their
perception but not of them. This is, as it were, the objective counterpart to the subjective ghostliness associated with its preconcep-
tuality, but now clearly as part of the outside material world and
not just its affective experience. We might say that *Stimmung* is
present as a *force* that binds together the world of things (and notably in a noncausal but still determinative fashion); or as Johann
Gottlieb Fichte has it, that Stimmung is a *movement*.

Second, as the earlier-cited phrase "of echoing tone variations" implies, what holds together and produces the sense of unity, what establishes the relations, is a complex web or chain of similarity, analogy, and resemblance between parts, with no necessary first term in either the external or the subject world.[19] What this alerts us to is that, outside of the musical sphere proper, the often almost invisible operations of mimetic, analogical, and metonymical forces account for the effects of *Stimmung* every bit as much as they do for those of sympathetic magic: *Stimmung*, too, is a matter of the similar, imitative, and contiguous. But third, insofar as the likenesses hint at a unity that is not in the things themselves but only invisibly between or behind them, *Stimmung* seems also to present an opening for the *allegorical* to assert itself, a "something more" (and different) coursing beyond the given: every bit as much as with the symbolic logic of the Neoplatonists, the logic of *Stimmung* pushes the orders or forces of likeness and similarity beyond the visible material and into the magic space of a supersensible realm—of allegory.[20] However, it does so without ever presenting anything more than the material things of the visible world.[21]

Wellbery also insists that, although both objectively and subjectively diffuse and difficult to pin down, *Stimmung* must nonetheless be communicable or, as he also puts it, *contagious*, operating suggestively at a level that might escape explicit formulation or even notice. Here, too, *Stimmung* functions similarly to ancient magic, which (as Armstrong also stresses) is by nature contagious, which is to say, works by contagion, by contact and contiguity—by affective relation. To some extent, this point is already implicit in what was said above about the needed contact and susceptibility of the aesthetic subject, of the artist to the order of things, and of the order of things to him. But what Wellbery's focus on the contagious communicability of *Stimmung* is meant to foreground is a second order of contagion, that which needs to occur at the site of a third term: in visual art, the viewer, and in literature, the reader. This is where the magic must (also) happen.[22] Almost by definition, *Stimmung* requires the viewer or reader to be drawn into these invisible relations, to become participant, and in a way that is not only receptive but active, even productive as well. In the end, *Stimm-ung*, like magic and like realism, is an effect, and one not only on but inevitably also by the engaged, targeted subject, who must be capable of (clairvoyantly) sensing, even of divining—this would be Schleiermacher's term (Carus's, too)—its presence behind or beyond the visible world or articulated words themselves.[23]

There are three final points about this theoretical model to raise before (re)turning to Keller's text, none of crucial importance to Wellbery's analysis, but all to mine. The first concerns temporality. The temporality of magic (and the magic of temporality) is of course one of my major concerns, but as perhaps befits the linkage with landscape painting, it seems decidedly secondary to Wellbery's: at most, apparently, a matter of whether *Stimmung* is momentary or durative. And although the momentary (i.e., occasional) is certainly important for us, it is not really the kind of temporality my concern with narrative magic requires, which also calls for sequence and, even more, for futurity. Still, there are two moments in Wellbery's discussion from which such a temporality may be teased out.[24] The first comes in a rather Freudian citation from Nietzsche that Wellbery specifically cites as introducing a (new) "temporal depth" (*zeitliche Tiefe*) to the discourse. The passage describes how recent experience can awaken unconscious, prereflexive memories and affects that echo it, combine with it (*mit-stimmen*), but are then experienced as a singularity, as one present emotion or experience: it is the temporal echo-effect or *Stimmung* that determines its present force.[25] The second comes much earlier in the essay when, in keeping with one part of the original musical metaphor, *Stimmung* is described as a state of readiness: an anticipatory, even premonitory *Bereitschaft* (an already tuned-in-ness) to enter into relations with what is to come, but in such a fashion that the "readiness" also predetermines the shape or order of what has yet to unfold.[26] A similar point is made by Jochen Hörisch, who speaks of a "presentiment" (*Vorahnung*) or "foreknowledge" (*Vorwissen*) as intrinsic to *Stimmung*, a disposition that "aims to predict" subsequent effects and permits one to choose or direct the *Stimmung* that will recursively and afterward determine one in turn.[27] In any case, these two passages from Wellbery suggest how the basic idea of *Stimmung* allows for relations that are linked temporally as well as spatially, and that aim at and even anticipate what is to come even as they reach back and echo what came before—both important factors for the retrospective medium of narrative.[28]

The second final point to be raised is the specific relation of *Stimmung* to art, or more broadly, the relation between representation and world. At one point Wellbery notes that art or rather the artist is required to activate the communicable contagion that is intrinsic to *Stimmung*, to bring about its continuability (*Fortsetzbarkeit*). And at another, Alois Riegl is cited as noting that landscape painting is meant to gift us, as it were, with an intimation of the immanent formal connection (*Formzusammenhang*) behind the appearances of ordinary life, conveying a sense of connectedness (via echoing similarities) that is otherwise unapparent in our everyday experience. Both are important, but equally so is Wellbery's apparent reluctance to distinguish between, say, the direct experience of a landscape and the mediated experience of a landscape painting—which is to say, the indifference to matters of mediated representation versus immediate experience or sensation. Far from an oversight, this seems an essential insight, and in two ways.[29] First, insofar as it reckons representations themselves to be part of and not separate from the world of things, and thereby potentially to participate in the force of their relations. From this perspective, part of the function of the realist principle of transparent mimesis would be not so much to efface the role of the artwork as to encourage this play of forces through the very porosity of its supposedly separate spheres—where the hidden-but-present (meta)level of representation can itself double up as the hidden-but-present allegorical order of *Stimmung*; or phrased differently, where the artwork qua artwork can become the portal for that allegorical order to enter the representation's "real" world.[30] And second (although clearly related), insofar as this indifference, this porosity, once again underscores the reading experience itself as an immersion, a "mystical participation" in the presented world. This would represent a negation of the post–eighteenth-century distinction between sign and world, including the twentieth-century distinction between story and discourse, and in their place a reaffirmation of early models of magic reading in which textuality remains firmly part of the one world, and where reading, like representation, itself becomes a potentially powerful site for the contagion of *Stimmung* that oversteps the boundary between representation and the real.[31]

The last point is in many ways the trickiest, but hopefully enough context has been established in what precedes to make it. Insofar as *Stimmung* implies a kind of force, a movement and communicability between spatially and temporally separate parts—a movement and communicability that takes place both between objects and events in and of themselves and between that objective world and individual subjects—*Stimmung* also implies a mode of action and activity, an *energeia* or *Tatkraft*, but of a particular kind.[32] Certainly the previously mentioned impulse for *Stimmung* to appear, to make itself manifest and to move toward communicable articulation—or from a slightly different perspective, to move from an anticipatory state of readiness to a realized state of engagement and fulfillment—is part of this *Tatkraft*, and as such *Stimmung* shares key features with the related concept of presentiment or *Ahnung*, and with it the directional, self-unfolding action of aesthetic experience per se.[33] But even more than this, the particular mode of action *Stimmung* implies in its intrinsic relationality is that of *actio in distans*.[34] One of the most ancient examples of *actio in distans* is one with explicit connection to the idea sets of both *Stimmung* and sympathetic divinatory magic (Cicero cites it in *De divinatione*): how when one musical string is struck it can cause a remote other string (or even strings) to vibrate as well.[35] In the absence of explicit, visible connection, a system of cause and effect is established that makes itself invisibly available for things to happen—a force field that grounds both *Stimmung* and divination, and, as I hope to show, the fictional realist world of Keller's novel as well.[36]

Meretlein

I'd like to start my discussion of the painting magic in Keller's text with the painting and story of the "little witch," Meretlein.[37]

Introduced early in the novel and drawn from the early modern period, this inserted exemplum clearly engages the issues of *Bildung* and erotic desire that figure so prominently in both Freudian and Foucauldian approaches to the *Bildungsroman* genre. But it also presents a kind of surplus meaning that exceeds the parameters of these approaches, which is to say, a witchery that properly belongs both to its own early modern setting and to the realist text in which it is placed.[38] As I hope to show, the form of witchery introduced in the Meretlein story is a kind of binding magic. Forms of binding are, of course, central to both psychological and socially oriented readings. And as just described, they are also central to the idea of *Stimmung.* As we'll see, the discourse of witchery allows for an almost seamless transition between these three, in ways that push the operant field of binding beyond the narrow confines of the first two and into the more comprehensive field of the last, of *Stimmung.* But it extends our understanding of the binding forces at work in *Stimmung* as well: for witchery encompasses not just the affirming but also the threatening forces implicit in the relations of *Stimmung,* the sympathetic forces behind both it and traditional magic, and whether these are thought of as emanating from nature or from art.

The Meretlein story is actually inserted into the text to explain a particular bind, Heinrich Lee's peculiar tendency toward obduracy (*Verstocktheit*), a condition also variously described as his clamming up (*Verstummtheit*), his constraint (*Befangenheit*), and his rigidity (*Halsstarrigkeit*).[39] This hinge immediately suggests that Meretlein serves as an analogue for Heinrich himself, and there are certainly significant resemblances between the story of this obstinate and unruly girl-child and Heinrich at this moment in his own story (not praying, going hungry, etc.) that link her figure to his. But there is also a great deal of material apparently dissimilar and superfluous to the immediate context and figure of Heinrich himself; and what emerges retrospectively is that Meretlein also serves as a proleptic projection or likeness for the figure of Anna and *her* binding, a shift in which Heinrich comes to occupy two other figure positions in the Meretlein story: that of the painter who produces a portrait or *Bild* of the witch-child; and that of the pastor

charged with her corrective "Education" or *Bildung*, who also
serves as the writer whose first-person text Heinrich incorporates
into his own—although in the complicated way such displaced
doublings can work, the position of the pastor will also be taken
by Anna's father, who as mentioned is as occupied with Anna being
educated (*gebildet*) via "Instruction" as Heinrich is with her being
depicted (*gebildet*) via painting.[40] Between them, the producers of
Bild and *Bildung* represent the two media in which Heinrich's relations to Anna will be mostly carried out, which are also the two
media in which the realist poetics are most thematized—although
as the focus on *Stimmung* anticipates, music will also play a significant role.[41]

The particular way the relevant resemblances and (binding) connections of Meretlein shift from the present Heinrich Lee to the future Anna is itself significant. To begin, it proleptically reflects the
way we'll see Heinrich shift his own condition of constraint or *Be-
fangenheit* directly onto Anna in a completed and ultimately fatal
process of rebounding reversal: taking the arrest or *Starrheit* she
causes him as lover and transforming it into the arrest he imposes
on her as painter and writer.[42] Second, the shift itself—the projection onto Anna of his own unruly desires and of the constraint
they make him feel—will prove absolutely central to the *Bildung*
project of Heinrich's subject formation and socialization. But third,
the shift is significant because, for these things actually to happen,
for the reversals and reinvestments to occur, somehow more than
"real" causalities will need to be operant in the textual world.

As we'll see, a good part of this added causality will be active
and present at a metatextual level: at that usually hidden level
of activity and presence that is only accessible to—and activated
by—the reader, remote from, but then summoned into, the more
manifest workings of the narrated world. But the point of the text
and painting of the Meretlein being inserted into the story is that
the metalevel (with its own temporalities and causalities) is being
inserted into it, too, where it will serve as a portal for certain magical effects to penetrate into the story world—effects marked *as*
magical through their association with Meretlein. In this respect,
it is worth noting how the Meretlein story will itself operate as

an omen, as a magic charm determining the later fate of Anna for and via the reader, setting up a not necessarily causal but still determinative force by which the text will bind her future, precisely via the similarities and coincidences—the *Stimmung*—between the two figures.[43]

The figure of the witch-child is first presented to the reader in three forms: as a worn grave tablet Heinrich discovers in a church wall, as a portrait he finds in his uncle's house in the country, and then as the text by the pastor he reads and incorporates into his own. That Meretlein's story is first introduced as a worn grave tablet is immediately important, and not least in that it seems to suggest something long past about her "early" witchery *(früh-zeitige Hexerei)*: that she herself was both a mere child and is now dead further reinforces the temporal distance of her story, set as it is in a similarly "early" pre-Enlightenment, pre-realist period. That is, the grave tablet seems to suggest the death of this whole earlier childlike era, together with its superstitious magic and sorcery.[44]

But that Meretlein is first introduced as a grave tablet is also crucial for our understanding of the following two forms of her appearance, in ways that multiply the role that death plays in its connection to her figure. This is especially true for how it figures in painting. By signaling the child who will become the subject of the portrait as lifeless, it brings into play the essentially life-less dimension of painting itself. The topos is a not uncommon one in nineteenth-century literature, and is doubly underscored here by not only having the subject of the painting introduced as dead, but also in the portrait having Meretlein holding a child's skull—and the specific relevance to painting is further signaled in the story by having the painter claim not even to need a real skull in order to include it in his portrait, since such belongs to "the very first elements of his art." Painting—and the same holds for writing and art in general—is recognized as a sphere intrinsically opposed to the life it is meant to re-present, and the portrait of a dead subject self-consciously includes painting as a potentially, even intrinsically deadly force in the realist world—or rather, behind the world, in a suggestively allegorical (and metatextual) space.

The painting of the dead child reflects, then, a basic paradox of realist representation, one that pushes it away from life and toward allegory.[45] But part of the same topos and its paradox is how the painting also proves uncannily alive and its subject to live on in this other but still present realm. We find this to be the case here as well, as in the portrait "the living child" (*das lebendige Kind*) seems fully there to the present-day viewer: and part of what is there is not just the child but the magic, the witchery of her figure, as even the present-day viewer is involuntarily charmed and fascinated by her living portrait. The achievement of the very ideal of realist representation (life) has brought with it a doubly contradictory effect: not only does the supposedly superceded magic return, it returns imbued with an added deadly force. But as mentioned at the outset, this has perhaps always been part of magic, which almost always traffics with the dead as part of its other world, and no less so when that world is an artful one. Thus, it foregrounds an aspect to the traffic with the things of the natural and the aesthetic worlds overlooked by our earlier account of *Stimmung*, but still essentially part of it: its spectral nature and connective force are not just of hidden life, but, at least at times, hidden death as well.[46]

The particular kind of witchery associated with Meretlein is first described by Heinrich in terms of erotic desire. Grown men, he tells us, had only to look at the child in order to become seduced and to fall fatally in love with her: these grown men include both the painter of her portrait, who was "completely charmed" (*ganz charmiert*), and the disciplining pastor, who, too, became "bewitched" (*verhext*) by her. Although the bewitching forces seem to originate in Meretlein and only to affect the men, Heinrich actually sketches out a more complex series of displacements that involve both causal and temporal reversals—the same series we will see again between Heinrich and Anna, and that, as mentioned, is also implicit in the shifting identification of Heinrich and Anna with Meretlein herself. Heinrich shows how the aroused fantasies and erotic forces are centrally and properly sited in the viewing males and only become projected on or bound to the viewed child, so that she rather than they becomes the site and source of their wild unruliness; and he shows how the potentially fatal effect of those forces on the men becomes redirected at her as well, constraining her instead of them. In this respect, it is telling that one of the primary aspects of the disciplining of Meretlein in the story proper is a hunger cure, a starving of appetites, imposed by the pastor. But the "Correction" also extends to the painter, who needs *her* to hold still so he can practice his artistic control—and so, as the text says, his painting is the continuation, not disruption, of the pastor's "Education" of her. That is, painting itself, in its own life-depriving way, participates in this same arresting or binding project, of removing the child—qua repository for unwanted erotic and fantastic forces—from the realm of the real: and it does so in part by joining silence to hunger as both means and end. In any case, Heinrich describes how the alleged initial stubborn rigidity (*Halsstarrigkeit*) of the child becomes replaced by the arrest (*Starrheit*) imposed by the men, itself a displacement of the arrest they experienced in themselves, a displacement and arrest completed by those of painting itself.

This attempt to bind the child fails, and in ways that double up on the paradox of realist painting just mentioned. We're told that the painting of Meretlein "aroused in the viewer an involuntary longing to see the living child and to be allowed to fondle and kiss her," even as—breaking the painting's silence—it also generates "stories and legends," "all sorts of fantastic and fabulous tales," inspired by an equally "involuntary sympathy" in the community. The witchery doesn't go away, not by abjecting it into the child, fatally "correcting," starving, or silencing the child, nor fixing and removing her via painting. It continually reappears at the level of both desire and imagination and refuses to leave "this world"—and in this, Heinrich's description of the painting and of Meretlein's narrative afterlife is again reflective of events in the story, indeed of its central event. For when Meretlein was finally apparently killed off by the corrective efforts of the pastor, she fantastically resurrected herself from the grave and returned to life (on the Buchberg, no less).[47] At the level of both representation and world, the magical bindings do not, indeed cannot, go away.

The complicated reversals and persistence of Meretlein's witchery are also evident in Heinrich's description of its magic workings and bindings not so much in terms of individual erotic desire as in those of a more communally centered socialization process. We get a hint of this in Heinrich's mention of how "old women would use this tale as a bogeyman for the children when they were not pious, and would add still other strange and fantastic details."[48] Again, the intent is to arrest, charm, or bind an ungovernable youth and produce a proper docility; and as the echo of the pastor's own ideal of piety suggests, this subjection is to be done in the name of and by means of a kind of instruction, of *Bildung*. But the remarkable thing is how the means chosen and deployed to rein in and bind the unruly subjects are themselves explicitly "strange and fantastic," or differently put, how the strange and fantastic are put in the service of achieving sober, normative bounds; in other words, enchantment in the service of disenchantment. This is the context in which the painting of Meretlein is properly introduced: it underscores how the magic of painting, every bit as much as magic stories, is meant to put an end to the witchery.

In fact, the scenario described by Heinrich shows remarkable similarities to the powerful description of Joshua Reynolds's painting of the Bunbury boy that Nancy Armstrong uses to launch her analysis of how nineteenth-century novels work (or "think").[49] Armstrong relates the anecdote of how the painter used the telling of fantastic ghost stories to get his restless young subject to sit cooperatively still and fix his gaze back on the painter, who could then in turn fix him on his canvas: she argues that this use of a fantastic, supernatural fiction to control the subject is foundational for the emergence of the individual constructed by nineteenth-century novels and *Bildung* alike. We have much the same elements operant here, with the subjects bound by the fantastic stories and the painter who captures the controlled, spellbound subject—except that in this case, the subjects are split in two, with the latter-day children subject to the fantastic stories and the earlier Meretlein subject to (and of) the painting. On the one hand, this underscores the parallel between the way the children are bound or educated (*gebildet*) via the stories and Meretlein is bound and painted (*gebildet*) via the portrait. On the other hand, it opens up the space for a different fantastic means for subjecting Meretlein, means associated with an earlier period: binding her not via fantastic stories, but via fantastic clothes, which is also to say, via things.

The use of clothes in the early modern era as a means of enforcing social identity is well known: sumptuary laws have long been recognized as one of the external coercive mechanisms for subject formation that become displaced by more interiorized disciplinary means—such as ghost stories—with the advent of the Enlightenment.[50] As befits its early modern setting, the story of Meretlein retains this use, but the particular way her clothing coerces and constrains her is still very much in keeping with the later use of fantastic tales. The painting shows Meretlein as

> a young girl of extraordinarily delicate build, in a pale green damask gown whose hem was spread stiffly (*starrte*) in a wide circle and concealed her feet. Around the slender, fine body a gold chain was hung. . . . On her head she wore a headdress formed like a crown, made of small, shimmering gold and silver leaves, braided with silken threads and pearls.

> ein außerordentlich zartgebautes Mädchen in einem blaßgrünen Damastkleide, dessen Saum in einem weiten Kreise starrte und die Füßchen nicht sehen ließ. Um den schlanken feinen Leib war eine goldene Kette geschlungen. . . . Auf dem Haupte trug es einen kronenartigen Kopfputz aus flimmernden Gold- und Silberblättchen, von seidenen Schnüren und Perlen durchflochten.[51]

It is not so much signs of class or even gender that these clothes embody as it is those of the marvelous; and her fantastic sartorial accoutrements bind Meretlein to their own "strange and fantastic details." She becomes, as it were, magically trapped by her trappings: from the border (*Saum*) that locks her within its circle and deprives her of feet, of any means of movement or escape, to the chain bound about her body and the straps (*Schnüren*) about her head. The pale green of the damask cloth (itself a woven net) seems to transform itself into the extraordinarily delicate build of her body, the gold of the chain into its thin fineness. Every enchanting aspect of her clothes, every fantastic prop of the painter's art, come to charm her and bind her, to discipline her into an appropriate, contained, but also distressingly lifeless subject, doubling the work of the painterly medium itself: every thing seems to reinforce the metonymical regime of the child's skull Meretlein holds in her hand. In short, bewitching magic is not just the end to be controlled. It is also the means of control.

Of course, the deployment of such sartorial enchantment to constrain the witch-child results in its own foreseeable failure. For one thing, and as befits the place of this story not only in the early modern but also in the nineteenth-century novel, this external constraint yields an inward turn, the production of a spirited (*geistreich*) interiority in Meretlein that bears all the marks of its imposed cruelty (in the form of sadness and melancholy) and aestheticization (in eyes beautiful and shining), that for that very reason comes to exert a new bewitching force all its own, more or less behind or beyond either the merely material trappings of the painting or the original physical corporeality of the girl. A new, invisible "spirit-ed" realm of unruly and now deadly binding forces comes to the fore, every bit as seductive as the external realm of visible things. (This interior "spirit" realm becomes, as it were, the subjective correlative to the metatextual allegorical space painting opens up behind its own objective representation: both spectral, both at once a source of other life and death.)

For another thing, even insofar as Meretlein's external trappings impose their binding power on her and so produce in her a seemingly contained, interiorized subjectivity, they also cause that subjectivity to be bound to and dispersed among those (in)vestitures: the very metonymical means for forming a contained and disenchanted subject seem to prevent that from fully succeeding and, in the process, to reenchant the object world—and not least because the very means to create stilled subjects in this case relies on a continued active relation to an external world of things.[52] This underscores a point somewhat downplayed in Armstrong's account: the nineteenth century in general, and its novels in particular, are the setting for a world newly populated not only with "subjects" but also with "objects," indeed with subjects bound to objects. The two proliferations are, if not causally, still consequentially linked, as is their mutual enchantment.[53]

This last point tips the analysis in a new direction. Both the more Freudian and Foucauldian models for binding followed so far present complex pictures for how magical effects are turned against themselves in an effort to eliminate the excess forces of magic from the world; and both also offer sophisticated explanations for why those efforts fail and these forces remain a part of the (realist) world. But even in their accounts of systematic failure, both models themselves work systematically to disenchant the picture, not least because both restrict the operant field of magic to its strictly human dimension.[54] But there are additional elements to Keller's story that, for this reason, these models can't quite accommodate, but that I believe the model of *Stimmung* can.

Part of the sorcery exercised by Meretlein in her story is not only over men, nor only over the human community, but also, we're told, over birds, snakes, plants, and fish. This can be connected to the little leaves (*Blättchen*) in her pictured crown, which she later mimics with one made completely out of beech leaves (*Buchenlaub*) on the Buch-berg, adding sashes similarly formed: all these signal, and celebrate, her intimate connection, her boundness to the natural world (itself signaled at another level as [also] a *Buch-welt*).[55] This also helps explain her initial response to her fantastic outfit for the painting, which was one of great joy and wild dancing—the same response she has when naked outdoors, and one only transformed into its opposite by the addition of the child's skull, which works to enforce a different, one-sided reading of the magical binding forces at work between her and her things (and behind them, the text). But that the skull is not the end of it can be seen in the weather on the day of her intended death and, instead, of her magical resurrection. In ways that exceed the merely human world altogether, the heavens prove strangely attuned to and echoing of that human world, with the sky at first completely dark and lowering and then, at the moment of her resurrection, "as the sun, strangely penetrating (*seltsam und stechend*), pierced through the clouds, she looked, with her yellow brocade and her shimmering crown, like a fairy- or goblin-child"—an instant of human and cosmic *Stimmung* or sympathy in which even the pastor is forced to believe in the existence of a kind of magic (*habe in diesem Moment steif an ein Hexenthum geglaubt*).

All this points in a direction similar to that seen in the double bind between Meretlein and her trappings, where at the same time that they chained and constrained her she became joined up with and broadcast into them. But here Meretlein's relation to objects extends beyond a social human world—and thus, to bonds with objects whose meaning and power do not only arise out of such a human world. Instead, connections are being made to a natural world of things—or more precisely, to a world of natural but also invisible and allegorical forces that are only communicated via natural things—in a way that can only be weakly or "subjectively" accounted for by either a Freudian or Foucauldian model, but that is fully supported by the idea of *Stimmung*, which admits both a nonhuman external world and, crucially, a world behind that world: a world and set of relations that needn't be dismissed as merely part of the story's early modern setting, but might prove intrinsic to both the subjects and objects of Keller's realist novel, and to their relations, in both their happy and threatening sympathies.

The sign of the necessary inclusion of this natural and other allegorical world in the text, indeed in the portrait, might be seen in the white rose the painter introduces into the painting. He does so without explanation, and the pastor accepts it as "a good symbol" (*ein gutes Symbolum*), although of exactly what he does not, and perhaps cannot, say. Meretlein holds it in one hand as she does the skull in the other, and like the skull, the painter's rose clearly harnesses and re-presents allegorical forces lurking within and behind the painting. And as with the skull, the re-presented forces seem to some extent also metatextual, signaling an equally essential *Element* of the painter's art to be taken in by the viewer (qua reader). But the rose pushes the allegorical and metatextual forces entering the painting in a rather different direction, away from deathful containment and toward some kind of undefined natural life—as crucial in its indeterminacy and lack of explicit referent as in its naturalness. The white rose hints at something else, something more—a something else that, along with the rose, will reappear in the figure of Anna.[56]

Landscape (*Vorbilder*)

The portrait of Meretlein is introduced out of chronological order: it makes its first actual appearance in the novel at the moment of

Heinrich's own exposure to this natural world of interconnected things, an exposure that coincides with the beginning of his *Bildung* as a painter, soon before the introduction of Anna.[57] Heinrich has left behind his formal schooling in the city and journeyed to his uncle's house in the country, carrying with him his books and painting supplies. He wakes up after his first night in this new setting "on the breast of mighty Nature," in the midst of a teeming tableau of men and animals—a marten, deer, dogs, cows, horses, goats—both inside and outside the house, with an expansive landscape glimpsed out the window: all things described in almost excessive realist detail, but also in language laced with metaphors of music and weaving and images of wild, communal joy. As Heinrich sits in the midst of this chorus and weave, the portrait of Meretlein reappears:

> I sat at the window and breathed the balmy morning air; the shimmering waves of the swift stream flickered back again on the white ceiling, and their reflection lit up the countenance of that strange child, whose antiquated [*altertümliches*] image hung on the wall. It seemed, under the play of the changing silver light, to live, and increased the impression everything made on me.

> Ich saß an dem offenen Fenster und atmete die balsamische Morgenluft; die glitzernden Wellen des raschen Flüßchens flimmerten wider an der weißen Zimmerdecke und ihr Reflex überstrahlte das Angesicht jenes seltsamen Kind, dessen altertümliches Bild an der Wand hing. Es schien unter dem Wechseln des spielenden Silberscheines zu leben und vermehrte den Eindruck, den Alles auf mich machte.[58]

As an omen anticipating Heinrich's relation not only to the natural world but also to his painting of it—and beyond that, to his not-yet-begun relation to Anna—the Meretlein portrait here introduces a rather somber undertone to the animating harmony. The carefully constructed image of nature and man as a concert of sympathetically echoing elements finds its visual analogue in the web of reflections surrounding Heinrich: the morning light that blends into the air and water and then reflectively appears again on the ceiling, and from there reflects onto the portrait, infusing both the child and her portrait with their reflectively communicated life—even as then Meretlein and the *altertümlich* portrait communicate themselves back into that life, that web ("the impression every-thing made on me").[59] It seems fitting that Heinrich's description of this natural world culminates in the humming concert of insects weaving its web amid the abundant plant life in the nearby grave-yard: Meretlein has already sounded this deadly note behind the *Stimmung* of the bounded world.

We see here that the particular magic of Meretlein is from the outset of Heinrich's country stay inserted into the weave of forces connecting both the world of natural things to itself and Heinrich to that world. We see, too, that the avenues of insertion for that magic are those of conjoining re-presentation, in the form of both the "natural" reflections of the nonhuman world and the ancient or antiquated (*altertümlich*) aesthetic representation of the human one. And there is a third site in this relation, one placed between the reflections of the natural world and the representation of the witch-child, namely, the reflection of the room's white ceiling—a site that adumbrates the white wall on which Heinrich will paint his landscape of the Heathen Chamber in Anna's room, that in dif-ferent but closely related ways will again activate the relations be-tween nature, painting, and a "little witch," with death foreboded again as their joining force.

That blank reflecting space between the outside world and the painted girl seems, then, already to mark the medial and mediating space about to be occupied by Heinrich's landscape painting; for his first response to the reciprocating activity (*Tätigkeit*) of nature and man he experiences upon waking is to want to become actively part of it himself by means of his paper and brush.[60] This impulse inspires Heinrich to attempt his first nature painting en plein air, as he ventures into the nearby woods to sketch a beech tree (*Buch-baum*) and a young ash (*junge Esche*). This is a crucial step in his *Bildung* as a realist artist, his first contact as an artist with the "real," and so we'll want to look closely at it for what it shows landscape painting to entail: to see what relations obtain between Heinrich as painter and his subject (his landscape), how these re-lations reflect those found already in the Meretlein painting, and what these might reveal about the magic behind the world—and behind realism—even here. But first we need some background.

While the painting of the trees is Heinrich's first real exposure to nature as a subject of landscape painting, it is not his first exposure to landscape painting itself, which actually happens in the absence of nature. This occurs at several different junctures. The first comes when, after his own unruly behavior in the social world, Heinrich is confined to his mother's house and made to suffer the further constraint (*Be-fangenheit*) of her punishing silence. While in this house arrest and profoundly still (*gründlich still*), Heinrich undertakes to copy an old landscape painted in oils that hangs on a wall. Although apparently (i.e., empirically, in itself) mediocre in quality, it is nonetheless a "wondrous" work (*ein bewunderns-wertes Werk*) that inspires Heinrich's wonderment (*Verwunder-ung*): and "the peace that breathed in the well-intentioned picture arose in my soul, too, and might have shone from my face over to my mother."[61] The "incomprehensible," melding connectedness of seemingly opposing elements (*der unbegreifliche Übergang des Roten ins Blaue*) and the pervasive unity (*Gleichmässigkeit*) that Heinrich discovers in the painting spill out of it and, via reflection, draw into its charmed circle, its happy or *glückliche Stimmung*, the warring/loving human players outside of it, in the "real world." This leads Heinrich to "forget himself" and actually begin singing while painting—both symptoms of *Stimmung*—and by the time the painting is completed the silence and arrest are over and he has become reconciled and reconnected with his mother. That the reconciliation is at least in part the result of natural (musical) forces working through the painting is suggested by Heinrich's description of the mother's words breaking her silence as "like snow-bells in early spring."[62]

The second instance of Heinrich's exposure to landscape painting remains closely linked to the first, not least in the continued absence of nature—but now not only of nature. It occurs after he has been expelled from a school linked to his dead father and has again been confined to his mother's house. He again occupies himself with painting landscapes; but "since I didn't possess any more models (*Vorbilder*), I had to call them [i.e., landscapes] into being all on my own." Or as he also puts it, "I invented my own landscapes" (Ich erfand eigene Landschaften). That this is not quite the case is underscored when Heinrich explains how he draws on a store of miniature landscape motifs that he gleans from an old album (*Stammbuch*) of his mother, from a small library of out-of-date ladies' almanacs from her youth, as well as from the painted oven in their shared room.[63]

Two closely related points emerge from this. First, the evident exclusion of examples derived from his mother's world as *Vorbilder* suggests that, at some not quite articulated level and by a hidden associational logic, their absence for his painting is linked by Heinrich with other missing *Vorbilder* as well: most notably that of the dead father, but with him all the other, older male models of the patriarchal order outside the maternal home, including those from his father's school. Second, when Heinrich speaks of lacking a *Vorbild* and inventing his own landscapes, he shows that what he means by *Landschaft* is not so much the individual things or motifs visible therein—the mountains, bridges, columns, or lakes he finds in his mother's books—as the invisible force that connects them and makes them whole. The missing *Vorbild* is, as it were, the missing *Vor-bild*, the space before or behind the picture. Without it, instead of a unity he produces only a pile of motifs heaped together (*zusammengehäuft*); instead of a tone-setting *Stimmung* coming to him from some outside and connecting him to that outside, he has only his own isolated mood and person to project into the picture (which he quite literally does)—a person ultimately as disunified and disconnected as the painting he produces. Landscape painting emerges here as the place for "magical thinking" in the narrowest, most restricted sense: unbound by any connection to the outside world, projecting onto it the fantasies or moods of a self-regarding subject, and so finally reflecting more of the "reality" of that subject than anything of the world itself—indeed (and in this, very different from the first example) having no real connection with or effect upon the world at all.

The third early exposure comes only after Heinrich has left his mother's home and arrived at his uncle's, in the narrow time-space between his morning awakening in the country and his encounter in the woods with the trees. It moves the focus from the isolated individual to the social: and it does so by providing contact with precisely the kind of *Vorbilder* that were missing when Heinrich was alone with his mother.[64] In his uncle's house, Heinrich comes across texts and images from the long tradition of landscape painting.[65] Significantly, almost all of these come from an earlier, Enlightenment period, thus evoking both an ideal of *Bildung* and, inevitably, an aura of the antiquated past, even of the dead—evoking in both respects the world of the father.[66] These texts and images (this traffic with the dead) stand at the outset of the *Bildung* proper that the novel will trace out, wherein Heinrich will join his solitary magical thinking to the unifying order and binding norms of this *vor-bild-lich* realm: they will serve as the source for the conventions (the magic formulae) that will bind Heinrich's "fantastic nature" not only to a properly socialized realm but also, through them, to the natural world of landscape itself.[67]

It is against this background that we now approach Heinrich's own approach as a painter to nature—an approach that, in the first instance, proves a complete disaster.[68] Equally inspired by his early solitary fantasies in his mother's house, his recent book-learning in his uncle's, and his morning awakening to the weave of nature and man, Heinrich goes into the woods to draw. At first he is unable to separate out a single object as subject for his sketch, but eventually a mighty beech-tree (*ein gewaltiger Buchbaum*) seems to stand out from the closely conjoined ranks of trees, and Heinrich imagines himself able to subjugate its form (*seine Gestalt bezwingen zu können*). But rather than mastering or arresting it (*[ihn] festzuhalten*), it masters him, and he falls into his own state of constraint (*Befangenheit*). He does draw, but produces a sketch lifeless and meaningless (*leben- und bedeutungslos*); composing his picture one piece at a time, he proves incapable of bringing the fragments into relation to the whole (*in ein Verhältnis zum Ganzen*). The figure on his paper grows monstrous: "When I looked up and finally ran my eye over the whole, there grinned back at me a ridiculously distorted picture, like a dwarf in a concave mirror; but the living beech (*Buche*) radiated in even greater majesty than before."

How to understand the failure of Heinrich's first attempt at painting nature, or, as we could also say, at realism? An answer is perhaps best approached by noting the most remarkable aspect of this first contact with the "real," and that is how it is primarily presented in allegorical terms. We need to consider both sides of this remarkable aspect: both the specific allegorical terms in which the scene is presented, and the bare fact that it is presented as an allegory.[69]

The terms of the allegory are suggested in the mention of "majesty" with which Heinrich concludes his account, but they are present throughout in the image of this mighty tree, "with noble trunk and magnificent cloak and crown," challenging Heinrich, "like a king from olden days who summons his foe to single combat," stepping forth from the joined ranks of the forest's "sons" (her trees). The image confirms what our earlier examples portended: that landscape painting is deeply implicated for Heinrich in a relation—both psychological and social—to a patriarchal order, a notably ancient, even antiquated order of male figures that represents a unity all its own that stands between Heinrich, nature, and his drawing; and that Heinrich's failure is in part due to his not being properly connected to that order, the order that alone is capable of binding nature and bestowing life and meaning on his painting, but only once it has bound and bestowed life and meaning on him.[70] Without that *Stimmung* (that connection), the final product of his painting—the ridiculously distorted image that grins back at him, like a dwarf in a concave mirror—remains more a reflection of his own interior subjectivity than of any external, objective world.

There is another explanation embedded in this scene for why the attempt fails, one that engages more directly with the novel's natural world—an explanation that gives a rather different and perhaps more integral reason for the allegory itself. This explanation notes that what Heinrich attempts to represent, to copy, as the natural world is in important ways never really there in the material things themselves, but only in an immaterial realm beyond them—which is to say, in a necessarily allegorical space: that the reality he seeks to capture isn't there, but only behind or between what is there.[71] This is evident from the outset. The forest presents itself to Heinrich not as isolated things, but as a unity and web of relations: as the great whole (*das große Ganze*), intertwined, nestled, and folded together (*verschlungen, sich schmiegten, verschränkten*) and everywhere bound to itself (*sich überall verbunden*). And the *Buch-baum* itself proves to be not a thing, either, at least not a thing that can be arrested or represented, but rather some well-nigh immaterial being behind a constantly changing and moving, appearing and disappearing, set of relations and effects:

> Sunbeams through the foliage played upon the trunk, lighting up sap lines and then letting them disappear again; now a gray silvery spot, now a lush bit of moss would smile out from the half-darkness, now a small branch sprouting out from the roots swayed in the light, a reflection revealed a new line of lichen on the side deepest in shadow, until everything disappeared again and made room for new appearances.

> Die Sonnenstrahlen spielten durch das Laub auf dem Stamme, beleuchteten die markigen Züge und ließen sie wieder verschwinden, bald lächelte ein grauer Silberfleck, bald eine saftige Moosstelle aus dem Helldunkel, bald schwankte ein aus den Wurzeln sprossendes Zweiglein im Lichte, ein Reflex ließ auf der dunkelsten Schattenseite eine neue mit Flechten bezogene Linie entdecken, bis Alles wieder verschwand und neuen Erscheinungen Raum gab.[72]

Through all the shuttling in external appearance, the *Buchbaum* itself maintains a removed wholeness, an interior and decidedly spectral harmony: as Heinrich says, "The tree stood there as calm as ever in its greatness, and from deep within let a ghostly whispering be heard" (Der Baum in seiner Größe [stand] immer gleich ruhig da . . . und [ließ] in seinem Innern ein geisterhaftes Flüstern vernehmen).

We needn't listen too hard to hear inside this description a whispered allusion to the "great" notion of stillness in motion (*Ruhe in Bewegung*), a principle that in the novel is closely allied with *Stimmung*, and not least because both are allied not only with nature but, behind it, with "the great shade" of Johann Wolfgang Goethe—who, I suggest, is also spectrally behind or within the figure of this *Buchbaum* (the main reason it is a *Buch-baum*).[73] As we discover later on, the demonic-divine (*dämonisch-göttlich*) shade of this Goethe exists in a uniquely present-tense temporality in this novel, one that stands outside of simple narrative time and, although introduced late, exerts its presence even here.[74] The stillness or *Ruhe* into which the *Buchbaum* retreats itself bespeaks this other removed dimension, and the Goethe who stands within and behind it unites all three aspects of Heinrich's relation to the *Buchbaum*.[75] He reflects key elements of Heinrich's psychological relation to the world of his father, especially in his identification with both a program of *Bildung* and death.[76] Similarly—and via the same double identification—he embodies key elements of Heinrich's relation to aesthetics, as the primus inter pares in the order of mentors, models, and *Vorbilder* that determines Heinrich's relation to art and, through art, to the world. But beyond these, Goethe also represents for Heinrich (as narrator) the life force or *Lebensgrund* behind the natural world, a force or ground that Heinrich defines as the very principle of connection that animates and empowers all the things and events of the narrative world. He is, as it were, a figure for *Stimmung*, for the magisterial spectral force and movement of relational unity that, while remaining largely hidden and untouched behind the world, binds together subjects, and subjects and objects, and mimetic representations and their objects, in webs at once psychological, social, aesthetic, and natural.[77] It is a blending of the metatextual, patriarchal, and natural every bit as evident and decisive as we saw in the case of Meretlein and her portrait.

This spectral nature that is at once the *Buch-baum*, Goethe, and *Stimmung* is a *force*, and a potentially threatening one. But that it appears here in the form of *Ruhe in Bewegung* is important for two reasons: it shows how the potential violence of this force can operate even in its most gentle, affirmative form; and it hints at a potential way out from under its threat for Heinrich—both of great significance for understanding what happens next, and for what will be Heinrich's relation to Anna, or rather, the relation of his painting to Anna. In elaborating on this principle once it is formally introduced into the text— after he has read Goethe—Heinrich writes in the present tense, which gives everything identified with Goethe its unique power and reality:

> It is only stillness in motion that upholds the world and makes the man; the world is calm and still within, and so must a man be as well, if he wants to understand the world and, as an effective part of it, reflect it back. Stillness draws on life [Ruhe zieht das Leben an].

> Nur die Ruhe in der Bewegung hält die Welt und macht den Mann; die Welt ist innerlich ruhig und still, und so muß es auch der Mann sein, der

sie verstehen und als wirkender Teil von ihr widerspiegeln will. Ruhe
zieht das Leben an.[78]

For all its apparent calm, the *Ruhe* at the heart of the world is
a form of stillness and arrest; and as something that makes "the
man," it threatens him with a kind of arrest and stillness as well—
with precisely the kind of constraint or *Be-fangenheit* to which
Heinrich succumbs when faced with the *Buchbaum*. The (magical) trick, as Heinrich describes it, is for the artist to learn how to
redirect the threat of *Ruhe* by turning it (*dies anzuwenden*) back
upon the world; to join with the hidden order behind the world, to
share in both its distance and unseen action, and from there reflect
its endangering force back on and into the world.[79] And in its own
indirect way, Heinrich's language also makes plain where the *Ruhe*
is to be redirected: from "the man" and onto "the feminine" that
Ruhe here replaces (as the subject of *zieht an*).[80]

   This at least is what we see in Heinrich's next attempt. Defeated
in his direct power struggle against the (male) beech-tree, Heinrich
takes refuge in praying to God—which is to say, in invoking the invisible male order he failed to master—and turns to a new subject,
a different tree: a young ash (*eine junge Esche*). The turn clearly
correlates to the turn we see him make in two other instances: first,
in the shift of his identification in the Meretlein episode from one
with the rebellious child to one with the disciplining male adults,
the painter and pastor; and second, in response to his own losing
struggles with the male social world (i.e., his father's school), in his
coming to identify himself as painter with Anna's father as educator over and against his beloved Anna. These other instances are
not mere parallels to the present scene: rather, the young ash is deliberately described in ways that recall Meretlein and predict Anna,
beginning with its gender.[81] The task—the opportunity—here is to
see even more clearly how Heinrich's landscape painting is implicated in his relation to his female subjects.

   The young ash—also called "the little tree" (*das Bäumchen*)—
"had a slender trunk only two inches thick and above a delicate
crown of foliage whose leaves, in regular rows, could be counted,"
recalling the figure of Meretlein in both its marked, even starved thinness and its delicate, ornamented, leafed crown; the identification

is furthered when Heinrich speaks of "the childlike little trunk," "its beautiful figure," its "fineness," and so on—all features that turn the tree into an echo of Meretlein, and all features that will connect both Meretlein and the tree to Anna.[82] Moreover, the tree first presents itself to Heinrich sketched (*gezeichnet*) against "the clear gold of the evening sky" in such a way as to make it a shadow image (*Schattenbild*) of itself, which is to say, like the portrait of Meretlein, already aestheticized, already a *Bild*, removed from the (material) real and in spectral form—a state that will also be passed on to Anna, about whom Heinrich will say at the end of the first day he sees her: "Doused in the glow of the setting sun, the feather-light, transfigured form (*verklärte Gestalt*) of the young girl floated before me."[83]

When Heinrich sits down to sketch the childlike little trunk— or as he puts it, to "steal" it onto his paper—he does so by first drawing two parallel lines. The verb choice and the parallel lines reveal what is at stake in the painting: a magical attempt to bind the subject via its mimesis (literally, to draw it into his page).[84] Tellingly, the tree does not easily submit or succumb to the attempt and displays an unruly, energetic movement that threatens to frustrate Heinrich's drawing—repeating the struggle with the beech tree, but more importantly, also that with Meretlein (which was also, we remember, a displaced struggle with disruptive forces originating in the male sphere). But Heinrich persists and clamps onto "every movement of my model" (*jede Bewegung meines Vorbildes*), until he has captured it as his picture or *Gebild*:

> Once under way, I reverently added the grasses and small roots growing in the ground nearest it, and now I saw on my paper one of those pious, little long-stemmed Nazarene trees that cut across the horizon with such charm and simplicity in the pictures of the church-painters of old and their epigonal followers of today.

> Ich fügte, einmal im Zuge, mit Andacht die nächsten Gräser und Würzelchen des Bodens hinzu, und sah nun auf meinem Blatte eines jener frommen nazarenischen Stengelbäumchen, welche auf den Bildern der alten Kirchenmaler und ihrer heutigen Epigonen den Horizont so anmutig und naiv durchschneiden.[85]

When the drawing is complete, Heinrich feels as if he has done something wondrous *(als ob ich Wunder was verrichtet hätte)*. And it truly is a "wondrous" thing he has performed. To see this we need also see that, for all the apparent absence of the "real" tree itself from Heinrich's final, thoroughly conventional, and antiquated sketch, it is somehow still present as its subject—every bit as much as Meretlein is present in her painting. In fact, the conventions must be understood as working in strictly analogous fashion on the tree to the way Meretlein's clothes do on her eroticism (or for that matter, the way the same conventions work on Heinrich's fantasy): they work to capture or bind its unruly reality, and do so by drawing on, but turning back against the "real" the magical forces that emanate out of it (drawing as at once a drawing on and mirroring back). That the binding magic is once again a death-filled one is marked both in the overt, lifeless aestheticization and in the antiquated, epigonal character of the evoked conventions (as we've seen with both Meretlein's portrait and Heinrich's own relation to conventions); that somehow the surrounding natural world of objects is to contribute to the binding effect is brought home by the inclusion of the grasses and small roots in the ground nearest it— the very same sense of a surrounding world that, in the case of the beech tree, marked its boundedness to the natural world and frustrated Heinrich's attempt at binding here becomes utilized by him to accomplish that binding of the ash: again, the double nature or power of sympathetic relations. All told, then, Heinrich's landscape painting really does aim to perform a *Wunder*, to practice a magical art of drawing on forces of binding and, inevitably, of death; and that magic can really happen precisely because the real world of the novel itself is grounded in forces of binding and death that art can draw on: on nature, the demon-god Goethe, and *Stimmung*. And this brings us to Anna.

Anna (Narcissus and Echo)

Anna enters the novel immediately following Heinrich's painting of the two trees, and she is just as immediately linked with all three dimensions of his relation to landscape painting: the psychological, the social, and the natural. All three figure prominently in the erotic bonds that from the outset bind Heinrich to Anna, and by which she will soon be bound by him, and as we'll see, they do so in a process that echoes the binding of both the original witch-child, Meretlein, and the young ash-tree—and that not just echoes, but actively engages the witching forces of the one and the drawing powers of the other.

All three dimensions are summoned up as Heinrich goes to visit Anna for the first time. The psychological appears in a manner that combines the clothing motif of the Meretlein episode and the (absent) *Vorbild* motif of Heinrich's landscape painting in his mother's house. Heinrich dresses himself for the visit in a fantastic and (for him) painterly (*malerisch*) fashion, drawing on items borrowed from his mother's wardrobe. But rather than as with Meretlein enforcing a fixed identity, his outfit as with his painting betrays a sense of disunity and in particular a lack of gender definition, all evidence, he says, of the lack of a fatherly *Vorbild*. He becomes in his clothing, as it were, an embodied reproduction of the magical thinking in his earlier landscape painting.

The social is evoked more directly, in the brief sketch of Anna's father, who, much as the masters of painting encountered in the uncle's house, will become a (fatherly) *Vorbild* for Heinrich, but here in relation not to landscape but directly to Anna. He is introduced as a former village schoolmaster deeply invested in matters of *Bildung*, which he pursues both in his own person and, reflectively, through the figure of his daughter. And the natural is evoked most directly, in the detailed description of the walk through the woods that Heinrich takes to reach Anna in her father's house, a description that deliberately echoes that of the first morning's awakening in his uncle's house described above.

This is the background against which Anna first appears, and the passage needs to be quoted at length. Heinrich stands in the woods and looks down at a "still and calm" (*still und ruhig*) lake that suddenly comes into view:

> A narrow strip of cultivated land surrounded the lake, and behind it the forest continued upward in every direction. . . . On the sunny side lay a vineyard of considerable extent, and at its foot the schoolmaster's house, close by the lake; but immediately above the highest rows of wine-grapes hung the pure deep heaven, and this mirrored itself in

the smooth water, up to where it was bounded by the yellow rows of corn, the emerald fields of clover and the woods behind them, all of which re-presented itself, unaltered but inverted, in the lake. The house was whitewashed, the woodwork painted red and the window-shutters painted with large shells and flowers; white curtains fluttered out of the windows and out of the door and down a dainty set of stairs stepped the young cousin, slender and delicate as a narcissus, in a white dress belted with a sky-blue band, with golden-brown hair, blue eyes, a somewhat willful brow and a small smiling mouth. One blush after another welled up on her narrow cheeks, her fine bell-like voice rang out almost inaudibly, and died away again at every moment.

Ein schmaler Streifen bebauter Erde zog sich um den See herum, hinter demselben setzte sich überall der ansteigende Wald fort. . . . Nur auf der Sonnenseite lag ein ansehnlicher Weinberg und zu Füßen desselben das Haus des Schulmeisters, dicht am See, unmittelbar über den höchsten Weinreihen aber hing der reine tiefe Himmel, und dieser spiegelte sich in dem glatten Wasser, bis wo er durch den gelben Kornstreifen, die smaragdenen Kleefelder und den dahinter liegenden Wald, welche alle sich gänzlich unverändert in der Flut auf den Kopf stellten, begrenzt wurde. Das Haus war weiß getüncht, das Fachwerk rot angestrichen und die Fensterladen mit großen Muscheln und Blumen bemalt, aus den Fenstern wehten weiße Gardinen und aus der Haustür trat, ein zierliches Treppchen herunter, das junge Bäschen, schlank und zart wie eine Narzisse, in einem weißen Röckchen und mit einem himmelblauen Bande gegürtet, mit gold-braunen Haaren, blauen Äuglein, einer etwas eigensinnigen Stirne und einem kleinen lächelnden Mündlein. Auf den schmalen Wangen wallte ein Erröten über das andere hin, das feine Glockenstimmchen klang kaum vernehmbar und verhallte alle Augenblicke wieder.[86]

The theme of binding—even of binding magic—runs throughout this passage, engaging the natural and human worlds in ever-tightening concentric circles, first around the lake and then around Anna. The initial antiphonic tension, as it were, between the natural and human is set in the contrast between the narrow "cultivated" band of earth that draws itself around the lake and the still wild woods that remain outside and around it.[87] The same contrast reappears in the more circumscribed (and humanized) form of the vineyard paired with the schoolmaster's house, the one hinting at wild bacchanal unruliness, the other (hugging the lake) countering with protective *Bildung* (with both acquiring a further circumscription in their future inculcation into a human subject, the one in the form of the wine and the other of schooling). In both cases, the bind between the two realms seems a double one, suggesting the equal force and pull of both worlds: but the balance is then immediately (*unmittelbar*) tipped in the direction of containment or arrest by the addition of a new set of binding forces operating both without and within this first pair: the "pure" heaven that encompasses everything (including the woods and vineyard, but also the house and cultivated strip) from the extreme outside; and the lake's reflection that similarly encompasses everything (including the heaven) from the very center. Both sky and lake are, significantly, still part of the natural world, and so partake of its forces; but both also begin to exceed this world and introduce in allegorical form an "other" dimension into the landscape, at once (quasi-) divine and metatextual.[88] The peculiar binding or *begrenzend* force of the heavenly is conveyed by its purity, countering the wildness of the woods and the riot of grapes; the peculiar force of the reflection is conveyed by the suddenly markedly painterly, color-oriented character of the language of the narrator, who works in collusive connection with his intradiegetic painter-character (which is to say, from the very center of the text).[89] In this way, the lake's reflection positions representation itself with the (natural) divine as a force encompassing the entire setting: indeed, in its reflection, the lake binds together as one the divine (heaven), nature (cultivated earth), *Bildung* (schoolmaster), painting, and narration as one unified force working from both outside and inside the natural human world. Not incidentally, that final frame of the divine sky and the metatextual lake also introduces into the scene the haunting intimation not only of other, supranatural forces, but also of another temporality, that of the suddenly assertive, self-manifesting narrator: one in which the future is already reflected in the present, and in which the present is—spectrally, preconceptually—already contained by its own future.

Even as the lake is set at the center of these encompassing circles, so too Anna seems both metaphorically to double the lake and to be set metonymically within an even tighter circle beside it. She first appears framed by the house of her schoolmaster father, suggesting the binding force of his *Bildung* program on her. But the framing house is also described in terms of painting, and again mostly through colors: it is "whitewashed" and "painted red," "painted with large shells and flowers"—and those shells augur forth a frame Heinrich will place around one of his pictures of Anna later on, again drawing attention to the spectral presence and futural power of the narrator. But already, even without that augury, we see the same collusion of *Bildung* and *Bild*, of schoolmaster and painter, that we saw with Meretlein, here directed at Anna by her father and Heinrich in ways that fulfill that earlier omen (i.e., Meretlein), or are haunted in turn by its premonition—not causally, but still determinatively. Even as Meretlein's clothes (magically) transformed themselves into her body to control her, so here does this painterly schoolhouse mimetically/metonymically reproduce itself on Anna, and both outside and in. Her "somewhat willful brow" and "small smiling mouth"—recalling the unruliness of not only Meretlein but also the ash tree (and within the description, the wild woods and wine-grapes)—are countered by the white of her dress, which draws on and in the white of the house and of the curtains inside (the latter suggesting interiorization); and similarly, the "blush" that appears on her cheeks draws on the red against white of its woodwork. Even the "dainty set of stairs" (*Treppchen*) on which she stands reappears as both Anna's "delicateness" (*Zärtlichheit*) and the diminunizing -*chen* of her dress, eyes, mouth, and voice.

All of this binds her, constrains her, in ways that practically force the slenderness of her figure (think of Meretlein's starving, but also of the ash's trunk): and that it does so by means of this mimetic, re-presenting relation gives the peculiar force to what is the very center of this description, the moment when it dissolves into pure symbol or allegory (like the white rose or beech tree) and presents Anna as like a narcissus. The image draws together crucial strands. Most obviously, it sets Anna up as the site for Heinrich's self-regarding, subjective projection, for the kind of magical thinking we saw already in his landscape painting: his erotic relations will prove equally narcissistic, equally a matter of displaced self-projection, and equally denying of the subject's own reality. And as part of that, the symbol foretells the death that always inhabits the narcissistic gaze and from the start haunts this erotic relation as well. But the image of Narcissus (which is to say, of mirroring) also marks Anna as the site for just the kind of reflecting relations that we see here actively at work between her and the house, an image that metonymcially links her to the lake and is inscribed in the reflectivity of her very name (An-nA): and that along with the lake (and house) is deeply implicated in the matter of painting.

It is not, however, only the house, with its double binding force of *Bildung* and *Bild*, that seems reflectively reproduced at the site of Anna; the surrounding natural world also reappears here in microcosmic form. This is true of the encompassing sky, which finds its echo in the "sky-blue band" that girds Anna as surely as the heaven itself does the entire scene; but the yellow of the cornrows is also echoed in the golden brown of her (presumably braided) hair and the dark blue of the lake in and as Anna's own blue eyes.[90] The chain is, of course, also mediated in the form of the flowers (and shells) that appear painted on the house's shutters, as it will be again in the hat and shawl Anna soon dons for her woods walk with Heinrich, the former bound with cornflowers and poppies, the latter "a grand white shawl, used long ago on state occasions, strewn with asters and roses" (*ein prachtvoller weißer Staatsshawl aus alter Zeit mit Astern und Rosen besäet*).[91] In all these various ways, Anna is uniquely, forcefully, reflectively bound in sympathetic relation to the natural world, or rather, to both the social world (in the form of the house and, in the case of the shawl, the state) and the natural world, or even more fully: to the present world of both human and natural things, mediated by a more invisible but no less present world of divine forces (that blue sky), *Bildung* (that house), and, within and behind it all, the metatext of painting and narration.

All told, the entire passage seems a deliberately composed illustration of *Stimmung*, in its "coordinately colored relational weave" (*einheitlich gefärbtes Beziehungsgeflecht*), an "interplay of echoing tone variations": in the way the relationality plays itself out contagiously both in and among things themselves, and then between Anna's subjectivity and those objective things; in the unity between the elements brought about by the work of similitude, analogy, and metonymy, but also at its very center, allegory; and in the almost excessive visibility of the scene coupled with the haunting presence of the invisible forces that connect things. These invisible forces seem at once natural, social, supernatural, and metatextual; and as we've seen (particularly in the shells), the last implicitly brings an added element to the description and its play of *Stimmung*: temporality. The final line of the passage cited brings this added element more explicitly into play, by subtly shifting the metaphorical field pervading the description from painting to music. The shift keeps the metaphorics of *Stimmung*, but—especially through the focus on echoes—also extends them to include additional matters of time and action, making these aspects of *Stimmung* integral to the workings of the text world as well.

Music and echoes are as inseparable from Anna as painting and reflections, and equally integral to her connection with the natural and social/human worlds. Here at the end of this passage we have just the single line "her fine bell-like voice rang out almost inaudibly, and died away (*verhallte*) again at every moment" and, immediately following, mention of "the house re-echoing with cleanliness and order" (*das vor Reinlichkeit und Aufgeräumtheit widerhallende Haus*).[92] But a second scene during this same first visit develops the motif in detail, and in ways that go well beyond Anna and the house. After a shared meal (of fish raised and caught by Anna, echoing Meretlein) the schoolmaster opens up his organ, "so that the inside of both folding doors displayed a painted Paradise, with Adam and Eve, flowers and beasts"—making the link not only between music and painting, but also, in the reference to Eden, to the harmonious union of man and nature (and the divine) broached in the first day's awakening (and implicit in the opening description of Anna)—all three (painting, music, natural harmony) integral to *Stimmung* (and Anna's relation to it). The unifying effect is furthered as Heinrich, Anna, and all the visitors are made to stand in a circle around the schoolmaster and, "after he had charmingly played a bit as a prelude," sing in unison, and in such a way that, Heinrich tells us, "I myself let my inner happiness stream forth unconstrained and freely into the singing" (Ich selbst ließ mein inneres Glück unbefangen und frei in den Gesang strömen)—with both the joined circle and the self-dispersal into that circle again representative of *Stimmung*. Then comes this:

> Whenever we came to the end of a verse, an echo sounded from across the lake, given back by a rock wall in the woods, dying away harmoniously, fusing the organ notes and the human voices in a new wondrous tone, and trembling into silence just as we ourselves raised the song again. Joyous human voices were roused at different places in the heights and depths, which sang and shouted their delight into the still, weaving air, so that the canon with which we closed spread itself, so to speak, over the whole valley.

> Wenn wir einen Vers geendigt hatten, erklang über den See her, von einer Wand im Walde, ein harmonisch verhallendes Echo, die Orgeltöne und Menschenstimmen verschmelzend zu einem neuen wunderbaren Tone, und zitterte eben aus, indem wir selbst den Gesang wieder anhoben. An verschiedenen Stellen, in der Höhe und Tiefe, wurden freudige Menschenstimmen wach, welche ihre Lust in die still webenden Lüfte sangen und jauchzten, so daß unser Kanon, mit welchem wir schlossen, sozusagen sich über das ganze Tal verbreitete.[93]

Four aspects of this passage interest me most. First, how as with the previous, painterly description of Anna, the effect—a "wondrous" one—is to create a web (*weben*) to bind the group with the entire natural world, or rather with the world of both nature and men (and the strangely indefinite origin of those "joyous human voices" augments the fusion). But whereas in the previous case this web was one of enclosing containment (contracting, vortexual), in this case it is in the first place one of dispersive broadcast (expanding, centrifugal). Second, how unlike with the painterly description, the binding effect is here presented as something that happens: as action, as a kind of contagious movement—and one with a built-in system of recursivity, of displacement, redirection, and return, in such a way that the broadcasting, centrifugal force is also transformed into a back-turning, centripetal one. Third, and as part of its emanation and reversion, how this movement introduces a complex temporal schema into the binding web, one not generally associated with painting (or painterly reflections) but intrinsic to echo, creating the conditions that not only transform its action into an *actio in distans*, but also allow for a projected futurity—or if you will, a belatedness—to become part of the force field established by *Stimmung*.[94]

The fourth point of interest only emerges later, when, so to speak, that belatedness is realized, that future comes home (and the extended infectiousness of its *Stimmung* beyond just this moment is evident, for instance, in the continued singing of the group throughout the day, long after they've left the schoolmaster's house): and that is how this web, here so seemingly benign, eventually returns as the means for Anna's (enchanted) entrapment—and it does so in good part by once again displacing its center from the male figure (here, her father) onto the female—turning its echo effect onto her. As mentioned, the schoolmaster will soon send her away to a city to further embody his program of *Bildung*. When she returns as "the fullfilment of his ideal, beautiful, delicate, and cultured (*gebildet*)," she takes his place at the organ while he stands, watching, behind her: as Heinrich says, "She really looked like a Saint Cecilia" (and for Saint Cecilia, compare the "church-painterly image" [*kirchenmalerische Bild*] of the young ash-tree).[95] The same system of radiating broadcast and echoing return as earlier is evident, except that, with Anna at its center, the forces have all, in their return (their reflection, their echo), become both art-ful (*künstlich*) and deadly. On the one hand, Anna has become an active force and the world around her transformed through her into art, into a (quasi-painterly) echo of her music. Her father now appears clothed in garments she embroiders, the house outfitted with pillows and a flowered (*großblumig*) carpet she devises, and outside "the little garden was no longer a disorderly rose and alpine-violet garden, but rather, more suited to Anna's present appearance, fitted out with foreign plants (*fremden Gewächsen*)": the schoolmaster, the house, and even the natural world have been transformed into an echo of Anna, and resonate with her new appearance, in an outward movement of broadcast, communicative contagion.[96] But on the other hand, Anna has herself become transformed and ever more tightly bound by that world: "She had become a completely different figure, . . . her golden hair lay smooth and genteelly bound (*gebunden*). . . . Her facial features kept themselves much stiller now (*viel ruhiger*), and her eyes had lost their freedom and were under the constraints (*in den Banden*) of conscious propriety . . . so that I was terrified."[97]

Magic Realism

A complex shift in agency is at work here: while both Anna and the natural world about her seem empowered, seem the site of active force, it is her father at one step removed (in both place and time) who has become the all but invisible agent (merely watching, no longer doing), working on the one hand through Anna and on the other through art and nature (the garden) to bind her in the deadly, echoing web: working through the time-delayed echo-effect of sympathetic relations. There is as much a realist as a magical effect to this mix of hidden (authorial) agency and apparent subject autonomy. And the question becomes, how does Heinrich also become such a removed invisible agent, working through similar sympathetic relations, similar echo-effects—and what has this to do with both the magic and realism at issue in his relation to painting and to Anna?

There are two parts to answering this question. First, we need to note how Heinrich himself—as lover—engages in a similar echoing system of broadcasting Anna into nature and then having it (or her) recursively turn back on him. We see this in a dream he records shortly after this first visit: "As I went to sleep, it spooked (*spukte*) and rustled . . . I never dreamed of Anna, but I kissed tree-leaves, flowers, and the air itself and was everywhere kissed in return."[98] Anna becomes spectrally dispersed into nature, and nature becomes a charged, macrocosmic version of her person. In his waking life, this becomes a particular invisible force invested in—but also with—the landscape that is at once sympathetic and erotic, and in both cases capable of exercising its attractive force from a distance, as Heinrich reports when he returns to the city: "Anna's dwelling, invisible to me, acted magnetically over all the land between (*wirkte magnetisch über alles dazwischen liegende Land her*)."[99] Something similar is also at stake when Heinrich takes on

Anna's flower-covered shawl after their walk through the woods: "Anna handed me the shawl . . . and I threw the soft, flowered wrap around my head and shoulders. . . . The stillness had now become, near and far, so deep that it seemed to turn into a ghostly roar (*ein geisterhaftes Getöse*). . . . As I stood for a moment as if spellbound (*wie festgebannt*), the whole horizon round seemed to tremble with a blissful shudder, [moving] from the mountain in ever narrowing circles right in to my heart."[100] In each case, an echo effect is achieved that binds Anna and the landscape, and that then turns back on Heinrich with its invisible, ghostly, magnetic forces—in the last case in ways that leave him, however joyfully, "spellbound" within their ever-tightening circles.

Second, we need to note how Heinrich manages to change the direction of these forces so that they target not him but Anna—and how in doing so he transforms their magic into realism, but without losing their magic. As anticipated by what we saw with Heinrich's tree painting, both these aspects are managed by the same double move: by introducing painting (and not so much as a reflected image of the visible as a de-flected echo of the invisible) into his relation to Anna and nature; and by himself retreating to the position of invisible agent, much like Anna's father while she plays (letting her and her world operate seemingly autonomously, untouched). It is hardly coincidental that it is in between the first singing session centered on the father and the second centered on Anna that Heinrich will paint his picture of the Heathen Chamber, charged as it will be with its magic echoing forces—nor that the "rock wall in the woods" that initiates those first echoes turns out to *be* the Heathen Chamber. And similarly, it is hardly coincidental that in Heinrich's first meeting with Anna, in between the first description of her and the group singing, comes one of the novel's most sustained theoretical discussions of landscape painting and realism—nor that that discussion focuses primarily on the significance of the invisible powers behind the visible world.

Almost as soon as Heinrich meets Anna, he begins a conversation with her father—forging a bond that, like that between the pastor and painter in regard to Meretlein, will secure the chain of *Bildung* and painting that encloses "the little witch." The

conversation that focuses first on matters of *Bildung* moves seamlessly on to landscape painting; the thread that joins the two is the
tenet that invisibly behind both efforts stands the divine as their
guiding and supporting force—joining together not just *Bildung*
and painting, but also the schoolmaster and Heinrich with God as
a united (male) group with shared interests and powers (a group
to which, of course, Goethe also belongs). While gazing steadfastly
at the surrounding landscape and directly inspired by it, Heinrich
explains to Anna's father that the art of landscape painting entails,
on the one hand, a faithful and exact reproduction of the natural
world "according to the laws of the Creator" (*nach den Geset-
zen des Schöpfers*) and, on the other hand, a self-creation of the
natural world "as if they [i.e., the trees, etc.] must grow and be
seen somewhere" (*als ob sie irgendwo gewachsen und sichtbar sein
müßten*), which is to say, an imitation not of God's creation but
of his creating power.[101] The seeming contradiction between these
two modes of imitation is deeply embedded in realist poetics, often uncomfortably so; it is also central to landscape theory, where
the model of *Stimmung* that requires both an objective world and
its productive subjective correlative makes it seem less jarring.[102]
But more immediately important is the schoolmaster's reply to this
claim and Heinrich's response. Anna's father asks whether this
means that the landscape they are now looking at is an adequate
object for art "simply because of the gentleness and power of God
that are manifest here as well," to which Heinrich replies, "Yes,
certainly . . . nothing more is needed here to make it meaningful
(*bedeutend*)."[103] What one paints and seeks to reproduce is not
the visible world itself (although that is also all one paints), but
the divine power that, invisibly behind it, makes it signify: one approaches the seen world only as an echo of the unseen—an unseen,
moreover, that is also a form of pro-vidence (*Vor-sehung*), even
foresight (*Voraussehen*).[104]

In order to ally himself with this removed immaterial realm and
draw on its powers, Heinrich becomes constrained, as it were, to
adopt a position of removal from the merely material condition of
his relation to the world—and in particular, from a merely material,
direct relation to the figure of Anna. The strange, determinative

distance (he calls it the enchantment [*die Verzauberung*])[105] that comes almost immediately to characterize Heinrich's relation to Anna—wherein he hesitates to touch her or address her directly, and deals more easily with her image or *Bild* in her absence than with her bodily presence when they are together—can be accounted for in psychological terms: as an extension of his ever-apparent constraint (*Be-fangenheit*), of his inability to deal with the real, and so basically of his *Ohnmacht*, his powerlessness. But while it is this, it is also the condition for his exercise of power, the indispensable condition for his magical relation to the real—which is also, I'll say, his realist relation to the real and, as we'll see, his "objective" relation to Anna. It is no coincidence that this distance (this love) begins immediately after Heinrich's talk with Anna's father about the poetics of landscape painting, nor that he concludes his visit by claiming to have acquired two things at once: an alliance with the invisible power behind the natural world and an erotic relation with Anna. The invisibility of the one dictates the immateriality of the other; both equally the foundations for realism and magic.

The Anna Paintings

Three paintings made by Heinrich are directly linked to his relation to Anna: one of a bouquet of flowers, another of the Heathen Chamber, and a third of Anna herself. Each exhibits magic binding forces that—in increasingly explicit ways—aim at harming Anna; each engages a complex relation between Anna and the natural world that draws on sympathetic powers to do so; and each contributes not only to Anna's death, but also to Heinrich's *Bildung* and the work's realism. We need to look carefully at each in turn.

Flowers for Anna

> The ancient Greeks and Romans used two basic types of binding magic to do something to someone else. Generally, this someone had wronged them or it was someone whose love they wished to keep. One type of binding magic is the binding spell or curse, written and sometimes pierced, and

the other is the figurine, erotic or otherwise, that may also
be pierced or twisted or bound. The names of the victims are
written in the subject (nominative) or object case (accusative)
probably to show the person is being acted upon by the
binding. There may be a verb of binding, like *katadein*,
in the first person, so the curse tablet reads, "[So and so]
I bind her . . ."[106]

The first painting is in some ways the least obviously charged with
magic force and intent, and also the least directly involved with
Heinrich's landscape painting and *Bildung*.[107] But it is also the one
most clearly linked to the Meretlein episode, with Anna explicitly
referred to in this episode as a witch (*Hexe*); and it is also the
one that follows Heinrich's discussion with the schoolmaster about
landscape painting and is positioned as its realization or fulfillment. The reason for both its seeming marginality and its centrality is basically the same: the episode and its painting are heavily
invested in a principle of metonomy, of contiguity, a principle that
underwrites their particular forms of both sympathetic magic and
literary realism.

Heinrich returns to Anna's father's house shortly after their conversation to fulfill his promise to paint a picture illustrating the
divine, supernatural power behind the natural world. To some extent, this signals the continued collusion of the father's *Bildung*
program and Heinrich's painting, the way Heinrich will paint
within the framework of the schoolmaster's plan for Anna—and as
we'll see, this does in fact prove to be the case (much as the painter
and pastor with Meretlein). But a difference is also marked in the
way each—the father and Heinrich, *Bildung* and painting—will
work to realize that plan. Here, when Heinrich arrives, the father
organizes his household to work together in the vineyards; Heinrich, however, stays behind and works apart; Anna meanwhile is
shuttled between the two, starting with Heinrich, then leaving to
join the others before returning to him, with them, later on. Although Heinrich will purport that his mode of work is more or less
the same as the others, equally a form of mundane social activity
(he refers to himself as "like a worker who is worth his wage"),
this is but one of several screens (*Vorgeben*) he maintains about

his painting. For the real work his painting is to do hardly belongs to the mundane, commonly shared world at all, but rather to one apart from it, drawing on quite different forces to achieve its ends.

The painting itself is to be not of the landscape per se, but rather, "for a change, [of] flowers from nature," already a symptom of the metonymic nature of this painting and its scene.[108] Still, as a nature painting, it is also supposed to be a painting of Anna, and one that affects Anna (is "for" Anna)—however not directly, but through the binding powers of the same metonymy and contiguity at work between the flowers and landscape and already at work between Anna and nature in general. In this respect, it is important that the reason for painting the flowers given by Heinrich is "so that I could stay in Anna's proximity": this is both because the painting is from the start connected to her, and because "nearness" (proximity) or "next-to-ness" (contiguity) is the condition through which that connection is made.

The need for some means to bind Anna is also evident in this scene—although again, indirectly, through metonymy and, especially, metonymic evocations of the Meretlein episode. Even before Heinrich decides on the "object of his activity," we're told "Anna had a mighty tub full of green beans to rid of their little tails and strings and to arrange in rows on long threads" (Anna hatte eine mächtige Wanne voll grüner Bohnen der Schwänzchen und Fäden zu entledigen und an lange Fäden zu reihen). This seemingly simple task set beside Heinrich's own is disarmingly realist in its mundane nature and mode of action; but it also becomes charged with allegorical force via textual echoes and premonitions in ways that pose an implicit, immediate threat to Heinrich. The beans resonate with the bean field (*Bohnenplatz*) in which Meretlein ensconced herself, communicating indirectly—contiguously, contagiously—some of her witchery to Anna: this will become fully realized later on that same night, in the famous "bean-night" (*Bohnenabend*) scene wherein Anna breaks free from her customary restraints, grows wild, unruly, and erotic, and earns the appellation "you witch!"[109] The very same superreal, nonpresent pathways that the reader activates to link the beans and Anna to these "other" scenes, and particularly to Meretlein's witchery, remain spectrally active in the scene, in Anna and the beans as their witching power: the power to link, to bind superreally—and thereby, too, to carry an "other" meaning, another force spectrally behind the scene, into the scene itself.

It is this in turn that charges the twice-repeated threads or *Fäden* with their particular force, signaling the kinds of threads or strings at issue to be not just the visible ones of the real material world but also the invisible ones of the magical allegorical one—and again, that the latter is magical is signaled by how those threads connect to Meretlein. As with the erotic ties between Meretlein and her male counterparts (including both the pastor and the painter), the existence of those threads represents a power struggle, as indicated here in how Anna's task is "to rid the beans of their little tails and strings and to arrange them in rows on long threads" (*der Schwänzchen und Fäden zu entledigen und an lange Fäden zu reihen*). The *Schwänzchen . . . zu entledigen*, especially coupled with the little pocketknife with which Anna does her cutting, might well suggest a form of castration, especially to a Freudian reader, with castration itself engaging the same metonymic logic at work between the flowers and landscape, the beans and Meretlein, and both and Anna.[110] But equally important, the two different threads or *Fäden* with which the "little tails" are serially paired suggest the displacement of power, of super-powers, at issue, the threatened loss of the binding threads of the "little tails" themselves and their (serial) displacement onto Anna's own—very much the same displacement we saw originally with Meretlein, who "bewitched" the men into losing control of themselves and becoming bound by and to her in ways that then needed remedy by *Bildung* and painting.

It is in implicit response to this that Heinrich decides to paint a bouquet of flowers, or more precisely engages Anna herself in making such a *Strauß* (with overtones of *Strauß* as altercation—for that is what his bouquet becomes to her beans).[111] That for this purpose the flowers, too, need to be broken off or cut is perhaps also in response to Anna's knife work on the beans. Moreover, although the cut and gathered flowers are not explicitly bound, they are put into an old-fashioned ornamental glass vase (*altmodisches Prunkglas*), a bundle of deathful binding motifs—the deadening antiquation of "old-fashioned," the conventionalization of "ornamental," and the reflectivity of "glass" that all evoke the nonlife of art—we will see again shortly in the painting's own container, its outside frame: certainly the reclaimed and reversed binding that is implicit here will become far more explicit in the closely connected "bean-night" scene itself, when Heinrich captures the wild Anna and sings, "The little mouse was already caught / and tied by its foot / and around its tiny fore-paw, / a red band was put," after which the mouse is killed.[112] But the main points here would be these: that behind its realist trappings and gentle, almost idyllic setting, the scene of Heinrich's first Anna painting is a highly charged one full of power plays and dangerous unseen forces, working through its natural visible objects and mundane activities; that what charges the scene with those powers is not only a more or less present erotics but also a literarily evoked set of binding echoes and adumbrations that is not present and not (simply) real, but is nonetheless only present and only works through the real objects and activities in the scene; that while both erotic and literary, these forces nonetheless work as one in and behind the scene itself, entering into the scene through metonymic links; that the way they work is considered magical, as the evocation of Meretlein assures; and that, once again, the kind of magic they work is a binding one, activating the same metonymic chains that allow them to enter the scene in the first place. Just as Heinrich's activity or *Tätigkeit* operates alongside but completely otherly than the mundane social work in the natural world (the vineyards), so do these allegorical forces work alongside but completely otherly than the material objects (the beans, flowers, etc.) and real events of that world.

The spectral presence, then, of these magical forces and, because of them, the need for some (magical/unseen) means to bind Anna is conveyed almost exclusively in the displaced context of the material things next to Anna and Heinrich and their side-by-side but seemingly unconnected activities. The question then becomes how painting becomes that magical means of binding, or in language we've used before, the portal for those magic forces to enter the text world; and how it avails itself of both the presence and the distance of contiguity or metonymy to do so. For we need to stress

again that this picture that is to bind Anna is not directly a representation of Anna, as was the case with Meretlein's portrait and
will be later with Anna's, but of a bouquet: the powers of painting
at stake are not strictly speaking mimetic but rather, as I've said,
metonymic, syntagmatic—which, as Frazer reminds us, are still intrinsic to sympathetic magic and, as Jakobson reminds us, equally
so to realist fiction.[113] But we need to ask how.

The answer has first and again to do with the ability of painting to draw on and produce conditions of *Stimmung*. Once he
begins painting—and in ways that clearly recall his first attempt
at painting in his mother's house—the gathering (*Zusammenstell-
ung*) of the bouquet spills out and extends itself contagiously into
the human world, into a togetherness (*Zusammensein*) of Heinrich and Anna, filled with movements and interplays (*Bewegungen
und Zwischenspiele*), a sense of communion in which they communicate freely about their interrelated life stories (*gegenseitigen
Lebensläufen*), a sense that also spills back into the painting of the
"brought-together" flowers, and later proves capable of expanding
out again to include other viewers, including Anna's father and all
the others who return from the vineyards. For all the sense of unity
and sociability it produces, this *Stimmung* still involves a certain
asymmetry of relation and private advantage: it empowers Heinrich
as its producer with a singular sense of superiority (*Überlegenheit*),
while it positions Anna as its viewer as a-stonished, *erstaunt* (and
thus, "of my mind [*meines Sinnes*]"). That this power might also be
harnessed for the binding purposes of *Bildung* is conveyed by the
lessons (*Belehrungen*) Heinrich would, however fatuously, impress
upon her as he paints. In this way, the painting again produces
conditions of *Stimmung* joining together the human world—both
the loving/warring pair and, later, the broader social group—and,
albeit more weakly, the natural world, for, as Heinrich admits, at
first his painting pays minimal attention to the flowers themselves
and relies on mere convention, as befits the dominant sociability of
the *Stimmung* that at this point pours into and out of the picture.

The force field of sympathetic relations activated by the painting
is put to darker, less common, and even more personal ends a moment later, when the painting momentarily sheds its alliance with

the social binding forces of *Stimmung* and draws more directly on its alliance with nature and the asocial desires of Heinrich's interior life, which is to say, when it links the hidden or "dark" forces behind both nature and Heinrich. The larger group that had gathered to view the painting departs, taking Anna with it and leaving Heinrich alone, aggrieved and annoyed: and he chooses to direct his anger and aggrievement into a renewed focus on his painting, in a way that is to restore the sense of connection with and power over Anna that he has just (actually) lost—no longer openly and benignly but now, rather, covertly and malevolently. Tellingly, this renewed focus expresses itself as an increased effort "really to make use of the natural flowers before me and to learn from them" (*die natürlichen Blumen vor mir wirklich zu benutzen und an ihnen zu lernen*).[114] That the learning and use to which he "really" intends to put the natural flowers does not reach its end in the mere improvement of his representative craft through more exact observation of his visible subject is made clear by his channeling of psychic violence; rather, he seems again to be learning to use painting to draw the invisible binding forces of nature—and especially their binding relation with Anna—to harmonize with and answer to his subjective ends; the emphasis on mimetic exactitude and replication is simply one of the means most required to connect to those invisible forces.[115]

That the painting is thus meant to "charm" Anna in the most traditional, primitive way is signaled when Heinrich inscribes the finished work with her name, in "beautiful" script, and adds as well (as nowhere previously) "Heinrich Lee fecit," all with an eye on its future (*künftig*) recipient: in this way, he directly links Anna to the flowers and painting, and the flowers and painting to Anna, in ways he designs and invests with future force. But the truly remarkable and significant factor is how, once he has done so, the natural world seems to respond and infuse his picture with its summoned force, in ways that subtly echo the moment of Meretlein's bewitched resurrection, albeit with reversed effect. We're told, "The sun went down and left behind a deep, rosy radiance, which cast a dying afterglow on everything and wondrously reddened the sketch on my knees, together with my hands, and made it look like

something right" (Die Sonne ging hinab und ließ eine hohe Rosenglut zurück, welche auf Alles einen sterbenden Nachglanz warf und
die Zeichnung auf meinen Knieen samt meinen Händen wunderbar
rötete und etwas Rechtem gleichsehen ließ).[116] The light—at once
flowery, evoking the nature in the painting, and a dying *Nachglanz*,
evoking the reflection that is painting—touches and so binds together Heinrich's work (his hands), his painting, and the natural
realm with "wondrous" unifying force, establishing that the psy-
chological/subjective binding force with which Heinrich would imbue the painting will be aided and abetted, even taken over, by the
natural/objective force of the world itself, and thus made "something right" (*etwas Rechtes*).[117]

It is a testament to both the presence of this power and Anna's
intuitive recognition of its threat that when she is presented with
the picture, her first impulse is not to dare touch it herself and
only even to look at it when hidden protectively behind others, and
that her second impulse is, as soon as she has the chance, to bury
it (*begraben*) "in the most inaccessible reaches of her room," exactly as Meretlein tried to do with the skull.[118] Both the threatening
force of the painting and the parallel with the Meretlein episode are
reinforced by the father's addition of a frame the following morning, after the interceding witchery of the "bean night." He compels
Anna against her will to retrieve the painting and places it within a
frame and behind a glass that up to this moment held a commem-
orative tablet (*Gedächtnistafel*) of the famine of 1817. Although
ostensibly a process of replacing "the melancholy memorial" with
"this blossoming picture of life," the principle of contiguity (and
temporal echo) that has dominated the entire scene is at work here
as well, and infects the present *Bild* with the earlier one, or rather,
brings out their hidden resemblance—and transfers that contagion
to the subject whose name is inscribed beneath the "picture of
life." Even as the frame resonates with the framing constraints of
both the father's *Bildung* and Heinrich's *Bild* within which "Anna"
is placed, and even as the glass reflects the lifeless realm of aesthetic representation behind which "Anna" is placed (paralleling
the ornamental glass vase within which the flowers in the picture
are placed, making for yet another bracketing outside/inside frame

very much like the heaven/lake earlier), so does the reference to the famine resonate with the starvation regimen to which Meretlein was subjected as part of her *Bildung*, the starvation that itself reflected the constriction of *Bildung* and painting alike, and that we also saw in the thinness of the young ash-tree drawn between its parallel lines and have seen, too (and will again), in Anna herself. All this indirectly—by the same indirection that turns the bouquet into a figure for Anna, and painting into a form of *actio in distans*: that works through sympathetic relations and simple contiguity to imbue things with symbolic, allegorical force, invisibly, magically and yet for all that still realistically—all this transforms the picture into an unspoken spell leveled against Anna by her father and Heinrich, the educator and painter, just as the portrait became against Meretlein at the hands of her educator and painter.

It is, then, no wonder that when the father does speak, in his incantatory dedication of the framed picture, he closes by referring to it and the flowers in it as "these works of God," recalling the discussion of realism that this painting was to actualize, for in its final form it does illustrate the hidden (patriarchal) powers—his own, Heinrich's, the pastor's and painter's, even God's and Goethe's—working through and behind the natural and represented world that are so central to the realist agenda.[119] And it is no wonder that he also refers to it as Anna's memorial plaque (*Denktafel*), proleptically figuring her as dead (indeed killed by this very picture and frame) and analeptically figuring it as parallel to Meretlein's grave *Tafel* (indeed turned into a grave by the very parallel). What does seem a wonder, but what these both help explain, is how in this context he also declares the painting a model or *Vorbild*, in a manner that seems completely different from how this term has been used before. Previously, it always indicated precisely the hidden male order behind or before the picture that invisibly joins it together and that Heinrich seeks to imitate and draw into his painting—something usually imagined as situated in the past (even among the dead) and behind the painting. Here, however, it suggests an admonition, even a command for how Anna is to live in the future and before the picture, "with a soul adorned and innocent as these delicate and honorable works of God!"[120] A second look, however, reveals the connection: it is the *Vorbild* qua (male) hidden order that through the picture would determine how Anna is not so much to live as, in living, to die. But most significant for us is how, as a *Vorbild*, the painting here is charged with an active, future force, which is to say, the forces—both subjective and objective, erotic and natural—that Heinrich has magically and realistically/metonymically harnessed or bound into his picture become imbued with a literally ominous, futural thrust. And this brings us to the picture of the Heathen Chamber.

The Heathen Chamber

The Heathen Chamber (*Heidenstube*) that becomes the subject of Heinrich's painting on Anna's wall (in her absence, awaiting her return) is formally introduced just after her father's framing of the flower-bouquet painting, when Heinrich and Anna enter the woods alone.[121] As mentioned, both the place and painting represent a kind of lovers' paradise, a variant on the topos of the *locus amoenus*, with all its traditional echoes of eros, nature, and aesthetics—but here given a characteristically deadly turn. We need to describe exactly what the *Heidenstube* means to Heinrich and Anna (and to the reader) to understand the peculiar significance and force with which the painting becomes charged.

As might be expected—given the setting in nature, always the site for sympathetic relations, and the figure of Anna, always a magnet attracting those relations—the scene is spectrally haunted by echoes of earlier textual moments; and rather than just remaining invisibly active in the background, this metatextual play (again) enters into the scene as a central determinative force. The flower-bouquet painting is drawn in as Anna collects yet another bouquet of flowers as they approach the site; both it and she are then linked to Meretlein as Anna "wove a delicate crown out of the small, genteel forest flowers and put it on."[122] The resultant literalization, aestheticization, and, in the case of Meretlein, magicification that these links impose on Anna become activated the moment they reach the Heathen Chamber, "a place where the water gathered itself and stood still," and Anna says, "Here one rests" (Hier ruht man aus):

> Now she looked exactly like a lovely fairy-tale, her image looked up smiling out of the deep, dark-green water, the white and red face fabulously shadowed over as if through a dark glass.

> Nun sah sie ganz aus wie ein holdseliges Märchen, aus der tiefen, dunkelgrünen Flut schaute ihr Bild lächelnd herauf, das weiß und rote Gesicht wie durch ein dunkles Glas fabelhaft überschattet.[123]

This is not only about the transformation of Anna into an unreal, aestheticized object, making visible the literalization already allusively begun—although it certainly is that. The reflection in the water—which captures Anna's *Bild* and becomes at once the object of attention and the medium that enchants and transports her into a fairy-tale world—bespeaks her transposition into both the world of art and the world of nature, and if we put slight pressure on the "dark-green," into the (specular) world of the "green" Heinrich.[124] That the connection to Heinrich is a dark one is conveyed by the *dunkel*; that the connection to art is, too, is conveyed by the *dunkles Glas*; that the connection to nature is similarly dark, even deadly, is conveyed by the stillness of the water and its replication in Anna's "Here one rests (*ruht*)" In all cases, Anna is "shadowed over" (*überschattet*), in ways that suggest not only the lurking presence of death and stasis, but also the almost visible presence of the shadow world of diffused, linked, shaping forces of the psyche, the landscape, and the text—by the "light-darkness" (*Helldunkel*) that envelops the entire scene.[125]

The threatening darkness to the setting is amplified by the rock wall on the other side of the water, itself reflected in the water. This wall contains the Heathen Chamber proper, and it has already implicitly been implicated in the reflecting relations and connections affecting Anna and Heinrich as the unnamed origin of the echoes in their earlier song.[126] Now they are, as it were, at the site of that origin (paradoxically, an origin of projection and reflection, but also of connection). And by the same connecting pathways activated by the echoes and reflections of the physical natural setting, the story of the Heathen Chamber that is attached to the wall becomes part of the place, or rather of the power of the place working on Anna and Heinrich, reflectively—even as, by a similar kind of metonymy, the entire site becomes the Heathen Chamber. We can even say that as the reflection in the water is at once of this rock wall and Anna, it comes to resemble the flower-bouquet painting inscribed with Anna's name: the backstory that Anna tells becomes like the frame her father places around the painting, with its backstory of the famine, and so like the earlier painting, Heinrich's subsequent painting of the Heathen Chamber will be more a metonymic representation of all these elements than just a mimetic one of the place itself. Like the bouquet of flowers, it too will be a painting of Anna; and it, too, will be charged with the ominous force of its backstory; and this is secured by the combined metatextual and natural (metonymic) forces active in the place.

There are a number of key elements to the story of the Heathen Chamber—a hollow or depression (*Vertiefung*) in the rock wall that echoes the *Vertiefung* of the reflecting pool—that are of significance. For example, that it bespeaks a place where, with the advent of Christianity and implicitly modern society, the heathen was forced to hide itself—and that would include not only currently taboo erotic drives but also the magic beliefs of earlier times: a spatial counterpart to the figure of Meretlein. Or that it is a place with no apparent entrance from this world, but once entered, with no way out other than death. Or that death comes to its occupants by starvation, a motif placed so closely next to that of the famine as to almost touch it, but that again evokes (more remotely) Meretlein as well; or even that the bones of the victims fall into the water below, turning the dark-green still reflecting water into a grave, or rather into yet another variation on the grave it already is and already reflects back communicatively in the *Bild* of Anna. But one aspect is of particular importance: that yet another layer is added to the story when Heinrich and Anna actually see a strange-looking (*fremdartige*) family in the Heathen Chamber that matches the story Anna has just told, and Anna "firmly believed she was seeing their ghosts" (*glaubte fest, die Geister derselben zu sehen*) and offers up a sacrifice (*Opfer*) to propitiate them. Specters—and apparently dangerous ones—enter directly from the background text into the natural landscape and realist world, summoned up, as it were, out of its own past and present setting.[127] Although later Heinrich and Anna are offered a realistic explanation for the apparition, this seemingly magical and unreal world still persists side by side with the factual realist one and retains its own reality. Indeed, it is the former, not the latter, that will be evoked as the subject of Heinrich's "realist" sketch: whose image is meant to bind Anna when she sees it, to haunt her with its spectral forces, and to portend the fate that will become her own—and to which she will be the sacrifice.[128]

As mentioned, this Heathen Chamber painting will eventually succeed in killing Anna: she will die in the bed adjacent to it, with Heinrich at her (and its) side—which is to say, via a kind of metonymy, a communicative contagion. But in a crucial scene shortly before this, Anna comes close to being killed off by Heinrich in the Heathen Chamber itself, and it is worth considering both how this scene functions as a precedent and why it necessitates the later death by picture and metonymy instead. Doing so will allow us to reemphasize one of the key conditions for the kind of sympathetic magic associated with realism and, not incidently, with *Stimmung*—namely, distance, or more fully, *actio in distans*.

The scene is the real climax of Heinrich and Anna's romantic relationship, the moment they come most directly into physical contact, and it forcefully combines the dominant motifs of landscape, erotics, and metatextual entrapment. The latter is especially evident in the scene's placement as the sequel (*Nachspiel*) to a communal performance of Schiller's *Wilhelm Tell*, in which Heinrich has set the trap of casting the unsuspecting Anna in the role of Berta to his Rudenz, and has had her costumed accordingly.[129] This literary entrapment is a textual variant on the pictoral entrapment Heinrich has mostly practiced, with the same engaged issues of death by aestheticization, convention, and so on: the sartorial equivalent to painting is also something we already encountered with both Meretlein and Heinrich himself. In any case, by seeming accident

Anna recognizes the trap, leaves the communal drama, and takes off on her horse for the woods with Heinrich close behind. It is here that the landscape reasserts itself.

The landscape description that frames Heinrich's and Anna's ride to the Heathen Chamber is the most expansive in the novel, and it features some of the key conditions for *Stimmung* in landscape painting.[130] The view extends to the distant mountains on the horizon that surround the scene, "infinitely still and remote":

> Above them lay a wonderfully beautiful, mighty mountain range of clouds in the same radiance, light, and shadow of just the same color as the mountains. . . . The whole was . . . a wondrous wilderness, drawing powerfully and close to the heart and yet so soundless, unmoving, and remote. We saw everything at once, without taking a particular look at it; the wide world seemed to revolve around us like an unending crown, until it narrowed in as we gradually rushed downhill.

> Über ihnen lagerte ein wunderschönes mächtiges Wolkengebirge im gleichen Glanze, Licht und Schatten ganz von gleicher Farbe, wie die Berge. . . . Das Ganze war eine . . . wunderbare Wildnis, gewaltig und nah an das Gemüt rückend und doch so lautlos, unbeweglich und fern. Wir sahen Alles zugleich, ohne das wir besonders hinblickten; wie ein unendlicher Kranz schien sich die weite Welt um uns zu drehen, bis sie sich verengte, als wir allmählig bergab jagten.[131]

We note the "wondrous" and powerful echoing harmony of the mountain and cloud formations; the sense of a dominant unity ("the whole," "everything at once") not lodged in any particular thing; and the way this echoing harmony and unity that originate in the object world forcefully but imperceptibly impose themselves on the subjectivity of the viewers, who are themselves drawn into its echoing, sympathetic relations in a macro-/microcosmic exchange. This last is especially caught in the play of the "unending crown" of the encircling world, which narrows down to focus on Heinrich and Anna, the latter of whom is riding "with the sparkling little crown" (*dem funkelnden Krönchen*) of her costume on her head: the encircling natural world comes almost literally to encircle and bind Anna herself.[132] We note, too, how the play of imaginary and real, immaterial and concrete, that might seem to mark the two sides of the human-natural link first appears within and between the things of the natural world in the links between the clouds and mountains—by implication setting this link, too, in the object world, and so effacing this boundary between the human and natural world as well. But most importantly, we note what Alois Riegl stresses most about landscapes: the need for distance and seeming inactivity for the Stimmung effect to emerge and assert itself—no matter how "powerfully and close" it presses on "the heart" (*das Gemüt*).[133]

The effect of the landscape and its *Stimmung*—spun out at great length—is to create a dream setting, highly aestheticized and eroticized, the former a continuation of the literary echoes of the Schiller play and the Meretlein episode Anna attracts, the latter an extension of the play of natural attractions in the landscape and between it and the human figures. But the key moment comes when Heinrich would break free from his sense of dreaming and embrace reality directly: "As I saw the charming, almost fairy-tale-like figure walking thus through the fir trees, I believed again that I was dreaming, and it took the greatest effort not to let the horses go, in order to convince myself of the reality (*der Wirklichkeit*) by rushing after her and clasping her in my arms." When he does actually embrace and kiss her—and so venture out of the dream into the empirical—the result is predictably deadly: Anna "became deathly pale (*totenbleich*)," and Heinrich says, "I felt as if I held some utterly strange, insubstantial object in my arms" (Es war mir, als ob ich einen urfremden, wesenlosen Gegenstand im Arme hielte).[134] They move apart, and the misstep is only overcome and the *Stimmung* partly restored when Heinrich goes back to looking at and contemplating Anna via the reflection in the water, at the remove of representation.[135]

What is striking in this shuttling between the dream world and the real is Anna's shifting status as object or *wesenloser Gegenstand*. For at one level, when she's ensconced in the aestheticized realm of Heinrich's fantasy—whether via the trap of the Schiller text, the *Stimmung* of the landscape, the echoes of the Meretlein, or the reflection of the water—she is no less an object than when all these are stripped away and she becomes real, actually touched and held by Heinrich. But in the latter case she seems to become a different kind of object, to transition from what Bill Brown might call an object to a mere thing: to lose the connections invested in her not only by Heinrich's subjectivity but also by the surrounding world and to become almost *too* real—or more precisely, to become at once both more and less real, less participant in the complected whole.[136] Certainly the restoration that follows involves regaining the distance Riegl claims is inseparable from landscape, which requires "far-sight" (*Fernsicht*) to overlook the real that disturbs its *Bild*; that Wellbery sees as inseparable from *Stimmung*, that cannot result in actual action without ceasing to be itself; that Freud sees as inseparable from narcissism, and Horkheimer and Adorno from the magic circle required for mimesis—all claims, we've seen, that seem seconded by Keller's Goethe and his vision of both art and the world.[137]

The point is, then, that in this scene, Heinrich's connection to Anna is *too* real, too direct: it lacks the distance everyone claims is necessary for landscape, *Stimmung*, subjectivity, and art—a distance I claim is also necessary to realism, which, we've seen, works not directly on its subject matter but only indirectly, through metonymy, mediation, and echoing correspondence, and whose objects are thus never just themselves, but always also metonymies, allegories—socialized, textualized, invisibly chained objects.[138] This distance that separates realism from the real (and not only realism, but landscape, *Stimmung*, subjects and objects) is what allows its magic—its reality—to work, in ways that are impossible in the real world alone; and this is why Heinrich must paint his magic realist pictures to get to Anna.

Anna's Portrait

The last of the Anna paintings is a portrait of Anna. But even as the paintings of the flower bouquet and Heathen Chamber turn out to be not of their mimetic subjects but rather of Anna, or rather, of metonymies of Anna, her own portrait turns out not to be of her either, but rather of the metonymic relations in which she is held: the nexus of "dark" imaginings that bind Heinrich to her and with which he would bind her in turn; the aesthetic conventions that bind his imaginings and also have come to bind her; and both the natural elements and the metatextual connections that are so inextricably entwined with both of these and with her figure. In an almost uncanny fashion, it is a portrait or *Bild* in which Anna is at once captured and disappears, fading into a kind of invisibility in response to (in tune with) the forces visibly forcing her appearance. It is, as it were, the means by which Anna is finally forced out of the real world and into the next; and by which the forces of that other world enter fully into her place in this one.

The implicit relation of this portrait to Heinrich's nature paintings is made evident in the setting for Heinrich's drawing. We're told, "I spent the days deep in the forest. . . ; however, I drew very little from nature, but when I had found a completely secret spot where I was sure no one could surprise me, I pulled out a beautiful piece of parchment, on which I painted Anna's likeness from memory, in water-colors."[139] This seems at first to echo Heinrich's earlier practice (during a period we skipped), when he first entered into a formal apprenticeship in the city with a man named Habersaat, and would disappear into the woods for hours at a time and return with impossibly romantic drawings of twisted trees, jutting rock formations, rushing waterfalls, even deformed humans, and claim they were all drawn "from nature," when clearly they were mere products of his uncontrolled even if still conventional imagination, with no relation to anything actually seen. Here the admission that he draws "very little from nature" and instead "from memory" seems to suggest much the same, especially when the actual painting turns out to be every bit as fantastic (*phantasievoll*) as those earlier landscapes. As Heinrich says, "I couldn't draw [well], and so the whole came out rather Byzantine. . . . It was a full-length figure and stood in a rich bed of flowers, whose tall stems and crowns rose with Anna's head into the deep sky; the upper part of the drawing was rounded off in an arch and framed with interlaced tendrils [or scrolls], in which sat shining birds and butterflies." One can hardly imagine a painting more distanced from the real, from both the natural world in which it was made and from Anna herself. Nor is it easy to imagine a less effective portrait with a less promising future.

But there are also indications that something different and more is at stake here, something that aligns this painting not with the ineffectual romantic paintings for Habersaat but rather, again, with the magically effective paintings of the flower bouquet and Heathen Chamber. To begin, although his work was painted from a distance, from memory, and crowded with aesthetic convention, Heinrich also assures us, "Every day I observed Anna secretly (*verstohlen*) and openly and improved the picture accordingly, until at last it became completely like (*ganz ähnlich*)." That is, despite the indeterminacy as to exactly what the painting comes to be "like," there is still a forceful assertion of realist mimesis and relation to its ostensible subject, Anna—although, on the other hand, that the mimesis again involves "stealing" (*verstohlen*), as it did in the case of the young ash-tree, suggests that something more than *just* realism is at stake in the mimesis as well (more anon). Second, although Heinrich may not be painting "from nature" (*nach der Natur*), in this case that he is painting in nature is of paramount importance. This is brought home by a textual echo that makes it seem that, if not at the Heathen Chamber, Heinrich is painting this portrait at a place significantly like it: "The greatest happiness for me was when I set myself up comfortably beside a clear reflecting pool beneath a thick roof of leaves, the picture on my knees." The representation that is his art is closely linked to the representation (the reflection) that is nature, such that—even as with the earlier image of Anna in the water-mirror (*Wasserspiegel*) of the Heathen Chamber—the portrait of Anna is to draw equally on the reflecting forces of art *and* nature (in all their likeness), to become a site for both, and so like the picture of the Heathen Chamber something that binds Anna not only to the aesthetic but also to the natural world. As unreal and even primitive as the conventions of Heinrich's blossoms, birds, and butterflies so obviously are, they are still intended, as the Habersaat conventions are not, to summon nature into the drawing and have its powers join with those of convention to bind their subject, much as we saw with the added grasses and flowers in the drawing of the ash tree and as we see here in the subtly constraining features of the arch, framed with interlaced tendrils (or scrolls [*Rankenwerk*]), and the flowers' crowns close beside Anna's head, which has so often been encircled by a crown of its own. That the natural riches (the rich [*reich*] flower bed) in which Heinrich sets his image of Anna are matched by the fantasy riches (*phantasievoll bereichert*) of her clothing transposes both the artful and natural forces of the painting onto her body in ways we've also seen before with both Heinrich himself and Anna—and of course with Meretlein as well.

Finally, the particular intent, or intended effect, of this portrait is conveyed by the art Heinrich practices next to or alongside it. As he says, "I only interrupted this work to play on my flute." Ever since the introduction of Anna, we've marked the equivalence of landscape painting and music as artful means for engaging nature's sympathetic powers (its *Stimmung*) and creating the macro-micro connections of the natural and human world (*Stimmung* again), with the important distinction that music broadcasts these binding relations outward rather than just drawing them in, and that it converts them into something that happens, into an activity with displaced, recursive force, and so, too, into a kind of temporal force working over distance. In our previous example of the organ playing, these powers were evoked by a larger human group and recursed back to that group; here, Heinrich summons them up alone and directs them at Anna alone, who is of course the intended object of the accompanying portrait as well. We're told that while making this painting, Heinrich would approach Anna's house at night without leaving the woods, where he would let his flute music "ring out through the night and moonlight":

> No one seemed to notice this or at least not to react; for I would have stopped immediately if anyone had been affected by it, and yet this is exactly what I sought and I blew my flute like someone who wanted to be heard.

> Hierauf schien kein Mensch zu achten oder sich wenigstens so zu stellen; denn ich hätte sogleich aufgehört, wenn irgend jemand sich darum bekümmert hätte, und doch suchte ich gerade dies und blies meine Flöte wie einer, der gehört sein will.[140]

The flute transposes both the aesthetic and the natural forces of the painting into a more active, temporal form, in a way that makes clear how Heinrich's art, for all its hiddenness and restriction to the natural world, and for all its isolated origin in his secret fantasy, is still made with the intention of having its effect elsewhere (and at another time), on the real and human world: on Anna.

That the intended effect of the portrait is a dark or deadly one is already evident in the fact that Heinrich has by this point openly been declared a "women-hater," committed to "perpetual misogyny."[141] But it is made more specific to the painting when the portrait is accidently discovered by his girl cousins and Heinrich is subjected to a trial of sorts to expose its purpose. His inquisitors ask, "What do you have against Anna that you behave in this way towards her?"; and more particularly, "By what right and to what purpose are innocent young girls copied (*abconterfeit*) without their knowledge? . . . It could not be a matter of indifference to them that their portraits were being prepared secretly and to unknown ends (*heimlich und zu unbekanntem Zwecke*)."[142] Although Heinrich is forced to divulge his secret, he does so in a manner that preserves the portrait's hidden purpose: he claims that he has made it for the schoolmaster, Anna's father, thus proleptically handing it over to the figure whose *Bildung* designs on Anna so powerfully complement those of his own picture or *Bild*. But more basic than this is simply the expressed recognition in this scene that the painting has a hidden purpose (*Zweck*); that this purpose is directed against Anna in potentially harmful ways; and that mimesis here, far from an innocent or neutral practice, is one that draws or steals its subject into its representation and can then subsequently (recursively, futurally) be used against it—which is to say that painting embodies real magic binding properties.[143]

Once the painting has been exposed and destined for transfer to Anna's father, it acquires an added dimension in the form of a frame that becomes as much a part of the portrait as did that for the painting of the flower bouquet that the schoolmaster himself supplied. In fact, we are given a far more detailed description of the frame than of the portrait itself, in good part because the portrait is, as we've seen, itself a kind of frame, a means of enclosing and arresting Anna (and so, too, in a sense, of pushing her out of the picture). On the day of the transfer, Heinrich's cousins show him the portrait:

> Only now did I get to see my picture again, which had been quite finely framed. On a deteriorated copper engraving the girls had found a narrow wooden frame, most delicately carved, which might well have been seventy years old and, on a slender moulding, depicted a row of little shells, one half-covering the next. Around the inner border ran a fine chain of square links, almost completely free-standing; the outer border was drawn round with a string of pearls. The village glazier, who practiced all kinds of arts and was particularly strong in the obsolete kind of lacquer-work done on old-fashioned boxes, had given the shells a reddened shine, gilded the chain and silvered the pearls and added a new, clear piece of glass.

> Erst jetzt bekam ich mein Bild wieder zu sehen, welches ganz fein eingerahmt war. An einem verdorbenen Kupferstiche hatten die Mädchen einen schmalen, in Holz auf das Zierlichste geschnittenen Rahmen gefunden, welcher wohl siebenzig Jahr alt sein mochte und eine auf einen schmalen Stab gelegte Reihe von Müschelchen vorstellte, von denen eins das andere halb bedeckte. An der inneren Kante lief eine feine Kette mit viereckigen Gelenken herum, fast ganz frei stehend, die äußere Kante war mit einer Perlenschnur umzogen. Der Dorfglaser, welcher allerlei Künste trieb und besonders in verjährten Lackirarbeiten auf altmodischem Schachtelwerk stark war, hatte den Muscheln einen rötlichen Glanz gegeben, die Kette vergoldet und die Perlen versilbert und ein neues klares Glas genommen.[144]

One of the main ways this frame affects Anna with well-nigh annihilatory force is through the many (meta)textual overtones that engage in their own *Schachtelwerk*, boxing Anna into their own earlier frameworks. Most obviously, there are echoes of the frame for the flower-bouquet painting Anna's father supplied: we hear these in the way this frame, too, is taken from an old, "deteriorated" print from years past, and the emphasis on its archaic quality—itself echoed in the "obsolete" and "old-fashioned" arts of the glazier—again has the effect of assimilating Anna to a world already past and infecting her with that pastness. There are echoes, too, in those seashells of the schoolmaster's painted house, the house in or before which Anna first appeared framed in Heinrich's first (painterly) description of her, anticipating how she would be jointly bound by the father's *Bildung* and Heinrich's *Bilder*: their appearance here transforms their earlier one into an omen that now finds fulfillment. But most tellingly, in the fine golden chain with square links—the chain that captures the binding motif in all these echoes, and the links that, in their squareness, present in miniature how chains are also frames—as well as in the "string of pearls" that frames the chain itself, there are echoes of that other portrait of that other "little witch," Meretlein. So many key terms here—"narrow" (*schmal*), "delicate" (*zierlich*), "fine" (*fein*), "old-fashioned" (*altmodisch*)—that originated in the portrait of Meretlein and became fractally dispersed throughout the text, including in the earlier Anna pictures, each time loaded with the witching overtones their back-pointing echo of Meretlein entailed, are here brought home, summoned to their fulfillment and unloading their belated, futural force on the portrait of Anna, in ways that all but efface the appearance of Anna herself. Heinrich ends his description of the frame by briefly returning to that of the portrait instead, but foregrounds only those elements that most resemble the frame and themselves recall the binding of Meretlein—the "flowers and birds, as well as the golden clasps and gem-stones with which I had ornamented Anna"—and finishes by mentioning, "The face was not modelled at all and very light" (Das Gesicht war fast gar nicht modelliert und ganz licht): she herself all but fades out of the painting under the pressure of the encompassing forces mobilized to hold her.[145]

While it is the older arts of the village glazier ("who practiced all kinds of arts") that seem most to bind Anna (and so, too, most to assist Heinrich), he also places her beneath a new glass cover—and this, too, has its effacing or fading effect, drawing on the reflecting forces of nature and art at once. This is already implicit in its echo of the clear reflecting pool (*klarem Spiegelwässerchen*) beside which the portrait was drawn, itself reflecting both Anna's *Bild* in the Heathen Chamber pool and the glass behind which the picture of the flower bouquet was placed. But it becomes all the more so when Heinrich takes the framed portrait outside, into nature, to transport it to the schoolmaster's house. We're told, "When the sun was reflected on the gleaming glass, it proved true that no thread is so finely spun that it doesn't finally come to light" (Wenn die Sonne sich in dem glänzenden Glase spiegelte, so erwies es sich recht eigentlich, daß kein Fädelein so fein gesponnen, das nicht endlich an die Sonne käme).[146] Most obviously, this turns the portrait into a mirror reflecting back to Heinrich not Anna's image but his own, in keeping with her earlier description as like a narcissus and the painting itself as more a portrait of Heinrich's imagination than of Anna's image. But it also matters that the portrait here is touched by nature's light, much as Meretlein's tiara was touched by the shaft of heaven's light or the painting of the flower bouquet by heaven's "dying afterglow," setting up a fine web of woven threads between natural and subjective forces connected to the portrait. Both have the effect of seeming to make the picture itself—Anna herself—disappear from within the frame: and both seem underscored when the *Bild* finds its destined place "over the sofa in the room with the organ where it looked (*sich ausnahm*) like the portrait of a fairy-tale saint," which is another way of saying, not of Anna, but of the aesthetic and echoing forces that take her out (*ausnahm*).

Ahnung, Art, and Eros

Even as Anna seems forced out of her portrait by these various invisible powers, so, too, does she begin to be forced out of the textual world itself. This occurs shortly after Heinrich has completed his reading of Goethe and begun the final stage of his *Bildung* in landscape painting under the mentorship of Römer. Heinrich returns one day to find Anna's black coat ("the light-weight pleasant thing") on the same rest bed (*Ruh-* or *Lotterbettchen*) on which he had read his Goethe, and this is the first sign that Anna is soon to be consigned to a deathbed of her own. The question becomes, what does Anna's actual death tell us about the *Bildung* and realism at stake in the novel, or rather, about the magic at stake in the *Bildung* and realism of the novel?[147]

Certainly the easiest answer would be that Anna's death, her disappearance, represents a crucial abjection of the magical (and romantic) from both the world and Heinrich's subject. Realism demands a disenchantment of its textual realm, including its natural realm (so long the stronghold of romantic convention and thought), and an exclusive focus on the sensible and empirical; *Bildung* requires the abjection of the unruly desires and fantasies of the male subject, their projected conscription onto a female other, and then a final detachment of the male subject from that female other, whose death would signify his devotion to a properly restricted, sensible, and empirical existence—indeed, the suitably abjected subject of *Bildung* would be the condition for the disenchanted objects of realism. The two decisive figures for Heinrich's acquired realism and *Bildung* in this reading would be Römer and Judith, whose marked prominence at this point coincides with Anna's fading, signaling Heinrich's turn away from the enchanted world of Anna and toward a sensible world of real things.

There is textual support for such a reading. When Heinrich returns to the village after Anna has become ill, the schoolmaster tries to engage him in religious, otherworldly debate, "but during the last summer I had almost completely lost my pleasure in such discussions, my sight was directed toward material phenomena and form (*sinnliche Erscheinungen und Gestalt*)," and it is primarily his apprenticeship with Römer that has, he says, redirected him in this way.[148] Still, this orientation is immediately challenged by the other new *Erscheinung* that appears on the scene just as Anna begins to fade from it, namely, the reports of her "premonitions and dreams" (*Ahnungen und Träume*). These would obviously exceed any simple materialist or realist explanation, and it is not at all clear that the newly advanced aesthetic sensibility succeeds in dismissing them from the world.

The issue of Anna's premonitions and dreams is appropriately introduced by Katherine, the old hag who presided over the earlier "bean-night," who now, with "many a dark and occult allusion," first reports on Anna's new condition.[149] But it is left to Judith to clarify the changes that have followed Anna's illness:

> It's said that the poor girl has had strange dreams and premonitions for some time past, that she has already prophesied a few things that really happened, that often in dreaming as well as awake she suddenly gets

a kind of vision and presentiment of what persons at a distance, who are dear to her, are doing or not doing at the moment, or how they are.

Man sagt, daß das arme Mädchen seit einiger Zeit merkwürdige Träume und Ahnungen habe, daß sie schon ein paar Dinge vorausgesagt, die wirklich eingetroffen, daß manchmal im Traume, wie im Wachen sie plötzlich eine Art Vorstellung und Ahnung von dem bekomme, was entfernte Personen, die ihr lieb sind, jetzt tun oder lassen oder wie sie sich befinden.[150]

As the supposed embodiment of the materialist or *sinnlich* in matters of love—every bit as much as Römer in matters of art—it is not surprising that Judith adds, "I don't believe that kind of thing," nor that this dismissal is repeated in Heinrich's uncle's house, long the bastion of a plump empiricism.[151] But even with this widespread support for a disenchanted world (such as Römer, too, promotes), Heinrich is not completely convinced; and at some level, I believe, neither are we—not least because, as readers, we, too, have experienced such dream states and premonitions in the novel. Heinrich says, "As I shook my head in disbelief, a light chill still went through me" and "Even so a mixed feeling (*gemischte Empfindung*) stayed with me." He returns to see Anna, and "as she herself now, in the presence of her father, began softly to speak of a dream she dreamt a few days before, and I saw from this that she was willing to draw me into the supposed secret, I straightaway believed in the thing," adding:

I thought about it further and remembered having read reports of such things, where without assuming anything wondrous or supernatural, certain still unexplored spheres and potentialities of Nature were hinted at, just in the same way as, by more mature consideration, I had to hold many a hidden bond and law as possible.

[Ich] dachte mehr darüber nach und erinnerte mich, von solchen Berichten gelesen zu haben, wo, ohne etwas Wunderbares und Übernatürliches anzunehmen, auf noch unerforschte Gebiete und Fähigkeiten der Natur selbst hingewiesen wurde, so wie ich überhaupt bei reiflicher Betrachtung noch manches verborgene Band und Gesetz möglich halten mußte.[152]

All this is couched in suitably tentative terms, and the sense of dubious reliability is maintained in Heinrich's almost comical response, first to Judith's report—"Almost in the same moment, I had the feeling that she [Anna] must be seeing me now . . . ; I was terrified and looked around me"—and then that night when he goes to bed "and assumed an extremely choice and ideal position, so as to come off with honor, if Anna's spiritual eye (*Geisterauge*) should fall upon me unawares," and continues upon waking to try "to control my thoughts and be clear and pure at every moment," as if watched and seen through by Anna.[153] But the fact remains that, as comical and even naïve as it seems, this imagined connection with and power of Anna are very much the same *Band* and occult force Heinrich as narrator has been employing toward himself as character and, as painter and narrator, has been (deflectively) employing toward Anna, now reversed, broadcast out by her and back at him. And they have the same policing *Bildung* effect, including the penetration into or, rather, production of an interiority, or more fully, a spirituality. For at some level, much as with Meretlein, the *Bildung* (and painterly) constraints on Heinrich's subject and Anna's person have not eliminated the abjected, unruly forces from the world, but merely forced their appearance—along with those of the policing itself—elsewhere, in a newly spiritual or ghostly (*geistig/ geistlich/geisterhaft*) realm, whether conceived as now interior or exterior to the sensible world. Realism has clearly not succeeded in disenchanting its world, but only in displacing its sorcery into a parasitic space, which is neither "wondrous" nor "supernatural" only because, on the one hand, it is recognizably metatextual and, on the other, because that metatextuality has consistently entered the text through the natural world.[154] The appearance here of Anna's "strange dreams and premonitions" merely makes explicit— concrete, visible—the magical forces that have been there all along for the reader as part of the "spheres and potentialities of Nature," and so, too, as not separate from the novel's program of *Bildung* and realism; that they are Anna's simply reinforces how she has been the site of the reflection, the echo effect of these forces all along. As with the double bind we first described with Meretlein, so too here with Anna: the very natural bonds that were mobilized to constrain her become the threads by which she extends out into nature's world; she doesn't so much leave the text world as join the invisible forces behind it.[155]

The same survival or persistence of the magical that we witness in such broad strokes with Anna's clairvoyance and premonitions we also see in more subtle but no less telling form with Römer and Heinrich's aesthetic education and with Judith and his erotic education. As mentioned, Römer represents an aesthetic devoted to a simple empiricism: he continually champions a mode of landscape painting that focuses on what he calls "the truths of nature" (*die Naturwahrheiten*), "the immediate truth" (*die unmittelbare Wahrheit*), and "the simple truth of nature" (*die gemeine Naturwahrheit*).[156] When Heinrich's own painting exceeds this focus and attempts to introduce spirit-ed relations and meanings (*geistreiche Beziehungen und Bedeutungen*), Römer calls him a sorcerer (*Hexenmeister*) and accuses him of a "presumptuous spiritualism" (*anmaßenden Spiritualismus*) that thwarts the "immediate truth" and "natural truth" when it seeks to represent the "complete truth" (*Gesamtwahrheit*) of nature.[157] Römer claims that the kind of landscape painting Heinrich pursues is "a dangerous thing," a mode that requires more basis in the study of the human than of trees and bushes—which is to say, a mode of landscape painting based on projection and echo, on seeking out sympathetic relations between micro- and macrocosms—a procedure Römer rejects as inadequately objective and true.

Römer refers to this style as based in "invention," and given both Heinrich's earlier propensity toward self-projecting fantasy obscuring or missing the real and a realist aesthetic and *Bildung* program that require the elimination of such magical thinking to attain the real, the reader might expect Römer's position to be authoritative and Heinrich's achieved *Bildung* and realism to consist in accepting it.[158] But Heinrich does not yield to Römer's definition of the true and truly natural, and notes instead Römer's own inability to recognize and reproduce the significant (*bedeutsam*) and "speaking" in nature. He describes how "already more than once in correcting my groupings, he had completely failed to see beloved spots in the mountains or woods I believed fully significant, as he mercilessly hatched over them with his thick pencil and levelled it all out to a forceful but insignificant [or unspeaking] ground" (schon mehr als einmal hatte er, meine Anordnungen korrigierend, Lieblingsstellen in Bergzügen oder Waldgründen, die ich recht bedeutsam glaubte, gar nicht einmal gesehen, indem er sie mit dem markigen Bleistifte schonungslos überschraffierte und zu einem kräftigen aber nichtssagenden Grunde ausglich).[159] That is, the realism of Römer that would reject Heinrich's "sorcery" and "spiritualism," his "spirit-ed relations and meanings," and participatory merging of the artist and his subject is recognized by Heinrich as far from representing the "complete truth" of nature, and in fact as conspicuously reductionist and exclusionary, even as untrue. And so Heinrich's own *Bildung* and realism will consist not in accepting but in moving beyond Römer's model and seeking a mode of representation that can accommodate into its real, natural world this added dimension.[160]

Admittedly, Heinrich is not yet at this point, and so the desired harmony of subject and object, of the spiritual and real, still more closely resembles the earlier dissonance of subjective fantasy and objective world. But there are two intimations of what this harmonic mode will look like and how it will differ from Römer's "truth of nature." Significantly, both come in more or less immediate proximity to the issue of Anna's premonitions and dreams (as does the just mentioned exchange between Heinrich and Römer). The first appears in Heinrich's narratorial description of the morning landscape to which he awakes when he arrives back at Anna's house, and of the fog in which he then becomes entangled on his way (unknowingly) to see Judith.[161] These extremely accomplished nature descriptions are notably distinct from the aesthetics of Römer to which they are juxtaposed, and while firmly bound to the visible objects of the external world clearly open up to an allegorical dimension that sees the human/spiritual world (reflecting first Heinrich's relation to Anna, then to Judith) in the natural, imbuing the scene with "spirit-ed" relations and meanings and presenting a world in which Anna's dreams and premonitions would be fully natural.[162]

The second intimation comes in Römer's studio, shortly after Heinrich returns to the city after his visit with Anna, and it comes in Heinrich's own intimations of his painterly ideal, momentarily glimpsed in his own activity:

> When I succeeded in hitting upon the verisimilar tone that would have been diffused over Nature in similar conditions—as one saw immediately, since a true tone always exercises an absolutely peculiar magic—then there stole over me a pantheistically proud feeling, in which my experience and the weave of nature appeared to be one.

> Gelang es mir, den wahrscheinlichen Ton zu treffen, der unter ähnlichen Verhältnissen über der Natur selbst geschwebt hätte—was man gleich sah, indem ein wahrer Ton immer einen ganz eigentümlichen Zauber übt—so beschlich mich ein pantheistisch stolzes Gefühl, in welchem mir meine Erfahrung und das Weben der Natur Eins zu sein schienen.[163]

This is a notably more complex representation of the immediate and "true" at stake in landscape painting than we get from Römer, and as the way "tone" here evokes at once painting and music suggests, this representation brings us much closer to a poetics of *Stimmung*—indeed, the very model of *Stimmung* that Wellbery ascribes to Goethe, that seems implicit in Heinrich's reading of Goethe, and that seems notably absent from Römer's poetics. That we are still dealing with realism is evident in the equation of the like (*wahrscheinlich*) and the similar (*ähnlich*) with the immediate (*gleich*) and true (*wahr*). But rather than a reductive empiricism, realism here is a mode of magic (*Zauber*), a magic explictly based in and productive of the sense of sympathetic connection and unity between the self, the mimesis, and the weave of nature (*das Weben der Natur*)—which is to say, in an experience of *Stimmung* that includes the natural world, the human artist, and the painting connecting them. Far from disenchanted, landscape painting for Heinrich is pantheistically charged—an embrace, as it were, of the magic within and not apart from the human or natural.

We see much the same persistence of the enchanted world in Heinrich's relation to Judith, even with—or perhaps, especially with—the fading of Anna from the scene. Judith has consistently been cast by Heinrich as representing the sensible, sensual world and the object of his sensual erotic desires, with his connection or attraction to her contrasted with his "spiritual" (*geistig*) and "platonic" connection and bond (*Band*) with Anna.[164] Thus, Heinrich's turn to her at the moment of Anna's fading could be read as the parallel in his erotic education to his turn to Römer's material phenomena (*sinnliche Erscheinungen*) in his aesthetic education—both as a turn to the "real" on the far side of a flirtation with *Spiritualismus*. That the relation with Judith also turns out to be the telos, as it were, of the entire *Bildungsroman* in its final version would seem to give added weight to this reading.

But the same reservations that hold in the case of Römer hold in that of Judith as well: the only difference is that it is Judith who represents the winning argument against Heinrich, rather than Heinrich against Römer. It goes something like this. Even as Heinrich's incessant aestheticization of Anna—the magic he has worked on her via his painting and writing—had the effect of constraining her, binding her within a constricting frame and eventually forcing her out of the picture altogether; just so does Heinrich's incessant sensualization or materialization of Judith. Judith as a representation of a *sinnlich* realm or principle—of a reality principle, as it were—is as reductive of her reality as Römer's poetics are of nature's reality, and no one is more aware of this than Judith herself, who from the start fights for a recognition of a more encompassing sense of herself, one that includes the spiritual and aesthetic dimensions of the world that Heinrich would otherwise associate only with Anna. Just as Anna's premonitions and dreams need to be acknowledged as part of the natural world, and just as Heinrich's "spirit-ed" relations and meanings need to be acknowledged as part of landscape painting, so, too, does the magical need to be included as part of Judith's character and Heinrich's attraction to her. Indeed, if there is a realism to be glimpsed in Heinrich's turn to Judith, both here and, especially, at the end of the novel, it is to be found in the rejection of Judith as the embodiment of a disenchanted, despiritualized realism: this at any rate would seem the peculiar symbolic force of the emblem beneath which Heinrich and Judith are finally joined, the glass painting from 1650 in the Golden Star tavern featuring "Emerentia Juditha" and her man—with Heinrich there as both lover and glass painter (*Glasmaler*), and with Meretlein and Judith joined in a single, encompassing figure and *Bild*.

This added enchanted dimension to Judith's character is conveyed most powerfully at the moment of Anna's physical fading and premonitions appearing, and of Heinrich's break with Römer and his *Spiritualismus* intact, in the novel's final Heathen Chamber scene—which belongs not to a costumed or dying Anna but to the naked and very much alive Judith.[165] Heinrich has expressed the wish to see the female figure revealed, unveiled (*entblößt*), and Judith, with an explicitly realist impulse—she will "magic away" (*wegzaubern*) Heinrich's illusions—decides to oblige him, but at the Heathen Chamber and from a distance. And at the Heathen Chamber, she attracts to her unadorned, natural body all the magical forces of both nature and textuality that otherwise seemed reserved for Anna but instead persist in the world without her. The textual magic is there in spectral allusions to Ariosto and, more immediately, to the Witches' Kitchen scene in Goethe's *Faust*; but more importantly, the natural magic is everywhere, in the setting as well as both participants, and between the setting and both participants. Heinrich says, "It seemed to me as if Judith had dissolved herself and soundlessly disappeared into the nature that teasingly rustled its ghostly elements around me. . . . It truly became uncanny to me, as the still of the night seemed completely saturated with daemonic intent" (Es wurde mir zu Mute, wie wenn Judith sich aufgelöst hätte und still in die Natur verschwunden wäre, in welcher mich ihre Elemente geisterhaft neckend umrauschten. . . . Es wurde mir wirklich unheimlich zu Mute, da die Stille der Nacht von einer dämonischen Absicht ganz getränkt erschien). Judith has shed her clothes, "like a lifeless, earthly hull," and in her naked truth—as the very embodiment of the real, the natural, the erotic—she appears ghostly (*gespentisch*) before Heinrich, singing magically (*zauberhaft*) and drawing him magnetically (*magnetisch*) to her appearance. And so on. But the point of Judith at the Heathen Chamber as "the nocturnal phantom" (*der nächtliche Spuk*) is this: even with the death of Anna, the magical does not leave the novel's world, does not yield a disenchanted erotic subject, a disenchanted natural realm, or a disenchanted aesthetic ideal. At its most basic level, the world of the novel remains an enchanted one.

Anna and Objectivity

The last word belongs not to Judith but Anna: it is with her, or rather her death, that the "Story of My Youth" comes closest to realizing its properly magic realism—its *Stimmung*, its seamless unity of the real and allegorical, the human and natural, the live and dead. It is one of the most powerful tour de force moments in German realist literature.

Once Anna dies, a process begins that extends what we just saw with her premonitions: even as with her physical fading her spirituality doesn't disappear but rather disperses, broadcast into the invisible and immaterial forces behind the natural world, so with her death her life doesn't disappear but rather disperses, broadcast into the visible and material things in the natural world—into the very things whose bonds to her were the means for constricting her, and which now become the means through which she flows out to inhabit those things and imbue them with their "spirit-ed" meanings and relations without ever being anything more than their concrete selves. The result is an amazingly freed and complete signification, freed of needed external (or transcendent) referent and complete in the things themselves; and a sense of all-embracing relation and unity that, for both Heinrich and the reader, produces an almost ecstatic sense of aesthetic bliss: an objective state and a subjective sense that Heinrich will call *Stimmung* and equate with the achieved end of his *Bildung*.

When Anna dies, her corpse is laid out "beautifully adorned" by old Katherine and Heinrich's mother in Anna's room:

> There she lay, according to the schoolmaster's wish, on the beautiful flowered throw that she had once embroidered for her father. . . . Above her on the wall Katherine . . . had hung the picture that I had once made of Anna, and opposite one still saw the landscape with the Heathen Chamber that I painted years before on the white wall. Both folding doors of Anna's cupboard stood open and her innocent possessions came to light and lent the still death-chamber a helpful appearance of life. [The schoolmaster helped the two women] take out and look over the most delicate and memory-rich little things that the blessed girl had collected from early childhood on. . . . Some of these were even laid beside her on the throw, such that, unconsciously and against the usual

practice of these simple people, a custom of ancient tribes was practiced here. The whole time they did this, they spoke with one another as if the dead girl could still hear them.

Da lag sie, nach des Schulmeisters Willen, auf dem schönen Blumenteppich, den sie einst für ihren Vater gestickt [hatte]. . . . Über ihr an der Wand hatte Katherine . . . das Bild hingehängt, das ich einst von Anna gemacht, und gegenüber sah man immer noch die Landschaft mit der Heidenstube, welche ich vor Jahren auf die weiße Mauer gemalt. Die beiden Flügeltüren von Annas Schrank standen geöffnet und ihr unschuldiges Eigentum trat zutage und verlieh der stillen Totenkammer einen wohltuenden Schein von Leben. [Der Schulmeister half den beiden Frauen,] die zierlichsten und erinnerungsreichsten Sächelchen, deren die Selige von früher Kindheit an gesammelt, hervorziehen und beschauen. . . . Einiges wurde sogar ihr zur Seite auf den Teppich gelegt, so daß hier unbewußt und gegen den sonstigen Gebrauch von diesen einfachen Leuten eine Sitte alter Völker geübt wurde. Dabei sprachen sie immer so miteinander, als ob die Tote es noch hören könnte.[166]

Among the objects that are brought forth and placed around and next to Anna are her father's letters, her books, her artworks, and the crown she wore on her last visit to the Heathen Chamber; also her own embroidery of Heinrich's flower-bouquet painting. It is an enchanting moment: all the object-devices that were deployed to bind Anna and ultimately deprive her of life and movement are on display, beginning with Heinrich's *Bilder*, but also extending to her father's instruments of *Bildung*; with nature there, too, in the mediated form of the flowered throw and Heathen Chamber landscape; and, too, those echo effects of her *gebildet* status, the letters she writes back to her father, the blanket she embroiders for him, and the flower-bouquet embroidery she makes for Heinrich. As if in unconscious (*unbewußt*) acknowledgment of the ancient heathenish way these objects have worked their sympathetic magic through metonymic connection, proximity, and contagion, they are placed next to the corpse, giving concrete expression to the powerful and ultimately deadly relation that has obtained between Anna and these things.

The end effect of these objects is, however, not only the deadly one on her: if the inanimate objects have communicated their binding force to Anna, she has communicated back her animate life to them. This is especially evident in the case of her "echo-effect" artworks, such as the flower-bouquet embroidery, which are at once signs of Anna's complete, even interior and active, subjection to her father's and Heinrich's designs, and of her own recursive, back-turned, dispersive agency. But it is the case with all the things in the room, including those produced by Heinrich and the father. It is the objects placed next to and around her that communicate the sense of life, Anna's life; it is the objects that, bound to Anna, communicate in turn to those in the room the sense that she can still hear (is still part of the *Mit-stimmung*). The sense that the bonds have not dissolved but remain in the things that originally drew them is reinforced when Heinrich takes into his own hands the flower-bouquet embroidery and says, "I felt myself bound to Anna by an unbreakable bond" ([Ich] fühlte mich durch ein un-auflösliches Band mit Anna verbunden).[167] Things stay enchanted, metonymically charged forces, and no less so—even more so—with the loss of their explicit human referent. (Marx and Freud would say things thus become fetishes, Brown that they become objects, Benjamin that they become auratic and look back; I will say they become realist.)

The same contagious communion that we see between Anna and the objects in her room we see again between Anna, the things in her room, and the natural world outside her window—at least in the experience of Heinrich. He has been keeping the nighttime death-watch over Anna's corpse:

> The dead white girl continued to lie unmoving, but the colored flowers of the carpet seemed to grow in the pale light. Now the morning star rose and was reflected in the lake. . . . With the morning graying . . . it seemed to live and weave around the still figure . . . as at the same moment I timidly touched her hand, I drew back my own in horror . . . : for the hand was cold, like a lump of chilly clay.

> Das tote weiße Mädchen lag unbeweglich fort und fort, die farbigen Blumen des Teppichs aber schienen zu wachsen in dem schwachen Lichte. Nun ging der Morgenstern auf und spiegelte sich im See. . . . Mit dem Morgengrauen . . . schien es zu leben und zu weben um die stille Gestalt . . . als ich zugleich zaghaft ihre Hand berührte, zog ich die meinige entsetzt zurück . . . : denn die Hand war kalt wie ein Häuflein kühler Ton.[168]

The same set of connecting, sympathetic forces that we saw active while Anna was alive we see still active once she has died: first between the natural world and Anna's artwork that imitates it, as the embroidered flowers appear to grow; and then, via the mimesis in the mirroring lake, more directly between nature and Anna herself, as the stilled corpse seems to live in the weave of light, reflection, art, and Heinrich's (attracted) imagination. In some ways, we seem at a moment much like when Heinrich first encountered the Meretlein portrait on the wall in his uncle's house; but even more we seem poised before a moment that will repeat the actual resurrection of Meretlein—both in her person and in her portrait—and not least because we seem poised again before the same paradox of realism, the same double-bind of that which stills life also preserves it.[169]

The results, however, prove far different from the case of Meretlein, or rather, the same paradox is played out in a rather different fashion, one that appears more "realistic," more disenchanted, and yet still manages to keep faith with witchery. There is no resurrection: Anna remains undeniably dead, and the cold factuality of her inert corpse acts as a forceful rebuke of what now appears as Heinrich's magical thinking.[170] But the disruptive force of this all-too-material touch is immediately countered by the "harmonic force" (*harmonischer Kraft*), the "powerful tones" (*kräftigen Tönen*) of organ music Heinrich hears coming from the next room over; the music that, as always in this novel, speaks of a larger reality: of *Stimmung*, of the invisible, occult connections between the human and natural, their shared "spirit-world" (*Geisterwelt*) that keeps even the dead Anna implicated and present.

As I said, the nighttime communication between Anna, the natural world, and Heinrich that makes her seem alive in its weave can be read as only Heinrich's magical thinking, rudely but properly dispelled by the subsequent material contact. And the almost immediate restoration—even resurrection—of the sense of sustained spiritual contact brought about by the music can be read as a defensive retreat to that magical, reality-denying thinking: for music is also a medium for aestheticization, and is in this case tellingly played by the schoolmaster, and so perhaps Anna is only successfully recuperated, aesthetically and psychologically, as object after her momentary recognition as thing—much as happened in the last meeting between Heinrich and Anna at the Heathen Chamber. Such a reading would comfortably assign the "spirit-world" to the subjective and aesthetic alone, and would leave the natural, nonhuman world safely untouched, or only represented in the physical touch that denies spirit(s). But as I also said, music seems always to exceed just the aesthetic, to convey the sense of (micro/macro) cosmic connection that is *Stimmung*; and this suggests that the same extension of sympathetic forces into the nonhuman that we witnessed with Meretlein and throughout with Anna persists here as well. As indeed proves the case.

The sense of *Stimmung*, of a harmonious blending of the human and the natural, the subjective and the objective, the significant and the concrete—the sense that is first conveyed "magically" during the night in Heinrich's fantasy in Anna's room is achieved far more "realistically" in the clear light of the next day, outdoors and in the woods: as Heinrich says, he goes "into the living green" (*ins lebendige Grüne*), himself of course dressed in matching green ("like a heathen").[171] The effect comes about through a mode of description that manages only to describe what is there, without any obvious projecting subjectivity on Heinrich's part, and yet still to resonate with attendant, not-quite-represented significance and connection.

At the center of this description is the coffin that is being built for Anna's corpse. It is made from the boards of a "slender little fir-tree" (*schlankes Tännlein*) that had been intended for the schoolmaster's own coffin, boards that had served for many years as a "resting bench" (*Ruhebank*) on which he would read and Anna play, and whose ends are now cut off for Anna's coffin.[172] With no explicit elaboration or needed symbolic loading, the "little fir-tree" speaks of Anna, the "resting bench" of arresting stillness, the father's reading of the *Bildung* that will be the arrest of the playing "slender" child, the cut-off boards of both Anna as an extension of her father and his now lost connection to her. But most speaking of all is the relation between the boards themselves and the tree from which they come, which conveys in simple, concrete fashion a unity between the human aesthetic and the nonhuman natural that becomes the coffin, which is at once a fashioned artwork and still, always, also the tree itself.[173]

The merged unity between the human aesthetic and natural material worlds is furthered by the decision to build the coffin in the woods, on the far side of the reflecting lake. Heinrich and the carpenter (who does the actual physical work) set up a workplace by clamping cut boards to living trees; Heinrich helps build a fire out of combined wood-shavings and twigs; the carpenter planes, and the rolls of shavings, "like delicate, shining satin bands," drop to the ground and mix with falling leaves. The sense of *Stimmung* is especially captured when Heinrich describes how the planed shavings loose themselves "with a bright singing tone, which was a seldom-heard song beneath the trees," and adds the echoing hammer-blows and cries of startled birds to the chorus—all at once nothing but themselves and still indices of a harmony between man and landscape, art and nature in the external world. The high note comes in the completed coffin itself:

> Soon the finished coffin stood before us in its simplicity, slender and symmetrical, the lid beautifully vaulted. . . . I saw with wonder . . . ; I had to laugh. . . . As [the carpenter] polished the coffin all over with the [pumice-]stone, it became as white as snow, and only the faintest reddish breath of the fir-tree still shone through, like with an apple-blossom. It looked far more beautiful and dignified than if it had been painted, gilded, or even studded with bronze.

> Bald stand der fertige Sarg in seiner Einfachheit vor uns, schlank und ebenmäßig, der Deckel schön gewolbt. . . . Ich sah verwundert . . . ; ich mußte lachen. . . . Als [der Schreiner] aber den Sarg vollends mit dem [Bims]steine abschliff, wurde derselbe so weiß, wie Schnee, und kaum der leiseste rötliche Hauch des Tannenholzes schimmerte noch durch, wie bei einer Apfelblüte. Er sah so weit schöner und edler aus, als wenn er gemalt, vergoldet oder gar mit Erz beschlagen gewesen wäre.[174]

The coffin is art, but also wood; the more polished art it becomes, the more it brings out the wood, in colors like snow and as with an apple blossom; and the more it becomes at once art and nature, the more it becomes like Anna—even metonymically to be Anna: slender, beautiful, and white with the faintest breath of red shining through. It is, I'd say, this truly magically charged moment of micro-macro relation, where the aesthetic and natural merge and the coffin becomes Anna without ceasing to be itself, and Anna present in the coffin without even being there, that forces from Heinrich (and the reader) both wonder and almost involuntary laughter—both effects of *Stimmung* perceived, a *Stimmung* that originates in the things of the external world and only then communicates itself to the internal one of his (and our) subjectivity. And it is as much this sense of the objectivity of the effect as it is the complete integration of the artful and natural, the apparent absence of a projected, superimposed aesthetic dimension (painted, gilded, or even studded with bronze), that makes this moment also seem a realist one.

This is not to say that the mediation of the aesthetic—of both a perceiving aesthetic subjectivity and intervening aesthetic conventions—is absent from the scene; but rather that this, too, is brought into *Stimmung* (porous accord) with the rest in ways that bind them tightly, sympathetically together (and keep them natural, real). We see this in the glass pane Heinrich himself adds to the coffin, the pane that will cover and frame Anna's face and that repeats and varies in significant ways the glass panes that covered both the flower-bouquet painting and Anna's portrait and echoes, too, the several reflecting waters in which she appears. Heinrich leaves the woods and returns to the house to fetch the "forgotten" glass from an old picture frame whose original *Bild* had long since disappeared. When he gets back to the coffin he dips the glass in the lake's water to rid it of its darkening dust:

> Then I lifted it up . . . and when I held the shining glass up high against the sun and looked through it, I beheld the most lovely wonder I have ever seen. I saw three charming angels making music; the middle one sang, the two others played . . . but the apparition was so aerially and delicately transparent that I didn't know whether it was hovering in the rays of the sun, in the glass, or only in my fantasy. When I moved the pane, the angels immediately disappeared, until suddenly, with a different movement, they appeared again. Since then I've been told that copper engravings or drawings, which have lain undisturbed for long, long years behind a glass, during the dark nights of these years impart

themselves to the glass, and leave behind upon it, as it were, their lasting mirror-image.

Dann hob ich sie empor . . . und indem ich das glänzende Glas hoch gegen die Sonne hielt und durch dasselbe schaute, erblickte ich das lieblichste Wunder, das ich je gesehen. Ich sah nämlich drei reizende, musizierende Engelknaben; der mittlere sang, die beiden anderen spielten . . . aber die Erscheinung war so luftig und zart durchsichtig, daß ich nicht wußte, ob sie auf den Sonnenstrahlen, im Glase, oder nur in meiner Phantasie schwebte. Wenn ich die Scheibe bewegte, so verschwanden die Engel auf Augenblicke, bis ich sie plötzlich mit einer anderen Wendung wieder entdeckte. Ich habe seither erfahren, daß Kupferstiche oder Zeichnungen, welche lange, lange Jahre hinter einem Glase ungestört liegen, während der dunklen Nächte dieser Jahre sich dem Glase mitteilen und gleichsam ihr dauerndes Spiegelbild in demselben zurücklassen.[175]

As with the glass panes covering both the flower-bouquet painting and Anna's portrait, this one, too, speaks of aesthetic mediation, and especially, as with the flower-bouquet painting, brings with it the contagion of its earlier image. And as with those earlier panes, it brings with it as well the suggestion of a back-reflecting mirror, a *Spiegelbild* that reproduces more the artist and his representing conventions (or medium) than the matter behind it. But something new is happening here, suggested by the way the image's contagion is materially and not just metaphorically (or metonymically) evident; by the way the glass does not simply mirror Heinrich's image back to himself but stays transparent; and by the way the lake's water proves not so much a reflecting medium as a clarifying one. The aesthetic here is at once material and porous, its interceding conventions (and medium) at once evident and invisible, everywhere and nowhere; and as a result, its image seems at once and without distinction to exist in the glass, Heinrich's fantasy, and the natural light. And while it seems equally important that the image is of angels and of music—the one hinting at the divine, the other the harmony at stake—it seems even more important that the image, the *Bild*, is produced or transferred by nature itself, without a human agent, or a transcendent one. The process of imparting (*mitteilen*) and leaving behind (*zurücklassen*) is exactly the kind of contagious, contiguous exchange between proximate realms that the novel has long been working toward (an *actio in distans* that seems the visual equivalent to one musical string communicating its vibrating tone to a remote other): here nature itself is responsible for the transfer, the representation, that joins both the human and the divine together in itself and in the aesthetic. And it is no less a "wonder" for being a form of natural magic—and for being real.

All this comes to one final representational crescendo with the actual burial of Anna, a moment when the concept of *Stimmung*, the aesthetics of realism, the end(s) of *Bildung*, and the fate of magic become, as it were, the very objects to be brought into accord. The magic comes both first and last, and it does so in the form of echoes, especially of Meretlein. Anna's coffin is bedecked with flowers, including many a bouquet, but also, and chiefly, a wreath or crown of white roses. The coffin is carried over the mountain, where "radiant white clouds drifted high in the blue sky, and they seemed to stand still for a moment over the flowery coffin and peep curiously through the little window that almost roguishly sparkled forth between the roses, reflecting the clouds," recalling the portrait being similarly carried over the mountain, but even more—and especially in that "roguishly"—that witching moment when the sun burst through at Meretlein's funeral and touched her crown.[176] The *Stimmung* that is implicit here in both the temporal echoing of these earlier moments (Meretlein, the flower bouquet, the portrait) and the present accord of the several realms (the personal, the aesthetic, the earthly flowers, the heavenly light and clouds) is also here in the chorale and "figural-song" (*Figuralgesänge*) sung at the graveside "with bright and pure voice" (*mit heller und reiner Stimme*), and helps instill what Heinrich calls his "elevated and solemn *Stimmung*" as he stands there, observing, experiencing, and *enjoying* the moment—because it is a moment not only of death but also of *Stimmung*, with all the enchantment that brings with it, even when death is also what it brings.[177]

This key doubleness to the moment (as both death and *Stimmung*) is also intrinsic to its *Bildung* and realist thematics. The ends of *Bildung* are expressed when Heinrich looks through the coffin's glass pane and declares, "In elevated and solemn *Stimmung*, but in complete calm (*Ruhe*), I saw that which it enclosed being buried, like a part of my experience, my life, held in glass and framed."[178] This seems to enact the reductive scenario we described earlier: the abjection of the unruly desires and fantasies of the male subject and their projected conscription onto a female other, whose death marks his detachment from those same forces. And at first glance, this model of *Bildung* seems to find its expected counterpart in a similarly disenchanted, culminating aesthetic perception or experience:

> The singing continued. . . . The last ray of sunlight now shone through the glass pane onto the pale face that lay beneath it; the feeling that I now had was so odd that I can designate it in no other way than with the strange, grand, and cold word "objective" that German aesthetics has discovered.

> Der Gesang dauerte fort. . . . Der letzte Sonnenstrahl leuchtete nun durch die Glasscheibe in das bleiche Gesicht, das darunter lag; das Gefühl, das ich jetzt empfand, war so seltsam, daß ich es nicht anders, als mit dem fremden hochtrabenden und kalten Worte "objektiv" benennen kann, welches die deutsche Ästhetik erfunden hat.[179]

It is indeed an odd or *seltsam* response to Anna's death; and its oddness is only increased when we note that Heinrich reaches for the word "objective" in the exactly functionally equivalent moment wherein the pastor reached for "witchery" (*Hexentum*) at Meretlein's death. Thus, it invites a double reading. On the one hand, objectivity has successfully displaced and replaced "witchery," which goes into the grave along with both "the little witch" Anna and, with her, Heinrich's immature, desire- and fantasy-filled subjectivity, leaving only a disenchanted world and subject—and whether this objectivity represents a strength or weakness (*Stärke oder Schwäche*) is not decided.[180] But on the other hand, and as we've seen, "witchery" has also, as it were, become "objective." The object world, quite apart from either Anna or Heinrich's subjective fantasy, has come to resonate with both, has become charged with unseen, unrepresented connecting forces that Heinrich, and the reader, have been trained to respond to and connect with themselves—and that is why this is a moment not only of negation but also of fulfillment, not of abjection but of completion, not of lost but of sustained connection—a moment that calls forth Heinrich's and our aesthetic bliss. "The singing continued," Heinrich remains "in elevated and solemn *Stimmung*," and for all its seeming dissonance, the moment is still one resonant with the cosmic harmonies of the novel's realist magic.

2

Speaking Magic in Fontane's
The Stechlin

Theodor Fontane is generally considered Germany's most important novelist between Goethe and Thomas Mann, indeed its most important realist author; and his last published novel, *The Stechlin* (*Der Stechlin*, 1897), as among his most important texts. The work displays many of the qualities that distinguish Fontane's realism and make it so different from the works of the so-called poetic realists, including Keller, and more akin to its nineteenth-century European counterparts in France and England, often considered the gold standard of realism per se. But it also displays many qualities that seem to push beyond this standard and to anticipate the poetics of a postrealist, even modernist period. My concern is with both these aspects, especially the transition from the one to the other, and with respect to a set of questions similar to those posed about *Green Henry*. How does magic constitute an intrinsic element of its realist and then almost postrealist world? In its temporalities, causalities, and relation to objects and the nonhuman world? Or more particularly, how does "magic reading" function both for characters in its world and for readers of its text? What role does futurity and its divination play? And what kind of forces must be active in that textual world—such as those we identified with *Stimmung* in Keller—to make such reading, such magic, happen?

Premonitions I

The distinctive, more European mode of realism usually associated with Fontane's work is based on both temporal and spatial coordinates that closely link the literary world to a particular extraliterary historical moment and setting, or *Umwelt*, that help define its "real."[1] History and setting both act as shaping forces determining the literary world and its subjects, the one imposing a kind of contingent occasionality and direction, the other a surrounding affective environment that impinges more or less directly on characters' lives. The idea of history also lends the narrative itself a teleological force in both its forward-looking sequence and backward-looking retrospection, in ways that extend beyond the singular case of the protagonist's individual biography or development. And the *Umwelt* becomes increasingly socially, even politically defined, with matters of class, region, and nation coming to the foreground— and thus becoming active forces—and with a marginalizing of two of the factors that played such a crucial role in Keller's text in supporting its magical dimension: namely, the downplay of psychology as grounded in a kind of otherness or unconscious as opposed to one shaped by social forces from the *Umwelt*; and the downplay of the natural world, which becomes more and more consigned to the outskirts, as both setting and force.[2]

All of this is evident in Fontane's first novel, *Before the Storm* (*Vor dem Sturm*, 1878), which has its referential basis in both a major historical event—and so draws on extraliterary historical sources for its plot—and its setting, which draws heavily from material from Fontane's earlier nonfictional work, *Wanderings through the March of Brandenburg* (*Wanderungen durch die Mark Brandenburg*, 1862–89). The novel depicts the fortunes of the family Vitzewitz during the retreat of Napolean's troops from Russia through Prussia in the winter of 1812–13, with special attention to the romantic entanglements of the young adult children, Lewin and Renate, with their Polish cousins, Kathinka and Tubal, but including a wide array of secondary characters, historical intrusions, and geographical specificities. These features have helped mark the work as what some consider "the greatest historical novel in German literature," and as such one of its most representative realist works, quite different from the so-called *Sonderweg* of the German *Bildungsroman* and its "poetic" realism.[3]

But while it is this, it is also the novel of Fontane's that is most conspicuously invested in what we might call the supernatural, by which I mean precisely those conditions that ground and promote, even require, magic reading, including omens, prophecies, and divinations—and already in the deliberately ominous, premonitory title of the work. And while some critics see this as something of a flaw in the novel, an early literary tic in tension with its realist poetics, I will argue that it is in fact intrinsic to Fontane's realism, something that never disappears but only becomes more refined, even dominant in his subsequent works leading up to *The Stechlin*—as Peter Demetz notes, Fontane is consistently the most omen-invested of the German realists, early and late, and this deserves to be read as part of, rather than apart from, his literary realist poetics.[4] And so I would like to introduce an initial consideration of *Before the Storm* as representative of Fontane's realism and magic thinking, and their relation, as a background starting point for understanding both what persists and what changes on both these fronts in *The Stechlin*.

The function of omens, prophecies, signs, and their divinatory readings in *Before the Storm* can be divided into two levels, although as we shall see it is at their point of interplay that they are most interesting (which is to say that, as in *Green Henry* and despite the turn to third-person narration, the division is largely illegitimate in this regard): the evocation of omens that are more or less available only to the reader and both structure and require his divinatory reading of the novel, set against a future known to be set or fixed; and those available to and experienced by the characters in the textual world, for whom the future is not known to be fixed. The novel features the former first, in the form of both those immediately and explicitly recognizable as such, such as the narrator's account of the apparition of old Matthias Vitzewitz, of the split beech-tree before the manor, or of the Vitzewitz family prophecy, all presented to the reader prior to being presented to the characters themselves for interpretation; and those that are only subsequently (which is to say, retrospectively) recognized as such, for instance, the line "And she can walk on stars" or the unfolding motif of fire, and that are never fully presented or recognized as omens by the characters themselves.[5] This opening presentation of portentous signs is symptomatic of Fontane's sense that, in his narratives, the beginning must always be "pregnant with the future," establishing a temporal dimension and a signifying system supplemental to but also permeating its sequential historical present world, suggesting itself as the ground of historical consequence—although, again, a ground not immediately accessible to those "in history."[6]

Even though the narratorial level comes first and in many ways remains primary for our reading experience, it is really only by considering the divinatory reading of the characters in the work that we learn how to experience this added dimension and system ourselves. The means for introducing such omens and the occasions for their appearance to characters are, as we'll see, many and varied. But perhaps the most characteristic for Fontane, with the most integral relation to realism, is the one featured first and then sustained throughout, in the form of the omen as anecdote, such as the story Lewin tells—with much self-conscious commentary—to Renate early on about the mysteriously red-glowing window at the palace in Berlin, about which "people say it means war" ("An easy prophecy," replies Renate) and to which, "to bestow upon it profounder significance, to make it appear as signs and wonders" (*eine tiefere Bedeutung zu geben, so etwas wie Zeichen und Wunder*), Lewin then immediately adds a second anecdote he theatrically titles "Charles XI and the Apparition in the Throne-Room at Stockholm," thus inaugurating a chain or series of like anecdotes that will manifest itself intermittently throughout the text.[7]

That these omens are presented to the characters in the form of anecdotes (and the same could be said of the story presented to us of the split beech-tree or of the family prophecy, which are formally identical) is itself of "profound significance" for considering the relations of magic reading and realism. As Paul Fleming has argued— drawing on the work of Joel Fineman, Stephen Greenblatt, Peter Fenves, and Hans Blumenberg—the anecdote might well be the prose form best suited for capturing prosaic reality, engaging a cognitive mode "at the nexus of literature and experience, literature and the real."[8] As the narration of a singular, detached historical event that is "of little effect but great significance," the anecdote is a literary form that, in the words of Fineman, "uniquely refers to the real"—whether or not true or verifiable—and so produces the effect of the real, while at the same time it provokes interpretation of the more-than-real, the hidden significance beyond itself that the anecdote might entail for the present or future. It introduces an opening into the teleological fabric of the grand historical récit (and in a historical novel such as *Before the Storm*, this would be in both the narrative and history itself), a moment that seems to embody a different, independent logic or significatory structure, both "within and yet without the framing context of successivity," and so posing questions of "the historiographic integration of event to context"—of this "real" to the ordinary prosaic real.[9] It is precisely this quality of hidden, indeterminate context and connection that Lewin foregrounds as essential to his own anecdotal narratives, and not because it is inconvenient or insignificant, but rather the opposite. As Renate says, not seeing how events are connecting excites the imagination to more mysterious interpretive moves, "like knights on a chessboard" (but a chessboard unseen).[10]

In the case of particularly ominous anecdotes such as those narrated by Lewin, the question of interpretation—of the relation of the anecdote to the context in which it is uttered—is, as it were, doubly determined: by the need to ask, what does this mean in the present context? and what does it bode for the future? (with the immediate context already a future one in relation to the past time of the anecdote itself). The first relation is, of course, never a direct or causal one—the two historical moments are neither sequentially nor consequentially connected—but rather based upon a certain analogical mode of connection. It is a matter of resemblance, of like to like, of a similitude read into and then out of the anecdote; and insofar as these tales seem to suggest a certain supernatural force behind or beside or attendant upon the anecdoted world, they also establish that force as one that operates *via* similitude. The second relation is an extension of this: again as Fleming says, there is almost always a "predictive, futural, almost prophetic character to the evidence presented" by anecdotes in that, for all their singularity, they seem to participate in an ongoing chain of similitude: what makes them sign-ificant is this quality of futurity, a quality independent of, even if embedded and only manifest in, ordinary historical sequentiality.[11] Both relations are captured in the characteristic way Lewin supplements his first portentous anecdote with another one, albeit drawn from a completely unrelated historical moment (further underscored by how, within each anecdote, the ominous event occurs multiple, and usually three, times). While no causal relation is proposed either between the two anecdotes or between both and the present context (as Renate says, "I do not see how these events are connected" [Ich vermisse die Beziehungen]), the sense of similarity as a connecting force, acting in but beyond historical causation by establishing repeating patterns across time, suggests itself to the characters as a determinative (if noncausal) force for their own future.[12] And this leads the characters in the course of the novel to connect these anecdotes up with subsequent, future omens or events as well—even as it also leads us as readers to connect them to repeated patterned images of the narrator's taking place over the characters' heads, as it were, reinforcing a similar sense of ominous, determinative forces operating behind the simple causation of the plot.[13]

Two additional points. First, for all the sense of determination, fate, or necessity that emanates out of such anecdotal readings, they actually "prove nothing," as Fleming notes.[14] One can infer, but there is no necessity to anecdotal evidence, even when what is inferred is necessity (which is to say, fate). This is a form of withheld acknowledgment that is regularly represented by Fontane's characters in the novel, and it is an essential part of his realism—but also, we've seen, an essential aspect of all magic read-ing: its foundation is both there and not there, both forceful and without substance; indeed, it is just this spectral quality of its hid-den world that persists even when the text's many specters are open to dismissal.[15] Whether or not a particular character assents to the ominous quality of the given anecdote is often at issue in the text, and it is one of the critical tests of character in the novel—and by no means are those who dismiss or disavow the ominous, nor those who embrace only a closed predetermination or fixed necessity, the ones most in touch with the "real": quite the contrary (more anon). But in all cases, the anecdote presents characters with a world of signs (at once real and supernatural) rather than simply realia; and it presents that world of signs as fundamentally unreliable, open, and ambivalent: as spectral.

Second, and a bit more difficult to formulate, anecdotes have a way of both thingifying their subject matter—presented as some-thing of a foreign body in the main body of the text, a piece of dug-up, materialized language that becomes an autonomous object for the characters' and readers' contemplation—and emptying it out at the same time, turning it into a sign of something else, some mean-ing beyond itself. Narrative enters, as it were, into the text's world of considered objects, with all its particularity and singularity, even as it turns itself, qua object, into allegory.[16] Indeed, in this, anec-dotes resemble the role and reading of archaeological objects in the novel, such as Wotan's wagon, which the characters Seidentopf and Turgany place on a table between them and read and interpret vari-ously for its significance and place in Ur-Germanic history—and by implication for the present and incipient history of Germany as well.[17] Just so do anecdotes become things, and things as signs, in the narrated world.

Besides such anecdotes—and there are many throughout the text, all of which become objects of interpretation, and their interpreta-tion itself a subject for interpretation, and all inviting readings of their connection to the immediately contiguous moment as well as to more remote but similar series of other portentous anecdotes or events[18]—besides anecdotes, there are numerous other sites for the practice of such divinatory readings: we might say that anecdotes train characters in the novel in a certain mode of reading experience that they then extend into other areas. Many of these sites, like anecdotes, take place at a juncture of the literary (or aesthetic) and the real: the names of things and places that seem to forebode future events for the characters, at times accompanied by one of Fontane's favorite lines, "nomen et omen"; similarly portraits, chanced upon snatches of poetry or song, and on several occasions dreams.[19] All are approached as signs or *Zeichen* of something beyond themselves, beyond their ordinary intention, something at once intensely personal and infused with future significance, but also with uncertain significance: whether the portrait of the mother of Kathinka, whose startling resemblance to Kathinka herself suggests a similar betrayal in her (Kathinka's) future of her beloved (Lewin); or a chance verse from Herder that is immediately read for its possible portentous significance for Lewin's situation.[20] As with anecdotes—and archaeological objects—these instances stage the very process of reading in the text, and in so doing underscore its magical, divinatory qualities.

This mode of reading extends beyond that of anecdotes, or of aesthetic, lingual, and archaeological objects, to encompass all manner of events and things in both the social and the natural worlds. So, for instance, it regularly appears in the context of such social rituals as playing forfeits, "casting lead," or gambling—all games that, as E. B. Tylor reminds us, carry the vestiges of magical thinking and divination into the modern world.[21] The first (playing forfeits) is explicitly described in such a way as to foreground these qualities and to draw out the similarity to anecdotes: Turgany says, "The profoundest mysteries of nature are revealed in the playing of forfeits. . . . To choose something of indeterminate value without lapsing into the trivial: that is the art."[22] As with anecdotes, the emphasis is on the seemingly insignificant—what stands outside ordinary modes of valuation—as the bearer of another, more profound, and mysterious significance for those there and then. And in additon to the focus on the ostensibly trivial is the further suggestion of the importance of the element of chance or coincidence that again—like anecdotes or snatches of poetry—opens up a space in the teleological fabric of cause and effect for some other meaning, some other contingency, to enter the textual world. For this reason, characters in Fontane's world learn to attend to the apparently immaterial, nonhumanly intentional, chance moments of their experience as of special significance, and reality, for their future. And this extends beyond such controlled, to some extent artificial or ritualized settings to encompass the whole human and natural *Umwelt*: whether it be the appearance of reapers in a field, northern lights in the sky, crows in a tree, or the chance name of an inn or street, the wide world becomes charged for the characters with signs, and signs with the futurity that makes them signs—and with uncertainty.[23]

This way of reading and experiencing the world extends into the most quotidian and conventionally realist encounters in the novel. So, for instance, in a relatively trivial moment "of little effect but great significance," Lewin happens to catch a glimpse at a ball of Kathinka dancing with another man, the Polish Count Bninski, soon to emerge as his rival. Watching them, "he seemed to himself insipid, prosaic, boring":

> Catching sight of him, old Countess Reale again raised her lorgnette to her eyes and, after briefly inspecting him, lowered it again with an expression that seemed designed to set the seal on the verdict he had just passed on himself. Fräulein von Bischofswerder's two plaits were hanging even lower and looking even more despondent. It all seemed to him a sign.

> Die alte Gräfin Reale, seiner ansichtig werdend, setzte wieder die großen Kristallgläser auf und ließ nach kurzer Musterung das Lorgnon fallen, mit einer Miene, die das Urteil, das er sich selber eben ausgestellt hatte, untersiegeln zu wollen schien. Die beiden Locken des Fräuleins von Bischofswerder hingen noch länger und trübseliger herab. Es schien ihm alles ein Zeichen.[24]

Both the disapproving stare of Reale and the drooping plaits of Bischofswerder have other immediate causes (given earlier), having little to nothing to do with Lewin and nothing at all to do with Lewin's relation to Kathinka or with each other. But Lewin reads their momentary contiguity in terms of their perceived similarity to his own situation, and discovers connections that together become a sign or *Zeichen* whose meaning and relation are apparent to, and meant for, him alone—and whose binding chain seems charged with future force. In this way, chance similarities in the text beyond any character's intention become omens of a kind of necessity, a fate that seems destined whether or not anyone in any way acts to promote or parry it.

It helps, of course, that in the event the omen proves accurate: that Lewin—regularly identified as one of the more superstitious characters in the novel—turns out to be right, and that in this and other ways the narrator confirms his reading; both contribute to their concord with the presented realist world and to the principles governing the reading of that world. To some extent this also belies the assumption that such omens are only a function of subjective, psychological projection; rather, character prophecies succeed or fail in the novel according to their congruence with the narrator's ominous imagery system and not necessarily according to their individual psychological acuity.[25] The same point is also made in a more negative manner, by the representation of characters whose reading of the world excludes such magic.[26] At one point, Marie—the fairy child of the novel and Lewin's eventual wife—condemns a rather pedestrian author by saying, "He is no poet because he knows only the real world," and something similar can be said about the most nonsuperstitious characters: they turn out to be unskilled readers.[27] The two most prominent of these are Pastor Othegraven and the Herrnhuter Aunt Schorlemmer, both of whom, not incidently, share with the disparaged poet a strong Protestant ideology. Othegraven, on his way to propose to Marie, chances upon some unrelated bad news, and we're told, "If he'd been one of those people influenced by signs or omens, he'd have turned back." "But there was no superstition in him"; he goes on, and in the event his trip is indeed ill fated.[28] Aunt Schorlemmer, who throughout vehemently denies a supernatural world but still enjoys making prophecies, is nonetheless singularly poor at it: as Renate tells her, "You see truly what ought to be (*das Rechte*), but not always what will be (*das Richtige*)." Interestingly, in both these cases it is not so much the strict this-worldliness of these characters that makes them less than optimal readers as it is their religious commitment to a doctrine of predestination—and so not a rejection of a fated future per se (no less than that implied in either teleological history or narrative), but rather, perhaps, a rejection of openness and ambivalence toward that future.

Besides Lewin, there are a host of other characters whose superstitious nature encourages their magic reading of the world, some consistently, such as Major-General von Bamme ("Rob me of the little superstition I have and I have nothing at all and collapse") and others occasionally and, as it were, only retrospectively, such as Berndt von Vitzewitz—in both cases, largely accurately in their reading.[29] Interestingly for Fontane as a "social" realist, there seem to be no clear distinctions in terms of social class as to who is most invested in such readings: aristocracy and servants, peasants and merchants, seem all equally to inhabit and participate in the same portentous world. There is, however, a distinction in terms of gender: in the novel, female characters—and especially those of undefined or marginal social status and of unusual proximity to the nonhuman natural world—seem the most immersed in the magical world, and to be not only the most magical readers but also the best readers.[30] Of the three most important—Hoppenmarieken, Marie, and Renate—the first two are the most interesting to us. Hoppenmarieken, whose dwarfed and oddly distorted body puts her on the edge of the (non)human world, even as her social status is oddly outside human law and custom, is regularly referred to as a witch (and sometimes as a specter or clairvoyant): in a significant pairing, she is associated both with fortune-telling through cards and with a herbarium of potent plants and a menagerie of companion birds. For all her asocial status, she is also the unofficial, extra-ordinary connecting force and binding power of the local *Umwelt*, bringing the various houses and social groups into relation by delivering letters (which is to say, signs); this might be thought together with her "jackdaw's nest" of collected (stolen) objects that contrast so noticeably with Seidentopf's "systematic" display of archaeological objects, representing a different mode of connection, outside of normal (law and) order or semantics, but for that very reason charged with hidden significance. In any case, she is most important to us as the character who performs the magical feat at the center of the novel, "charming" the fire (*et bespreken*) that threatens to engulf the Vitzewitz manor, making "two or three signs" and uttering "a couple of incomprehensible words" before jamming her crooked stick into a key opening in the building's architecture and marvelously stopping the flames—flames, moreover, eidetically connected to Lewin's much earlier prophecies (mentioned above).[31] Her decisive intervention into the novel's "real" *and* symbolic worlds seems to confirm the authority of (her) magic presence in Fontane's novel: and again, not only in how she affects the actual fire in the text's real, immediate setting, but also in how this functions as a reliable omen in the text's symbolic fabric for the subsequent fate of family and nation (the house, as it were).

The fairy child or *Feenkind* Marie is the character most associated throughout with the realm of magic and, as with Hoppenmarie-ken, with that of nature as well. She is also perhaps the most prominent subject of prophecies by various others in the novel and, more significantly, the nodal point (the opening) for the governing portentous symbolic systems of the novel as a whole—and, as it turns out, the novel's most perceptive reader. Like Hoppenmarieken, she is of uncertain social status, by birth associated with magic through her magician father; she is from the start described as "of the world of nature, not man" and—in a most Meretlein-like moment—is once discovered asleep in the corn, poppies in her hand, a little bird at her feet, all of which inspires the prophecy that "she will bring blessings to the house, like martins under the roof"—which turns out to be fulfilled.[32] Most significant are the connections her figure makes between the realms of the supernatural, the natural, futural prophecy, and realized fate, which is to say, the novel's governing principles (its nature magic). This is primarily secured through the motif of stars in the novel—long the site of divination, not only qua fate but qua *deuten*, a site often evoked in Fontane's later novels as well.[33] Marie's magical, "other" background is signaled by her childhood dress decorated with little stars; the movement from the "humanly" intended joining of Lewin and Kathinka to the fated one of Lewin and Marie is marked by inserted descriptions of the appearance of actual stars, whether noticed by the characters or not; and so on. It is by reading these juxtaposed, unarticulated connections and resemblances that the novel's reader discovers and learns to anticipate the hidden reality governing the novel, and in such a way as to assent to its necessity and credibility; and that reality, that imagery system, for all its metatextual origin, is presented in the novel as "nature": entering into the novel through such "chance" moments as the game of forfeits that first brings Lewin and Marie together, revealing "the profoundest mysteries of nature" (*die tiefsten Geheimnisse der Natur*), and culminating in the union about which the narrator declares, "What had come to pass was simply that which ought to have come to pass: the demand of nature, that which had been determined from the very beginning" (Denn es war nur gekommen, was kommen sollte; das Natürliche, das von Uranfang an Bestimmte hatte sich vollzogen).[34] As the figure most connected to the natural and the supernatural worlds—and so, too, least restricted to the merely human—Marie is thus also connected to the narrator's metatextual world, most governed or affected by, but also open to, its portentous forces, and for this reason, she is also their best reader. We see this especially when she divines the otherwise unexpected reversals of fortune of Lewin and Tubal at the climax of the novel's action, and does so because "deeply embedded in her nature was a belief in a balance and compensation, the sacred mystery . . . inscribed in her heart"—the sense of a poetic, natural governing order or principle beyond human intention or ordinary knowledge.[35] And it is worth noting how this sense makes Marie not only the best reader of the future in the novel, but arguably also the best appreciator of art—for as we see, these are intimately related.[36]

Marie, then, is the figure most responsible for bridging the gap between the magical, divinatory readings by characters in the text and that by readers of the text; she not only brings the metatextual into the textual but also, in the textual world itself, seems to have access—connections—to the governing principles of the novel itself, and thus, a reliable, even privileged intuition of its future actuality (its real), an intuition shared by the reader. This textual/metatextual connection or exchange is one crucial aspect of the micro-macro relations intrinsic to the reading of Fontane's novelistic world. But there is another that is equally decisive for the intended significance of his text, and grounded in a similar mode of divinatory reading. This is the never articulated but central micro-macro relation between the fate of the individual characters—which is to say, of the Vitzewitz family—and that of the broader historical world or moment in which they find themselves, namely, Prussia in the winter of 1812–13. So, for instance, the reader is required to divine the relation between the breakdown in Lewin and Kathinka's relationship—or more broadly, between the Prussian house and the Polish (foreign) one—and the looming revolt of Prussia against the Napoleonic (foreign) forces. The relation is established by searching out similarities and resemblances even among supposed contrasts— for example, in the common push here toward a Prussian identity detached from foreign alliances, in the one case resisted, in the other pursued—and by reading apparently chance contiguities as in fact meaningful metonymies. To take a particular example from a passage mentioned earlier, the moment of Lewin's catching sight of Kathinka and Bninski dancing at the ball, which he immediately connects with Reale's disparaging stare and Bischofswerder's drooping braids to constitute a "sign," is itself immediately followed by the news "York has capitulated," the opening action in Prussia's break with its foreign allies.[37] The reader extends Lewin's own divinatory practice to link this news in its perceived similarity to the case of Lewin's "capitulation," and in such a way as to constitute it, too, as a sign—not only of the accuracy of Lewin's reading that the break with Kathinka is inevitable (and the reader's extra-literary, retrospective knowledge of the historical outcome provides this insightful force), but also of the possibility that, contrary to Lewin's own present evaluation, the break could prove positive. This is not quite to say that the characters and their relations function as allegories for the political situation, nor that the historical narrative context determines the fate of the characters, although both of these are nebulously true. But it is to say that, very much as with anecdotes for the characters, the reader is asked to look at the microstory and its seeming embodiment of an independent logic and significatory structure and to pose questions as to the integration or connection of its events to the macrocontext—and to seek out the connection not in a causal or verifiable link but rather in one suggested by contiguity and similarity.[38]

Such, then, are some of the key features of the magic reading at stake in Fontane's first novel, his historical novel: and while, as mentioned, some critics ascribe this to a residual romanticism later overcome, it is worth stressing the aspects of these features that seem proper to realism itself, indeed both producing and generated by its realist world. So, for example, one might wish to foreground as particularly realist the undeniable skepticism toward superstitious beliefs that is expressed by so many characters; but this needs to be balanced by the fact (noted at the outset) that such skepticism is almost always part of divinatory practices—and also by the fact (just noted) that such skepticism is not always expressed by the characters who best read the world. Or one might wish to emphasize the characters' magical reading practices as (only) historically appropriate to the novel's admittedly romantic historical moment; or conversely, as a mere cover or proxy language for, actually, a still futural (from the perspective of the story) psychological rendering of experiential insight. Both of course are true, and accord well with a conventional model of realism: but both leave a remainder, an excess that still belongs to the novel. After all, the magic reading practices of the historically romantic characters are reproduced by Fontane's contemporary "realist" readers to generate or uncover its operating system; and the accuracy of characters' reading of portents too often depends on nonpsychological factors such as chance, or impossible-to-realize coincidence with narratorial imagery systems, to be reducible to subjective projections alone.

We need, then, to accept a far more basic and integral relation between divinatory reading practices and realism, a relation evident in and inseparable from both its temporal and its spatial coordinates. In regard to time, the very retrospective dimension of realist narrative sets up another temporal dimension to that of ordinary historical experience, one in which the ending, even if not known, is known to be set: which leads to a pairing of each present or past event with its excess future meaning—a meaning beyond itself, deferred, still at a hidden distance. This meaning, we've seen, is sought in something like anecdotal fashion—utilizing actual anecdotes or converting ordinary objects or events into such independently signifying (but unverifiable) moments, moments that seem to provide a privileged opening to this other temporal dimension that exists and houses this other meaning. And although, strictly speaking, this other dimension and its meaning are not causal, they are still that through which the reader constitutes the sense of consequence and determination in the novel; indeed, contrary to conventional opinion, it is here, as it were, that necessity resides and not in the historical events themselves.[39]

As regards space, or rather our reading experience of the novel's *Umwelt*, the case is similar. We learn to read objects and object-like things (paintings, quotations, stories, etc.) as signs signaling something about the human events, often communicating a prescient, authorial truth (communicated by an otherwise hidden author): we attribute excess meaning and power to things beyond themselves and beyond the intentions of the human characters; indeed, the more embedded in a world unaffected by human intention—the more "natural"—the more privileged the conduit for authorial communication.[40] We learn, like Lewin at the ball, to build metonymical chains linking seemingly unrelated things and words to protagonists' fates, to look for meaning in "signs" of contiguity and resemblance; we learn to see perceived coincidences and correspondences beyond characters' human intentions as special sites for authorial/authoritative significance.[41] We learn that everything communicates; everything connects.

And perhaps of greatest, most lasting significance for Fontane's realism: in coming to occupy a world of signs at once futural and author-itative, the reader learns of the fallibility of signs; their polysemy and ambiguity, their openness to multiple, even contradictory behavior, and often enough, their dependence on the person and occasion of their reading, utterance, or understanding—their contingency. One might even propose that the most characteristic aspect of Fontane's realism is the one most grounded in its conditions of magic, divinatory reading.

Premonitions II

Omens, the world that supports them—the world of the text as well as the text itself—and the divinatory reading practices of both characters and ourselves that engage them all persist through Fontane's fictions written between this first book and *The Stechlin*, his last, with an ever more seamless integration into the fabric of his realist poetics. From the immediately following historical tale of *Grete Minde* (1880) to the historical Berlin novel, *Schach von Wuthenow* (1883), to the great contemporary Berlin novels for which Fontane is chiefly celebrated—*L'Adultera* (1880), *Cécile* (1887), *Delusions, Confusions* (*Irrungen Wirrungen*, 1888), *Effi Briest* (1896), and (contemporary but not Berlin) *Irretrievable* (*Unwiederbringlich*, 1892)—portentous signs or *Zeichen* and their reading, whether accurate or not, remain firmly in place for both characters and readers. And this is true even as the narratives move into clearly more "realist" milieus of the present time and social *Umwelt*.

Some things stay the same, such as the tendency to open stories with premonitory signs, signaling the presence of, and opening access to, the narrative's other temporal dimension and meaning; or the proclivity to bind such signs to the natural world and works of art—as in *Green Henry*, coupling the natural and metatextual—and to bind both to the reading practices of quasi-magical female characters. Perhaps the best example of the first is the ominous opening of *Irretrievable*, with its explicit discussion of premonitions: these are connected both to the natural world, in the form of the female protagonist's anxious attitude toward her new home, a castle literally built on sand, and to a textual world, in the form of her equally anxious reading of an Uhland poem cited by her husband.[42] And perhaps the best example of the second tendency more generally comes in *Cécile*. Here the novel's initial setting in Thale, with its Witches' Dance Floor, Devil's Wall, Horse's Hoofprint, and *Todentrode*, but also its flowers (especially its foxglove), birds, and animals (especially the Newfoundland who attaches himself to Cécile)—all become charged with magical meaning that communicates itself to Cécile via a kind of metonymic contagion, imbuing her with its witching force and presenting itself more or less uniquely to her as a sign system to be read.[43] The engagement of the aesthetic world is made in similar fashion through the animal painter Rosa Hexel, who throughout the stay in Thale seems always nearby, and both parts of whose name have their significance not in relation to Rosa herself but only in relation to Cécile, the witch (*Hexe*) associated with both the flower and the animal world.[44] Moreover, the way that the Witches' Dance Floor becomes contiguously linked to the all but demonic train to Berlin; the way that once Cécile returns to the city, the countryside flora reappear in the gardens among the streets and buildings, and the foxglove in the digitalis that she takes for her ailing heart (more anon); or the way that Rosa Hexel appears here, too—all this illustrates both the persistence of this coupled magical, natural, and aesthetic world and the extension of its realm into the decidedly modern *Umwelt*, whose technological and social forces themselves come to carry a similar attendant charge (of excess, allegorical significance). And of course, we see both these tendencies, and their persistence and extension, in Fontane's best-known works—*Schach von Wuthenow*, *Delusions, Confusions*, and *Effi Briest*—as well.

While much remains in place, some things do develop, contributing to a more integrated realist poetics and to a more pervasively symbolic, even allegorical world—for the realist effect is achieved not by the elimination of its ominous qualities but by their all-permeating dispersal. We see this already in the example from *Cécile* of both Rosa and the natural world as displaced sites for magical presence, linked to the protagonist's fate through the simultaneously realist and (sympathetically) magical qualities of contiguity and metonymy. But the dispersal can be seen more generally with respect to all the features most central to Fontane's poetics: conversation, description, and characterization. With respect to the first, the distinction between ordinary conversational subjects and embedded anecdotes seems to weaken, such that the reader learns to attend to the most banal, seemingly insignificant utterances or accounts for their other, allegorical meaning—for what they suggest, via similitude, for the primary story and its future.[45] With respect to description, here too we have a sense of broadening diffusion: rather than just such specific "signs" as northern lights, reapers in a field, or shining stars (although we have such things as well), we have extended descriptions of landscapes, domestic settings, or city-street scenes represented not (just) for their own sake but for the "other meaning" they metonymically convey about character and plot—something approaching the conditions of *Stimmung* that we explored in *Green Henry*. And as for characterization, there is arguably an increasing tendency to bring the realms of magic experience, ominous appearances, and divinatory readings further into the characters' social sphere, whether in the somewhat insidious form of instrumentalized manipulation as in *L'Adultera* or *Effi Briest*, or in the more common form of a conventionalized, socially conditioned "superstition."[46] And with this comes an expanded emphasis on a decidedly social "something" (*Etwas*) as the source of active, hidden binding forces affecting characters' fates, a role earlier more limited to the binding forces of both nature and metatextual art.[47] This is not, however, to say that these latter forces disappear: they simply become more discreetly present—and often enough, the wrongness of social forces is exposed by their dissonance with still more authoritative natural ones, every bit as much as the wrongness of characters' divinations appears in their contrast with the author's portentous designs.[48]

All this could be illustrated, and qualified, through the analysis of numerous examples drawn from Fontane's many novels, but for the purpose of setting up the discussion of *The Stechlin*, I would like just to concentrate on certain aspects of the last point—the continued, albeit muted presence of the natural nonhuman world in its underwriting of the magical one—and to illustrate these with just two examples. The first comes very near the beginning of *Irretrievable*, and it concerns a conversational exchange about (animal) homeopathy, one of the chief discourses in which the *Naturphilosophie* of the romantics—and by extension, the sympathetically magical world of the early modern—projected itself into the late nineteenth century.[49] We're told:

> The whole story meant nothing more nor less than the final triumph of a new principle and, through the treatment of animals, the success of homeopathy could no longer be held in doubt. Until now, the old-school quacks had never tired of talking about the power of the imagination, what naturally was supposed to mean that the minute particules themselves didn't heal: but thank God, a Schleswig cow was free of imagination, and if she got healthy, then she did so by the remedy and not by faith.

Die ganze Geschichte bedeute nicht mehr und nicht weniger als den endlichen Triumph eines neuen Prinzips, erst von der Viehpraxis her datiere der nicht mehr anzuzweifelnde Sieg der Homöopathie. Bis dahin seien die Quacksalber alten Stils nicht müde geworden, von der Macht der Einbildung zu sprechen, was natürlich heißen sollte, daß die Streukügelchen nicht als solchen heilten: eine schleswigsche Kuh aber sei, Gott sei Dank, frei von Einbildungen, und wenn sie gesund würde, so würde sie gesund durch das Mittel und nicht durch den Glauben.[50]

The conversation continues, leading up to an anticipated future appearance of the doctor who practices this animal homeopathy—which, however, never happens, and the topic seems unexpectedly dropped. But this is not to say it proves insignificant. Quite the contrary, its apparently unmotivated, singular occurrence marks this matter as an opening in the diegetic fabric, one whose meaning seems to derive from and point to a different realm, and to require a different (nondiegetic) knight's move of interpretation to integrate it into the narrative—to make the connection.

That connection is made by recognizing the metatextual relevance of homeopathy: how it functions as a link or portal connecting the metatextual to the textual, a shared principle joining the operating conditions governing the natural world and Fontane's fiction.[51] Characters argue about whether there is something mysterious, mystic, or wonderful about homeopathy (and that hermeneutic openness is part of both realism and magic), but they all agree to its two underlying principles, each of which has its counterpart in Fontane's realism. The first is that of micro-macro relation: as one character puts it, "It's simply a question of large or small quantities and whether one can do as much with a grain as with half a hundredweight."[52] As we saw in *Before the Storm*, this principle coincides with Fontane's own representational tactics for portraying sociopolitical history through the "particules" of single characters and their small fates—in this case, Schleswig's troubled German/Danish identity via the failed marriage of Christine and Holk—and moreover, those small fates through the often small, even trivial events that trigger them (omitting the "weightier" ones).[53] These relations are neither directly causal nor simply symbolic, but rather operate in the same suggestive, hidden, and ambiguous (dubious but real) space as that described for homeopathy. It is a space that, with respect to homeopathy, the novel explicitly identifies with *Sympathie*, because grounded in homeopathy's second principle, "similia similibus"—the same principle that, we saw, grounds the micro-macro relations of Fontane's poetics, not least in the case of his anecdotes.[54] This principle of like to like, of sympathy and resemblance, transforms one thing into a sign of another, forging a connection of one to another—but always, as Holk says of homeopathy, in ways that keep the interpretation open, even as they necessitate the hermeneutic reading practices of divination to animate and reveal the operant world of binding links.[55] Crucially for us, the novel itself connects both of these principles and their reading effects to those of storytelling in general and anecdotes in particular.[56] But equally significant is that Fontane presents them (and their *Sympathie*) first and foremost as elements of the natural, nonhuman world, keeping the link between the work's metatextual and natural forces, and in both cases to the partial exclusion of its merely human dimension.

Unlike the first, the second passage suggesting the continued presence of a world of natural magic is a far from marginal, incidental one. Indeed, it is one of the best-known moments in *Delusions, Confusions*, and it illustrates how this magic world of sympathetic connections that exists in part apart from the merely human world of the characters nonetheless engages or encompasses them. Lene and Botho have left Berlin and escaped into nature at Hankel's Depot. Once there, in an open meadow, Lene composes a bouquet of flowers, and she and Botho take turns naming them—forget-me-nots, devil's bit, everlastings, and so on—turning each one, via its name, into a sign, an omen for them and their affair, and as is typical of Fontane, it is Lene, the woman in this natural world, who proves the more authoritative, discerning reader.[57] Botho then asks Lene to bind the bouquet with a strand of her hair, and Lene famously hesitates, "Because the saying is, 'hair binds.' And if I bind it round the bouquet, you're bound with it" (Weil das Sprichwort sagt: 'Haar bindet'. Und wenn ich es um den Strauß binde, so bist du mitgebunden). Although Botho would dismiss this as mere superstition, Lene insists, "even if it does seem like superstition," that the claim is still true (*richtig*)—and in the event, as Botho must belatedly acknowledge, it does prove true, the omen or spell to be real. He says, "There certainly are such riddling powers, such sympathies from heaven or hell, and now I'm bound and cannot get loose" (Ja es gibt solche rätselhaften Kräfte, solche Sympathien aus Himmel oder Hölle, und nun bin ich gebunden und kann nicht los).[58] Although these sympathetic and "riddling" forces that attract and bind Lene and Botho are themselves in part socially conditioned and even produced, they also run notably counter to the dominant social order, and remain associated by Fontane with the natural order. Sometimes in his work they prove stronger, such as in *L'Adultera*, where the happy ending to the lovers' affair (their "elective affinity") is described as simply a case where "the law of nature triumphed once again" (Das Naturgesetzliche habe wieder mal gesiegt).[59] But even when, as here, they prove weaker and less binding than the forces of the social "something" that seems to govern Botho and Lene's world and fate, they nonetheless persist, and persist as the standard against which the wrongness or unnaturalness of that social world is gauged. And the more open or bound to that other world's forces a character such as Botho or Lene proves to be—and so too the more disjointed from the merely social world—the more connected to both the narrator's and the reader's sympathies, and precisely because more connected to the novel's governing sense of the real behind its (mere, its social) realism.

The Stechlin: "The Stechlin"

Such are some of the principal ways that the magical world and the divinatory readings it occasions persist in Fontane's texts, even as they transition from the early historical novels with settings in the romantic or early modern period to the mature works set in contemporary, social, and often cosmopolitan contexts; where even as they transition to historical temporalities, social causalities, and an extraliterary, urban, and predominantly human *Umwelt*, all features that distinguish Fontane's poetics from that of the poetic realists and, in the eyes of many, make his works more truly realist—where even then the magical world persists as intrinsic, inseparable, and necessary to his realist art, instilling the sense of a necessity unfolding in time and of the intricate connections between character and world. And so the question we began with remains: how does this magical world and the kind of readings it supports both persist and change as Fontane's realism itself persists and changes in his last, almost postrealist work, *The Stechlin*? That it does persist, and retains its futural force, can be glimpsed in such seemingly minor moments as when Melusine—the work's most magical character and astute interpreter, the one most connected to the elemental natural world and to presentiments (*Ahnungen*) that are "positively prophetic" (*schon geradezu was Prophetisches*)—has an itching in her little finger that foretells a visitor, a premonitory experience later shared by the work's other most connected, grounded, and reliable interpreter, Dubslav.[60] And we see it, too, and more generally, in the residual superstition of other characters, such as Dubslav's son, Woldemar, or Melusine's father, Count Barby.[61] Ferreting out the forces that allow for such experiences, however apparently circumscribed, is part of our task; but so too is describing the conditions that make them seem different—both more fragile, elusive, and pervasive—from those in Fontane's earlier work.

The best place to begin is at the beginning, since, as we said earlier, an opening presentation of ominous signs is symptomatic of Fontane's narratives early and late, an opening "pregnant with the future," establishing a temporal dimension and signifying system supplemental to its sequential, historically embedded world.[62] That proves as true here as it did in *Before the Storm* or *Irretrievable*. As in *Before the Storm*, the novel's setting derives from Fontane's nonfictional *Wanderings*; and as there and in quite a few others, it is initially provincial, in the country, a counterpoint to the Berlin setting to come. The text begins, famously and emphatically, with a description of "the Stechlin," the lake whose ominous and supernatural character provides the background for the entire narrative, instantly binding the natural and the metatextual, the lake and the novel itself, in ways similar to what we saw in Keller and in other, earlier Fontane works.[63] (As one of his artists says elsewhere, "Water is nature, and nature is landscape."[64])

The lake that is presented to us as the framing *Umwelt* and "the Stechlin" is first described as part of a "chain of lakes" (*Seenkette*), and this "chain" provides our first indication of the operant conditions for the lake's portentous quality. The chain image works in two ways. First, and seemingly more minor, we learn that "the Stechlin" refers not just to the lake (and the novel), but to the adjoining wood, the adjoining village, the manor or *Schloß* on its edge, the family in it, its present and perhaps, too, its future inhabitant.[65] Second, and seemingly more major, we learn that the lake itself, the first "Stechlin" in the intradiegetic series, seems to anchor a great chain of interconnected things and events—what Melusine, echoing a phrase from Hermann Lotze's *Mikrokosmos*, will call "the great connectedness of things" (*den großen Zusammenhang der Dinge*)—that undergirds the natural and human world: a chain of "secret relations," of "world relations."[66] We're told:

> When far off in the outside world, perhaps on Iceland or in Java, a rumbling and thundering begins, or when the ash-rain of the Hawaiian volcanoes is driven far out over the southern seas . . . then it starts heaving *here*, too, and a waterspout erupts and then sinks down again into the deep.

> Wenn es weit draußen in der Welt, sei's auf Island, sei's auf Java, zu rollen und grollen beginnt oder gar der Aschenregen der hawaiischen Vulkane bis weit auf die Südsee hinausgetrieben wird . . . dann regt sich's auch *hier*, und ein Wasserstrahl springt auf und sinkt wieder in die Tiefe.[67]

Through the lake, the novel's narrow, microcosmic setting is joined with the great, macrocosmic world to form a communicative network, binding every (great) there with this (small) here, by means of signs produced via contact and similitude. Although first presented as a purely natural system—and in this, clearly analogous to that of sympathetic homeopathy (more anon)—this network will in the course of the novel be extended, via further analogies and similarities, to encompass such social eruptions as revolution and such modern communicative technologies as the telegraph and telephone, linking together the (timeless) natural and (present-day) human worlds in one great binding signifying chain.[68] But even more crucially for us, this natural, signifying *Umwelt* is also extended right at the outset into the frankly fantastic and supernatural. We're told, "But when something truly big happens . . . then instead of the waterspout a red rooster rises up and crows loudly across the land." And with that we have our first truly magical opening in the fabric of the novel—and our first omen as well.

Two aspects of this ominous lake and the world that supports it need to be emphasized right at the outset. First, for all the suggestion of a world connected by hidden, subterranean sympathetic relations, the lake also clearly evokes a principle of antipathy as part of that world, and not only in its contrasting pairs of the great and small, the there and here. As many critics have noted, it joins the "still" and the earthshaking, the ever-abiding and abruptly changing, the humanly political and elementally natural, and the natural, political, and everyday (all signs of the real) with the frankly fantastic and symbolic or allegorical, forging chains of interconnecting similitudes *and* differences absorbed into and ramifying out of the one "Stechlin."[69] This inclusion of a principle of contrast or opposition is, of course, quite like the inclusion of antipathy among the forces sustaining the sympathetic cosmos in both the classical and early modern periods, and perhaps, too, like that of allopathy alongside homeopathy in Fontane's natural-medical symbology.[70] It is something we saw already, albeit in more modest proportions, in our reading of *Stimmung* in *Green Henry*, and that we see elsewhere in Fontane as well, not least as part of the polysemy that allows for competing, open interpretations of his ominous world. Here, however, the principle of antipathy so prominently featured in the lake's opening description seems exceptionally (and formally) foregrounded, and thus to feature as well its always latent double nature: as a force that is at once part of the world of sympathy and capable of tearing it apart (echoing the world-shattering violence of its earthquakes and volcanoes).[71]

Second, a changed, even collapsed temporal dimension seems to accompany the spatial expansion embodied by the lake, which has important consequences for its futural force. While connected to Java, Iceland, Hawaii, and Spain, the waterspout or crowing rooster does not seem to appear before or after the distant event, but simultaneously with it. While this rather neatly corresponds with the principle of *actio in distans* underlying the sympathetic cosmos of both ancient divination and nineteenth-century *Stimmung* (the note struck here resonating there), and equally with the near simultaneity attached to the novel's most modern technological communication systems that deliver their signs-for-reading all but instantaneously, regardless of the great distances covered—it still suggests that in one crucial sense the temporal futural dimension to the omen that is embedded in the natural *Umwelt* has changed, almost disappeared. That is, the eruptive sign of the lake does not in itself seem to point to any future: it is an omen only insofar as it might happen again (although in this its sign functions very much like what we saw at work in anecdotes).[72]

Such, then, is the portentous opening. The surprise, however, is that this initial emphasis on a world of intimate and far-ranging connections that appears to forbode a violent event on the order of an earthquake or volcano—an event, moreover, of world historical importance—turns out to be in such open tension with the novel that follows, in ways that seriously challenge both its traditional realist and divinatory structures. It proves to be a novel in which almost nothing is especially connected to anything, at least not in any conventionally motivated way, and in which nothing "eventful" happens at all, not even locally (or microcosmically).[73] In particular, there is no real plot to be developed, no sense of action or character development, let alone conflict or violence, that might forge links in a chain that leads to something significant. And after its opening paragraphs, it proves a novel of rather restricted description as well—including of the natural world.[74]

The absence of a plot is perhaps the most significant challenge to both the traditional realist and divinatory dimensions of the novel—unusual for Fontane, who usually had quite engaging plots, among the most memorable of German nineteenth-century novels.[75] Fontane himself emphasized the absence of consequent action in this particular work; critics like to quote his description of *The Stechlin* as a five-hundred-page text in which two young people get married and an old man dies—otherwise, little to nothing

"happens."[76] And while a few events do generate some anticipatory, futural force—the question of whether the younger and rather
staid Stechlin, Woldemar, will get married, and if so to whom, the
unruly Melusine or her younger, rather reserved sister, Armgard
(it's Armgard); whether the elder Stechlin, Dubslav, will win the
election he halfheartedly stands for (he doesn't); and most important for us, whether the crowing rooster will make an appearance
(it doesn't)—none deeply energizes the novel, generates or resolves
personal or political conflicts, or provides a story line or trajectory
that binds together its various threads. This eliminates one of the
major props of traditional realism, one of its major mechanisms
for generating significance and binding together its world, what
Walter Benjamin calls its "meaning of life" (*Sinn des Lebens*): the
temporal structure that turns sequence into consequence, that creates beginnings, middles, and ends, and so imposes its teleological
logic on the narrative design and its significatory system, in ways
supposed to reflect the realist faith in historical successivity and
directionality.[77]

At the same time that it thus compromises or refigures the novel's realist basis, so too its magical divinatory one, which in its
own right requires the futural dimension of a plot, in fact in ways
we've seen that underwrite the essential compatibility of realism
and divinatory reading—where every realistically motivated event
can thus also have its magical dimension. For whether we stress
that omens, too, have a teleological temporal direction that moves
from sign to fulfillment (or miss), with a middle ground, too, of
suspenseful alternative outcomes, or conversely, that omens, like
anecdotes, open up a portal, a gap in the teleological fabric of the
grand historical récit, allowing another temporal dimension outside of ordinary experience to enter into the narrative world in its
mere successivity—either way, both the omens and their reading
would seem to require a sequentially unfolding plot every bit as
much as traditional realist narrative.

While this development, this absence of a future, as it were,
seems in keeping with the changed temporal status of the waterspout omen opening the novel, it also seems in tension with the fact
that no other novel of Fontane proves so insistently preoccupied

with the question of reading the future. But then, the disappearance of traditional narrative teleology and the lack of faith in the future as knowable and determinative that this brings with it can make the question of the future all the more pressing, even if its reading becomes all the more difficult or even, in the absence of any concept of the future, impossible. In any case, this is a circumstance we will have to explore.

Besides the near absence of plot, there are also notable (even if more minor) dimunitions in the roles played by character psychology, description, and even conversation in the novel, all mainstays of realist narrative and all with various implications for divinatory reading. Character psychology is of course central to much of realism, and not just in the *Bildungsroman* tradition; in fact, the representation of a protagonist's psychic conflicts arguably comes more and more to replace the representation of external, action-based conflict.[78] And as we've seen, this subjective focus also typically grounds many realist divinatory readings, in the form of either psychological projections or their situational, subject-centered interpretations. Fontane, however, despite his status as a realist, his increasing independence from "action," and even his deserved reputation for creating memorable characters (Melusine and Dubslav among them) and character-centered narratives, does not really emphasize psychology, at least not in a traditional way, and this is all the more the case in *The Stechlin*. Even in earlier works he rarely invests characters with interior lives, and what psychology and psychic conflicts they do have are more the consequences of internalized, often self-contradictory social norms than of the intervention of "other" dark forces, following "other" principles.[79] But in *The Stechlin* even these conflicts, these glimpsed interiorizations, are more or less absent; with the exception of a very few retrospective moments on the part of Dubslav (to be discussed below), there are almost no interior lives at stake in the novel at all and hardly even any single protagonist-focused representations.[80] Indeed, as twice asserted in the text itself, characterization almost comes to border on caricature in this novel.[81] And the result is a flattening of not only a traditional realist dimension, but also of a magical one: there are also few omens that appear to individual characters that correlate with that individual's interior state. However, as in the case of the near absence of plot, this is not to say that the magical dimension disappears; just to prepare for its being refigured without futurity or subjectivity.

The dimunition in the role of description and conversation is a bit harder to formulate and perhaps more questionable an assertion, not least because, from another perspective, both gain in importance. But descriptions of personal appearances or the *Umwelt* for its own sake seem notably pared down, again diminishing a realist effect, and instead become more restrictedly focused on key instances of landscape—though even here the description can be emphatically abbreviated, such as that of the view caught by the characters from atop Dubslav's lookout tower (*Aussichtsturm*).[82] And conversation, in which all of Fontane's novels are so rich, and in some ways none more so than this one—conversation is almost never of a kind that addresses significant topics in the extraliterary world or even in the novel, and certainly not in any connected, continuous, logical, or particularly conflictual way; and along with the lack of conversations that are consequential in themselves (i.e., bearers of narrative significance), there seems also to be a severely restricted number of conversations that the "knight's move" of interpretation opens up to a different, foreboding reading.[83] Rather, the novel is almost completely taken up with conversations of the order of what Kierkegaard calls chatter, *Geschwätz*, and what the work itself calls *Plauderei*, small talk—not striving for, even resisting, both sustained, explicit logical connection and weighty (real, true) significance, and avoiding too the kind of personal relation that often yields the nonintended chance significance with futural force.[84]

And yet it is precisely here, in a realm of small talk—a realm without event or action, without conflict or obvious connections, without deep psychological investment or rich subjective coloration, and without governed, significant direction forward, all obstacles for the readers of traditional realism—that the novel commits to recreating not only its realist world but also that more magical world that supports divination. That is to say—and it is almost obligatory to say—that the novel's great theme and organizing

principle of interconnection that is adumbrated in and interconnected with the opening representation of "the Stechlin," is to be
language itself: conversation or *Gespräch*, but also, more broadly,
language or *Sprache*—as, of course, we saw that "the Stechlin"
was in the first place a word, and a word producing connections
even before it becomes the connecting lake.

The theme is presented in a twofold manner. On the one hand,
Sprache is represented in its most trivial, quotidian, almost oppres-
sively ordinary form, as "small talk," and in this respect continues
to stake its claim to a kind of realism, isolating and accentuating
a feature that had long been part of realism's *Technik*, and in the
case of Fontane a large part. But on the other hand, language—and
language *as* "small talk"—is also engaged in its almost metaphysical form, in a way that deliberately and insistently looks beyond
its ordinary communicative function. And in this respect, in drawing language itself into its represented world, the novel not only
anticipates a more modernist orientation, but also, we'll see, engages anew some of the most important operant conditions for
magic reading and experience we know from the early modern
and romantic periods.[85] That is, language is approached as the
medium or, better, the "life-form" (*Lebensform*) that envelops or
encompasses the world of man and man's relation to the world, in
ways that insist on the near inseparability of language and world,
or rather on language as inseparably in and of the world; as the
"life-form" producing within itself and on its own terms attractive
forces and conflicts, similarities and differences, sympathies and
antipathies.[86] In this way, it takes up and refigures many of the
traditional elements of realist narrative, but as we'll see, it does so
in a realm almost beyond—if still dependent on—semiotic content
or even explicit representation.[87]

In considering, then, how the novel refigures its world so as at
once and inseparably to support both its realist and its supplemental second-order magical dimensions, I would like in the following
more intense engagement with Fontane's text to concentrate on
three primary and somewhat overlapping areas. First is the role
of language in the narrative world in general and how it is experienced and thematized by the characters themselves, much as how
we considered how signs were experienced by the characters in

Before the Storm. Second is its role in shaping the realm of human interaction, and especially social interaction through seemingly casual conversation (*Plauderei*). And last is its role in shaping or producing that realm seemingly beyond language, and especially the connections between the human and the nonhuman natural world that, we've seen, are so crucial to the workings of both ancient magic and modern *Stimmung*—and to the premonitory dimension of Fontane's own earlier works.

But before proceeding to these particulars, I'd like to raise two more general points. First, I want to note how the focus on conversation entails a different relation between language and mimesis from that more broadly associated with realism, and an apparently less problematic one. When addressing the description of a nonlingual, objective external world such as we had in the pictorial representation of landscape in Keller's *Green Henry*, the inevitable conventionality of painting's mimetic sign system causes, we saw, an unavoidable distance or mediation between the physical reality and the aesthetic copy; and this mediating gap would seem all the greater if, instead of the "natural" signs of painting, we focused on the arbitrary ones of language.[88] When considering the depiction of conversation, however—or more broadly, reported speech or writing—the plausibility of verisimilar representation in language becomes much less dubious an enterprise.[89] With regard to both subject matter and, equally important for us, its temporal unfolding, the veracity of the imitation—the presence of the model in the representation—would seem secure, and this would hold regardless of any extraliterary referential basis the conversation might be imagined to have.[90] In this respect at least, the conversations in Fontane's novel would seem almost by default to have as secure a claim to realism as the most accomplished paintings or descriptions in Keller's. But just as Keller was concerned with paintings not only of the world but in the world, and so too not only with their realist but also with their magical properties, and not least through emphasizing their metonymic powers over their mimetic ones, so, we'll see, is Fontane in regard to conversation: drawing language into the world, and depicting a world consisting largely of language, are as much a matter of exceeding a representational realm as achieving it, and not least by (again) stressing language's metonymic properties over its mimetic ones—or, in the terms to be deployed below, by stressing its connotative over its denotative powers.[91]

Second, although in some ways the focus on language is thus very much in keeping with a realist poetics, in others, as mentioned, it seems also to adumbrate key aspects of modernism—and this impacts its magical properties as well. Certainly, and as Fontane critics have often noted, there is an incredible faith in language here as in all of Fontane's earlier works: *Sprache* seems at once personally adequate to Fontane's characters, fully capable of communicating meaning between them—in keeping with which, all seem to speak or share in the same Fontanesque language and eloquence—and completely capable of representing the external world.[92] In all this, language seems securely realist.[93] On the other hand, the very self-conscious attention to their language shared by the novel's characters occasions a kind of thickening, a loss of transparency to its representational medium that poses a challenge to any simple realism and approaches instead the modernist foregrounding of the representing medium itself—but in ways that also, curiously and yet characteristically, seem to undercut the very prominence they impose. That is, anticipating the "language crisis" (*Sprachkrise*) that becomes full-blown by the end of the decade, language in the novel is also shown to be breaking down, no longer capable on its own—without the concerted effort of its speakers—of holding together either the human social world or, for that matter, the human and natural worlds.[94] In this, the novel becomes almost post-realist and modernist, but at least one aspect of its response to this tattered, dissolving fabric of language also looks to the point where modernism itself becomes, as it were, pre-realist: where the weakening of the conventional understanding of language leads to an interest in its nonhuman, natural ground—and in this, to a far more basic "magical" ground as well.[95]

"Everything Is a Sign" (Nomen et Omen)

I'd like to begin my discussion of the novel proper, or rather, of the role of language in the novel proper, by first considering a few items that do not appear to be language, but rather, decisively, things. So, for example, in the more extended opening description of the Stechlin manor, there are two such things: "as the only ornament, a large, shiny glass sphere" in the courtyard and the somewhat sickly aloe plant nearby.[96] The reflecting glass ball is placed prominently in the middle of the setting; is later connected to the nearby glass factory that produced it; finds its counterpart in the garden of Dubslav's older (and narrower) sister, Adelheid, albeit without the underlying, self-reflecting foil; is briefly looked into as if a mirror (*Spiegelbild*) by Woldemar's two traveling companions, Czako and Rex; and is casually mentioned by some other marginal characters as well (e.g., "Oh, when I see these glass-spheres").[97] The aloe, though sickly, is nonetheless Dubslav's "favorite . . . and that came about because . . . a foreign seed" found its way into the aloe's pot and now blooms entwined with it, easily and often mistaken for the aloe itself.[98] In the case of neither the glass ball nor the aloe plant does the novel go beyond these concrete descriptions. Even so, just in what it does describe, it awakens an impulse to transform these things into symbols or, better, allegories: to imbue them with a supplemental significance beyond themselves, and one intimately connected with, or at least intimating via connection, the novel's already suggested "world of relations." The glass ball's locally produced globe that nonetheless reflects the greater world around it, inviting too self-reflection; the aloe's contrasting blend of the near and far, the native and exotic, the dying and the unexpectedly (or deceptively) thriving: without ever exceeding their simple realist dimension, and equally important, without ever being assigned a specific meaning, both come to assume an allegorical dimension as well, via the connections they suggest with the world of connections they inhabit. And what is true of these two things at the outset proves true of just about every thing in the novel. As Dubslav declares near the end, "Everything is a sign" (Ein Zeichen ist alles): the characters themselves inhabit a world in which every thing is, or can be, a sign of something else, something beyond itself; a world in which the world of things has become a world of language, a charged site for divinatory reading.[99]

Although in the case of the world-reflecting globe and the near-and-far entwined aloe the novel declines to assign a singular significance, this kind of discretion is rarely exercised by the characters in the novel in their relation to its things. Almost any thing in the novel can incite in them an allegorical reading, and although certain characters prove particularly adept at this metamorphosis of their immediate, ordinary world into a charmed (and charming) speaking one—Dubslav, Czako, and Melusine chief among them—the impulse is more or less universal. So Czako, upon perusing his and Rex's guest room in the Stechlin manor, immediately reads such incidentals as a Meissner figurine and Bible as having personal significance for each of them, respectively (prepared by an unspecified "prescient ability" [*Ahnungsvermögen*]), and says of the bed, "I'll bet this little thing of a sofa has a story to tell."[100] When shown the schoolmaster Krippenstapel's beehives, he just as quickly coaxes them into an allegory of human government; when eating chicken wings at Adelheid's cloister, he immediately transforms a comparison of them with the breasts of thrush enjoyed the day before at her brother's place into one of the otherworldly (*Jenseitiges*) and this-worldly (*Diesseitiges*).[101] Similarly, Dubslav cannot stand the flowers on the table because of what they signify to him about social standing; he chooses his drink—*Goldwasser* as opposed to *Lacrimae Christi*—based not on its taste but on its symbology; and judges bottles for their political significance, as "signs of our time" (*Zeichen unserer Zeit*).[102] And Melusine, to give just one example, cannot try on hats with her sister Armgard without taking into consideration how the "language" of the hats' flowers must determine their selection.[103]

While these three might be the main instigators, such "readers" of the everyday world are endemic to the novel. Some of the signs so read have futural force, as when Adelheid reads the red stockings of the child Agnes as a portent of a coming socialist revolution, or when the Barbys' coachman, Mr. Robinson, reads the paintings on a teapot as signs of Woldemar's looming choice between Melusine and Armgard; and to these signs we might add two central items of the Stechlin manor, the rococo clock on the landing of the central staircase, "with a Chronos (*Zeitgeist*) on top, bearing a scythe," and the museum of weathervanes Dubslav collects (also called weathercocks [*Wetterhahnen*], evoking the lake's portent)—neither one explicitly "read," and so like the globe and aloe, but both still harboring a distinctive, directive temporality as part of their quality as signs.[104] But much like the lake itself, and unlike most such signs in earlier Fontane texts, the vast majority of these *Zeichen* seemingly lack futural force. On the other hand, while both Czako and Dubslav have a distinct tendency to turn "things" into allegories or signs of the political, a tendency shared enough by other characters that the weight of its signed world might seem political—and certainly if it is to be taken as a "political" novel, this is primarily based on how people read its signs, or rather, its things—it would still be mistaken for ourselves to read the significance of its sign world merely in political or even social terms.[105] Far more important, I believe, is for us to focus on the more general procedure: the tendency to transform or metamorphose the thing world into language based on principles of sympathy and similarity, of asssociations with the human and what lies close to hand; where the thing world is assumed to bespeak the human world, and to enter into the human world in the form of language, of text; where the thing world is there *to be read*, at and for the moment, but, also more simply, there to be drawn into and joined with language. And in this respect, as the main instigators of these transformations, it is worth noting that, rather than being linked with the political, Czako is linked with poetry (*Dichtung*), Dubslav with both sympathy and metamorphosis, and Melusine, as with so many of Fontane's other gifted female readers of the world as sign, with something elemental—at once natural and (almost) supernatural, and certainly, as her name implies, magical.

The same impulse toward allegorical reading that drives characters' relations toward the things in their world also drives the narrator's descriptions of the object world per se—although as in the case of the glass globe, the sick-but-blooming aloe, the clock, or the weathervanes, these tend not to be explicitly read by him, or, put differently, tend only to be offered as signs for the reader. As mentioned, such descriptions seem comparatively rare in the novel, but all the more significant for that, and not least for the combined effect of implicit allegory and omitted commentary (which is to say, silence) they entail, an effect perhaps most evident in nature descriptions. So, for example, the description of the "so-called" but decidedly prosaic Poet's Walk (*Poetensteig*) that leads to the "viewing tower, cobbled together out of all kinds of beams" (aus allerlei Gebälk zusammengezimmerte Aussichtsturm), whose color-tinted windows Dubslav has had removed and through which one now contemplates the lake and wood; or that of stuffy Adelheid's salon with its low ceilings, oversized old-fashioned furniture—"nothing not inherited," with chairs no longer trustworthily functional—and birdcage in the window, all of which clash and refuse to harmonize with the room's few more modern things; or even better, the description of the cloister's courtyard, dominated by a "high-rising, mighty gabled wall" that seems at every moment ready to collapse and bury everything beneath it, but is nevertheless topped by nesting storks, "whose keen predictive sense (*Vorgefühl*) always knew if something is going to hold or fall" (and here one juxtaposes Woldemar, who is among those viewing this and on a visit to [not] discuss his marriage plans with the aunt so devoted to upholding the house of Stechlin).[106] Like the sunset vistas so favored by the aging Count Barby, all of these descriptions—and perhaps especially when they touch upon the natural world—seem charged with a gently insistent allegorical force, but one that does not necessarily rise to the level of language, or rather, requires no other language than that of things themselves to function as *Zeichen*. This is, as it were, the property of realist objects that we saw achieved late in *Green Henry*; it is also the counterpart to the novel's characters' urge to transform every thing into allegory, or into language—the counterpart in both its sameness and its difference. (We'll have to return to the difference this difference makes: i.e., the significance conveyed through the muteness of the world beyond the novel's communicative language, already implicit in the opening description of the lake in all its stillness.)

Something quite similar to what happens to things in the novel happens to names as well: they too get taken up into the novel's language or *Sprache* and then transformed into signs for the characters—much as in the primary case of "Stechlin," they even start as words before transforming into characters (characters who are then in turn transformed by them).[107] Names, or rather proper names, hold a special place in the novel, as indeed they do in language in general.[108] Although Fontane's near contemporary, J. S. Mill, proposed that "a proper name is a word that answers the purpose of showing what thing it is that we are talking about, but not telling us anything about it," this is far from the case in this work, which seems rather to draw on the more ancient understanding that "the personal name itself constitutes an omen, an oracle of identity . . . an attempt to control or predict through predication the future life of a child"—and Hans Blumenberg is certainly right to emphasize "name-magic" as one of the most significant "ominous" themes of *The Stechlin*, in keeping with Fontane's signature phrase, "nomen et omen"—although again, it must be said, with a greatly diminished futural force to such omens.[109] But far from the primarily denotative function described by Mill—a referential one much like that often ascribed to realism in general—names here seem instead to have overwhelmingly *connotative* force, to be grounded in the associations, relations, and connections they evoke, in what Gottlob Frege calls the sense or *Sinn* that characters, both those bearing the name and all others, need orient themselves to.[110] And the characters do so explicitly, out loud, as it were: names are repeatedly taken up as the subject of interpretive readings, are—very much like things—transformed into language and then explored for what the novel calls "contiguous" meanings (*Nebenbedeutungen*): for the connotations and associations, similarities and sympathies, and paradoxes and antipathies that invisibly surround them and give them life.[111] Indeed, we can even formulate this as a more general truth about the novel: even as, expanding on the insight of Roman Jakobson, we identified metonymy, not mimesis, as the realist principle behind Keller's *Green Henry*, so, expanding on a claim by Roland Barthes, can we designate connotation, not denotation, as the principle at stake in *The Stechlin*.[112] And quite simply, connotation requires divination: reading what is communicated by what is not there in what is.

Sometimes names seem precisely, "naturally," to represent their person or thing, as in the case of one Baron von der Nonne, "whom nature seemed to have formed while taking particular attention to his name."[113] At other times, they seem to stand in open conflict with their signified objects, such as in the case of "the green glass hut" (*die grüne Glashütte*), whose fairy-tale-like (*märchenhaft*) connotations are the opposite of the completely quotidian reality—and this would be evidence of the world and language beginning to fall apart, dissolving the connection on which both realism and magic depend in an inchoate *Sprachkrise*.[114] And in still other instances, names are of the kind Blumenberg shrewdly describes as the most important, namely, "names heavy with meaning, but from which one can hardly make out *what* they mean," a state provocatively suspended between the two others. Such is the case of Krippenstapel ("named Krippenstapel, which all by itself already will say something") or even, as Blumenberg notes, of Armgard, where "even impoverished meaning is meaningful" (sogar *Bedeutungsarmut bedeutsam* [ist]).[115] In such cases, the "name-magic" is particularly "ominous," because while it invites reading of its significatory, shaping force, it also presents its ultimate indecipherability, its place beyond ordinary language or semiosis—and at the same time retains the possibility, as in the case of anecdotes, that there is nothing, or no necessity, there at all. (Which is to say, there is more at stake in "Armgard" than Blumenberg's pun on *Armut*.[116])

But perhaps even more important than these instances are those cases where characters live in conscious relation to the connotations of their names, in both their sympathetic and antipathetic implications, producing the bonds of attraction and repulsion that give their names peculiar significatory energy and force, with all the openness and undecidability of a compressed anecdote.[117] This is comically—and one-sidedly—the case with the composer Niels Wrschowitz, whose antipathy toward the connotations of his first name, and its contradictions with his last, drives him to great lengths to disavow it, and with it, with all sympathies with the Scandinavian world per se.[118] It is similarly, though less one-sidedly, comical in the case of both Dubslav and Czako, who, too, are in conscious and continued relation to the undesirable, but also unavoidable, associations of their names.[119] But it is most fully and complexly the case with Melusine, whose name carries the most, and the most magical, connotations. Woldemar says, "Anyone named Melusine should know what names mean" (Wer Melusine heißt, sollte wissen, was Namen bedeuten), and Armgard adds, "Oh, you never think of anything but fairy tales and, because your name is Melusine, you think you have something like an obligation to do so": she must actively engage, in her self-understanding, with the contingent meanings (*Nebenbedeutungen*) of her name as a determinate sign of magical character or identity.[120] And even as in *Before the Storm* the potential absence of a supernatural world itself created a spectral space in the novel, so here the sense of secret connections to the natural world implicit in the name Melusine, even if "factually" absent, is reproduced in Melusine's concerned connections to her name. And beyond even this, the magical connotations of her name are inextricably bound up with connections to the natural world, and these connections are themselves bound up with water, all of which connects her, and her name, with the ruling imagery system of the novel, grounded in the ominous, supernatural lake: at least for the reader, the connotative connections of her name connect her with the whole world of connection, and with the very principle of connotation itself.[121]

It is not just things and names that are being treated as signs in this way: even the most everyday words are continuously being singled out, held up, and "read" for what they might mean as signs quite apart from the specific context within which they occur, and so, too, transformed into allegories of "another" significance beyond their immediate one. Characters incessantly talk about their talk, or rather, they incessantly read their talk for the other meaning hidden, and revealed, in ordinary language itself.[122] The examples are almost too numerous to warrant selected examples, but word choice is constantly being parsed for what it connotes about class ("enter into matrimony" [*vermählen*] vs. "get married" [*sich verheiraten*]), generation ("novel" [*Roman*] vs. "tearjerker" [*Schmöker*], "timely" [*zeitgemäß*] vs. "opportune" [*opportun*]), profession, region, or the personal associations (*Vorstellungen*) one can or cannot link to it. As these examples attest, the associations themselves can suggest a breakdown of shared associations, a sense of division within or dissolution of the common fabric of language: but even then, the disassociations are eliciting associations, connections, and extended commentary from the characters.[123] Over and over again, fine-tuned attention is paid to the connotative as opposed to the denotative dimension of words—which is to say that words are read both as apart from the manifest order or associations in which they present themselves and, instead, as very much part of another, hidden order of associations; as both independent and enmeshed—again, like omens and anecdotes.

With this downplay of denotation, and so too "content," comes, as it were, a downplay of the language world of the text as, strictly speaking, mimetic or referential. Rather, with the focus on connotation comes a figuration of the world in more metonymical, relational terms, terms dependent on a different kind of likeness, that of relation itself—a transformation, I'd suggest, of the classical notion of a sympathetically linked cosmos into the abstract and ordinary of language itself: of world *logos* into lingual *logos*, material *Umwelt* into symbolic *Umwelt*. Characters are keenly focused on divining the *Verbindungen*, the *Beziehungen*, the connections and relations that a word (every word) sympathetically evokes—including the sympathies and antipathies that can inhabit a single word and grant it its polysemous character, such as when Melusine declares, "*Nice* is not a nice word," or Adelheid, "There is always a difference between *reckonings* and *reckonings*," or Wrschowitz insists that *Dame* and *Madame* are incomparable in meaning.[124] Even as "things" assure that the characters inhabit a world readily transformed into allegory by entering into language, and even as names assure that characters inhabit a world of omens in which they themselves are transformed into and bound by language, so the foregrounded associative character of speech itself assures that the world those things and names and characters inhabit is itself of the same order and nature as that which has long supported such allegories and omens and connections (even in its dissolution): the supernumerary, supplemental world of "magical" correspondences that accompanies and interpenetrates the "realist" world of mere reference, content, and ordinary meaning.

There is a related, albeit different thematization of language in the novel, one that is also part of the same reimagining of the traditional magical world of sympathetic relations in more abstract and everyday lingual terms. This is the aforementioned thematization of language as *Gespräch, Plauderei, Klatsch, Causerie*— as casual conversation, small talk, chatter: which is to say, the transformation of both language and *sympatheia*, and language as *sympatheia*, into a form or medium of social interaction and connection.[125] We see this from the beginning to (almost) the end: in the dinner party at the Stechlin manor early on; the tea party at Adelheid's cloister; the gatherings at the Barbys and the outing to the Egg Cottage; the after-party to Dubslav's failed run for political office and that to Woldemar and Armgard's wedding, and so on (and on). Such a foregrounding of the conversational mode is a hallmark of Fontane's novels, but it functions rather differently here, due in large part to its subsumption to the overriding concern with the topic of "the great connectedness of things"—that is, with the theme of connection itself, in both its constitution and its threatened demise.[126]

Sympatheia as Sociability (Simmel)

This shift in the realm of connectedness not only into language but also into the social relations experienced behind and through language is decisive for the form that the magical, sympathetic world assumes in the novel, and so too in Fontane's late realism. It is a form of connectedness that was brilliantly theorized under the name of sociability or *Geselligkeit* by Fontane's younger contemporary, the sociologist Georg Simmel, himself a pivotal figure in the move toward modernism.[127] Other critics, most notably Willi Goetschel, have recognized some of the affinities of Simmel's analysis to Fontane's novel, although none with an eye toward the magical and sympathetic dimensions at stake for both writers.[128] For this reason, I'd like to consider in some detail Simmel's account of "sociability," to contemplate how it maps onto our concern with

the magic dimension of Fontane's novel, and especially in its relation to language.[129] We will then need also to explore how the
novel challenges, inflects, or exceeds Simmel's model, and how that
impacts the role of the sympathetic relations at play in the work.

Simmel bases his account of sociability on two guiding principles. First, that society, or *Gesellschaft*, is to be defined as an active,
reciprocal relationality, whose significance lies in its formation of
a unity out of its individualized (but similar-ized) elements. It is an
interaction or *Wechselwirkung* of certain forces of both attraction
and repulsion that draw men into "a being together" (*ein Zusammensein*), a correlation of relations that work reciprocally.[130] It is,
that is, a participant realm without distinct subject/object positions
but instead one of mutually determining, affecting, animating relations. Second, Simmel posits that a distinction can be made between the material forces of sociation or *Vergesellschaftung* and
their immaterial, well-nigh spectral "Form," which transforms the
mere juxtaposition of isolated individuals (*das isolierte Nebenein-
ander der Individuen*) into a (momentary) "unity."[131] That is, it is
a supplemental, attendant, invisible realm in which the real binding power and significance of the unity lie, a binding power and
significance that Simmel designates as sociability or *Geselligkeit*.
Of course, sociability has always been a quality of the sympathetic world model; and in defining its nature in terms of these two
principles—as an attendant immaterial realm and as a reciprocally
unifying relationality of forces—Simmel reproduces in sociability
key terms of classical *sympatheia*.[132] What is new or different is
that here *sympatheia* is, as it were, being defined *only* in terms of
sociability, of a purely human realm, and so is also, though this
goes unsaid, about nonrelation, nonsympathy, nonunity.

In addition to this unspoken removal of connections to a
broader ideal of natural life, there is a second removal, one that
Simmel does speak of, this one based on the distinction between
the material and immaterial forms of those forces on which sociability is based. A *dissociation* occurs in which these forces are
no longer fully connected to what Simmel calls "life," no longer
inseparable from or bound to their material objects and conditions. Instead, they come to interact freely among themselves and

for their own sake: they establish a dynamic of their own apart from or alongside that of their "entanglement" (*Verflechtung*) in material life, becoming "shadow-bodies" (*Schattenkörper*) in a "shadow-realm" (*Schattenreich*).[133] This is the basis on which Simmel draws his analogy between the conditions of sociability and those of art and play. We've seen the intimate connection between the hidden worlds of sympathetic relations and art (qua metatextuality) before.[134] But the addition of play, while in a certain sense nothing new, does seem introduced to underscore the new, more fragile or tenuous condition under which the sympathetic world is functioning—which is to say, to underscore the possibility of detachment or dissociation from the real world, of an unreality distanced from any actuality.[135]

Simmel delineates three modes of relation that may obtain between this abstracted, spectral realm and "life." First, sociabilty can become wholly disconnected from life; even as "art" (*Kunst*) can become "artifice" (*Künstelei*), and "play" (*Spiel*) "playing" (*Spielerei*), so too can sociability become the equivalent of what conversation might often seem to be in Fontane: mere chatter, *Geschwätz*.[136] Second, this abstracted immaterial realm of forces can in turn come to shape the very stuff of life (*Lebensstoff*). Simmel doesn't dwell much on this, but the way this "shadow-realm" can invisibly and forcefully impact and determine material life is of course decisive for an understanding of the sympathetic *Umwelt*—and often enough in Fontane, as "a social something" (*ein Gesellschafts-Etwas*) that seems both to function as such an immaterial binding order and to be strangely alienated from a more expansive, sympathetically conceived nature.

Third and most significant for us, Simmel also insists that for all the autonomy and immateriality ascribed to these spectral forces, they still retain an essential connection or link to their origin in the "realities of life," which keeps them "always still laden with life" and imparts "their depth and power."[137] The dynamic of the one is underwritten by the other: "life" remains a determinate category or force, and it is the shaping and abiding power of life on or beneath the forms of the sociable (and the aesthetic, and the playful), and not the reverse, that proves decisive—or should.

It is this crucially and surprisingly realist—and also magical—connection and claim that lends the realm of sociability what Simmel calls *symbolic* significance, and which he several times mentions as going unrecognized from the perspective of a mere naturalism or rationalism.[138] Rather, the realm of sociability is an inherently symbolic—or, as we've called it, allegorical—realm, and it is this that makes it realist, and keeps both the sociable and the realist intimately connected to the contagious forces of a sympathetically conceived "life." (This might seem to be already hinting at vitalism, a proto-*Lebensphilosophie*, but not quite: life is still exclusively social life for Simmel, a major point of difference from Fontane.)[139]

Simmel further defines sociability as a feeling, an affect, but not a personal one. Rather, he sees it as a shared, connecting, contagious experience, as a mutual or reciprocal determination (*gegenseitiges Sich-Bestimmen*) of attractive forces—which is to say (though he doesn't), sociability is a mode of *Stimmung*, socially rather than psychologically conceived.[140] In fact, Simmel insists that for the affect (or *Stimmung*) of sociability to emerge, the particularities and uniqueness of the individual must be momentarily dissolved or left behind; sociability is a relation or condition in which, for all its sense of heightened engagement, subject identity and autonomy are subsumed into the associate whole. For this to happen, there are two modes of *dis*sociation that, Simmel says, must be enforced, two sets of bounds that need to restrict the realm of interactions. On the one hand, objective, external attributes such as wealth, social position, or erudition must be left out or behind—the very distinctions or realia on which one would imagine a social realism to depend. And on the other hand, so too must subjective, internal attributes such as mood or individual disposition—the very elements or factors on which a psychological realist identity would depend. But sociable man is neither socially real nor psychologically constituted, and "exists nowhere except in sociable relations."[141] This momentary opening in the objective "historical" fabric of life is a feature sociability shares with anecdotes, which not surprisingly play a key role in Simmel's account (more anon); the relinquishing of mere psychological subjectivity is a feature it shares with other manifestations of sympathetic engagement or participation—of the kind of identificatory participation we have designated as key to magical experience, with its characteristic mix of complete self-engagment and negation.[142]

The reason for the required suspension of both the socially, objectively real and the psychologically, subjectively real is equally important for understanding sociability as a variant manifestation of the sympathetic world (and so too of *Stimmung*). Sociability calls for interaction, *Wechselwirkung*, among *Gleichen*, those who are "like" one another; it must constitute a realm of homogeneous similarities and resemblances out of the myriad heterogeneous elements of its material universe.[143] Properly speaking, only what is—or better, can be made—"like" is part of its interactive, relational unity (that contiguity, even contact, is also requisite seems to go without saying: only elements or subjects in immediate contact with one another can participate in sociability). The gift of discovering, constituting, and maintaining that order of similarity—and Simmel stresses that it is never really quite manifest on its own: the world of multiplicity and difference is what is apparent, every bit as much as it was for the Neoplatonists—is one that Simmel calls "tact" (*Takt* or *Taktgefühl*).[144] And tact is a mode of reading: not only in negative terms, in its divining the differences in both oneself and the others that are to be left unnoted, but also in positive ones, in its reading of resemblances, similarities, co-incidences, and impersonal connections. Again, the reciprocality of these similarities and of their reading is significant: while everything depends upon the interpretation of the momentary conjunctures of the social occasion in terms of a similarity to the self, that self is also in some sense moot, and the center and even source of the similarities must lie outside oneself, in the interactive whole. Indeed, an individual's capacity for sociability might be measured by his or her ability to read and so realize this shared realm outside the self; and to bring as wide a field of different elements into active relation as possible and still have the sense of unity or concord prevail.

Simmel singles out three occasions within which sociability is especially likely to manifest itself: social games, coquetry, and conversation or *Gespräch*. The first two are for the most part marginal to our concern with *The Stechlin*.[145] But for both Simmel and us, the single most important location or occasion for sociability is the third, conversation or *Gespräch*. It is the presence of its immaterial "shadow-realm" that distinguishes sociable conversation from mere empty chatter or *Geschwätz*, as which, from a purely naturalist perspective that does not recognize this unspoken dimension, it must appear. The actual matter of the conversation, its semantic content, serves only as the material vessel for the manifestation of this other, symbolic order: the subject matter does not have significance in itself but only derives its true or real meaning "from the fascinating play of relations that [it] create[s] among the participants"—a play or realm or experience of what Simmel also calls binding or *Bindung*.[146] And as he stresses, it is in order that the symbolic significance of this attendant, parasitic, and unspoken play of relationality dominate that the significance of the "matter" of conversation must be, or become, secondary, relatively *insignificant*, even apparently trivial—in a word, small talk (*Plauderei*) as the purest form of language that embodies the connecting forces of sociability and so produces its sympathetic realm.[147]

Simmel specifies two formal elements of conversation that facilitate the play of sociability. Both touch upon issues of temporality in determining how small talk comes to embody this "other" play of forces. First, he notes how the animating flow or movement of the conversation must be maintained without in any way becoming goal-directed or purpose-driven. Rather, its connecting thread must display the qualities of *Zufälligkeit* and *die ganze Austauschbarkeit*, of chance and complete exchangeability.[148] With respect to the former, this means that it needs to remain outside the teleological fabric of sequence as consequence—an attribute of conversation in the ordinary real—and embedded instead in the seemingly aleatory serial logic of chanceful, "happy" correspondences and connections, open to the knight's move of mildly magical connections or associations. With respect to the latter, what Simmel calls "exchangeability," this means that the logic or force (the *logos*) connecting the individual elements of the unfolding series must be both grounded in perceived or discovered resemblances or similarities— in a perceived likeness between them, or even in the language in which they are couched, that allows one to be easily exchanged for or linked to another—and sufficiently part of the common shared context, external to but encompassing each individual participant, that the thread can be taken up, ex-changed, and extended along a relay of participant speakers, exercising alike the knight's move of reading out of each present moment the omen of one's own similar, upcoming addition, spreading contagiously outward and onward at once.

It is this latter point that Simmel especially foregrounds when he defines sociable conversation as the purest and most sublimated form of "a relation that wants to be nothing but relation" (*einer Relation, die sozusagen nichts als Relation sein will*)—perhaps the clearest expression of how sociability is indeed a modern variant or relation of classical *sympatheia*.[149] And it plays a key role again in the second of the formal elements he discusses, namely, the special place of the anecdote in such conversation—an element we've already had occasion to note as of special significance to the magic reading of Fontane's novels. For Simmel, anecdotes are important first because of their temporal quality: they are short, self-contained, without immediate temporal connection to the present moment, and without needful extension, all of which makes them ideally suited to maintaining the mobile pace of conversation in its nonteleological unfolding. But they are equally important for the kind of extension they do invite. On the one hand, the anecdote is a form in which the context of the individuality of the teller completely disappears, vanishing into "the shared consciousness of the circle," a dissolving of subjectivity (and psychology) through participation we've noted before as characteristic of magical being.[150] But on the other hand, the anecdote is a form, an opening, in which all can participate equally (*gleichmässig*), can read, interpret, or simply receive and make connections to his or her own *Umwelt*, unencumbered by the teller's original context—and so of course not only receive but also supplement or relate with another similar one, so as to continue to forge and relay the contiguous chains founding the realm of similitude on which sociability is based.[151]

Simmel ends his discussion by returning to its original theme, namely, the necessary relation between the realm of sociability and "life," its ties with the reality of life out of which it weaves its own fabric (die Fäden, die sie mit der Lebenswirklichkeit verbinden und aus denen sie ihr . . . Gewebe spinnt).[152] And he adduces several different historical examples to illustrate what happens when this "life-form" of pure connectivity and relationality loses its connection and relation to the sphere of life itself—and so, too, by implication, underscores the importance of preserving this broader, more encompassing mode of relationality at the heart of sociability. As he emphatically phrases it, "All sociabilty is only a *symbol* of life . . . but it is even so a symbol of *life*."[153] The examples he offers for the potential dangers of lost connection are historically remote, the knightly brotherhoods of the German Middle Ages and the courtly society of the French ancien régime. But clearly the aristocracy of his own Prussian present provides the more proximate impetus for his analysis as a whole. It is just this example that Fontane's novel addresses as part of its exploration of the "great connectedness of things" as resituated within language, and especially language as the site for sociability—and to which we now return.

Stimmung (Space)

Like Simmel in his essay, Fontane in *The Stechlin* is engaged with sociability as a modern manifestation of the magical "shadow-realm" of sympathetic relations and with language in the form of conversation as the primary vehicle for its realization. Even as things such as the glass globe, the aloe plant, or the clock dissolve or are taken up into lingual allegories, so does language itself dissolve into symbolical "sociability"; even as names and words in general transform from denotation into connotation, from referential meaning into associational linkages, from identity into similarity, so too do talk and its participants pass over into the unspoken, immaterial realm of connective *Geselligkeit*. And like Simmel, Fontane too—and even more insistently—is concerned with the complex relations that obtain between the realm of sociability and "life," in all its objective material reality; with both the necessary exclusions or dispersions of the latter for the realization of the former, and the desired connections or obtrusions without which "small talk" becomes mere "chatter." Finally, like Simmel, Fontane too is interested in the formal means by which the magic of sociability is achieved and momentarily maintained, particularly in the realm of language.

However, there are two distinct ways in which Fontane's engagement with sociability—and more specifically, with sociability through language—is fundamentally different from Simmel's, and both have consequences for the sympathetic relations (the connectedness of things) at stake in the novel. First, although sociability is undoubtedly at the center of the unifying relationality behind and within conversation in *The Stechlin*, it is not actually a term or vocabulary that Fontane employs to characterize or explore this spectral play of forces. Rather, the governing model for thinking about sociability—and especially in and through language— is one mentioned as only implicit in Simmel, but that we know as central to the magical realm in Keller, namely, *Stimmung*. As we will see, *Stimmung* is a term that occurs almost obsessively in multiple, linked forms throughout the novel, especially in the context of conversation: as *Stimmung, Verstimmung, Mißstimmung, Zustimmung, Übereinstimmung, Bestimmung, Umstimmung*, and even as *Stimme(n)* and *Abstimmung(smaschine)*, as well as in numerous verbal and adjectival variants—all in various ways part of the *Verbindlichkeit*, the sense of ob-ligation, of binding ties, of the novel's social world and its imagery of binding threads (*Fäden*), "tying on" (*anknüpfen*), and so on.[154] As in Keller, *Stimmung* is thus also here hardly restricted to an interiorized subjective realm, but instead (and again) exists in the interaction between the participant subject and the external world, although as in Simmel and in contrast to Keller, the external relational sphere seems itself by and large restricted to the human world (and human language). Nonetheless, in ways not true of Simmel's "sociability," the concept of *Stimmung* as it emerges out of the nineteenth century necessarily brings with it the broad range of connotations we discovered in Keller, including a far more macrocosmic sweep encompassing the natural world or *Umwelt*, a world beyond the merely human and even beyond language itself. As we will see, Fontane draws in these connections as well, linking through the associate word–group of

Stimmung the realm of sociability to his overarching concern for the "great connectedness of things," with significant consequences for the magical, supernatural dimension of the work (suggesting, for instance, why divinatory presentiments [*Ahnungen*] can become, modestly, part of sociability).

The second distinct difference of Fontane's engagement with sociability has to do not with its greater outward extension and *umwelt-lich* vibrancy but rather with its inner retreat and temporal fragility; with the unraveling of the shared language on which sociability depends for its material basis. Simmel's model presumes a stable ground in common language, and we've seen how Fontane's novel shows that ground giving way under the strain of historical time, threatening a loss of sociability (or *Stimmung*). One of the several thrusts to this added factor, in both its solvent and its temporal qualities, is, we'll see, intimately connected with the greater extension inherent in sociability qua *Stimmung*—namely, as the novel progresses and the gaps in language and, concomitantly, in sociability begin to widen, there is an increasing tendency to attempt to (re)constitute connections to a realm beyond both the social order and language, indeed to that realm excluded by the modern restriction of the sympathetic *Umwelt* to these two, to (re)establish relations with the mute world of nature in its most magical, sympathetic form. Whether that attempt succeeds, whether access to the divined alternative world is opened up, whether such a participation, such a fulfillment, is indeed possible—this becomes increasingly integral to the future at stake in the novel.

But before exploring these differences from Simmel and their consequences for the sympathetic order and divined future in Fontane, let us consider where the two overlap, or rather where their differences emerge out of the shared context: in the constitution of sociability or *Stimmung* in and through small talk, and in the depiction of those forces that threaten its *Verbindlichkeit*, its binding sense of ob-ligation. As in Simmel, for the *Stimmung* that is sociability to emerge through such talk, there is a need in the novel for participant individuals to abstract themselves from the concrete realities of their material objective lives in order effectively to be joined and taken up into the conversational thread. This entails tactfully attending to the outer and inner boundaries barring the intrusion of objective, external elements such as social position or political views and of subjective, internal ones such as mood or psychological need. Peter Hasubek offers a perceptive reading of how the small talk between the Countess Melusine and the mayor Kluckhuhn happily unfolds between these bounds, deftly excluding differences in class, education, and their personal stakes in the occasion of their meeting in order to achieve a momentary bond of likeness or *Zu-stimmung* (accord). And there are numerous similar occasions, in some of which the narrator explicitly remarks on a character's efforts not to overstep these lines in order to preserve the *Zustimmung*.[155] These limits define what we might call the spatial extension of the sociable *Umwelt*, an *Umwelt* no longer simply synonymous with the world as a whole, limits that must be maintained for the unified relationality (the *Stimmung*) to hold.

The significance of these bounds is as evident in their breach as in their keeping, and in ways that can both threaten and, more surprisingly, strengthen the woven fabric of ob-ligation or *Verbindlichkeit*. Only occasionally are these breaches of a purely subjective nature. As mentioned, the narrator himself mostly abstains from crossing this inner border and so keeps us and his characters in the more sociable realm: as is said of Dubslav at his funeral, "His life lay open, nothing in it was hidden, for nothing needed to be."[156] And so it is often only the inability or unwillingness of a character such as the pastor Lorenzen or Armgard to enter into the talk that hints at the abiding presence of this purely subjective realm. However, breaks in the outer limits are quite common: perhaps most comically near the beginning, when Rex and Krippenstapel both interject into the conversation embarrassing surpluses of erudition about ecclesiastical architecture, bringing the sociable moment to an abrupt halt, an interruption only smoothed over (and so bounds and bonds restored) by Woldemar's remark "Nothing is harder than to arrive at certainties (*Bestimmungen*) in this area."[157] Equally harmlessly, the businessman Gundermann near the beginning works in an "equivocal" manner to pursue political ends beneath what should be mere polite conversation; far less harmlessly, Princess Ermyntrud inserts her religious interest in

Dubslav's conversion or *Umstimmung* beneath the apparent accord or *Zustimmung* of their talk, and Baruch Hirschfeld his economic interest in Dubslav's finances into their talk—with both leading to discord or *Verstimmung* and a breakdown in social relations.[158] There are also instances where Simmel's outer limits of objective life have become so personalized by characters as almost to become the otherwise absent inner limits: Adelheid with her fiercely imposed restrictions on matters of religion or class, the composer Wrschowitz on all matters related to Scandinavia, or the critic Cujacius on questions of art.

The effect of these transgressions is twofold. On the one hand, and as Simmel predicts, they often lead to a tear in the weave of the sociable, a momentary opening and intrusion of a gaping, almost uncanny silence needing as quickly as possible to be covered up to restore the sense of *Stimmung* on which the characters suddenly almost desperately depend.[159] We see this when Woldemar works to overcome the silence following Krippenstapel's architectural lecture, or when Wrschowitz's political rhetoric at the Barbys' house simply silences the others: "Everything went quiet, so that there was nothing for the Count to do but somewhat belatedly express his halfhearted *Zu-stimmung*."[160] Such opening silences expose the fragility of the unified realm, the anxiously foreboded loss of its communicative connective network. And they invite both characters and readers to divine an even greater looming silence behind the talk, a silence ominous and, in the anxiety it provokes, pregnant with both significance and futurity—indeed its significance in its very omened, apparently fated loss of futurity. (And we note the complexity of levels: if sociability is the unspoken immaterial realm behind the concrete matter of conversation, then this silence is the equally unspoken immaterial realm beyond sociability—a silence seemingly associate with that of the still, supernatural, always ominous lake.)

On the other hand, these moments of transgressive intrusion of the objective, material real into the (merely) sociable *Umwelt* also secure the micro-macro threads and ties to "life" that sociablity requires to sustain its vibrancy and vital force: whether in the form of Gundermann's or Dubslav's introjection of their political proclivities,

Wrschowitz's or Cujacius's of their aesthetics, or Adelheid's or Lorenzen's of their religiosity. Such intrusions not only secure and maintain relations and connections to the (social) world outside of sociability proper. They also occasion the generative friction or conflict that Fontane's novel, in contrast to Simmel's model, suggests as necessary for sociability to self-realize: the antipathetic repulsive forces that are a part of, rather than apart from, the sympathetic attractive forces at work in conversation.[161] In short, such boundary-overstepping moments can both threaten and secure, weaken and strengthen, the sociable order; its connective binding forces operate both from outside and within, extensively and intensively.

In either case, the reason for the observance of these restrictions in the first place is, as in Simmel, to generate a sphere of the similar or *gleich* out of the myriad, actually heterogeneous individual elements of the momentary assemblage.[162] For this to be achieved requires characters with a gift for divining, inventing, and sustaining similarities out of a world in which, materially, they hardly appear. This indeed requires tact: as Hasubek observes of the conversation Melusine manages with Kluckhuhn, it unfolds as if between two speakers of similar value and rank, because of her perceptive glossing over of their differences in social and educational standing; we see the same in the opening dinner party when Woldemar seeks to establish a connection or *Verbindung* between Captain Czako and the forester Katzler, one achieved as a result of the social graces of all concerned.[163] But it also requires more than simple tact: it requires a special kind of imagination and, as part of that, a special kind of reading, and this because, almost exclusively, the "like" must be sought in the language of the small talk itself. For the most part, the differences in subjective sensibility or objective social circumstances are either so great or so unknown among the momentarily contiguous conversants that they must look and attend to the actual words spoken to find a point of contact on which they can latch their similar, related, connected response, a "catchword," as it were, some turn of phrase or image that can be responded and added to in kind and in turn ("catching" like a cold, contagiously). We see this, for example, in the opening dinner party, where Frau Gundermann reads the insignia of the the Alexander Regiment on

Captain Czako's epaulettes and transforms it into a reference to Al-exanderplatz in her native Berlin, which then becomes transformed again, by Dubslav, into a reference to Russia in years past; or how, at the same event, Frau Gundermann's reference to rats in Berlin leads to Czako's reference to the Pied Piper (or rat catcher [*Rat-tenfänger*]) of Hameln and rat terriers as "rat catchers," and then to his underground adventure in Paris with such rat-hunting dogs. Reading out these correspondences, or rather divining in the speech of one's interlocutor the point of contact to which one can connect and out of which one can draw something similar, serially—this is what makes for the magic weave of sociable, catching conversa-tion, for the constitution of a space of similitude that binds.[164] And this proves another reason why so much self-conscious attention is paid to language in the novel and why there is a tendency to transform everything into language, associational, even allegorical language: language is very often the very basis for the likenesses, the similarities, on which sociability depends.

There are clear differences in the novel between the various characters' abilities to produce this realm of likeness, with respect to not only the limits that need to be set in relation to the broader world or *Umwelt*, but also the variety and quality of connective elements that can be encompassed within the conversational sphere itself—and so too the peculiar quality, fullness, and durability of the *Stimmung* at stake. This ability has much in common with what Simmel calls personality and Max Weber all-but-magical charisma: it is perhaps best compared with what Henry James calls the "as-sociational magic" by which a central character can render those around her "portentous," with that character's presence "spread-ing and contagiously acting . . . vibrating in the infected air" and thereby imparting the "tone" to the setting.[165] The primary repre-sentatives of the contrasting extremes of this ability are the Stechlin siblings as seen in their respective hosted meals, but each has, as it were, as-sociates (their "like"): Adelheid in Rex, Wrschowitz, and Cujacius, and Dubslav in Czako, Melusine, and Count Barby. Indeed, in the contrast and affinities between and within these dif-ferent sets of characters, the novel engages a wide range of similar and opposing realms of sociable extension.

Adelheid's sphere is the most restricted and the least magical, the place where sociable binding is the most difficult and the most open to discord or *Verstimmung*.[166] The narrowness of her sphere, which the narrator explicitly describes in both aesthetic and spatial terms ("her profoundly prosaic nature, her Brandenburgian narrowness"), is determined not only by the many matters that need to be excluded, but also by the need for the entire assembly of individuals simply to agree (*stimmen*) with her on those matters that are taken up—by the reduction of similitude to sameness.[167] This is especially experienced during the visit to Adelheid's cloister by Rex, who is in any case already the character most like her. He is repeatedly constrained to express his accord or *Zustimmung*, even his "complete *Zustimmung*," in order to secure her and the occasion's *gute Stimmung* and avoid anything discordant (*Verstimmliches*): anything that might contrast or be at all unlike occasions silence on either his part or hers, and neither one comfortably.[168] And despite or rather because of this almost exaggerated need for uniform, monotonal *Stimmung*, Adelheid is also described as lacking the power "to hold the conversation and circle together," leaving out those more given to playful poetic association (Czako and his momentary companion, Schmargendorf) as well as those simply left with nothing to say (Woldemar and Triglaff).[169]

Dubslav's joined assemblies and conversations also continuously strive for *Stimmung*, and are punctuated by repeated references to *Zustimmung*, by silent gestures of *Zustimmung*, such as nodding or joining hands, and by similarly repeated references to *Verbindlichkeit*, connecting threads or *Fäden*, and even *Sympathie*.[170] But unlike with Adelheid, the *Verbindlichkeit*, *Stimmung*, and even *Zustimmung* do not depend on sameness, but instead encompass a wide world of difference, contradiction, and even opposition without losing the sympathetic connections. Indeed, the heterogeneity and expanse of oppositionally (or antipathetically) joined elements and participants clearly strengthen the fabric of unifying relationality. This is paradigmatically the case at the opening dinner party, where revealingly Czako is more in his element and Rex more challenged to establish ties (*zu knüpfen*): where poetic associations of similitude animate the language; where contrasting

sides of the same catchphrase are given equal or like force ("Had
I said the opposite, it would have been just as right"); where the
boundaries of exclusionary tact can be innocuously crossed in matters of taste (Czako's rats) or of politics (Gundermann); where the
particular participants linked in sociable small talk can be joined,
loosened, and rejoined in new, different pairings and still maintain the binding unity in the increased interactions, wherein new
similarities and points of contact are sought out, discovered, and
spun out, so different from the fixed pairs at Adelheid's tea; and
perhaps most tellingly, where, like the moments of loosening, the
moments of silence are not interruptive or exposing but supporting, included, contributory.[171] Indeed, Dubslav can sit quietly and
simply listen to the weave of different conversational threads extending out around him and silently express his *Zustimmung* and
thereby display precisely that gift (that associational magic) that
Adelheid lacks, of holding the conversation and circle together.[172]
It is this wide-ranging, emanating connective force with Dubslav
as its silent sympathetic center that gives the spatial breadth to his
sociable sphere, with topics extending from Berlin to Paris to Mos-
cow and beyond, so different from Adelheid's "Brandenburgian
narrowness" at Cloister Wutz and so similar (and so connected) to
the magical Stechlin lake, with its equally wide-ranging, emanating,
world-encompassing connections and *its* underlying silence—with
its sympathetic/connective magic so modestly but also convincingly
replicated in the associational magic of Dubslav's sociability.

Stimmung (Time)

Although here presented spatially, as the sphere of sociability,
conversational *Geselligkeit* and *Stimmung* are also achieved temporally in the novel. After all, the connecting threads and their
various interruptions unfold only in time, and so display properties
best suited to allow the required pace, the mobile flow and freedom
from the all-too-real progress of purposive action or plot. As Simmel suggests, these properties include the serial logic of seemingly
chanceful, happy correspondences and connections outside the

teleological fabric of unfolding consequence, and grounded instead in discovered, linking similarities and resemblances; and a quality of "ex-changeability," a (contagious) capacity to be caught up and moved along a relay of participant speakers so as to constitute a shared nexus external to but binding each individual alike.

We have a glimpse of the building of such an associational chain in the example of "Alexander" just mentioned from the opening dinner party, as it moves from Czako's uniform to Frau Gundermann's Berlin to Dubslav's Russia, all in ways contrary to historical sequential time.[173] But a far more telling example comes in the outing to the Egg Cottage, where we can see not only the kind of links formed in small talk contributing to *Stimmung* and sociability, but also the contributions made to both by the surrounding natural setting and silence—precisely those traditional elements of *Stimmung* beyond the merely social and lingual that Simmel's model leaves out and Fontane's seeks to reengage. Moreover, while avoiding the kind of teleological thrust and purposive action Simmel notes as anathema to sociability and Wellbery to *Stimmung*, the conversation here also does seem to have a hidden direction, a remote if absent end, and thus to acquire a type of future force and ominous quality. However, like the divine communication that can occur only where human intention is absent, this direction or end is not that of the participants but of the author, whose metatextual presence will come to fill that of the text's natural and silent spaces.

The entire episode of the outing to the Egg Cottage takes place under the sign of *Stimmung*. It begins with the declaration "All were in that sort of cheerful *Stimmung* which inclines one to find everything beautiful and charming."[174] And it will end with the hand-clasping union or *Bund* among all the major participants—though notably not with the more intimate, exclusive, and plot-driven engagement bond between Woldemar and one of the Barby sisters (more anon). What occasions the opening *Stimmung* of the still loosely assembled group at the steamer landing is the ringing of bells—a well-established figure for *Stimmung*—both on the boat itself and from the surrounding towers of the city.[175] Melusine comments on the disparate variety of these towers and wonders whether all can be brought together in a single group; but her friend, the Baroness, decrees, "A tower's a tower," and so supplies the requisite *Gleichheit* or similitude at the level of language that will underwrite their unity—and so, too, in the chiming of those bells and linking of those towers, the omen of *Stimmung* that will structure the episode, the readiness or *Bereitschaft* that *Stimmung* always includes as a futural dimension.[176]

Although this prelude foretells the eventual binding experience of the episode, the *Stimmung* takes a modulated while to unfold, in ways that underscore its temporal quality. Dropping to a low point soon after setting out, it proceeds in three broad movements or chains—and it is important that the chains are movements, and the movements chains—that temporally speaking go from present to past to future, as if, in order for the temporal order of *Stimmung* to assert itself, it must first detach from the mundane order of present, objective sequence.[177] The outing proper begins in silence, with the role of talk taken over by that of landscape description, rendered temporal by the movement of the boat; a viewing of the "colorful alternation" (*buntem Wechsel*) and "rapid alternation" (*raschem Wechsel*) of the changing scenery, whose linked, serial unfolding takes the place of talk itself.[178] The scenery only slowly—and even then never completely—frees itself from "the things of the everyday and workaday world" and so opens up to the natural sphere; and even so does the talk, once it resumes, struggle to raise itself above, to move itself beyond, its prosaic ground and present ordinary time and into the free space of genuine sociability.[179] That is, natural *Umwelt* and conversational flow are related, connected, linked, and, as in *Delusions Confusions*, *Cécile*, or *Irretrievable*, the connection with the natural realm is crucial for the release of sympathetic forces and relations in the human realm.

We see the desire for such movement beyond the ordinary in Melusine's initiating attempt to elevate the "thing world" of the landscape into associative language, and thereby to activate the associative, sympathetic forces of both sociability and the natural setting. She points, in passing, to a small island and calls it a "Lovers' Isle," looking to provoke an associative, connected response from Woldemar that would touch on and so reveal his still unrevealed amorous attractions. But Woldemar works to frustrate the magic

(*Zauber*) of that name by evoking a more prosaic one for the same place (Rummelsburger) and, equally important, he claims that she has completely failed to "read" his soul with her remark: the name fails to connect or associate with either the objective or the subjective sphere.[180] The same initial failure of language to detach itself from, and so animate, the prosaic matter of the objective everyday comes when Woldemar similarly deflates the connotations of the name "Egg Cottage" and reduces it to the flat denotation of "a so-called pub (*Lokal*)," which almost leads to discord or *Mißstimmung* in the group and does lead them to avoid the Egg Cottage at first and instead try to recapture the opening *Stimmung* on a communal walk, again drawing on the power of movement.[181] Even this is not yet enough: Barby and the Baron fall into a conversation in which their "persistent differences" in matters of religion and politics prevent *Zustimmung*, and the others all but bicker at the sight of a factory marring the landscape on the farther shore—a factory that produces ladies undergarments that also renders what should be mysterious, hidden, and suggestive prosaic and all too present.[182] It is only when the group turns around and heads back downstream with the river, toward the Egg Cottage, with the intention of observing "life on the river (*Fluß*)" and, at the insistence of the old Count, the sunset, that the possibility of restored *Stimmung* asserts itself—which is to say, only when uncompromised natural imagery asserts itself—natural imagery, moreover, that easily yields to allegorical extension (temporal allegorization no less).[183]

The second movement or chain begins once the sun sets and the group reassembles in the Egg Cottage. The restored potential for *Stimmung* is signaled—indeed omened and abetted—by the appearance of connecting points of light both in "the whole pub" and along the river and farther shore; in the latter two cases, these are moving lights. Their appearance repeats or echoes the micro-macro chiming of the bells on the ship and in the city at the outset, and so too—in both the image and the echoing—reasserts in the setting a trope for *Stimmung*, and with it a somewhat elevated and dematerialized presence to the *Umwelt*.[184] And this time, the *Stimmung* implicit in the connected points, the movement, and the immaterial lift of the lightened setting manages to manifest itself in the conversation as well. It does so precisely through the building of the type of swift-moving, "chance-ful," and "exchangeable" associative chain Simmel specified, a chain that moves both the conversation and its participants out of the concrete present of their place and time.

The "thing" that provides the material anchor for the chain (much as the insignia on Czako's uniform did at the dinner party) is the Swedish punch about which the group now tightly assembles, and from which the word "Swedish" gently detaches to begin the conversational flow.[185] Melusine links it to the Scandinavian-averse Wrschowitz; his absence evokes in turn the freedom to venture forth beyond the type of constricted sphere associated with him (and with the first part of this outing) and into a more open, encompassing realm, such as we saw associated with Dubslav and his lake (both, we'll see, symbolically present beneath what follows). In a rapidly moving, animated conversation of world-encompassing sweep—moving from Sweden to England, Berlin, Ruppen, Portugal, and Russia—and oscillating freely between polar views ("I'd have thought the opposite"), the chain of linked, connecting points extends ever forward.[186] The Swedish punch that joins to the anti-Swedish Pole leads Woldemar to declare his own "Scandinavianism," and to embrace, in addition to the punch, the "Swedish glories" of "iron and courage" (*Mut und Eisen*) and "Säkerhets Tändstickors" (a kind of match), to which series Melusine then adds the Swedish Nightingale, Jenny Lind.[187] This in turn takes the conversational chain into a realm that is, significantly, detached from the material setting in both place and time: Melusine tells of her personal contact with Lind in London as a child ("Before my time," says Woldemar), to which Woldemar couples an account of his own past encounter with Lind's picture in the National Gallery in Berlin, and adds to this a description of a picture of Lind in the pastor Lorenzen's room in Stechlin and the story of his former teacher's long-ago, schoolboy "first love" with the singer—which leads to the spectral presence of the absent Lorenzen amid the assembled group.[188] The conversational chain has, by its own formal, linking, and abstracting force, led the assembled participants to a point of harmonized unity: "I think so, too," says Melusine in

agreeing (*stimmen*) with Woldemar's sympathetic reading of Lorenzen's love story, and "Armgard and the Baroness nodded": the
linked similarities in the conversation draw the participants into a
similarly linked similarity among themselves.[189] And that the end
point of the thread is Lorenzen is both chanceful—the conversation
breaks off only because the group must hurry to catch the boat
back—and fortuitous: *glücklich* or happy in both senses. Lorenzen
will return as the connecting thread of the third movement and will
yield there something of a premonition of the end of the novel: in
both ways, he becomes a figure charged with futurity. (To pick up
on the metaphorical potential of the Egg Cottage, first hinted at by
Melusine and then momentarily thwarted by Woldemar's literal-
ism and now, with language once again open to its associational
dimension, again available: this place has incubated and hatched
the future of both this episode and the novel as a whole.)

The third movement, which culminates in the bond or *Bund*
of joined hands, begins with a fortuitous, *glücklich* return to the
water. The two previous figures for *Stimmung* reappear in similar
(not the same) form, echoing, connecting, and extending their own
chain. The chiming of bells aboard ship and in town is picked up
by the clanging below in the machine room and the crackling of
distant fireworks on shore; the strings of connecting lights similarly
reappear, now along both banks and mirrored close up in the surrounding (and moving) river; and the sounds and lights get linked,
extended, and lifted up to new, otherworldly, immaterial heights in
the exploding fireworks that appear in the air.[190] And even more:
beyond or beneath these two figural frames of *Stimmung* for the
coming *Bund* comes another set, twinned and contrastive: the encompassing frames of silence and the darkened landscape. Despite
the clanging of the ship, "otherwise everything was still, so still,
that the women broke off their talk"; and although they can see
the fireworks, they are so removed from the actual ground and
earthly, social context that the explosions are not actually heard.[191]
The reigning silence brings the natural landscape to the fore: "Then
everyone became silent again and looked out on the landscape,
which lay there . . . in deep darkness," with the very darkness,
indeed invisibility, of the landscape adding to, even unleashing its

allegorical, dematerialized, suggestive potential, and reinforcing its link to the silence (similarly blank, open, ominous) as well.[192]

Such a silence and landscape are indispensable to the sociable bonding that the subsequent conversation is to generate, every bit as much as the movement of the boat and river. The silence is from the first associated with the presence of the ever-silent and all-but-invisible Armgard: as Woldemar says to Melusine, "It suits some to talk and some to be silent. Every being-together needs its silent one (Jedes Beisammensein braucht einen Schweiger)." And although Armgard is the most prominent *Schweiger* present in the scene, she is not the only one. After all, the absent-but-present figure who is manifested in and silently holds together the conversation, namely, Lorenzen, is also frequently identified as a *Schweiger*. And, of course, even beyond these two, we have the dominant *Schweiger* in the novel and in this episode, too—not a person at all but the lake Stechlin, and *its* presence-in-absence as the underlying force or figure behind the binding relations of this "being-together" seems everywhere signified. We have it in the landscape *as* water; in the conversation in all its binding geographical reach; in the nearby lights connecting to the distant fireworks' "cannon shots" as the lake to even more distant disruptions; even in the seemingly passing mention of the telegraph poles with "their wires strung from post to post" that emanate out from the shore.[193] That is, beyond the concrete world of this episode and its associated, manifest conversation and lending it its unifying significance and relationality is a silent invisible allegorical realm, closely linked to the natural world and, in the spectrally looming form of the lake, bringing with it its ominous force—not least in the way the "all still, so still" (*alles still, so still*) here portentously echoes the opening "All still here" (*Alles still hier*), and so hints at a different temporal (and communicative) order, one that proceeds by linked, repeated likenesses rather than causal sequence.

The conversational chain emanating out of "Swedish" and leading up to Lorenzen in the second movement is not directly picked up again in the third. Rather, a new, similar but different one begins, even though reverting to the same unifying center—and it is significant that a new chain, a "byway" back to Lorenzen's spirit-like presence, must be and can be forged: the associational pathways structuring this kind of conversation do not follow a linear consequential logic, just a serial one that takes off from the present moment's material and emanates out from there.[194] It is worth noting, too, that the new chain implicitly incorporates two elements of the earlier series leading up to Lorenzen that at the time seemed especially dissimilar and inert, namely, the "Säkerhets Tändstickers" and "courage and iron": the igniting match that transforms the earlier lights into exploding fireworks, and the spirit (*Mut*) that transforms Lorenzen from a figure of infatuated love into one of a new kind of heroism. Conversational elements do not need to be linearly or immediately present to become links in the associational chain; they evade even this kind of temporal restriction, much as in the "all still" that echoes the novel's opening or the upcoming funeral description that will adumbrate its end—the same sort of "other" temporality and imbrications we ascribed earlier to anecdotes.

The new chain begins with the fireworks and with them elevates the conversation into ever more ethereal realms. A discussion of the fireworks leads to mention of chance passing fancies "flying up into the air" (*in die Luft fliegen*), which "heightens the charm" (*steigert doch den Reiz*) of things such as "[hot-]air balloons" (*Luftballons*) and "airship battles" (*Luftschifferschlachten*), which leads to other topics that "float in the air" (*in der Luft schweb[en]*), and from there to Lorenzen as an "aeronaut, an 'Exclesior' man and climber, someone from the real higher sphere" (*Aeronaut . . . ein Exclesior-, ein Aufsteigemensch, einer aus der wirklichen Obersphäre*).[195] Two points are of special interest. First, how even as the imagery system of the fireworks lifts up that earlier one of the lights and leaves behind the material base of sound earlier embodied in the chiming bells, even as Melusine's whimsical embrace of "airship battles," as the Baroness says, entails forgetting "the reality" (*die Wirklichkeit*), even as the language itself leaves behind the concrete denotation of the fireworks and rises via associative similitude to ever more abstract, symbolic forms (to Lorenzen as a "climber"), just so does the sense of "reality" at stake rise into the symbolic, immaterial, spirit realm. Melusine's "forgetting the reality" opens up to "the real (*wirklich*) higher sphere," which houses the kind of spirit heroism and spirit love connected with Lorenzen and his desire "*really* to live" (wirklich *zu leben*): a heroism as far removed from noisy conflicts as the group from the exploding fireworks, and a love as elevated from earthy sensuality as those same fireworks. Not incidently, this "real higher sphere" is also associated, via a further link of Lorenzen to the poet João de Deus, with literary art or *Dichtung*—which, in its own metatextual presence at this (and every) moment in the novel, is also part of this silent and immaterial "higher" realm and reality, and porously imparts, invisibly communicates to, the scene its own binding, unifying force (parallel to, indeed indistinguishable from, that more "subterranean" force of the similarly absent-but-present lake).

The second point of special interest is how, even as the conversational chain works by continued extension of the similar without ever falling into mere sameness or repetition, with continued handing over and on of the linked chain with the prospect—even the requirement—of continuous extension on into the future to sustain it, so does this very property of extension and "exchangeability" become the concrete subject-matter that the conversation latches onto and then, via the knight's move of associative reading, omens forth for the assembled group itself, in both its macro- and microcosmic form. Woldemar quotes Lorenzen saying about João de Deus, "[Supposedly,] there aren't men like that any more. But there are the like, there must be the like or must be *again*" (Es gäbe dergleichen nicht mehr. Aber es gibt dergleichen noch, es muß dergleichen geben oder doch *wieder* geben).[196] The very associative, serial, and similarizing property of casual conversation that is needed to assure the maintenance of the "shadow-realm" of sociablity is also, we're told, required for the continuation of "our entire society" (*unsre ganze Gesellschaft*); and although this we're not told, we know that the futural imperative of that same property is of special, personal significance for the speaker of these lines, Woldemar. After all, the critical if unspoken side issue of this outing is Woldemar's unrevealed plans for his engagement bonds, about which we earlier saw Melusine attempting to solicit signs. Those bonds signify and embody a crucial part of the novel's overriding concern with the future itself, with the chain of similitude that will extend the Stechlin line: they signify to both Woldemar and the reader the need to find "the like" (*dengleichen*), a new but similar someone to succeed not de Deus but Dubslav, and so for Stechlin time to proceed forward by repeated likeness—by kinship, as it were.[197]

Even as the conversation seems to move from present "real" and denoted matter toward ever more abstract, immaterial, and absent connoted referents, and even to extend into an as-yet-unforeseen future ("be *again*" [wieder *geben*]), so too does the unifying end of its chain point beyond the conversation itself, the end point that invests it with its symbolic but real significance from that beyond, binding it together, significantly; the point that animates and inhabits the silence behind the spoken, and does so from some as yet unseen future.[198] That unspoken, spectral point—that "shadow-body"—binding together the conversation and its participants into a sociable unity (with futurity) is, I suggest, the absent Dubslav, the novel's belated "silent one" and the figure for whom, we just said, "the like" must be found and given again.[199] Just as the lake is the hidden allegorical presence lurking behind the natural *Umwelt* and investing it (or rather its *Stimmung*) with ominous force, so too is its human counterpart in Dubslav there (in the *Stimmung* of the conversation) as well, and to similar ominous effect—indeed, the presence of the one Stechlin, the lake, behind the setting silently and sympathetically summons forth the other, Dubslav, behind the conversation and accord (*Bund*). We see this in how the figure of João de Deus, first evoked for his associational resemblance to Lorenzen, subtly shifts, extends, and transforms in significance when an account is added on of his death and funeral, an account in which already can be divined the similar fated end not of Lorenzen but of Dubslav, as indeed comes at the novel's close. Even as the beginning of the novel has its echo here in the "all still" of the water, evoking the lake, so the end in the funeral, evoking Dubslav: the two Stechlins who sympatheticially share in the other, outside-of-time "shadow-realm" and to whom are attached the novel's ominous force.

In implicit confirmation of Dubslav's spectrally and ominously evoked presence and its crucial link to the very nature of language and sociability, when the present, associated group does join hands to materially manifest the bond or *Bund* of this outing, they do so in the name of the simple letter *D*, pointing at once to Dubslav and the quality of language that makes that point appear. As has been true of the novel in general but of this episode in particular, the conversation from the outset has engaged in name play and even name changes, as part of its foregrounding of the similar metamorphic, serial character of conversation as it transforms from one topic to the similar next, from one participant to the next, and often discovering and enacting those similitudes and exchanges at the level of language itself.[200] So too here, in the silent, unspoken transformation of *D* from de Deus to Dubslav: as the Baroness declares, they shall move, as it were, from *C* to *D* as the joining object of their *Bund*.[201] Language here, in its most elemental form—a letter—and in its most elemental, arbitrary series—the alphabet—does the work of both symbolizing, signing, or connoting an "other" referent beyond the immediate denoted context and, by that, binding together through its hidden associational ties its entire order in sympathetic relations. That is the real magic, the magically real of this binding moment, this micro unified world, this conversation: language itself.

One further point. The quality of *D* that is foregrounded to explain its binding force is the italicized feature that "he" (de Deus and Dubslav) lived "*not for himself*" (nicht für sich).[202] This underscores the essential impersonality, even nonsubjectivity that Simmel describes as intrinsic to sociability, that we have described as equally intrinsic to the immersion in *Stimmung* and *sympatheia* in general, and that proves inherent too in language once it has shed its merely denotative referential character and opened up to the associative play that allows *D* to reach out and attract connections to other referents, other subjects. It is, I suggest, just this essential impersonality that can also explain why this union (*Bund*) dominates the outing rather than the alternative in the more personal, purposive, and earthly engagement of erotic ties—even subsumes those attractive forces (that "love") within its own and so, too, determines the quality of its futurity. Woldemar's engagement will require the dissolution of his autonomous individuality in order for him to become, as it were, a participant element himself, a "like, again" (*wiedergegebener Dergleiche*): it will not be based on a present, material, individual feeling but on a perpetuated future of the Stechlin line through a chain of similitude. This is the same kind of perpetuated chain on which sociability and language—and sociability through language—depend. The connection between the chains of the novel's family line and its associative language is something introduced at its outset in the very word *Stechlin*, with all its open, nonspecific, multiple serial reference, and at the same time, and by that very property, its binding, connecting links. So it seems fitting that, in ceding to this serial, futural imperative, this unspoken and yet commanding force behind and within conversation proper, Woldemar should come to embrace the silent (and almost subjectless, almost invisible) Armgard over the voluble (and individual) Melusine, and thereby connect, too, to that other Stechlin in the linked chain, the lake, its biding omen, and its magic: for it is from this silent, and all-but-unfeatured, source that the present moment derives its principle of meaning, movement, and futurity. As Woldemar will later say to Armgard, "So the future lies with *you* (Die Zukunft liegt also bei *dir*)," as it always has in the silent "shadow-realm" behind the apparent real.[203]

Verstimmung (Anecdote)

While the Egg Cottage episode demonstrates the associative chains that, as a property of small talk (*Plauderei*), produce the immaterial, unspoken realms of sociability and unifying *Stimmung* and so, too, a future force, the following episode, "Election in Rheinsberg-Wutz," foregrounds instead that other element of sociable talk singled out by Simmel and already shown to be central to the ominous in Fontane, namely, anecdotal narration. But it does so in a context where the fabric of sociability and *Stimmung* is unraveling, loosening its connective threads and hence, too, its share in sympathetic magic and the future. The anecdote at the center of this episode—and arguably at the center of the novel—concerns the magically restorative blood-bath taken by a "compromised"

Siamese princess.[204] Significantly, it is the most magically and supernaturally charged anecdote in the novel. But even as the binding
power of the sociable realm seems threatened in this episode by its
own artifice or nonreality, so too is the magic—and magic reading
(which is to say, the futural force)—of its anecdote.

It might seem odd to characterize this episode, and particularly
the specific scene in which this anecdote appears, as suggesting the
breakdown of sociability and *Stimmung*, since the sense of social
bonding or *Verbindlichkeit* and the concentration of affirming references to *Stimmung* are no less present here than in the Egg Cottage episode. This is especially true of the day of the election itself,
which begins with Dubslav "in an excellent mood" (*in ausgezeichneter Laune*), a mood that becomes a heightened *Stimmung* when
linked to the "magnificent fall weather" and the circle of his closest
associates, all of whom converse in the most unified and ob-liging
or *verbindlich* manner on their own little boat trip and shared
repast, with "not a trace of discord (*Verstimmung*)" and instead
"accord and cheerfulness" (*Zustimmung und Heiterkeit*), with
everyone "in common accord" (*allgemein zugestimmt*)," nodding
Zustimmung, shouting, "Yes, yes" (*Stimmt, stimmt*), and even
joining voices (*anstimmen*) to sing in unison.[205] Nonetheless, it is
telling that this section actually begins under the sign of discord
(*Verstimmungen*), indeed potentially "fatal discord" introduced by
Adelheid, and this reveals something crucial about the *Stimmung*
at stake in what follows.[206]

The source of the foreseen *Verstimmungen* broached by Adelheid in a letter to Woldemar comes from her insistence that, in
forging his marriage ties, he limit himself to the sphere of the Mid-
dlemark aristocracy: any reach beyond that would occasion the
deadly discord. And as different as the Stechlin siblings otherwise
are when it comes to the sociable sphere, in this episode it is their
similarities that come to the fore. For the *Stimmung* of Dubslav
and his associate aristocratic circle is in near-fatal disconnect with
that of the larger social order within which they find themselves.
The disconnect is itself thematized in terms of *Stimmung*: counterpointed to the chain of accord or *Zustimmung* generated by
and binding Dubslav and his group is the *Stimmung* of the larger
social sphere or *Kreis* exposed through the election. Despite the

efforts "to unite all the votes behind Dubslav" (*alle Stimmen auf Dubslav zu vereinigen*), "what the *Stimmung* in the district really was" (*wie die Stimmung im Kreise wirklich war*) is captured by the votes, the *Stimmen* themselves, which go decisively to the progressive or modern party with their "voting machine" (*Abstimmungsmaschine*)—and "the people's voice, God's voice" (*Volksstimme, Gottesstimme*).[207]

This is notably different in effect from the counterpointed scenes with the servant class woven into the Egg Cottage episode (passed over by us). There the effect was to widen the expanse of the connected world in ways that increased rather than lessened the sense of unified relationality, whereas here it is far more to lay bare the loss of relation between the microcosm of Dubslav's social circle and the macrocosm of the wider social sphere. The two *Stimmungen* are radically unconnected, and hence under the fateful sign of *Verstimmungen*. As Lorenzen will later put it in his all but metatextual and prophetic exposition to Melusine, "The old families are wasting and throwing away the sympathies" (Die alten Familien . . . vertun und verschütten [die] Sympathien).[208] The former unity or *Einheit* of sympathetic relations within the social order is being dissipated, undone, and with it the connection to the broader world and future.[209]

This is the thematic context within which the anecdote occurs: the story of the princess of Siam and her restoration or *Wiederherstellung* by means of a bath in animal blood. The proximate cause for its telling is another incidental story, the gossip (*Klatschgeschichte*) about wayward Lilli and her abandoned but then returned-to fiancé cousin, that moves the conversation away from the immediate, objective political context into the more detached sociable sphere: one anecdote invites another, contagiously. Like other anecdotes in Fontane, these introduce an opening in the concrete, historical, and diegetic fabric of the text, and present a different logic or significatory structure that calls for a different interpretive approach for characters and readers alike—that approach we've called the knight's move of divinatory reading.

Reflecting this opening, the princess story lacks all objective temporal markers, is geographically far removed and set in the fantastic realm of the Orient, and is presented as at once marvelous (*märchenhaft*) and factual (*tatsächlich*); and it is just this combination of the magical and real that becomes the focal point of its reading.[210] Again like other anecdotes in Fontane, the interpretation involves not simply a reading of the story's event in itself, but rather its analogical reading, its connection to the immediate present context and its future. In this case that context is twofold, encompassing both the just-told, embedded story of Lilli and the occasion of Dubslav's failed bid for votes (*Stimmen*). But beyond this—for the reader if not the characters—it also involves a reading of how it might link up with other, similarly temporally detached anecdotes besides that of Lilli, other openings in the fabric, suggesting cumulatively an "other" force or order independent of ordinary historical sequentiality, or plot consequentiality, with determinative import for the future of the primary narrative.

It is in this last respect that this particular anecdote most stands out. While there are several such overarching serial chains of temporally discrete anecdotes built up across the narrative—such as that linking together significant acts accomplished in silence or from a distance—these have interpretive but little predictive force. But this story, although having only limited associational extension through linkage to other anecdotes, does attract predictive power, does acquire or draw upon an "other" ominous force and presence.[211] It does so through its links to the super/natural imagery system that dominates the novel as a whole: the water imagery that begins with the lake and then runs as widely and subterraneously throughout the text as the lake does throughout the world, uniting characters as diverse as Gundermann, Rolf-Krake, Melusine, Sponholz, and Dubslav, and episodes such as the Egg Cottage outing, the boat trip taken here by Dubslav and his group—and in this anecdote carried through in the image of the bathing princess. It is just this linkage to the ominous lake and to the ruling authorial metatextual imagery system—much like the more traditional stars in *Before the Storm*—that in-forms (parasitically infuses) the magical thinking at stake in the anecdote itself and gives it futural force for the novel: the crucial combination of the natural, the metatextual, and the magical that invites and supports divinatory reading.

The crux of the anecdote is itself a futural one, albeit in that involuted way in which the only future imaginable is a repetition of the past—an inextricable aspect of divinatory time in general, wherein a past event is read in the present for its similitude with what is to come, but also and for that very reason creating a tension with the relentless unidirectionality of historical time. The anecdote revolves around the issue of restoration (*Wiederherstellung*) or, more specifically, restoration of purity (*Reinheitswiederherstellung*), and the italicized catchphrase "*Blood makes good again*" (Blut sühnt): the princess, having lost her original purity after being violated by a foreign prince, undergoes a ritual bath in animal blood and emerges with her natural innocence restored, and so able to rejoin society and marry (once more).[212] The characters hearing the tale apply it to the story of Lilli and her fiancé, and use it to predict reconciliation. The reader, however, is led to consider the further resemblance to the broader but still immediate context of the lost election as well, and to speculate that the "restoration" at stake is also that of the Prussian aristocracy in the sociopolitical sphere.[213] Certainly the magical thinking—the belief in this restoration of the original state—that preoccupies the auditors of the anecdote seems as much if not more a reflection on this latter future than that of Lilli's return to her cousin. But there are still other details to the anecdote that point beyond even this immediate context to other readings of it as an omen of "restoration," details that also bring with them the same question of the magical thinking at stake in their predictive force.

First and most obviously, the whole anecdote, with its tale—seconded by that of Lilli—of a "compromised" woman given a second chance at marriage and finding happiness therein, and, moreover, a woman magically transformed and renewed through her immersion in a bath, would seem to suggest a connection to Melusine in both her actual (*tatsächlich*) and her fairy-tale-like (*märchenhaft*) identities, and especially to omen forth a restorative marriage of Woldemar and Melusine, restoring both her and the Stechlin bloodline, and perhaps even in ways that bring back a human connection to the elemental, magical world of the lake. This seems the nearest, most forceful divinatory reading of the anecdote. But, crucially, it goes unfulfilled: and this is of decisive importance for other, related readings also charged with futural force that, taken on their own, might seem to point toward a restored magic world in the novel— readings that place special symbolic weight on "blood."

"Blood" points in two directions independent of, albeit potentially subsumed by, that which tends toward Melusine. First, it links to the dominant theme of the widely desired continuation of the Stechlin bloodline. This theme is borne throughout by the issue of Woldemar's engagement and occupies the closing lines of the novel: the fervent hope that, at this incipient moment of Dubslav's and his social sphere's compromised condition, Woldemar will rise up, extend the line, and lead to a renewal that is at the same time a restoration, a return to an original state in which the new becomes the old and the future resembles the past. To quote again what Woldemar says to Armgard right after his father's funeral and just before moving back into his ancestral home, "So the future lies with *you*."[214] This is a hope—and so too an omen— that will factually be fulfilled in the novel. But its magical thinking, its faith in a stable temporal order independent of historical time based on extended chains of similitude—this faith is no longer fully embraced: its factual fulfillment is no longer truly fulfilling, not forceful enough to actually fashion the future.

Second and both more materially and abstractly, "blood" links the matter of renewal and restoration to the natural, even animal realm, and this in vital liquid form—connecting hopes for "restoration" to a literal immersion that links to the novel's water imagery. In this way, it seems also to point, at this moment of the dissipation of the merely human sociable sphere as the site of *Stimmung* and its magic, to the possibility of a restoration of the earlier conditions of sympathetic relations in the natural world with *its* magic—a magical restoration via a restored magical nature. This would seem an even more radical return to an original state; and while this turn, too—omened forth in this anecdote—seems fulfilled in the future of the novel, its magical thinking, its faith in a vital, healing, animating reconnection with "life" also falls short, for all its attraction, an attraction equal to that of a well-nigh mythical repetition of the family line, and equal, too, to that of a restored Melusine as

Woldemar's bride. In all three cases, the magic, the future, and the divinatory reading go unrealized.

"Everything Takes Place in Silence"

After the lost election, the novel's concern with "restoration" qua "social" futurity comes increasingly to center on Woldemar.[215] Indeed, the novel as a whole comes increasingly to focus on Woldemar and his social life and connections in Berlin. But the concern with "restoration" and magic—and, with magic, sympathy and *its* futural properties—continues to center on Dubslav and his life and connections by the lake. Once Dubslav loses the election—which is to say, once the *Stimmung* of his circle fails to connect with that of the broader social sphere—Dubslav enters a new phase, a different pursuit of connecting to the macrocosmic order, with a different relation to futurity, and a different relation to language and signs as well. Increasingly—though significantly never completely—we see Dubslav loosen his ties to social life and conversation, and, as it were, to the forward arc of historical time, including that of the narrative plot. Instead, we see him binding himself to the natural world and, closely allied with it, to both the lower classes (and their language-not-language) and "nature women" of the kind we first encountered in Hoppenmarieken and Marie in *Before the Storm*, and have here at the end of *The Stechlin* in the figures of the "witch" Buschen and her granddaughter, Agnes. It is a world that is at once an older, more primitive one and a more childlike, primitive one; a world that seems withdrawn even from the Christian era (embodied by Adelheid and Ermyntrud) and its faith in the Word and everlasting future life, into something far more ancient and earth-bound: a world of sympathetic magic, of silence—and of death.[216] For what we discovered in *Green Henry* proves true here as well: death is inseparable from the silent sympathetic ties of *Stimmung* in the natural (and the metatextual) world, is indeed a defining force, a binding future.

Already in the immediate aftermath of the lost election, on the ride home afterward, we see the beginning of this shift in Dubslav's relation to both the social and the lingual realms. Traveling alone with his servant, he comes across "the old souse" Tuxen passed out drunk in the road and takes him safely back to town.[217] The scene newly displays Dubslav's sympathetic relations with the people of the land and of marginalized social status, sympathetic bonds outside those of objective social relations—Tuxen voted against Dubslav in the elections—and powerfully supported by the dialect-laden language in which they converse, so different from Dubslav's, and the novel's, normative social speech and thus signaling a different, less socially determined and more "natural" set of bonds at work.[218] And we see the same shift again in Dubslav's first, relatively early, and more crucial encounter with Buschen and Agnes, where the move to a new relation to both the socially excluded and non-"social" language is further coupled with a new relation to the natural world and silence.

Dubslav has gone for a solitary walk to commune, as we say, with nature—significantly at a moment when, we're told, "the sun was already below the horizon, and only the red of evening still glowed through the trees."[219] Dubslav's shift toward solitary communion with nature is one that gathers momentum from here on out, and although not always so openly allegorical as with this setting sun, with its *Stimmung* between the human and natural worlds, his communion is always a matter of ever more forceful participatory identification.[220] One sign of this is that as he reflects on the lake and setting sun Dubslav also reflects on himself, in one of the very rare moments—even the first moment—of reflected interiority in the novel. It is a moment remarkable not for its content or insight (both endearingly simple), but for its connections with nature and for how it changes Dubslav's relation to language. Language becomes silent, indeed as silent as the natural world in which he finds himself, a reinscription of language captured in the lines "While he sat, he looked out and drew figures in the sand with his cane. The woods were completely still."[221]

This new, twinned relation to nature and language is then extended through its link to Buschen and Agnes, the novel's "nature-child," also a social outcast and uniquely associated with vegetal life.[222] Between them, these two women—very old and child-young,

and significantly women—encompass not only the temporal opposites of the present social order, the distant past and the still distant future, but also the twin sides of nature's ever-present, primal
originality, so independent of the present sociohistorical moment.
And while Buschen and Dubslav will converse both here and in
what follows in the same naturalistic language as did Tuxen and
Dubslav, and to the same sympathetic effect, Agnes and Dubslav,
both here and in what follows, will share in the same communal
silence as that of mute nature and the lake, and to the same effect
of silently forging sympathetic ties.[223]

Still, the shift in Dubslav's sympathetic relations with the world
is not really complete until he becomes entangled not with others but, instead, with his own natural, creaturely body.[224] This begins in the section portentously titled "Sunset," as Dubslav returns
by open carriage from Woldemar's wedding, again caught up in
contemplating the landscape and in a rare moment of silent so-
liloquy, and enters his house—now solely occupied by himself and
his dialect-speaking servants—and finds "his foot is swollen."[225]
This is the first sign (the first omen) of his body being touched by
hydropsy or "water sickness" (*Wassersucht*), contiguously drawn
into manifest, subsuming sympathetic relation to the novel's water
world: the world of the lake (his lake: "the Stechlin"), with its
own widespread subterranean sympathetic connections throughout the world; and of the text (his text: *The Stechlin*), with its own
wide, imagistic (and so nonlingual) net of associative connections
throughout the work.[226] And it is surely significant that it is only
with the emergence of his water sickness that Dubslav becomes
capable, however modestly, of divination, of "magically" and accurately reading signs for their future force, and so joins the only
other character in the novel invested with this gift, Melusine—
also a water figure, also connected to both elemental and magical
forces—with both thus now connected, too, to the lake and its
portentous force.[227]

Once Dubslav's body begins to be taken in and over by the
water—to become linked and one with it—there are three different attempts made at a "restoration" of his well-being, as well
as one, associated with the "new" doctor, rejected as "not very

sympathetic (*sympathisch*)," although one can also read his water sickness itself, and its slow dissolution of his body, as its own "restoration."[228] In any case, each of these three attempts is more or less explicitly a mode of sympathetic magic or healing; each is tied up with the "old" world of nature—and, significantly, with key elements of the novel's magical-realist poetics as well. In this way, the fate—the future—of Dubslav, sympathetic nature, and the novel's poetics become inextricably linked.

The first attempt is made by Dubslav's old doctor, Sponholz, himself a water man, off to spend weeks with his wife in healing, restorative baths. He prescribes "just a few drops" of digitalis to be taken with but a spoonful of water: as Dubslav says after taking it, "Now it starts. Foxglove (*Fingerhut*)."[229] That Dubslav uses the older familiar term and the doctor the more modern scientific one is itself significant.[230] From Fontane's early work on, the foxglove flower has appeared as a sign or *Zeichen* of the magical world, specifically of the witching world. It appears in *Grete Minde* (1880) as a "fairy-tale flower" (*Märchenblume*) whose petals fall on Grete as she lies in a field and portentously sign her as a witch.[231] And it appears again in *Cécile* (1887) as the flower linking Cécile to the nearby Witches' Dance Floor.[232] In *The Stechlin*, this magical dimension is left implicit, unspoken and merely silently connoted— although its connections to the wider natural world (of "forest and field") are underscored. But rather than appearing as the foxglove flower itself, and so an open sign of the magical or *märchenhaft*, it appears as a few distilled drops of digitalis, in what seems a sober, realistic, modern evocation of nature's forces.[233]

Nevertheless, and in just this form, these concentrated drops reveal their close connections to the magical: to the homeopathic "particules" and the micro-macro relations they suggest that we saw in *Irretrievable*, connections seconded here by the equally small doses of the equally supernaturally charged water Dubslav takes with the drops.[234] Homeopathy, we said, was represented as a kind of sympathetic magic that operated according to the same underlying principle as Fontane's realist poetics, of representing the macrocosmic through the microcosmic. So here, too, with respect not only to the foxglove flowers qua digitalis drops, but also to the greater (social) world qua Dubslav himself, and the even greater (social and natural) world qua the adjacent lake.[235] The wide world of magic is not so much absent as it is transformed into a concentrated kind of realism, one that aims to restore Dubslav to the greater world and, through Dubslav, to restore the greater world (of sympathetic relations) to itself. It is an attempt every bit as dependent on its associative magic as on its "realist" power to achieve its "restoration"—in its own updated way, not all that different from the blood bath of the Siamese princess and its restoration of her kingdom.

The second attempt does not so much displace as complement the first, and it draws on (or in) the second principle associated by Fontane with homeopathy and also with his realist poetics, namely, "similia similibus."[236] This time the attempt is specifically thematized as drawing on "witches' arts" (*Hexenkünste*).[237] Dubslav turns to the outside-of-the-social natural arts of the old witch Buschen, who prescribes remedies of tea with club moss (*Bärlapp*) and cat's foot (*Katzenpfötchen*) according to the witches' saying (*Hexenspruch*) "The water takes the water away" (Dat Woater nimmt dat Woater).[238] Dubslav repeatedly chants this formula to himself as itself an effective form of magic, even as he also works to allegorize the two teas and attribute their effective powers to their "world-history"-encompassing symbolic force rather than just some objective property.[239] But again, for all the emphasis on their witching nature, we note that the operating principles of Buschen's remedy are the very ones that have sustained the novel's poetics from the beginning: from the associative play of language in relation to things and names, always powered by similitude and drawing in an immaterial, allegorical sphere; through to the associative play of sociablity in characters and conversation, again powered by similitude and sympathetic relations and again drawing in a symbolic, immaterial world; to here, in the associative play of nature in the relation of plants to people—or rather, crucially, of water to water, thus evoking the overarching image of the natural but also supernatural and metatextual forces linking Dubslav (Stechlin) to the landscape (the Stechlin) and both to the novel (*The Stechlin*). Dubslav's turn at the end to Buschen's sympathetic magic in his pursuit of "restoration" is not, then, a turn away from the realist world of the preceding novel but rather a turn, even a return, toward its governing center, its "nature." It simply returns that sympathetic magic to its starting point, its ground in the natural world.

The third attempt or remedy completely encompasses the previous two—indeed, even as the traditional sympathetic cosmos might be said to subsume homeopathy—and brings the novel's overriding and formal concern with the "great connectedness of things" at once into natural material and allegorical form. This is Krippenstapel's honeycomb or *Wabe*, which is repeatedly described as embodying "the complete" or "the collective healing powers of nature," drawing or gathering into itself the concentrated essence of the entire natural order—and, Dubslav adds, "if *everything* is in it, then it's got club moss and cat's foot and naturally also foxglove in it, too."[240] Early on, Krippenstapel's bees had been representative of the social-political order; here that fades away, and the honeycomb becomes instead "a sign" (*ein Fingerzeig*) of the great web of interconnected nature. And Dubslav makes a point of taking into (and so of making one with) his body not just the liquid honey but the entire, more substantive waxen *Wabe* (from *weben*, "to weave") as well. As with the remedies of both Sponholz and Buschen, Krippenstapel's honeycomb translates or metamorphoses one of the dominant (and in this case, the dominant) poetic principles of the novel back into the natural world as the source of the desired "restoration"; and in turning to it as the embodiment at once of natural and allegorical forces, Dubslav (and the novel) is also returning to a mode of magic—indeed, the magic of the novel itself.[241]

And yet for all this reapproach to the sympathetic powers of the natural world, none of it is of any real effect. The magic doesn't happen: there is no restoration of Dubslav's health. The omen of the restorative bath fails in this respect, too, and not just, as mentioned, in its prediction of Melusine's "restoration." The only restoration arrived at is the dissolution of Dubslav's liquified body back into the watery world, and the only signs or *Zeichen* that prove reliable are those pointing to "the immediate future" (*die nächste Zukunft*) of death ("The signs are there, more than too many").[242] Similarly, the silent and "still" realm behind or beyond language that Dubslav comes increasingly to participate in and identify with, to find himself prepared for and attuned (*gestimmt*) with, seems to be not so much that of a powerful natural life force as that of death; or of death itself as a natural force and as whatever life and future one might expect by joining it, water to water, beyond the healing redeeming power of "the Word."[243] But also, apparently, beyond that of a restored, sympathetic nature as well.

And it is not only the restoration of Dubslav's health—and with it, of a natural sympathetic sphere—that comes up short at the novel's end and all but shuts out the future. The restoration of the Stechlin bloodline—and with it, of the aristocrats' sympathetic social world—that is associated with Woldemar, that was also omened forth in the anecdote of renewal-by-blood, and that, via Armgard as the vessel of "the future," is similarly linked with the silent realm; this seems similarly to be of no real effect, to have lost its power and hold on the future. As mentioned, this portended future seems strangely involuted, a wish to secure the future by turning it into a return to the past and shutting out the forward force of sociohistorical time; a future with no necessary relation to the "real" future, which seems something else entirely; a chain of similitude extended into a very different world. If Melusine's letter that closes out the novel is to be given its due force, then this particular future of Woldemar and the old aristocratic order is of no real significance ("It's not necessary that the Stechlins live on"), and its potential loss is of the same order as that of Dubslav and the sympathetic natural order.[244] Neither proves sufficiently real, neither omen of a sympathetic "restoration" sufficiently significant.

This leaves us with the only other future omened forth by the novel, the one associated with the child Agnes and her red stockings— Agnes, the silent child of nature and asocial status who is gifted with Dubslav's weathervanes and weathercocks, chief among them the one driven (metaphorically) by water, and who both wears and knits away silently at her red stockings. Adelheid fears these stockings, "because they are a sign," but Dubslav replies, "That doesn't say anything, Adelheid. Everything's a sign. What are they a sign of? That's what matters."[245] Adelheid will read them as a sure sign of a coming democratic or proletarian future, or more forcefully, of the end-time, das "*Letzte*."[246] And for all their different attitudes toward this possibility, Dubslav's response exposes one of its consequences for signs themselves, one directly connected to the breakdown in language we mentioned before as endemic to this novel; but where then the issue was how the breakdown in language threatened the social sphere (in ways unforeseen by Simmel), here it is how the breakdown in the social sphere threatens language, or rather, the future of divinatory language's futural force.

That is, Dubslav's question "What are they a sign of?" points to the necessary failure of such divinatory readings, and of such omens, in a world where the common ground or shared order behind its significatory systems—whether of nature, society, history, or poetics—has been lost, ended. If the omen of the bathing princess fails because none of its signed "restorations" seem fulfilled, then that of the stockings seems fated to fail because, in such a severed world, it could signify so many things—anything—that it means nothing, and the future is closed; or if it does succeed, then that is only because what it portends is the end of the known world or reality, and so again, a closed future, as closed as Dubslav's life and as in-significant as Woldemar's future child.[247] And I should stress how different this seems from the openness and undecidability of signs and omens in earlier Fontane texts and other realists as well, where the openness was still contained within a stable if polysemous world; here it is the signifying world itself that loses ground. Indeed, to give full weight to the novel's last line, the only realm of "connectedness," the only common ground of secure signification left standing is not of the world but of *The Stechlin* itself: which is to say, the very novel that is now finished, that we have just finished reading and that alone secures for the future the closed world of its significatory systems. Foucault claimed that literature was the last refuge of the ancient belief in magic and divinatory reading after the seventeenth century, and while I believe we have shown that not to be true through much of the nineteenth century, it does seem to come true here at its end, along with its faith in the future.

Of course, many of the directions that seem so melancholically arrived at and even ended in *The Stechlin* will have their own future life, their own restoration in the modernist movements to come.[248] The reemergence of immersion in an original, natural, sympathetic realm of forces outside language will occupy the vitalists and their *Lebensphilosophie*, even their blood talk, albeit with a symbolical sign system pointing more toward some distant past than future. Similarly, in the work of Freud, Proust, Benjamin, and others we will see the kind of temporal involution that turns the past into a secure repository for divining the future, albeit a future often enough itself already past: a reading forward that looks only backward and predicts the future only as a repetition of what has already been, leaving aside the truly new.[249] There will also be some magical, futural thinking closely tied to expectations of social revolution, and of course a renewed emphasis on art itself as an all-but-autonomous, magical realm of self-enclosed and self-referential significance. In all these various ways, magic and divinatory reading will survive into and thrive in the European literature and culture of the early twentieth century. But for Fontane, the point is this: in significant ways, *The Stechlin* represents the end of both a strictly realist poetics and magical thinking. The same notion of a future has been taken away from both; both are thereby together robbed of one of their chief supporting forces—and the reader, too, of one of the chief determinants of his engaged participation. The insight we are left with is just how much of a common ground realism and magic—and with them, literary and divinatory reading—always shared, in their similar modes of associative signification and allegorical structuration, and in their shared cosmos of sympathetic relations and reasonings: a cosmos in which the real was often magical, and the magical could be real.

3

READING MAGIC IN
WALTER BENJAMIN

This chapter will focus on Walter Benjamin and his modernist engagement with magic reading. But I want to begin elsewhere, with Hermann Hesse and a famous scene in *The Steppenwolf* (1927) that seems equally symptomatic of many of modernism's dominant preoccupations with magic and divination.[1] Hesse's protagonist, Harry Haller, in a somewhat distracted state of mind, is out for an evening walk when a man appears from out of an alley carrying a signboard and a box full of pamphlets. Haller reads the sign's "dancing reeling letters," fleeting, fitful, and almost illegible, announcing, "Magic Theater: Entrance Not for Everyone." He accosts the man, who mechanically hands him one of his booklets and then disappears through a doorway. The pamphlet seems to be—or rather, is—one of those poorly printed booklets that are sold at fairs ("Were you born in January?"), a "companion volume to fortune-telling books." But once Haller starts to read it, he sees it is entitled "Treatise on the Steppenwolf," and finds a detailed, deeply insightful reading of himself, his inner world, and his impending future, imparted to him from out of a seemingly timeless, metatextual realm presided over by the "immortal" Goethe, and promising release from the oppressive strictures of both his person and historical moment.

As the critic Theodore Ziolkowski points out, the magical experience that inserts itself into the otherwise realist setting here and elsewhere in this novel—indeed in much of Hesse's fiction—reflects a theory of magic reading that Hesse articulates in a 1920 essay, "On Reading Books" (Vom Bücherlesen).[2] In this essay, Hesse distinguishes between three types of reader, though he also stresses that each of us belongs intermittently (*zeitweise*) to now this, now that type: the different modes of reading are never entirely exclusive. The first is that of the naïve reader: "The book leads, the reader follows. The subject matter is taken as objective, is accepted as reality." The second type is more childlike, but also (and so) less naïve: even as a child "begins to play with things, bread becomes a mountain in which one bores a tunnel, and bed a cave, a garden, a snowfield," so this reader "regards neither the subject matter nor the form of a book as its only and most important quality. . . . He knows that every thing can have in it ten or a hundred meanings." This detachment from the intentional, objective meaning of the author and text is not only in the direction of enabling the reader's free play, but also in that of recognizing the restrictions on that of the author and his text: recognizing the external binding forces that invisibly determine the text world's and author's seemingly independent choices.

The third type of reader—and the one identified as the most intermittent, the most occasional—is, as it were, "a total child." He gives himself over completely to associative thinking: "He uses a book no differently than any object in the world. It is basically all the same to him, what he reads. . . . He doesn't read a writer in order to have that writer interpret the world for him. He interprets himself (*Er deutet selber*)." And, Hesse insists, we are all at times this reader: "At that moment, when our fantasy and associative ability are at their height, we no longer really read what is writtten on the paper before us at all any more. Rather, we swim in a stream of incitements and incidental ideas that come to us from what is read. These can come from the text; they can even come from the type-face." He suggests that even a newspaper insert can become a site of revelation for this reader—much, we suppose, as that fortune-telling pamphlet became for Haller.

Hesse does admit that this reader is no longer reading the text, and not least because he seems to be producing his entire experience— indeed, his entire world—out of his self alone (although the boundaries of that self seem as violently dissolved as those of the text). But he qualifies this concession in two ways. First, he explains that even if such a reader is, strictly speaking, no longer "reading" the book before him, he is engaged in a mode of "reading" that has become transferable to the world as a whole, to encounters not only with Shakespeare, Goethe, or Stendahl, but with carpets, stone walls, or cigarette packs. The whole world of things becomes again, as it was in ancient times, a riddling text to be magically read. And second, he insists again that this mode of reading is at best momentary and supplemental to other, more objective engagements—even if he also insists that no reading is complete without the complementary inclusion of this magical dimension.

Hesse's essay thus comes rather unreservedly to celebrate this mode of magic reading, ultimately extending it to embrace the world at large and infusing it as an essential feature of even everyday experience. His novel, however, poses an additional, more troubling perspective, one unbroached by the essay but nonetheless anticipated in its second mode of reading, the one that recognizes a broader, binding context that accompanies and encompasses this seemingly free play of the reading subject. That is, in the novel, Haller is led to divine the many affinities and sympathies between the magical thinking embraced by him in its psychological and aesthetic modalities and vehemently rejected by him in the popular culture and mass political movements of his day. And that uneasy, disturbing link between the psychological, aesthetical subject and his social, political *Umwelt* looms as an ineradicable factor affecting any and every consideration of this newly modern, magical order of experience.

Although unusually formulaic in his presentations, Hesse was by no means alone in his preoccupation with magic and magical thinking during the modernist period. Indeed, the overt irruption of the magical, in ancient as well as new forms and in both art and the world, is one of the key features often thought to distinguish modernism from realism, and even the most major figures of high modernism made it one of their central concerns.[3] Among the most important of these was Sigmund Freud, whose influence on Hesse's reading model is explicitly stated in the essay, and whose concepts of wish fulfillment, dream signs, and a hidden other realm of forces beyond the conscious or intentional represent some of the most dominant forms that the ancient tradition of magic, symbols, and their divination take in the modernist world, and so, too, some of the most powerful factors displacing the realist models of the preceding century. Freud himself, spurred by his studies not only of childhood and dreams but also of classical, romantic, and realist literature, eventually connected his psychoanalytic interpretations of the world back with the more ancient magical traditions being rediscovered by E. B. Tylor and James Frazer at the end of the nineteenth century, even as, in a more contemporary context, he was moved to consider the modern occult phenomenon of telepathy and the archaic forces animating the mass politics of his moment.[4] Although unlike Hesse (or for that matter Jung, ultimately the more profound influence on Hesse) Freud tended to understand psychology—including its mode of reading (*deuten*)—as a counterforce to magical thinking and not just its resurrection, he too was profoundly aware of the ambivalence toward the new world order his work had helped create. Certainly no study of magic reading and modernism, including this one, can overlook Freud, even if it chooses not to focus on him.

For again, he was by no means alone, nor was psychology the only sphere in which this new old world was emerging. So, for example, in *The Wasteland* (1922), T. S. Eliot also melded together the modernist world with Frazer's magical one, apparently quite independently of Freud, reflecting instead tendencies in vitalist philosophy and Christian theology. And part of this melding included the divinatory readings that formed part of both its archaic and the popular spheres, readings both derided at the surface and deeply engaged by the allusive associational and symboled aesthetics of the poem itself.[5] And such readings return in much more troubled tones during the much more troubled times of *Four Quartets* (1941), where Eliot also links them to psychoanalysis itself—not as the counter to magical thinking, but as one of its symptomatically modern forms:

> To communicate with Mars, converse with spirits, [. . .]
> Describe the horoscope, haruspicate or scry,
> Observe disease in signatures, evoke
> Biography from the wrinkles of the palm
> And tragedy from the fingers; release omens
> By sortilege, or tea leaves, riddle the inevitable
> With playing cards, fiddle with pentagrams
> Or barbituric acids, or dissect
> The recurrent image into pre-conscious terrors—
> To explore the womb, or tomb, or dreams; all these are usual
> Pastimes and drugs, and features of the press:
> And always will be, some of them especially
> When there is distress of nations and perplexity
> Whether on the shores of Asia, or in the Edgeware Road.
> Men's curiosity searches past and future
> And clings to that dimension.[6]

These closing lines occur in the context of the poem's own deep meditations on the convoluted intricacies of time ("Time present and time past / Are both perhaps present in time future / And time future contained in time past"), a concern that comes more and more to dominate modernism and that, we've seen, has always been behind divinatory reading.[7] Moreover, the pressing desire for release from the strictures of present historical time that Eliot suggests drives such magic thinking is also, of course, behind his own reflections: it is just that, in what might prove a signature modernist move, he seems to shut off the future as the place where such redemption might be found—looking instead to a "point of intersection of the timeless / With time," much as Hesse does in *The Steppenwolf* with the realm of the "Immortals" from which the "Treatise" apparently emanates.

And then, of course, there is Thomas Mann. *The Magic Mountain* appears in 1924, with its own radical rethinking of temporality in both thematic and formal terms. *Mario and the Magician* of 1929 explicitly explores the links between magic and the rising movement of fascism, while also implicating Mann's own art in the equation. Certainly we know that Mann had a keen interest in the occult movements of the Weimar period as well as a penchant throughout his life for signing his correspondence as "The Magician" (Der Zauberer) (even as Hesse signed as "Klingsor"). And he wrote his late, great novel, *Dr. Faustus* (1947), in such a manner as to equate early modern magic and modernist aesthetics, and both with fascist politics—and he did so by employing a *Technik* of his own that relied almost exclusively on the effects of analogy, sympathy, contiguity, and likeness among objects, events, times, and beings to establish its serial chains of significance, in ways that by default and design required magic reading (albeit of a far different kind than we find in Hesse).[8] This novel, too, struggles not only with the attractions and repulsions of magical modes, but also with its stubborn desires for redemption in the face of its equally stubborn refusal of the future as the site of their possible fulfillment.

Obviously, this list could be almost endlessly extended (Proust's magic lantern and correspondences! The surrealists' found objects! Even Hesse's own *Glass Bead Game*)—which is part of the point. But among all those who focused on the connections between the ancient and early modern traditions of magic and the new modernist milieu, on the convolutions of time and the inescapable weight of the present historical moment that made the equation of release and the future so problematic, and on links between the psychological and aesthetic subjects and the mass political and cultural context—among all those, perhaps no one was so concerned to understand the continuance of ancient practices in modern magic *reading* as Walter Benjamin—far more so than even Hesse, whose explicit interests in this topic were still restricted to contemporary models. And there are two additonal reasons why Benjamin proves singularly exemplary for our purposes. Both have to do with the fact that he is profoundly concerned with the connections of modernism not only to the ancient world (what he called primal history or *Urgeschichte*) but also to the world of the century just past, the nineteenth century, which has been our focus so far. For this

reason, we find him engaging with two of those strains of magic
we noted as lingering out of the nineteenth century and finding new
life in the early twentieth: the overt concerns with language and
with a vital natural world—a thing world—beyond language, with
a sympathetic world order reconceived to support the divinatory
reading of the modernist period.[9]

Divining Benjamin

That Walter Benjamin was preoccupied with issues of magic and
divination is clear. These figure prominently in his works, from the
first paragraph of one of his earliest publications, "Fate and Character" (Schicksal und Charakter, 1919), to the last section of one
of his last pieces, "On the Concept of History" (Über den Begriff
der Geschichte, 1940). But the exact nature of that preoccupation
is not as clear, even if it does seem remarkably consistent; indeed,
as is characteristic of Benjamin's thought in so many other respects
as well, the complexity of his position is not so much a matter of
change or development as it is of an intricate mode of negation and
affirmation that was there from the start.[10] On the one hand, there
is an undeniable suspicion, even rejection, of divination and "predicting the future" that runs throughout his work. We see it already
in "Fate and Character," but it is even more evident in pieces such
as "Light from Obscurantists" (Erleuchtung durch Dünkelmänner), his review of Hans Liebenstoeckl's *The Occult Sciences in the
Light of Our Age* (*Die Geheimwissenschaften im Lichte unserer
Zeit*, 1932), or his essay "Experience and Poverty" (Erfahrung und
Armut, 1933). Here, Benjamin unequivocally attacks what he calls
the "stupidity, low cunning, and coarseness" of the contemporary
modes of magical divination, "the last pitiful by-product of more
significant traditions," and he seems explicitly to include in his critique of magic and fortune- or future-telling the misguided "hunger
of broad sections of the people for happiness (*Glückshunger*)."[11]
The resistance to magical thinking is obviously of a piece with
his principled distaste for the tenets of *Lebensphilosophie*; for the
phantasmagoria of commodity culture; the emergence of fascism

with its "magic of blood and glitter"; and eventually, too, for that form of Marxism that divined future happiness in the fated progress of social history.[12] In all this, Benjamin could be said to share (along with Freud, Eliot, and Mann) in the skeptical, disenchanted enlightenment stance that gained such increased urgency amid the resurgent "barbarism" of the early to mid-twentieth century.[13] And added to this secular tradition, there was also a religious ground supporting Benjamin's suspicions of divination as well. As he reminds us at the end of "On the Concept of History," "Jews were prohibited from inquiring into the future," and while this ban on future knowing is perhaps most fully explored in the context of his famous essay on Kafka, it seems safe to say that "No Future" is an injunction implicitly guiding much of his thought.[14]

On the other hand, many of the most traditional and defining features of magic reading repeatedly reappear as central elements of Benjamin's thought, and are often explicitly identified with the practices of divination, and with reading as divination—and often enough in the very same essays that critique it. As I hope to show, alongside Benjamin's emphatic rejection of occult magic and its divinatory impulses there is an equally emphatic investment in precisely the magical traditions and divinatory practices we have traced from antiquity through the early modern period into romanticism and from there into realism. For this reason it seems more accurate to claim not that Benjamin is committed to the disenchantment of magic reading in his work, but that he is intent on clearing space for reapproaching and reasserting its truths. Not, then, to refute magic reading and assign it to some long-lost past but, in however "weak" a form, to redeem it and its future promise. And as we will see, to do so involves reimagining not only divination, but also the temporal, natural, and representational orders on which it has long depended.

Fate

As mentioned, Benjamin's preoccupation with divination is evident already in "Fate and Character," and some of the features that will shape his thinking on the topic throughout his writings are first formulated in this early essay, which strives to develop a concept of fate (*Schicksal*) that embraces both ancient Greek beliefs and modern fortune-telling of the most vulgar, popular kind (especially card- and palm-reading).[15] Crucially, Benjamin begins by posing the problem of fate as a matter of reading, and in particular as a matter of reading to predict the future (*die Zukunft herauszusagen*); and although he emphasizes right from the outset that such a reading practice is all but inconceivable for his contemporaries—and even that, in principle, he shares in the common critique and remains even more cautious than most about the idea of the future—he also sets out to show how the idea of such a reading is not nonsensical and how access to future fate need not exceed human powers of perception.[16] He bases his argument on a consideration of the relation between fate and signs—again, very much in keeping with approaching the problem in terms of reading. Fate, he says, like character, can only be apprehended through signs, not in itself, and such signs have a particular nature with particular features. First, the what they signify is always hidden, invisible, situated outside the immediately visible—in a realm, he says, that is not "present" (*gegenwärtig*) even if "there" (zur Stelle).[17] Second, what makes these signs signs, what determines their sign quality, is that they signify a relationship or connection (*Zusammenhang*) between this other realm (this fate) and the given subject: it is this connection that the signs signify. Benjamin insists that the relation or connection between the sign and signified cannot, strictly speaking, be considered a causal one, at least not in any simple sense of causality, and this is what makes determining the nature of these signs and of this connection so difficult—and has him decline in this early essay fully to explore what such a sign system might be like.[18] But he does provide an analysis of two key features: things and time.

First, he notes that all apparent phenomena (*Erscheinungen*) of external life, in addition to that primary site of the human body, can become signs of fate, of this hidden world and connection. This is in keeping with his insistence that between the active man and the external world all is interaction, their spheres interpenetrate, such that the idea of a discrete individual "character" as the defining core of man—or of man's relationship to the world—must give way to a far more porous boundary between the given subject and external world, to a connection in fact that surreptitiously binds him to all of life, natural life, or rather, binds him to the unseen world that determines both him and the external world and produces signs.[19] Benjamin defines this interpenetrating connection as based on guilt or debt, as a *Schuldzusammenhang*, although he also hedges on the implicit religious context and more straightforwardly calls it a natural life in man (*ein natürliches Leben im Menschen*).[20] It is this well-nigh ontological connection to everything— to what he also calls bare life (*das bloße Leben*)—that allows the clairvoyant to connect the subject's fate to cards, hand-lines or planets, sign-things that, simply by making the connection, make it visible—connect it.[21]

Second, Benjamin notes that the signs that make this connection— noncausal but binding, and unseen even if bound to everything visible—exist in a peculiar temporal modality. It is, he says, a very different kind of time, and "the complete elucidation of these matters depends on determining the particular nature of time in fate."[22] Adumbrating some of his later claims about messianic time (and recalling as well both Hesse and Eliot), he declares, "The fortune-teller who uses cards and the seer who reads palms teach us at least that this time can at every moment be made simultaneous with another (not present)."[23] It is not, he adds, an autonomous time, any more than its signs are autonomous, but parasitically dependent on another time (human, historical, sequential); it is a time that has no present and knows past and future only as particular (*eigentümlich*) variations.[24] And it is precisely the peculiar temporal dimension to the hidden world of fate and its intersection with a given moment in the inquiring subject's time world that informs and determines its signs, a temporality that both cuts against simple, causally conceived notions of a "future" and nonetheless keeps divinatory practices eminently viable.[25]

There is one additional issue raised in this early essay that is identified as essential but also left open: the question of happiness, fortune, or *Glück*. Benjamin poses the issue as a series of questions, asking: Has fate any relation (*Beziehung*) to *Glück*? Is *Glück* a constitutive category of fate?[26] His immediate response, much as with the question of predicting the future, seems to be no. But as in the case of predicting the future, the negative response might well be more about the limits of the present framework for posing the question—here the religious framework that interprets natural life as *Schuldzusammenhang*—than about the answer itself.[27] In any case, the link between the two questions—of *Glück* and of the future—is hardly a chance one for Benjamin, nor is the matter of his apparent ambivalence about both. These two issues, both singly and joined, will reappear repeatedly in Benjamin's thinking as points of contention, and remain central to his thoughts about reading.

Graphology

After this early essay, there are three more or less separate spheres in which the still early Benjamin pursues and elaborates his investigations into magic reading, each of which provides essential background for his most comprehensive reflections on the topic in the late essays "The Doctrine of the Similar" (Lehre vom Ähnlichen) and "The Mimetic Faculty" (Über das mimetische Vermögen), to which we will eventually turn.[28] These three precursor spheres are graphology, gambling, and childhood, and Benjamin approaches each as a modern avatar of more ancient traditions of magic and divination, and each as a site for a peculiar mode of magic reading and experience.

As a specialized mode of reading language, graphology is usually considered an invention of the nineteenth century, beginning in France with the work of Michon and Crépieux-Jamin and then migrating to Germany, where the *Lebensphilosoph* Ludwig Klages had a major impact on its development.[29] It was meant to be practiced by trained professionals, though well-read and gifted amateurs such as Benjamin himself could venture readings as well: the practitioner was to be guided by fixed points of reference in the script (direction, size, spacing, pressure, speed, etc.) with set meanings, but also by an intuitive sensitivity to the overall context and specific occasion of the writing.[30] For all the emphasis on its modernity and scientific basis, graphology thus still betrays its affinities with earlier traditions of magic reading such as entrail reading, not least through its purported scientificity and openness to the occasion; and for all Benjamin's emphasis on distinguishing its "genuine" tenets from its popular and vulgar or dogmatically vitalistic strains, the mode of graphology in which he was most invested was equally distinct from rational empirical approaches (influenced by Wilhelm Wundt et al.), and still devoted to addressing "the integral riddle of mankind."[31]

In reading, graphology attends to a form of meaning to written words that is ancillary to their semantic content; it seeks to read another, differently present realm of significance by decomposing words into the materiality and activity of their letters, even parts of letters; these are then construed as what Benjamin calls a set of hieroglyphs that, like allegories, function according to a differently ordered logic from that ruling their immediate, ordinary content and meaning.[32] That is, words are approached as signs of a different or additional kind from ordinary linguistic signs; this difference pertains at the level of both signifier and signified—and at the level of the connection between them, which is also established in different ways from ordinary language.

With respect to the signifier, graphology approaches words and letters as things, sign-things that convey something otherwise hidden, a meaning more or less unaffected by conscious intellection or intent—and therein lies both their status and their privilege as signs. Benjamin calls these sign-things images, and insists they are part of the visible world (although also, we'll see, with extensions into the invisible).[33] But he also describes them as natural, well-nigh animate things. He does so in part because he rejects the sign theory or *Zeichenlehre* of the French school that maintained a straightforward connection between image-sign and signified (e.g., cramped letters, cramped character), but that also and above all held to a monosemantic and *static* sense of signs. In this respect at least, Klages is privileged for his emphasis on the essential importance of *movement* for the sign-nature of script: it is only in the context of movement, the bodily material force of handwriting—which not incidentally introduces temporality into the line of writing, making it an essentially temporal space or realm—that the signs of script's "other" language, the one beyond intention, become manifest and fix their otherwise open, polysemic meaning in an associational chain.[34] (Robert Saudek will emphasize the special importance of speed to this movement, a factor that will become important to us later on.)

Movement only partly explains why the image-signs of language are described as animate things. It is also partly something more than this, something intimately connected to the materiality of these image-signs—and not only as the result of the bodily material movement on the (human) writer's part, but as bodily entities in their own right. Language, Benjamin says, has a body, and graphology is concerned with this bodily aspect of language, and he illustrates what he means by this with a "most revealing and appropriate" comparison between children's drawings and handwriting, wherein letters behave "just as their models—people, animals, and objects"—with tails and legs, heads, eyes, and mouths, and wherein reading them graphologically is a matter of transforming letters back into their bodily representations (*in körperliche Darstellungen zurückverwandel[n]*).[35] To some extent, this is about projecting the human condition onto externalized objects and animating them with a life or formative force that is not their own, and so reading them graphologically as a matter of transforming them back into human representations (more anon).[36] But to an equal and equally important extent, this is also about the direct, inherent connection of material words, qua things, with the material world, the thing world (*die Dingwelt*) and hence natural world, and reading them as transforming them back into the representations that body forth that world, that life, and writing's connection to it. Both of these readings—and the reference to children (as avatars of earlier times) suggests it—are of course very much in keeping with the ancient divinatory practice of reading animals themselves as animate signs, and of treating words in texts in the same way as animal-signs, even as themselves animate, natural signs (as what the ancients called "characters"); and it helps give added force to Benjamin's stress on reading the swoops of hand strokes—"right and left, top and bottom, straight and sloping"—like so many bird movements read by an augur.[37] In any case, in graphology as in ancient divination, the signs to be read are visual, moving objects—in this case words and letters—that operate apart from rational interference and from their normal significance and context; that function as animate signs—even as animals—implicitly grounded in a natural, bodily world; and precisely because they bypass the realm of human intent and participate instead in a subhuman, creaturely, non-(self-)conscious realm, they are privileged signifiers for knowledge about the human.

With respect to the signified, and in keeping with their designation as hieroglyphs, Benjamin again insists that words and letters do not behave as ordinary signs and do not convey ordinary, exclusively "human," much less conscious, meaning. In this context, he objects both to the French school, "whose proponents linked qualities of character to quite specific written signs," and to Klages, who "interprets handwriting basically as . . . expressive movement (*Ausdrucksbewegung*)."[38] In each case, his objection seems to be that they refer far too directly and exclusively to a characterological realm of meaning, which is to say, to a discretely human, individual, and ego-centered realm or core. This mistaken reading of handwriting as signs of character is the same error foregrounded (and sidelined) by Benjamin with respect to the signs of fate in "Fate and Character," in which he also faulted modern physiognomy—the practice of directly reading the body as sign—for the same misguided focus.[39] In each case, Benjamin is intent on rejecting a strictly individual and merely human contextualization and one that appeals primarily to known, present features of that individual.

Against the sign theories and readings of the French and Klages, Benjamin poses those of Anja and Georg Mendelssohn, who first institutionalized graphology in German universities. Their readings, he says, create a space for an ideographic interpretation of handwriting, "a graphology that interprets script in terms of the unconscious graphic elements, the unconscious image fantasies, that it contains."[40] As he will put it later with specific reference to "this magic aspect of language" (*diese magische Seite der Sprache*), their graphology teaches us "to recognize, in handwriting, images—or more precisely, picture puzzles (*Vexierbilder*)—that the unconscious of the writer conceals in his writing."[41] As the references to images as fantasies, to *Vexierbilder*, and to the unconscious all make clear, and as Benjamin explicitly declares, the Mendelssohns' sign theory and the "concealed" realm their images signify point to Freud's concepts of wish fulfillment, dream signs, and a hidden other realm of forces beyond the conscious or intentional. But for all the affinities to be explored between Freud and Benjamin with respect to magic reading, and for all the affirmation of Freud implicit in Benjamin's positive review of the Mendelssohns' work, Benjamin's position is still somewhat different from Freud's and the Mendelssohns', and in ways that, I believe, reveal his even stronger ties to the more ancient traditions of *sympatheia*.

The differences between Benjamin and the Freudians can be glimpsed most clearly in Benjamin's designating the "other" realm signified by the "other" dimension of handwriting not as the unconscious but as the body.[42] That is, Benjamin says not only that language has a body—even, we saw, an animality—but that the body has a language, and graphology explores both the bodily aspect of the language of handwriting and the "speaking" aspect of the body in handwriting (*was an der Sprache der Handschrift das Leibhafte, am Leibe der Handschrift das Sprechende ist*).[43] For Benjamin it is the body of the given subject that is projected on, speaks through, and is connected to the body representations of script, a natural, indeed physical and material connection that underwrites the "magical" correspondences between the two. As in "Fate and Character," the connections that although unseen bind the embodied subject to, and are made visible by, these sign-things are evidence of their common ground in a not-specifically human natural world—hence the shared basis of the twin sources for the natural, creaturely life of script, in the human subject and the material letters alike. It is just this hidden connection and correspondence, this common and shared ground, that on the one hand determines that the relation between the signifier and signified in the given word is not the arbitrary one of ordinary language and its ordinary semantic and cognitive modes, and is instead a well-nigh ontological relation—and herein crucially different from Freudian dream language—with its human projections always also natural connections; and on the other hand determines that the truth or fate signaled in and through script is not revealing of a discrete individual character but of a necessarily open relation, or participation, of each subject with the external physical world, including the natural materiality of words.

This, too, is part of Benjamin's distance both from the French school and Klages and from Freud, who not only overlooks the creaturely body in favor of the human unconscious but whose primary analyses also focus on individual character, even if unconscious. But Benjamin's position here remains much closer to that in "Fate and Character," when he claims that individual characters do not have a fate, or rather that the signs of fate do not pertain to individual character but only to a natural life in him—the same position he adopts regarding the signs of physiognomy, and a position also, of course, much closer to that of the ancient traditions, perhaps especially to that of the Neoplatonists.[44] This is emphatically manifest in Benjamin's closing thoughts in his main essay on graphology, which push the points of deindividualization and depsychologization and, instead, worldly connection, and do so in a language deliberately evocative of the magic, allegorical reading modes of the early modern world—which was already implicit in Benjamin's referring to words and letters in the first place not as dream images or even picture puzzles but as hieroglyphs, a word whose association for Benjamin with the allegorical traditions of the baroque can be traced back to his *Trauerspiel* book. In his final sentences, Benjamin challenges modern graphologists to consider not comparing different individual examples to prove discrete individualized identities, but to refer instead simply to a single sample of handwriting (*eine einzige Handschrift*), and declares, "Anyone able to share in this way of seeing would be able to take any scrap of paper covered with writing and discover in it a free ticket to the great *theatrum mundi* (*das große Welttheater*). It would reveal to him the pantomime of the entire nature and existence of mankind, in microcosmic form."[45]

Clearly, in positing this almost mystical connection or participation, this magical correspondence between the body-nature of man and of words—and by extension between man, language, and the great external world—Benjamin is approaching not only the sympathetic logic of earlier times, but also the *Lebensphilosophien* and occult sciences of his own, precisely those positions he claims to find intolerable.[46] And this seeming ambivalence is even more evident in those moments where his explication of graphology comes closest to those concerns most associated with magic reading: prediction and clairvoyance or telepathy.[47] On the one hand, Benjamin seems rather forcefully to deny any straightforward predictive power to graphology, especially when it comes to divining any future individual action or fate—indeed, he seems to suggest an ethical imperative against such reading.[48] But it is worth noting two points. First, that his reason for this restriction echoes the language he used in "Fate and Character" to describe the peculiar temporality of fate that likewise complicated its divinatory dimension: all possible actions and outcomes, he says, are essentially preexistent potentialities that remain hidden and unrealized and emerge into conscious realization only at the moment of chance intersection with a concrete specific occasion.[49] And second, although Benjamin doesn't foreground this point, the future does play a crucial role in the graphologist's reading of the signs, the moving line of writing itself, serving as a directional space toward which all script tends, and keeping open and then finally fixing the meaning, the sign-quality, of the hand strokes themselves—which without that implicit futurity and until that future moment remain hidden, unrealized, unknown. Graphology might not be required to read signs of the future, but it does require a future to read the signs at hand.

On the other hand, for all his reluctance regarding prediction, Benjamin seems quite willing to grant both clairvoyance and telepathy a place in graphological reading. He describes what he calls a "cubic" graphology, which sees beyond the only apparently two-dimensional surface of writing into an invisible realm both behind and before the visible material plane, a realm into which the visual script-signs extend in "immaterial curves," and he asks, "Could the cubic pictorial space of script be a copy in microcosm of a clairvoyant space (*ein mikrokosmisches Abbild des Erscheinungs-raumes der Hellsicht*)?" And he predicts "that one day it may be possible to exploit graphology to investigate telepathic events."[50] (We could speculate that this three-dimensionality brings out or accentuates the body-nature of script, but this would require our-selves to enter an immaterial and clairvoyant space.) What we see, then, in Benjamin's description of graphology that connects it back to earlier traditions of magic reading is this: it approaches words as conveying an ancillary mode of signification attendant on their ordinary, intended, and differently present meaning, where signs speak of a cognitive mode distinct from rational consciousness and point instead to another hidden world both inside and around us; that this world that animates signs—and so makes them signs—is in essential ways a natural, even animal one that connects man to language in ways that bypass the most exclusively human dimen-sion of the world, recognizing or realizing both as linked in invis-ible but fully natural ways; and that, precisely in this nonhuman and invisible form, the magic reading of script makes visible in micro-cosmic form the very nature of "the integral riddle of mankind" and its relation to the great external world or *Welttheater*. And we note how different this is from the case in Keller, where signs come between man and the natural world and are not a part of it, or from Fontane, where language remains exclusively a human so-cial affair, connecting men only to each other and not to nature, or even from Hesse, for whom the scrap of paper might well open up a great and magic theater, but one more or less only of the internal unconscious, not of the nonhuman external world.

Gambling

The two major elements of ancient magic reading that were also adumbrated in "Fate and Character" but play only an implicit role in the discussion of graphology are front and center in Benjamin's musings on gambling, namely, the elements of time, including the matters of both occasionality and futurity, and of *Glück*, includ-ing the matters of both chance and fortune, happenstance and happiness. As we noted in the previous chapter, on Fontane, E. B. Tylor specifically singled out sports and games of chance as one of the last remaining refuges for magic thinking in the modern world, supplementing Foucault's singular focus on literature. And as with Fontane, Benjamin's interest in such gaming is primarily (if not exclusively) concentrated on its magic thinking, which he explicitly identifies as a mode of reading and a form of divination—although in radical contrast with Fontane, such games and their reading are decidedly anti-social, focused on the isolated individual and his relation not to other humans but, we'll see, again to a nonhuman realm.[51] In any case, the interest in gaming links some of Benjamin's earliest work in a chain extending all the way to the *Arcades Project* (*Passagen-Werk*), and proves a somewhat surprising nodal point connecting some of his most crucial ideas about reading— and not only about reading.

Although in the *Arcades Project* Benjamin describes playing cards as modern remnants of more ancient fortune-telling cards, and card play itself as a "pejoration of ancient divinatory technique," insisting that "seeing the future is certainly crucial in card games, too," the primary example of gambling in his works is not cards but roulette and its particular mode of reading the table (*das Brett lesen*).[52] As we might expect from the previous examples of reading fate and handwriting, this reading is primarily performed by the player's body, what in this case Benjamin calls motor innervation "emancipated" from the interfering (but also present) promptings of rational waking consciousness (*rationale Wachbewußtsein*).[53] Motor innervation is to be understood not in terms of a discrete subject (i.e., as the communication between a brain and nerves) but rather as a special connection between the player and the table, what Benjamin calls a telepathic contact (*ein Kontakt telepathischer Art*).[54] Crucially, this telepathic contact, which allows the successful or *glücklich* player to divine the winning number, is between him and the ball—the rolling ball—and not between the player and the croupier who puts the ball in motion: the telepathic sympathetic link is not with the human world but with that of things, animated moving things.[55] Indeed, just as with the promptings of his own rational consciousness (his own self), the player

must fend off or parry the interfering, "hostile suggestions" generated by his human environment in order to remain open to the
communication of the object world and its winning number—or,
as Benjamin also puts it, to contact with the realm of fate where
all the winning numbers already are.[56] In fact, Benjamin supposes
that this human world, and more especially his own rational consciousness, are what keep the realm of winning numbers hidden
(*versteckt*) to the player: at the level of bodily sympathetic contact
at least, every winning number is known in advance, and it is only
when the player proceeds intelligently that he becomes blocked
from this advance knowledge.[57]

The distinction that Benjamin insists on between the promptings of consciousness and those of the body (or metonymically, the
hand) are familiar to us, both from what we already know from
Benjamin—in what he says about reading fate and handwriting,
but also what he says elsewhere about consciousness and trauma,
or consciousness and *Erfahrung*—and what we know from ancient divination and the reading practices derived from it.[58] But the
distinction is also at the basis of another, less familiar distinction
Benjamin draws, one crucial to deciphering his particular take on
divination and its relation to the future. He addresses this point not
only in his works on gambling, but also in one of his most explicit
and extended pieces on divination, the section "Madame Ariane"
from *One-Way Street* (*Einbahnstraße*): both are crucial to his notion of magic reading. In his works on gambling, Benjamin claims
that when a winning number is clearly predicted (*klar vorherge-
sehen*) but not bet on (*besetzt*), the genuine gambler will recognize
that he must stop playing: "For it is a sign that the contact between
his motor innervation and 'fate' has been interrupted. Only then
will 'what is to come' (*das Kommende*) enter into his consciousness
more or less clearly as what it is."[59] In "Madame Ariane," Benjamin declares that "omens, presentiments, signals pass day and
night through our organism like wave impulses. To interpret them
or use them: that is the question. The two are irreconcilable. If we
fail to [act and so use the omen, then] and only then the message
is deciphered. But now it is too late."[60] In both examples, a particular temporal gap based on a broken physical (albeit invisible)

connection has created a distinction within divination itself, one in which the telepathic reading of signs qua omens and consciously knowing what is to come (the future) are indeed acknowledged as legitimate possibilities, but only in a context in which the latter is no longer useful or timely.[61]

Against such reading qua future-telling, Benjamin poses a form of divination based on what he calls presence of mind, or, more precisely, bodily presence of mind (*leibhafte Geistesgegenwart*)— insisting once again on the body as the first, most ancient, and most reliable instrument of divination.[62] Crucially for us, he still insists that this presence of mind partakes of the future, is, he says, its extract: it still represents an inner intimation of what is to come (*eine innere Kunde vom Kommenden*).[63] It is just, I suspect, that it represents a different kind of knowing from that based on (belated) consciousness, and a different kind of "future" from that based on sequential temporality—very much as with the different kind of temporality first broached in "Fate and Character," one that aims to make this time simultaneous with another (not present).[64]

By reintroducing the issue of temporality to magic reading— both the idea of futurity and that of the difficult coordination or intersection of two different temporal dimensions—Benjamin also reintroduces the issue of occasionality and, with it, that of happiness as well. He notes that the genuine gambler (*der echte Spieler*) places his most important and usually successful bets at the last possible moment (*im letzten Augenblick*), for "it is only at the last moment, when everything is pressing toward a conclusion, at the critical moment of danger (of missing his chance)," that the ability to "read the table" shows up (*sich einfindet*).[65] This *Zeitmoment*, this sense that there is but one specific instance in which the true signs (the winning number) appear to the player and become legible, unhidden, present, is dependent on two factors: danger (I want to say, hazard) and acceleration.[66] The former, of course, is familiar to readers of Benjamin, adumbrating as it does the more famous formulations of the "Concept of History" essay and recalling that already mentioned in "Fate and Character": the particular danger that threatens the player lies in the fateful (*schicksalhaft*) category of arriving too late, of having missed the chance: it speaks

to Benjamin's well-known belief about the historical/temporal conditions for a moment from another time—whether of the past or
the messianic/divine—to be grasped in the present, as a present
with future force. But the latter factor, acceleration or *Beschleuni-
gung*, is less familiar, although just as central to Benjamin's concept
of both gambling and magic reading per se.[67] Benjamin says that
gambling produces the lightning-quick process of innervation at
the moment of danger—a process we will later see him explicitly
compare with the tempo, swiftness, and rapidity of reading (and
writing: handwriting)—that shuts down or outpaces the processes
of rational consciousness and its ordinary, progressive temporality,
and so creates the occasion for the unimpeded openness to telepathic contact or sympathetic connection with the nonhuman object world, its communication, and its other temporality (its other
meaning).[68] Acceleration, we might say, inflects the nowness, the occasion of the present moment, with a kind of future thrust, and in
such a way as to produce the borderline case (*Grenzfall*) in which
presence of mind becomes divination—which Benjamin calls one
of the highest, rarest moments in life (*in dem Geistesgegenwart zur
Divination wird, also einen der höchsten, seltensten Augenblicke
des Lebens*).[69] The gambler's reading, then, of this "hidden" (*versteckt*) world of signs is dependent not only on an open boundary
between himself and the nonhuman world, freed from the promptings of the rational human world, but also on a particular occasion
that alone opens up that boundary and provides that freedom—an
occasion itself dependent on an accelerated temporality to transform its mere presence into magic divination.[70]

In calling the moment of divinatory reading one of the highest
and rarest in life, Benjamin underscores what is at stake for the
gambler qua reader: happiness or *Glück*. And in doing so, he returns us not only to one of the defining conditions for magic reading in the ancient world—or for that matter, in Fontane's sociable
moment, and even, too, that happy moment of *Stimmung* in Keller
that has Heinrich rejoice at Anna's coffin—but also to the question
he himself left open in "Fate and Character" and returns to repeatedly in his own work (and not only, but also, in the context of
reading). In the earlier essay, Benjamin wondered whether *Glück*

had any relation or *Beziehung* to fate, and seemed to suggest that the answer was no: *Glück* was about being fateless, freed from the *Schuldzusammenhang* of the creaturely connection to natural life. Here his answer seems somewhat different, though he retains the same basic terms and does not really abandon his earlier position, either. Here, Benjamin focuses on the *Glück* and *Glücksgefühl* of the successful gambler, whose happiness and fortune result from the sense "of being rewarded by fate, of having grasped it, and being embraced by it."[71] The loser, on the other hand, is someone who has lost his relation or contact with fate, who has (fatefully) missed the chance, the singular occasion, for realizing *Glück*. To be sure—and returning more to the language and position of the early essay—Benjamin also stresses that once the game is over, the loser experiences a sense of release or relief (*Erleichterung*) at having somehow escaped fate, at having lost the connection, whereas the winner is burdened by the peril to which his success and happiness have exposed him at fate's hand.[72] As we will see directly, this failure on the part of the loser and his missed chance have a special place in Benjamin's thoughts, insofar as they can still hold out, in however weak a form, a promise of happiness redeemed, a future fulfillment that can reconcile his "irreconcilable" distinctions between immediately acting on omens and reading them belatedly, and so, too, between the fortunes of the winner and loser. But the emphasis here, in the context of gambling as a mode of divination, is certainly on the happiness in the moment itself, in all its power and peril; a happiness derived from divination and tied to a special, singular occasion, which is also to say, a mode of reading derived from the special connection between the player's present and the world of fate, mediated by animated moving things.

Childhood

The last of the three spheres in which Benjamin makes his early studies in magic reading is childhood. It is here that the affinity with Hesse's model of reading is most pronounced (and so it is hardly surprising that Hesse was so openly enamored with Benjamin's

writings on childhood).[73] And it is also here that, for many reasons, those early studies prove most important. First, because it is
in this sphere that Benjamin most directly addresses the practice
of reading not palms, cards, handwriting, or roulette tables, but
actual books. And he does so in a highly personal way, consistently approaching reading as an experience in which the self and
its happiness are equally at stake. Second, because like so many
of his contemporaries—and most notably Freud—Benjamin tends
to conflate ontogeny and phylogeny, and so to equate childhood
experience with that of primitive and ancient cultures. Hence,
many of his most direct investigations into the magical experience
(*magische Erfahrung*) that he claims binds together ancient cognitive modes with modern times focus in the first place on the child.[74]

Third, because it is here that, for the first time, Benjamin's notions of a natural, material, fateful, and telepathic connection or
contact between the human subject and the world of things come
to be formulated in terms of a logic of mimetic relation, linkage,
and exchange—a logic of resemblance and connection that secures
the strongest resemblances and ties between his take on magic
reading and the sympathetic world order that we have traced from
its earliest formulations through to the recent past of the late nineteenth century. That this order is once again the basis for divination and still grounded in Benjamin's focus on the body can be
seen in how he moves from calling the naked body the first and
most important instrument of divination to the body as the first
and most important site for the exercise of what he now calls the
(child's) mimetic faculty.[75] Once again, we will see the genealogy
of magic reading extending well into the modern era, and that of
Stimmung (qua *sympatheia*) extending well beyond isolated psy-
chologized subjectivity.[76]

But fourth, and in addition to these points that pertain to childhood itself, Benjamin's investigations into the magical experience
of the child are also always self-reflexively into the experience of
the memory of that experience—into the reading of that past—
and this is itself important in at least two ways. Most significantly,
the focus on remembering childhood allows Benjamin, as it did so
many of his modernist contemporaries—including Proust, Freud,

and, in a slightly different manner, Eliot—to relocate and reintroduce the practices of divination into the one sphere left open by the otherwise accepted ban on future knowledge. Memory becomes a form of divination, wherein childhood experience, events, and objects are read not in, of, or for themselves but as omens of a future, which in the present can be either already past or itself the present with future force. Memories become, as it were, "prophecies projected backwards": childhood is approached as the same type of retrospective domain or medium as history or literature, with the same complex temporal schemata and dimensions that turn all such reading into divination, a trafficking at once with the dead and the future alongside the engagement with the original time of the remembered, encountered moment itself.[77]

Two passages from Benjamin's works describe this backward-looking divination in particularly eloquent fashion. One addresses images, the other sounds; one is concerned with the childhood of photography, the other with the childhood of the author himself. The first comes in "Little History of Photography" (Kleine Geschichte der Photographie), in a meditation on an early photograph of Karl Dauthendey and his fiancée, who later committed suicide:

> He seems to be holding her, but her gaze passes him by, absorbed in an ominous distance. Immerse yourself in such a picture long enough and you will realize to what extent opposites touch here, too: the most precise technology can give its products a magical value. . . . The beholder feels an irresistible urge to search out such a picture for the tiny spark of contingency, of the here and now, with which reality has, so to speak, seared the subject, to find the inconspicuous spot where in the immediacy of that long-forgotten moment the future nests so eloquently that we, looking back, may discover it.

> Sie ist hier neben ihm zu sehen, er scheint sie zu halten; ihr Blick aber geht an ihm vorüber, saugend an eine unheilvolle Ferne geheftet. Hat man sich lange genug in so ein Bild vertieft, erkennt man, wie sehr auch hier die Gegensätze sich berühren: die exakteste Technik kann ihren Hervorbringungen einen magischen Wert geben. . . . Der Beschauer [fühlt] unwiderstehlich den Zwang, in solchem Bild das winzige Fünkchen Zufall, Hier und Jetzt, zu suchen, mit dem die Wirklichkeit den Bildcharakter gleichsam durchgesengt hat, die unscheinbare Stelle zu finden, in

welcher, im Sosein jener längstvergangenen Minute das Künftige noch heut und so beredt nistet, daß wir, rückblickend, es entdecken können.[78]

Adumbrating in an almost uncanny way Roland Barthes's notion of the *punctum*, the passage also echoes the divinatory practices of old.[79] We have the initiating, participant desire or wish on the part of the present reader, the stress on the chance (*Zufall*) that opens up the possibility for the other communication to occur, and an equal stress on the present occasion (*Hier und Jetzt*) required for that opening, that communication with the dead; where that *punctum*, that tiny spark of contingency, is peculiarly charged with a future force that makes its reading divinatory—albeit a future and reading that do not extend into the future of the reader himself.

The future divined in this photographic image is, in fact, itself a past, what Barthes will call an anterior future; that at stake in the second passage has more of a presence—indeed a double presence that differently inflects its divination, even if still backward looking. The passage comes in *Berlin Childhood around 1900* (*Berliner Kindheit um Neunzehnhundert*, 1934), in the section "News of a Death."[80] Benjamin is considering whether the phenomenon of déjà vu wouldn't better be spoken of in audial terms, as like an echo:

The shock with which a moment enters our consciousness as if already lived tends to strike us in the form of a sound. It is a word, a rustling or knocking, that is endowed with the power to call us unexpectedly into the cool sepulcher of the past, from whose vault the present seems to resound only as an echo. Strange that no-one has yet inquired into the counterpart of this transport—namely, the shock with which a word makes us pull up short, like a muff that someone has forgotten in our room. Just as the latter points us to a stranger who was on the premises, so there are words or pauses pointing us to that invisible stranger—the future—which forgot them at our place.

Der Chock, mit dem ein Augenblick als schon gelebt uns ins Bewußtsein tritt, [stößt] meist in Gestalt von einem Laut uns zu. Es ist ein Wort, ein Rauschen oder Pochen, dem die Gewalt verliehen ist, unvorbereitet uns in die kühle Gruft des Einst zu rufen, von deren Wölbung uns die Gegenwart nur als ein Echo scheint zurückzuhallen. Seltsam, daß man noch nicht dem Gegenbild dieser Entrückung nachgegangen ist—dem

Chock, mit dem ein Wort uns stutzen macht wie ein vergessener Muff in unserm Zimmer. Wie uns dieser auf eine Fremde schließen läßt, die da war, so gibt es Worte oder Pausen, die uns auf jene unsichtbare Fremde schließen lassen: die Zukunft, welche sie bei uns vergaß.[81]

Although still decisively a matter of retrospection, the divinatory experience here has a somewhat richer presence, enriched by the future twice over. On the one hand, the ominous moment sounding out from the past strikes its recipient in his present, and in being made present transforms that present into its own re-sounding future.[82] On the other hand, the past moment itself, in its own present, is charged with a sense of its own futurity. As Benjamin says of that remembered childhood moment, "I [took] special note that evening of my room and my bed, just as a person pays closer attention to a place when he has a presentiment . . . that one day he will have to retrieve something forgotten."[83] Admittedly, this presentiment is only fully realized later, retrospectively ("Only after many years did I learn what that something was"). But such is the characteristic paradox of this backward-looking form of divination: as Eliot will put it, "We had the experience but missed the meaning, / And approach to the meaning restores the experience / In a different form."[84]

There is a second, related way that this relocation of divination and of the future into the past (and especially, though not exclusively, the past of childhood) is important. Broadly speaking, it has to do with the redemption of that past, something found in Eliot as well. More narrowly, it has to do with the promised possibility of reconciling Benjamin's two irreconcilable distinctions between acting on and reading omens or presentiments, of reconciling those moments—the gambler's moments—of missed chances and failure with those other moments of success and fulfillment, and so, too, of reconciling the apparent contradiction opened up in the gambling essays about the happiness of the winner and loser, redeeming the latter's (past) miss in the former's (present) lucky hit. This is an aspect of backward-looking divination hinted at in Benjamin's recollection of the too-late arriving child (more anon), but it is most famously formulated in the second thesis of the late essay "On the Concept of History."[85]

Benjamin argues here that our idea of *Glück* is indissolubly bound up with the past, but the past understood as the missed chances of our lives: people we could have talked to, women who could have given themselves to us. Present happiness depends, as it were, on their redemption; on divining the past missed moment, now seen as charged with future promise—where the divining itself depends on the present wish for happiness as the demand made of the relation to the past. *Glück* depends on realizing the similarities that link together past and present moments in noncausal, transformative relation: "In the voices we hear, isn't there an echo of now silent ones? Don't the women we court have sisters they no longer recognize?" Our present *Glück* becomes their future fulfillment, a future and a fulfillment (a happiness) only possible because of the missed chance of the past, and a divinatory reading of that past based on the recognition of its future redemption. Which is to say, reading becomes a form of acting and of the future: the missed chance, the lost *Glück*, the past failure becomes the precondition for a divined and realized future—albeit a future that is now, in the present.

Elaborating further on the divinatory quality of memory in Benjamin threatens to take us too far afield from our immediate concern—or rather, too far ahead of our argument. What I want instead is to return to the points about childhood experience proper that are most indispensable to our topic, namely, those directly related to reading and earlier modes of magical thought, and then see how the features of memory just described reappear in this more defined context. I'll do so by concentrating on a few short sections from *One-Way Street* (1928), especially "Child Reading" (Lesendes Kind) and "Child Hiding" (Verstecktes Kind). These sketches incorporate some of Benjamin's earliest preoccupations with children and their relation to both books and the world of things: they form, too, the common ground for his later, far more extensive depictions of childhood in *Berlin Chronicle* (*Berliner Chronik*) and *Berlin Childhood*, as well as for the image of the child he (like Hesse) will evoke in other essays as the modern avatar of ancient magic.

Child Reading

"Child Reading" foregrounds two aspects of childhood reading that bespeak its magical dimension: the initiating demand and the sense of "mystical participation" that Miriam Hansen refers to as "mimetic blending."[86] The one-paragraph vignette describes the experience of a child in the lower classes of his schooling: it begins with the weekly distribution of books from the library, dispensed by seemingly invisible hands. Although the allotment itself appears governed by chance (or perhaps fate), it is accompanied by a wish on the part of the child, one that is often thwarted but on occasion "at last" granted: it then becomes attached to the essentially chance adventures of the presented (won) book and functions as the shaping force for the child's reading.[87] That reading is in crucial ways never quite the reading of the text itself; rather, the coincidence of his wishing self with the text opens up a realm of significance over and above the simple, generally available context of the text, a realm that can be read only by him—a modern variant of *biblicae sortes*.

As Benjamin says, the content of the book "did not much matter. For you were reading at the time when you still made up stories in bed. The child seeks his way along the half-hidden paths."[88] That is, the child seeks to read his own stories in or out of the text, a process that distorts and transforms its ordinary meaning content, which for this reason is "not so important." And he reads these stories not so much at the level of plot as in the swirl of letters (*im Wirbel der Lettern*) that function "like figures and messengers" from the enveloping text-world that covers him "like snowflakes."[89] This reading requires a porous boundary between the child and text: as much as its form of signification depends upon identification, it also requires a dissolving participation, or blending, that disperses the ordinary unity of the child-subject every bit as much as that of the book.[90] As Benjamin puts it, the child's breath becomes part of the air of the narrated events, and all the participants breathe it; the child is mingled (*gemischt*) with the characters.[91]

Clearly, this model of the child reading is, in both outline and detail, similar to both the earlier traditions of magic reading described in this study's general introduction and the version of Hesse's cited at the beginning of this chapter. But it also differs in subtle but significant ways from the latter (from Hesse), and in a fashion that aligns it more closely with the former (with the ancient traditions of *sympatheia*). The differences from Hesse can initially be glimpsed in the preceding paragraph, in how the child's reading is not only, or fully, a matter of projection onto the text, in which the text itself all but disappears, but is rather a more intrinsic matter of mutual relation and exchange (*Wechselwirkung*). Seemingly occupying an unmarked space between Hesse's second and third mode, Benjamin's child's reading is actually radically distinguished by being essentially nonpsychological in nature and, rather, based on an epistemology that is ontologically, metaphysically, and socially grounded in its understanding of both the subject and the thing world (*Dingwelt*), both the child and his book.

To fully understand Benjamin's model of the child's reading requires confronting his models of both the child's mode of cognition and the objects of its engagement—which is to say, both the child and children's books. In a series of early essays, Benjamin describes the child's distinct (but then linked) relations to color and form, and then similarly to pictures and words; and he describes the different kinds of books by which the child learns to read, is trained in the development and synthesis of his varied relations to the world of books, moving from colored to black-and-white picture books, and from ABC primers with personified, vocalizing, or figural letters to illustrated lexicons with words and pictures placed next to or substituting for each other—all leading up to the kind of adventure stories at the center of "Child Reading." The progressive, unfolding course of this book series constitutes at once the reading habits of the contemporary individual child and, more broadly, those of European culture itself from the early modern period through the nineteenth century (the heyday of children's literature) up to Benjamin's own modernist moment. And although

he continually stresses the singularity of the child's mode of reading, both his ontogenetic and phylogenetic models imply that the
reading experience of the modern adult is a complex compound
not only of loss but also of retained (or recovered) traces of that
earlier mode. Similarly, although he several times emphasizes that
children's books do not introduce children directly into the world
of objects, animals, and people, into so-called life, he does suggest
that they induce them, and so too adults, to perceive a world behind or beyond the ordinary apparent order (beyond the "blotchy
skin of things") that has its own claim, an even fuller claim, to being the world—or to completing the world, with its inclusion of the
magic side of things.[92]

We begin with the child's view of color and form and the picture books that are connected with it.[93] Benjamin argues that the
child's relations to color and to form are fundamentally distinct, a
circumstance often supported in early children's books by the great
autonomy between its coloring—whether by the illustrator or the
child himself—and the graphic medium of woodcut or engraving.
The relation to color is considered primary, even originary: it is
based solely on the sense of sight, isolated from all impressions of a
given object formed and synthesized—that is, "known" in a more
or less conscious, derivative way—from the other senses of touch,
taste, smell, or sound. To this extent, color is something immaterial, spiritual (*geistig*) but still sensual (*sinnlich*), detached from but
still attendant on the world of objects, or represented objects, or,
as Benjamin also puts it, "applied" (*angelegt*) to objects in a way
that avoids absolute synthesis.[94] But to an equal extent, color is
also what connects the child directly to an original realm of being,
nowadays all but lost to reading adults. Variously described by
Benjamin as similar to the Platonic anamnesis and as paradisial,
the experience of color directly links the child to the "spiritual
heart" (*geistigen Gegenstand*) of each object: even as it cancels
out the merely intellectual connections or *Verbindungen* synthesized from the other senses defining the object itself, the discrete
focus on color realizes a different set of "connections," a different
"interrelated totality"—without, Benjamin adds, thereby sacrificing the world.[95] He calls this other interrelated totality "the pure

Stimmung" (*die reine Stimmung*): it is another modern version of *sympatheia*, albeit at this stage at least accessible only to the child and otherwise lost (to the conscious adult) and, in this formulation, not fully synthesized with the material object world, but somehow out of sync and distorting.[96]

It is, then, by way of color that the child first enters into his reading, and in such a way that the boundary between his person and the text all but dissolves, allowing for the type of absorptive blending key to magic experience. As Benjamin puts it,

> The child enters into those pages, becoming suffused, like a cloud, with the riotous colors of the world of pictures. Sitting before his painted book, he makes the Taoist vision of perfection come true: he overcomes the illusory barrier of the book's surface and passes through colored textures and brightly painted partitions to enter a stage on which fairy tales spring to life.

> Im Schauen dringt [das Kind] selber als Gewölk, das mit dem Farbenglanz der Bilderwelt sich sättigt, in [die Seiten] ein. Es macht vor seinem ausgemalten Buche die Kunst der taoistischen Vollendeten wahr: es meistert die Trugwand der Fläche und zwischen farbigen Geweben, bunten Verschlägen betritt es eine Bühne, wo das Märchen lebt.[97]

To some extent, it is unimportant whether the pictures here were colored by the illustrator or the child itself, or whether we imagine the child as absorbed into the text or immersed in a dream state within itself.[98] The indifference is due in part to the effaced boundary between active and passive, object and subject, in this mode of reading, but in part, too, to the mutual reciprocity of their affective relation. For, on the one hand, given the gap between colors and their objects mentioned above, whether by the illustrator or the child the colors are always "applied" (*angelegt*) to the depicted objects in the book as an other, attendant, and differently ordered realm that cuts across their ordinary organized form (not hidden, but differently there), and thus, for all the "completion" of the absorption into the text, the text remains a distorted world— distorted by the child's discrete and pure view of color. On the other hand, Benjamin also suggests that this porous, outpouring realm— this "cloud at the core of things"—distorts the child in turn: as he says of his painting in *Berlin Childhood*, "The colors I mixed would color me."[99] As with *Stimmung* or *sympatheia* proper, the movement of projection and introjection is always reciprocal: as Simmel put it, it is a matter of relation, of *Wechselwirkung*.

This play of distortive, transformative, and similarizing reciprocity is even more pronounced in the child's relation to form in picture books. It is a relation that Benjamin insists is fundamentally distinct from the child's relation to color—and he adds, on the way to words. As we said, the experience of form is something derived from impressions generated by and synthesized from senses other than just sight, and especially by and from touch. It is based in the first place on the materiality and externality of objects in ways not quite true of the immateriality and im-position of color. As Benjamin says, if the colored picture immerses the child in a dream state within itself, the form of the black-and-white woodcut, the plain prosaic illustration of the picture book, leads him out of himself: much as with the posited materiality of letters in handwriting, drawings are assumed to have a body of their own that connects them, as objects, to the greater external world of things and nature.[100] And the child responds to that bodily form of pictures with his own body in a way impossible with color, which, we're told, the human body cannot produce.[101] As Benjamin says, "All form, every outline that man perceives, corresponds to something in him that enables him to reproduce it," and that something is his body, which he (Benjamin) designates as the organ of active relations and as the medium of the child's reading, which, he says, is always a form of enactment.[102]

This reproductive enactment also works in reciprocal ways, in both directions powered by and aiming toward similitude. On the one hand, the child "reads" drawings by making itself similar to them, in a way that manifests a porous boundary between the child and the world of things based on their common ground in bodily materiality—and in a way that is at once transformative and distortive of the child (more anon). On the other hand, the child is also compelled to reproduce the similarizing impression that the drawing has made on him at the site of the drawing itself, an active response on the part of his body, one that in turn transforms and distorts the original drawings, in ways meant at once to complete them and, Benjamin notes, to turn their mute form into language (again, more anon).[103] The child "scribbles" (*kritzelt*) on the uncolored drawings, draws or writes the bodily impressions the objects have made on him in his own bodily way on them: they touch him, and he (re)touches them.[104] This is, as it were, the inchoate equivalent of the language of the body that joins with the body of language in handwriting, here more disjointedly perceived; it shows, too, the basic equivalence of reading and (proto)writing in Benjamin's schema, where reading is always an active process of mutual inscription.

The term "scribble" leaves it unclear whether Benjamin imagines the child's scrawling to be in black only or to include coloring as well. If the latter, then something of the child's connection to an original immaterial nature and "pure *Stimmung*" (and the child's happiness in that connection) would be thought to infuse the material similitudes those scribblings produce. This would seem to be implied by the description of reading practices cited above, where the way of "applying" colors carries over to the child's reading of adventure stories, where colors proper no longer figure.[105] In any case, he does make clear that the child's scribbling encompasses both drawing and writing, both visual material pictures and immaterial symbolic language, in ways that impart to both the character of hieroglyphs: ushering the child into a world where every image or thing has a word or text behind it, and every word, even letter, remains both an image and a thing.[106] And if on this road to language and reading proper Benjamin leaves us somewhat in the dark about the continued presence of the pure realm of color, he does speak up about another realm of pure nature: sound.[107]

The early ABC primers that follow after the colored picture-books in teaching the child how to read begin by reinforcing this conflation of word and image, sign and material, keeping every word and even letter a hieroglyph tied to the world of things quite apart from or before any added sense or meaning (*Bedeutung*). The very earliest of these reading primers were, Benjamin tells us, voice-books (*Stimmenbüchlein*), with pictures of letters based on onomatopoeia, where *R* is a growling dog, *S* a hissing snake, *Sh* a woman shooing hens.[108] Letters are images—indeed things—connected to the greater world of things based on the similarity of sound, and although now the "pure *Stimmung*" of color seems absent from the equation, its place is filled by the "voice" (*Stimme*) or "natural sound" (*Laute der Natur*) that inhabits the picture-word qua onomatopoeia.[109] Much as did color, sound serves to connect the child to an original im/material realm of being before language or representation proper, a realm similarly serving as the basis for the realization of a different set of connections between objects and between words as objects, a different interrelated totality, resting now on the sympathetic similitude of sound alone.[110]

These *Stimmenbüchlein*, Benjamin says, soon give way to other things, both historically (after the Counter-Reformation) and in the education of the individual child—although it would be more accurate to say that they become complemented by other things, much as the child's engaged reading in terms of color becomes joined to that of form.[111] That is, the ABC primers come to present the child with the "majesty of script, full of clouds of arabesques," or more to the point, where letters are introduced "in disguise" (*vermummt*), as it were: *F* appears as a Franciscan, *C* as a clerk, *P* as a porter.[112] Although no longer linked to the greater world of things purely on the basis of (pure) sound, letters are thus presented to the child in the first place *as* things, animate things, as "characters" and bodies; as picture puzzles to be read visually for a significance differently organized from and all but independent of any word in which they might subsequently appear, even if only appearing along with such a word—and again, not so much hidden as just differently present.

In this respect, the image-sign of script functions much like the sound quality of language, opening up another realm of communicative connection and correspondence, another realm of similitude beyond that of either ordinary experience or ordinary language. And this occasions a mode of reading that Benjamin explicitly compares with the occult, magical, allegorical readings of the early modern period, linking the next stage of ABC primers to the emblem books of the baroque, and in particular to Johann Amos Comenius's *Orbis sensualium pictus*, whose system, arrangement, and method come "straight out" of Campanella's

book of magic.[113] Benjamin describes children's books from the end
of the eighteenth century that show, "on each page, a motley collection of objects without any pictorial connection between them,"
a "higgledy-piggledy still-life that seems mysterious until you realize what . . . Apple, ABC-book, Ape, Airplane, Anchor, Ark, Arm,
Armadillo, Aster, and Ax are all doing in the same place."[114] All
begin with the same letter of the alphabet—with the same sound
and image-form—and "not unlike Baroque pictographic combinations of allegorical objects," they initiate the child into a magic
mode of sympathetic reading, drawing linking *seirai* or associate
chains of similitude that function invisibly over and above either
the manifest images of the objects themselves or the semantic significance of their sociate words.[115]

In many ways, these emblem-book-like ABC primers, in which
letters connect otherwise arbitrary objects and images—and to say
it again, it is because letters are themselves objects and forms (and
through sound, nature) that the child himself connects with them,
reads their bodies through the enactments of his own body, quite
apart from any intellectual engagement—are a culminating moment in the child's initiation into magic reading. But in other ways,
they are the beginning of its demise—its loss for the adult and, inevitably, for the present day as well. On the one hand, these books
have induced the child, even if not consciously (and more by way
of anamnesis), to detect in every word or letter an image and sound
and object that keeps it a hieroglyph, suggesting another order of
meaning or relation within or beside the "sense" of the ordinary
context, an order in which he himself is essentially participant.
This mode of reading was further nurtured by the books of rebus—
a word Benjamin uses to link *res* or thing and *rêver* or dream, and
derives from the hieroglyphs of the Renaissance—that appeared in
the nineteenth century, the heyday of children's literature.[116] These
latter books taught children to engage in the turnstile substitution of words and images, to read for "hidden" combinations and
meanings beyond the apparently given; even as the "magic books"
(*Zauberbücher*) that appeared at this same time assured that the
picture puzzle would constantly change, and the *Anziehpuppe* or
"dress-up" books that the child could actively participate in the

change (through the application or *anlegen* of different costumes on the provided figures, a concrete variant of the child's earlier *anlegen* of colors).[117] All this persists as a mode of reading even as the child graduates to his nonpictured (and silent) reading of pirate stories or ghost stories, or whatever book chance might put in the schoolboy's hands, immersing himself "in the swirling letters like figures and messages in drifting snowflakes" (also called "sounding" [*tönende*] snowflakes).[118] And it persists, too, in however weak or submerged a form, in the adult reader as well—for this is how he has been trained to read, individually and historically.

On the other hand, these emblem-like ABC primers—and with them the rebus books "in which wherever possible all the nouns are represented by small beautifully painted illustrative or allegorical pictures"—also signal the beginning of the tendency "to separate the visual as far as possible from the word, and even more from the letter."[119] Word and image, letter and thing, are no longer presented as one unified element: where there is an image or object, there is no word, no language; and where there is a word or letter, there is no picture or thing. Even as color seems to disappear from the reading experience, and with it the direct natural connection to an immaterial realm of "pure *Stimmung*"; and even as sound (or *Stimme*) seems to disappear in now silent reading, and with it another connection to pure nature and its other order of things; so too does the image and its object-ivity seem to fade away, and with it the natural bodily connection that (literally) draws the reader into a sensuous, even if non-"sensical" relation to the text. But never completely: the sense of its loss persists in the form of a certain longing (*Sehnsucht*) or even guilt (*Schuld*) in the adult, and in however faint, distorted, or momentary a fashion, it looms as a substratum, as a potentially irruptive force in the child's future as an adult.[120]

Child Hiding

The second section from *One-Way Street* is "Child Hiding." It does not directly address reading, but it does expand upon the concept of the world that supports or underwrites it and on the child's mode of participation in it. It is a mode that Benjamin elsewhere describes as the natural heritage of mankind in its early stages, functioning now in an unbroken manner only in children. It is, I'd say, a reformulation of the basic connection between the subject and the natural world of things (*die Dingwelt*) that we saw behind his analyses of fate, handwriting, roulette playing, and children's books, and it reformulates it in a way that recasts that connection in terms most reflective of the earlier traditions of *sympatheia*— namely, in terms of an almost ontological logic or *logos* of analogy and similarity, resemblance and relation, that is key to magic's mode of both signification and identificatory participation.

In making this connection to the tradition of *sympatheia*, even as Benjamin is reaching far back to the ancient world, he is also extending the transformations of that same tradition in the nineteenth and early twentieth century that we mentioned earlier: the transformation of *sympatheia* into *Stimmung* in Keller; of *Stimmung* into sociability in Fontane; and the key place of something like *sympatheia* in the vitalist philosophies of Benjamin's immediate predecessors, such as Klages, Bergson, and their less reputable occult counterparts in theosophy and anthroposophy.[121] And as important as the resurrection of the ancient tradition is, so, too, is the transformation of the more recent one. So, for example, in almost direct contrast to Fontane, the sympathetic order is established by the child absent other people, in a more or less isolated, even alienated relation to the human world. "Child Hiding" describes a child playing hide-and-seek, but without others, alone in a room filled only with nonhuman things—a table, curtain, door—with which he engages: as in the case of interfering, "hostile suggestions" generated by the gambler's human environment, the exclusion of others, rather than, as in Fontane, their presence, seems the necessary condition for the experience of *sympatheia*.

This is not to say that the social dimension simply dissolves and yields to a connection with the natural world, such as still seemed possible in Keller, was yearned for anew in Fontane, and was so problematically reclaimed by the vitalists. Nor is it to say that the child in its alienation becomes psychologically or even individualistically conceived. Rather, the world of things with which the child is linked is overwhelmingly a humanly produced one: in "Child Hiding," although only lightly sketched, the site of the game is clearly a formal dining room in the child's bourgeois parental home, a dwelling in which "one is sure to find everything as it was (*beim alten*)."[122] The object world working its binding magic on the child is still a social one, largely keeping the child detached from a more naturally conceived order; indeed, as the *beim alten* indicates, the social world embodied in that object world is in important ways still the same nineteenth-century bourgeois world as in Fontane, and problematically (arrestingly) so.[123] As with children's books, these "things" (table, curtain, door) are complicit in a certain historicized socialization of the child over and above his natural relations, and both the social and the natural characteristics far outweigh any individual "character" of the child—as in "Child Reading" and other such vignettes, the child hiding never obtains a first-person pronoun that might distinguish him psychologically: he retains the neuter *es*.

Another point where Benjamin's transformation and extension of the more recent tradition are notable concerns the place of mimesis in the production of the sympathetic world. This is most evident in the comparison with Keller's realism, and on two fronts. On the one hand, whereas in Keller mimesis took place at the site of painting, as a medium mediating between the human subject and the (natural) world, in Benjamin the mimesis takes place more directly, without any mediation at all—or rather, with the thing world and the child's body as part of that world as the medium of mimesis itself. Gone is the sense of *in distans*; in its place comes a much greater sense of vulnerability to the active force of things, a far greater range to one's immediate "mimetic" relation to the *Umwelt*. On the other hand, whereas mimesis in Keller was based on relations of model and copy, of visible and sensible similarities— this tree and this drawing, this child and this portrait—in Benjamin the realm of similitude is no longer limited to such sensible appearances, and this vastly extends and transforms both the mode of mimesis and that of the sympathetic order that supports it. The child can be like a curtain or door: similitude is no longer restricted to verisimilitude.

One last preliminary point of extension, and perhaps the most important one. Whereas in Keller the achievement of *Stimmung* was considered the goal, the fulfillment of its realist ideal; and similarly, in Fontane the achievement of *Stimmung* in the form of *Geselligkeit* was the desired magic, and the threatened loss of sociability and, even more, the realized loss of sympathetic connection to the nonhuman natural world seemed sadly to signal the demise of the realist order; and whereas even in Benjamin himself, the adult's loss of his childhood's magic reading or the gambler's loss of his sympathetic connection to the realm of fate are both presented as just that, lamented losses of a once possessed and still desirable state—in "Child Hiding," this loss is also explicitly celebrated as a positive gain, as a desired condition. The realist poetics of connection give way, as it were, to those of a more modernist detachment.[124] Not that this desire is completely new or unexpected. In Keller, the demonic and deadly force of *sympatheia* was retained in his model of *Stimmung*, and emerged most evidently in the binding magic worked on Meretlein and Anna (where there was, however, no clear path of escape). In Fontane, the breakdown of the social fabric supporting sociability was looked on with sporadically muted approval by Dubslav. And even in Benjamin, we've had both the "fateless" gods of Hölderlin (mentioned in "Fate and Character") and the "relief" of the losing gambler to counter the happy child and fortunate player. No doubt part of this more pronounced affirmation of the loss of *sympatheia* can be attributed to the increased antipathy toward the (aging, arrested) social order, now embodied in the thing world.[125] But as our brief discussion of memory (or our linking it to missed chances as losses) also suggests, the affirmation of loss, especially of lost connections, might also be attributed to an expectation of belated recovery: to a future and a moment of happiness that might still be magically met.

"Child Hiding" describes the game of hide-and-seek, and both hiding and seeking are at stake in the vignette. But it begins with the hiding, or rather with the child's part in a hiding (*versteckt*) world, even as he otherwise seems right there, in plain sight; it is as it were about the invisible dimension of the visible world and the child's place in it—a world that is differently present. This world in whose hiddenness he comes to share (in which he is "enclosed" [*eingeschlossen*]) is, we're told, the material world, *die Stoffwelt*, a variant of *die Dingwelt* (perhaps somewhat more pejorative). Although we've seen this participation to be key throughout Benjamin, it is especially so for the child: Benjamin argues that childhood chains us to things (*uns an die Dinge kettet*) at a level and time that precedes human influence, knowledge, and even language.[126] The formative power of those chains—the force of things themselves—impresses itself on the child, and in such a way that he is made to become the things, or rather similar to the things, surrounding him.[127] It is because of this imposed form of mimicry that the child all but disappears, dispersed or bound into his *Umwelt*:

> Standing behind the doorway curtain, the child himself becomes something floating and white, a ghost. The dining-room table under which he is crouching turns him into the wooden idol in a temple whose four pillars are the carved legs. And behind a door, he himself *is* the door.

> Das Kind, das hinter der Portiere steht, wird selbst zu etwas Wehendem und Weißem, zum Gespenst. Der Eßtisch, unter den es sich gekauert hat, läßt es zum hölzernen Idol des Tempels werden, wo die geschnitzten Beine die vier Säulen sind. Und hinter einer Türe ist es selber Tür.[128]

In a later and more famous passage—"The Mummerehlen" from *Berlin Childhood*—Benjamin adds examples from the photographer's studio, where "we made ourselves . . . like the embroidered cushion someone pushed toward us, or the ball we had been given to hold."[129] Even more suggestive for us, he adds there as well the example of the child making himself similar to words read or heard, where language is once again positioned as itself part of the material world. It is, notably, a kind of "likeness" that is anything but manifest, and a kind of mimicry that remains entirely invisible and unseen. Still, the child's connection to the world is based on a sympathetic logic of contact and likeness that involves at once a binding identification with the object world and a (releasing, disappearing) dispersal of identity into that world.

In this formulation of the child's place in the sympathetically contagious order of similitude, the transformative powers emanate out of things themselves, and potentially threaten the child every bit as much as aid him (aid him precisely in allowing him to disappear, to be ghosted). As Benjamin's child puts it elsewhere, "I am distorted (*entstellt*) by my similarity to all that surrounds me."[130] Here, the sense of danger is no doubt linked to the fact that the *Stoffwelt* of the parents' dwelling embodies the nineteenth-century culture the child is anxious to escape, and whose "everything as it was" (*alles beim alten*) thus threatens, in binding the child, to arrest him (much as her sartorial trappings did Meretlein). But however specifically nineteenth-century that *Stoffwelt* seems, it also awakens in the child an ancient, primitive sense of the demonic— the *Dämon*, as Benjamin calls it—that inhabits its (more recently "ancient") things, a sense conveyed by references not only to the demon, but to the door as mask, the dwelling as a whole as an arsenal of masks, and the child himself as a wooden idol in a temple. This "fore-world" (*Vorwelt*) or "primal history" (*Urgeschichte*) that irrupts into and out of the present/past setting (Benjamin also calls it *Stimmung*) awakens the almost atavistic play of forces behind mimesis that keeps it active and potently magic.[131] But these forces do not emanate only out of things, do not only distort the child and bind him: the mimetic faculty is in him, too; it distorts, transforms, or disappears the *Stoffwelt* itself, and is the source of his own magic power. It determines his role as a shaman or *Zauberpriester*, able to bewitch (*behexen*) the world and make it anew.

We see this in how the table that transforms the child into a wooden idol is itself transformed into a four-pillared temple: it becomes *ent-stellt*, dis-placed from its own material present into another realm via mimetic resemblance.[132] The child joins in, becomes an active participant in the play or game (*Spiel*), and so, too, becomes not just a hider in but a seeker of similitude, and in ways that fundamentally transform his relation both to the thing-world and to the demonic forces, social or otherwise, they embody. Thus, although Benjamin stresses elsewhere that the play space or *Spielraum* and its things presented to the child "belong to the nation and class [it] comes from"—part of an adult world that is always "as it was," outmoded and arrested—it is precisely in such a setting that children "recognize the face that the world of things turns directly and solely to them. [And] in using these things, they . . .

bring together materials of widely differing kinds in a new intuitive (*sprunghaft*) relationship. Children thus produce their own smaller world of things within the greater one."[133] The child becomes the producer—or better, the seeker and diviner—of another world hidden in the material one, a spectral world of likenesses and relations.

Benjamin addresses this active role of the child in the section immediately preceding "Child Hiding," entitled "Disorderly Child" (Unordentliches Kind).[134] This child is presented as a hunter of things—stones, flowers, and butterflies, but also tinfoil, bricks, and pennies—and for him, every single thing "makes up one great collection." Strictly speaking, however, he does not seek out things, but rather "the spirits whose trace he scents in things" (*die Geister, deren Spur es in den Dingen wittert*). In order to capture (or release) these spirits, the child must first wrench them out of the greater, ordinary order in which he finds them, must, he says, disenchant them (*entzaubern*)—but his disenchantment is in the service of a reenchantment, his disordering in the construction of a different order. That is, for the child and in ways invisible to adults, these "things" are not only themselves but things they resemble, the similitudes scented in them: tinfoil is hoarded silver, bricks coffins, cacti totem poles, pennies shields. Even more, for the child, and again in ways hidden to others, these apparently scattered, random, "dis-orderly" things brought together in his room constitute an order, a structure that holds them in their other, spectral significance, a significance that disappears when only ordinary order is imposed (by the "sensible" adult, ordering "tidy up" [*Aufräumen*]). The child seeks the similitude in the thing, and the order that—as much as the thing itself—determines the similitude (e.g., would the penny be a shield were the chestnut not a club?). And he himself is part of that order, one of its invisibly transformed things: it is this that makes him a shaman (*Zauberpriester*) and his world bewitched.

Two additional points about this mimetic faculty in the child. The first is that the hidden similitude that the child divines is not static or single: the table needn't always be a temple, the cactus every time a totem pole. Indeed, as Benjamin says, "However unified and unambiguous the material is, the more it seems to embrace the possibility of a multitude of figures of the most varied sort."[135] Unlike in realist mimesis (or even realist *Stimmung*), a thing is never just like one other thing, or like in only one way. Rather, like the characters in Benjamin's graphology, the dresses in children's books, the letter *A* in the primer or all things allegorical in the baroque, the order of similitude and significance is an endlessly open one. And in keeping with that, the similitude that the world of things imposes on the child proves just as mobile, just as open: the table might turn him into a wooden idol, but the curtain turns him into a ghost, the door into a door, or as he writes elsewhere, sand turns him into a baker, a wagon into a horse.[136]

And yet, for all the plurality and mobility present to the child in this invisible world within the world to which he is so intimately connected, he nonetheless still fears its binding powers, its demon—and this not only insofar as those forces derive from the dreaded social imaginary of the nineteenth century, nor only insofar as they leave him vulnerable to manipulation or arrest by some other "shaman" ("Anyone who discovers him can petrify him as an idol under the table"—again, think of Meretlein). Rather, it is even the case of the binding power of his own mimicry on himself: "When he makes faces . . . all the clock has to do is strike, and his face will stay like that forever."[137] And so part of the game consists in driving out the demon who has so transformed him: just as when writing about fate (and for the same reason), Benjamin seems to celebrate both the connection with the world of things (and the invisible world behind the world of things) and its loss: both the magic powers to which the child has access through the connection, and the disenchantment or release that comes from its severance. The mimetic connection that on the one hand seems to lift the child out of his ordinary time and place and into an enchanted non-presence (an *Ent-stellung*) on the other threatens to keep him in that *Ent-stellung*, that fate, forever—and the magical world is desired only in its momentariness, its singular occasion, and not its duration. And so as with the gambler who loses or Hölderlin's "fateless" gods, being freed from the chain of mimetic relation is for the child also a welcome, desired relief—indeed, Benjamin writes, the "hiding" child actively seeks his deliverance, the loss of his place in the "hidden" world of similitude. In this way, the lamented sense of nonrelation to the natural world broached in Fontane's "sociability," along with the increasing break with the social *Umwelt* itself, is here finalized or taken as a good thing: a triumph of detachment over connection, of disenchantment over magic.[138]

This is not to say that the severance of these binding chains is the end of the story, is, as it were, without second thoughts. Rather, as with the adults who can no longer so immediately and easily be mingled with the characters in their books, there is also a sense that the loosening of these connections is truly a loss. But this loss, this loosening, proves to be the necessary condition for a new, more typically modernist sense of the occasionality of "magical experience"—and of happiness: an epiphanic occasionality far more rare than the almost always available situational reading of ancient divination, more complex than the simply present momentariness of sociability in Fontane or *Stimmung* in Keller, and more layered, too, than the one-off momentariness desired by the child mentioned above.[139] This occasionality involves a new, different version of hide-and-seek, and a different order of hidden similitude: looking not for like things but for like times—for the future hidden in the past.

That moments of sympathetic connection are still both valued by and possible for the modern-day adult can be seen in an example Benjamin repeats almost verbatim across several essays.[140] He writes, "Modern man can be touched by a pale shadow of this [magic connection to things] when he looks through a mask, or when, on southern moonlit nights, he feels mimetic forces alive in himself that he had thought long since dead, while nature, which possesses them all, transforms itself to resemble the moon."[141] Benjamin calls these moonlit moments "rare moments" (*seltene Augenblicke*), and they seem very much the same as those rarest moments (*seltenste Augenblicke*) of divination that, he says, gambling can produce, and to carry with them the same nascent promise of *Glück*—a sense of being touched and rewarded by fate.[142] Notably, the passage evokes the mask, seemingly the same mask worn by "child hiding" that transformed him into a shaman (*Zauberpriester*); and the nature evoked as the center of mimetic powers is seemingly again the nature of the ancient, "thought long since dead" world.[143] However, when Benjamin adds, "But [modern man] is transported into this very force field by his memories of childhood," this field seems as emphatically the present memory as the past childhood, a shift (or *Entstellung*) reinforced by the reflective moon and shadows as the condition for connection with sympathetic, mimetic nature.[144] In other words, memory itself becomes an active site—in some ways, *the* site—of the mimetic faculty for modern man, seeking the similitude to his present hidden (masked, reflected, and shadowed forth) in the past, with his bliss-producing divination of the future based on the same logic of likeness that the child or ancient brings to the things of his world, but now temporally cast and practiced by the adult, on himself, in his present-day.[145]

Two passages in Benjamin are particularly suited to elucidating this relation between the divining memories of childhood, the future of things, and the belated experience of *Glück*. The first is from one of the earliest essays, the section on the diary in "The Metaphysics of Youth" (Metaphysik der Jugend, 1913); the second is from the concluding sentences of "Child Hiding" itself. The first is one of the most portentous pieces in Benjamin's oeuvre, adumbrating in condensed and cryptic form many of his later key concepts. It is concerned with the role of the interval—the break—in the diary, and how it figures in both the fate and the future (the "resurrection") of the subject and the event-full world that surrounds him. In an especially lyrical moment, it designates that world as, significantly enough, landscape (*Landschaft*), and describes it as imbued with the same external agency we saw in the *Stimmung* landscapes of Keller and the childhood thing-world of Benjamin himself:

As landscape all events surround us, for we, the time of things, know no time. Nothing but the leaning of trees, the horizon, the silhouetted mountain ridges, which suddenly awake full of meaning because they have placed us in their midst. The landscape transports us into their midst, the trembling treetops assail us with questions, the valleys envelop us with mist, incomprehensible houses oppress us with their shapes.

Als Landschaft umgibt uns alles Geschehen, denn wir, die Zeit der Dinge, kennen keine Zeit. Nur Neigungen der Bäume, Horizont und

Schärfe der Bergrücken, die plötzlich voll Beziehung erwachen, indem
sie uns in ihre Mitte stellen. Die Landschaft versetzt uns in ihre Mitte,
es umzittern uns mit Frage Wipfel, umdunkeln uns mit Nebel Täler,
bedrängen uns mit Formen unbegreifliche Häuser.[146]

The new and complecting aspect of this is the inserted temporal
dimension to the sympathetic relation between the active world
and encompassed subject ("we, the time of things"), a dimension
stressed further when Benjamin adds, "Things perceive us: their
gaze propels us into the future. . . . We encounter nothing that
is not in landscape, and in it find nothing but future."[147] And it
continues in his description of the essentially reciprocal moment
of this arrangement, in the participant shaping force of the human
subject:

Knowing no answers but forming the center, we ascertain (*bestimmen*)
things with the movement of our bodies. By drawing nigh and distancing
ourselves once again on our wanderings, we single out trees from their like
and flood them with the time of our existence. We give firm definition to
(*bestimmen*) fields and mountains in their arbitrariness: they are our past
existence—that was the prophecy of childhood. We are their future.

Und wie wir antwortlos mit der Bewegung unseres Leibes die Dinge
bestimmen, Mitte sind und uns wandernd fernen und nähern, lösen
wir Bäume und Felder aus ihresgleichen, überströmen sie mit der Zeit
unseres Daseins. Feld und Berge bestimmen wir in ihrer Willkür; sie
sind unser vergangenes Sein—so prophezeite die Kindheit. Wir sind
zukünftig sie.[148]

What grounds and explains the structure behind this prophetic
relation (and *Bestimmung*) between the self and its landscape is
the fundamental context of that relation, namely, the diary, and
especially two of its determining features. The first is the interval
itself, which abrogates the continuum of developmental time (*die
Zeit der Entwicklung*) and opens up a non-time that breaks its
binding chain of experience (*Kette der Erlebnisse*); and the second
is the self not as writer but as belated, back-turned *reader* of the
diary, the temporally distinct place where, in Benjamin's elegant
phrase, we befall ourselves (*uns selbst widerfahren*).[149] The interval
helps explain the role here of the movement of our bodies: shifting

the animating mobility associated with divinatory signs from the object to the subject, this movement is about both connecting with the past (drawing nigh) and disconnecting from it (distancing once again), a disconnection in which, by virtue of the interval, the past landscape falls out of its original, ordinary connection with the subject. Instead, the subject as *reader* returns to that landscape anew, from his position in its future: and it is from this re-moved position that he ascertains (*bestimmt*) things, "singles out trees from their like" by flooding them with the time—the present time—of "our existence." He ascertains or *bestimmt* them from the perspective of how they are retrospectively seen to have prophesied his present self—it is in this sense that he declares, "Past things have futurity" and "All future is past"—and he defines this new connection of the landscape to the subject ("this countermovement of things in the time of the self") as both fate and prophecy.[150] And its realization in the moment of reading, of looking back with an eye to the future—"that time of the self in which things befall us"—that is the time and place of fulfillment, of what he calls resurrection (*Auferstehung*): when the past, in its likeness to the present, finds future life, afterlife, in a moment of mimetic reflection.

The second passage that sheds special light on the relation between divining memory and the future of things, and both in relation to the landscape of childhood, comes in the concluding sentences of "Child Hiding." It too is concerned with resurrection and, if you will, redemption. Benjamin has just concluded explaining the child's need to "drive out the demon" to prevent itself from being bound forever in the magical, mimetic realm of its dwelling (qua an "arsenal of masks"), and to preserve instead the open moment of the "magical experience":

> Yet once a year—in mysterious, secret places, in their empty eye sockets, in their fixed mouths—lie gifts. Magical experience becomes science (*Wissenschaft*). As its engineer, the child disenchants the gloomy parental apartment and looks for Easter eggs.

> Doch einmal jährlich liegen an geheimnisvollen Stellen, in ihren leeren Augenhöhlen, ihrem starren Mund, Geschenke. Die magische Erfahrung wird Wissenschaft. Das Kind entzaubert als ihr Ingenieur die düstere Elternwohnung und sucht Ostereier.

Everything hinges on that "yet" (*doch*), at the moment—with its time shift—wherein the child moves from being the hidden one to the seeking one, from "magical experience" to *Wissenschaft*, from shaman to disenchanting engineer. Everything, that is, hinges on seeing how this shift is at the same time to describing the work of memory as well as the game of childhood, to establishing the connective correspondences between the two that transform the one into a hidden allegory of the other—into a mimetic moment in a new way—and in the process revealing the identity (the similitude) between the child and the grown-up, the magic and the science: the one hiding in the other's seeking; the one a mask for the other to look back through and see his present self, his present work.[151] That is, it hinges on divining how the "gifts" hidden in secret places include this memory itself, liberated from its binding connections in the seemingly empty, dead, dusty, and fixed past (those binding connections that kept it past, and so fixed), and, once so released or *entzaubert* (much like the things of the "disorderly child"), available for new hidden connections, new mimetic connections, a new and different "arsenal of masks"; with a future of which they become a prophecy, a fate, hidden and revealed, in a state of resurrection and redemption. This, I suggest, is why these gifts are Easter eggs: at once dead (cooked or empty) and fertile, at once past childhood things and potent signs of future life—where the grown-up has found another kingdom hidden and present in the first magic kingdom of childhood, another, reflecting moment in the shadows of this otherwise lost sympathetic world.[152]

On Reading as Such (Reading Old & New)

Benjamin's most direct and comprehensive musings on magic reading (*magische Lesen*), indeed his take on its specifically divinatory dimension and on the sympathetic world that supports it, come in his essay "Doctrine of the Similar" and its somewhat later, abbreviated version, "The Mimetic Faculty," as well as in several, even shorter precursor essays. As a set, these essays differ notably from Benjamin's earlier studies of language and its magic that are couched in more ahistorical, exclusively metaphysical and religious terms. Instead, these later texts are written from the vantage of "students of ancient traditions" and seek to integrate his thoughts on graphology, gambling, and childhood into the tradition of ancient magic reading, and to derive therefrom the terms for a "new reading" (*neues Lesen*) appropriate to his own modernist moment—both in the resurgence of the archaic (*Urgeschichte*) and in the disruptions that transform it.[153]

Because they are couched in such different terms, the early studies of language and magic are not as directly relevant to us as the later ones. But especially the essay "On Language as Such and on the Language of Man (Über die Sprache überhaupt und die Sprache des Menschen)" has aspects that are crucial to understanding the rest of Benjamin, including the later language studies, and that, even if indirectly, impact his model of modernist reading—for while the early studies draw on a Judeo-Christian tradition and the later ones more on a Neoplatonic one, both of course are entwined in the early modern period that so deeply textured Benjamin's take on modernism itself. In any case, the aspects of the early work that are most important to us are the direct focus on language itself, including the language of things; and the description of the conditions that have dislocated or *entstellt* our relation to the language of things, indeed to language itself.

In "On Language as Such," Benjamin claims that "the primary problem of language is its magic," by which he means the immediacy of its communication in its connection to things.[154] This leads Kathrin Busch to suggest that even in this essay the magic at stake is a sympathetic one, whose communication or "contagion" conveys effects that are not "necessarily present or representable," but where "something else beyond the named content is given expression, something akin to a mood or atmosphere (*Stimmung*) that is neither semantic nor communicable at the level of word meanings."[155] This communication takes place in the first instance between and among things themselves, quite apart from the human: it does so through a more or less "material community" (*stoffliche Gemeinschaft*) that is im-mediate and magical—for, as Benjamin says, "there is also a magic of matter."[156] This is, we note, a somewhat different claim from that made earlier in relation to handwriting and children's books, where we said language has a body, or rather, a decisively material existence: the claim here is that the material—nature, things—has a language (albeit a mute and so imperfect one).[157] Man himself partakes of the magical community (of this *Stimmung*) insofar as he, too, is material; but human language is incomparable (*unvergleichlich*) in that its magical community with things is said to be immaterial.[158] Again, this is somewhat different from our earlier point, that the human body has a language that expresses itself, and closer to the point about how children, in reproducing drawings with or through their bodies, also transform them into words. Here, however, rather than emphasizing the smoothness and continuity in that transformation, the stress seems to be on the disjunction and difference at stake.

In fact, these two conditions—that things themselves have a language, albeit an imperfect one, and human language communicates "magically" with things, albeit on a different, immaterial footing—form the basis for the distortions inherent in both language itself and our relation to things, and Benjamin takes recourse to the biblical story of Creation and the Fall to explain this. Things have a language because Creation itself—nature and all its things—is the embodiment of God's creative Word: what a thing "is" corresponds exactly to the divine word that both made it and knew it.[159] In its original Adamic state, the name or word given to a thing by man corresponded to that divine word and hence thing, precisely because man, his knowledge, and his gift of language were of the same divine, creative word.[160] But with the Fall—both into knowledge (a fatuous knowledge distinct from that earlier "magical" knowledge of correspondences, one grounded in self-consciousness and so too in guilt) and into multiple languages—the Adamic correspondence of the divine word embodied in things and the human name given them no longer holds.[161] Instead, the relation between the names given to a thing by human languages and the name the thing had from God and retains in its silent, magical communication with other things becomes a matter of "overnaming" (*Über-benennung*), "the deepest linguistic reason for all melancholy."[162] Again, this seems rather different from the language of the body that melds with the body of language in handwriting—for there we do have connection, based on a shared material community—and closer to the child's scribblings that overwrite the book's drawings: the split between signifier and signified that becomes the (hieroglyphic) ground for allegory. There is still, Benjamin insists, a certain magic to human language in the "externally communicating" words and correspondences it produces: but how or whether this magic and these correspondences correspond with the magical community of things themselves and their language is essentially unknowable.[163] The sympathetic world, the "magical community of things," is there, but not, or no longer, for us, at least not for our language(s) and consciousness. And with it seems to go any direct route to divination, leaving us with only our material bodies, our lost bliss, and, Benjamin adds, the central metaphysical problem of linguistic philosophy: revelation.[164]

When Benjamin returns to the topic of language and its magic in "Doctrine of the Similar," many elements remain the same, but some emphases have notably changed. What remains is the posing of the question of "the magical side of language" in terms of the connections or correspondences of the human and world of things, and the insistence on the losses and distortions to those connections occasioned by what, in the earlier context, Benjamin called the Fall. What has changed is basically twofold: the divine dimension has dropped out of the analysis, and a different temporal dimension has entered in, with history in its extension now performing the work of loss and change earlier attributed to a single biblical event. Both developments have enormous consequences for the fate of divination or magic reading. Rather than framing his analysis in Judeo-Christian terms, with an inaccessible divine language as the determining factor affecting present-day reading, Benjamin turns to ancient traditions of natural magic absent any explicit, or required, meta-physical foundation.[165] This allows him to foreground the dimension of magical community and shared language between man and the world only hinted at in "On Language as Such," but underwriting his take on fate, graphology, gambling, and childhood: the magical community and language of matter, and man himself as matter. And the introduction of time—not just in its character as a diachronic operator in a synchronic system (the "Fall") but in its greater fullness as movement and change—allows for the twinned possibility of precisely those two experiences denied in the earlier essay: divination and *Glück*.

Benjamin's new starting point in ancient traditions of occult knowledge helps explain why he now approaches language, and especially reading, by way of similarity. His first formulation of this approach comes in a fragment entitled "On Astrology," and it begins with the rather Neoplatonic claim that the similarities we perceive in the world are nothing more than "tiny prospects from a cosmos of similarity" (*winzige Teilansichten aus einem Kosmos der Ähnlichkeit*) scattered throughout the material visible world that hint at vast invisible chains of likenesses.[166] That is, even as in the earlier essay he began with language as a property of the magical community of matter, so here he starts with a conception of similarity as a natural, macrocosmic principle. This principle is active in and between things quite apart from human projection: similarities are not only imported into things by chance comparisons on our part, but all of them "are the effect of an active mimetic force working expressly inside things." This force establishes an open network or force field—a chain or weave—of connection in which each thing functions both as an active productive center or subject, generating its similarity to other things, and as a passive receptive object, accepting or accommodating itself to other things qua centers; and in which the points or features within each thing as subject or object that might invite relations of similitude with others are multiple, indeed unlimited. It is this hidden, woven world of endlessly combinatory similarities that produces the "natural correspondences" that are also "magical correspondences": as in the case of the material community in "On Language as Such," magic is first in nature, in things, or rather, in the connection between things.[167] It is just that the foundation of "language" has been reformulated in terms of likenesses in ways that more closely resemble the conditions of *sympatheia*, of *Stimmung*, and even, in its community and reciprocal relationality, of Simmel's sociability (although realized here in the complete absence of humans).

The recognition of these similarities by humans might, Benjamin says, be limited, and is certainly more so in the present day than it was in ancient times. But when these similarities were recognized by men, this was not so much by virtue of their rational conscious-ness or even visual perceptions as it was by that of their shared participation in the web of resemblances.[168] That is, the human being, like every other thing, participates in the community of re-semblances as both mimetic subject and object, generating via the shared force within it its similarity to other things and accepting into itself the similarities produced by other things (qua subjects). This implies for man, originally, a kind of dispersed, broadcast, scattered web-identity inseparable from his unified bound connec-tion with things—similar to what we saw for Meretlein and Anna in the *Stimmung*-determined world of Keller, or for the "sociable man" in the more narrowly conceived communal world of both Simmel and Fontane.

Benjamin describes this associative, reciprocal relation in ex-plicitly archaic terms, as the magical, sympathetic resemblances between the human microcosm and nature's macrocosm. And he illustrates the archaic mode of divinatory reading based on this micro-macro relation with the example of physiognomy. While in both its ancient and its modern forms physiognomy considers bod-ies as legible signs of "something else" that is otherwise hidden but still determinative and binding, it is only in its recent degraded form that that "something else" is the realm of individual psychological character.[169] In its more original form it was devoted to divining the hidden connections and resemblances that bind the natural life in man to the external world. Benjamin underscores this with his very first example of the mimetic sensibility in "On Astrology," which describes the ancient practice of reading human physiognomy in terms of animal resemblances, itself a first step toward the more radical reading of the stars as animal beings, and from there to stars as connected back to human beings. As in ancient extispicy and modern-day graphology, this mode of reading sees the human in the nonhuman world, which is then mirrored back onto the hu-man as a way of knowing it. But because it is based not in a discrete human epistemology but instead in a shared natural ontology, this mode also divines more than the discretely human world and its self-reflective similitudes: it also reads or divines the nonhuman in the human, sensing man's connection with and similitude to animals, stars, and the whole external world of things in ways that far exceed mere rational cognition or visual perception: "non-sensuous" (*unsinnlich*) correspondences that belie the more humanly restricted psychology, and similarities, of the present day.

Both the ancient physiognomic and astrological divinations described by Benjamin are not only of similar things in the external world but also of moving, animate things;[170] and in intimate connection with that movement, Benjamin stresses that the successful reading of these similar things, the successful connection of the microcosmic human with the macrocosmic thing-world depends on a particular occasion, *ein Nu, ein Zeitmoment*, that can coordinate the movement—the time—of things with that of the human subject. Using the same language deployed earlier to describe the gambler's connection to the rolling ball and, through it, with the realm of fate, he says that the recognition of the realm of similarity is in every case bound to a "flashing up": "It flits past, can possibly be won again, but cannot really be held fast as can other perceptions."[171] This is the same occasionality that obtains in the ancient practice of kledonomancy that Benjamin refers to here, wherein the reading of chance words or events as omens is singularly dependent on their coincidence or similarity to the occasion of the reader himself. And it is the same occasionality that Benjamin also ascribes to astrological reading, where, he says, it is the addition of a third term (*das Dazukommen eines Dritten*), the astrologer himself, to the conjunction of two stars that allows him to recognize the sudden fleeting appearance of a constellation; it is the connection or similarity of his own occasion, his own momentary condition, that allows him to read the connection between the two objects and divine the order—the mimetic character—that makes them a constellation. Without the occasion of participatory identification or mimetic blending based on this coincidence, "the astrologer is cheated of his reward, despite the sharpness of his observational tools."[172]

We stated at the outset that, in the ancient world, magic reading was also always occasional reading, dependent on participatory identification to produce or perceive signification, and this was true again in our two nineteenth-century examples: the moments of *Stimmung* in Keller, the premonitions in early Fontane, and especially the moments of sociability in late Fontane, where the sense of ephemerality of the occasion, conveyed in part by its basis in movement and time flow, seems newly pronounced. But the temporality at stake in such occasional reading is even more pronounced in Benjamin's schema. We see this in the way the animation of signs is more insistently tied to movement and movement to temporality. We see it in how the coordination of the different realms required for magic reading is more emphatically one of different temporalities as well: where not only the hidden realm behind or beyond the present reality is conceived as temporal (whether in its form as the messianic, the past, or the heavenly movement of stars), nor only in the conception of the reader himself as fundamentally temporal (as in the figure of the diary reader, or childhood-remembering adult), but also with the occasion of their coordination itself as decisively, and even perilously, its own time, its own *Nu*.

All this matters.[173] But what most impacts the occasionality of modern magic reading is the phylogenetic equivalent to Benjamin's claims about the reading child turned adult: that the human micro-/macrocosmic connection with the world of things, "the natural heritage of mankind in its early stages," has become all but lost to modern man.[174] For Benjamin, this means that such magical connections become occasional for him in the new sense of becoming exceedingly rare, far rarer than in antiquity or its ontogenetic equivalent in childhood. But he also insists they can still happen, and apparently without the divine intervention needed for revelation in his earlier, more theological model: in those "rare moments" of mimetic experience on southern moonlit nights, or those "rarest moments" of divination for the gambler, or in those back-turned moments of resurrection for the diary reader or childhood memoirist—each of which seems to carry the same nascent promise of *Glück*: a sense of being rewarded by fate. What needs to be determined, then, is how these changed circumstances (the weakening of mimetic perception, and with it of the bond to the greater world of things) change magic reading and the sympathetic

connections that support it, and how these rare moments of divination are still possible, not for the ancient astrologer or the contemporary child, but for "modern man."

Benjamin insists that even with the loss or vast reduction of
the human connection with the world of things and so, too, with
the natural correspondences that exist between things quite apart
from ourselves, the impulse to magic mimetic thought, once stimu-
lated and awoken, does not disappear. Rather, in some form of
dislocation (*Entstellung*), removed or disconnected from the natural correspondences, it continues to function "in other fields."[175]
He singles out two such sites for this dislocation or relocation.[176]
The first is the unconscious, distinct from the natural body (as the
natural life in man). That is, the former connecting mimetic force
seems only to have disappeared from our conscious perceptions
and to have been lost in or to our natural bodies; but the human
unconscious still perceives and produces similarities and chains of
similarities out of the things of the external world and the subject's relation to that world. As mentioned, Freud also recognized
the affinities between the unconscious associational dream logic of
condensation and displacement and what Frazer calls sympathetic
imitation and contagion, and Benjamin seems to follow him in positing both this relocation and persistence of magical reading in the
unconscious—although unlike Freud he does not restrict its activity to dream-sleep or the mentally aberrant, but rather assumes its
constant activity alongside and in excess of our ordinary waking
cognition.

The importance of the Freudian unconscious to the modernist mode of magic reading we've noted before. But we also noted
Benjamin's resistance to psychological models, and his differences
from Freud. These emerge again when we consider whether Benjamin thinks the associational chains produced by the human unconscious line up or coincide with the natural correspondences
produced by the cosmos itself—which, unlike Freud, Benjamin
posits as existent. It is hard to say with certainty. On the one hand,
Benjamin describes the natural cosmos that produces its correspondences as one of infinite similarities, which makes it difficult to
imagine similarities that fall outside of it. On the other hand, the

gap between the two seems one of the determining differences between Benjamin and the vitalists (as earlier the mystics), and moreover seems required for those truly magical occasions (those southern nights or winning throws) where such a happy coincidence is
momentarily realized. That is, much like the distortion or dislocation described in "On Language as Such" for the postlapsarian
break between the divine, natural, and human realms, Benjamin's
model here for the modern-day adult appears to entail a disconnect between the two orders of magical similitude—for even in the
earlier essay he stressed that the reading of things produced by human consciousness was "equally magical," just incommensurably
different and so distortive of the magical community inherent in
things themselves.[177] The introduction here of the new realm of the
unconscious would seem to entail a disconnect not only between
the conscious and the unconscious, but also between the unconscious and the body qua "a natural life in man."[178] And this would
hold true whether the unconscious was conceived as discretely in-
dividuated in the subject's psyche or collectively socialized in the
subject's object world: in either case, we are left with a state not of
similarity per se but of what Sigrid Weigel perceptively calls "distorted similarity" (*entstellte Ähnlichkeit*).[179]

The other site to which the impulse toward magical thinking
has become dis- or relocated for Benjamin is language, in both its
spoken and written forms, which brings the question of magical
thinking and the world that supports it back to bear on reading as
such—or rather, comes more or less to restrict it to the case of reading as such (*das Lesen schlechthin*). As Benjamin admits, language
has always been included as a privileged site for the appearance
of magical signs, carrying some other meaning via similitude, and
in both its spoken and its written forms. We have only to recall
the case of the servant's (spoken) words in Homer, or of Homer's
own (written) words in the Neoplatonists, in both of which words
behave just like other animate things in conveying some other, divine significance that cuts across or through the ordinary logic of
their immediate context; or the case of sociable "small talk" in
Fontane, which similarly supported another, spectral significance
and sense of connection behind or beyond its apparent manifest

subject-matter; or, of course, that of Benjamin's own reading child. But the magic of language at stake for Benjamin's world also differs from that in both the ancient and the child's, and for the same reason as it differs for Fontane's—or more immediately important, for the same reason as the associational chains of the unconscious also might differ from those of the cosmos itself.[180] The direct connection of language to the world of things has been lost: even as human consciousness, and unconsciousness, have become separate from things, so too have words, including from the very things they represent. As Foucault puts it, words and world fall apart.[181]

Benjamin insists that words are no longer directly similar to things they signify. Although in "On Language as Such" this was still the case for Adamic language, and in the accounts of ABC primers something similar seemed suggested for the earliest children's books, this is not the case for the language of modern man. Still, even in its dis-located, dis-connected state, Benjamin does say that the imitative associational force of human thought continues to assert itself in language qua its own, discrete archive, repository, or *kosmos* of similarities. In the case of spoken words or *Sprache*, this manifests itself in its onomatopoetic dimension, at the level of sound. While he keeps his distance from the "most primitive" mode of onomatopoetic explanation that assumes a direct and singular similarity between sound and sense, signifier and signified, he still accepts the assertion that "every word—indeed the whole of language—is onomatopoetic."[182] We already encountered his description of children's voice-books (*Stimmenbüchlein*), where the initiation into letters was based on onomatopoeia, providing a social, individual ground for this claim; we also heard his description of language in "Trauerspiel," where alongside the signified meaning of a word came the "natural sound" by which nature itself strives for expression, thus providing a more material, metaphysical ground for the same assertion. But the present argument— for the present-day adult—is more than or different from this: the point here is that whereas sound and sense are not, or no longer, necessarily connected between signifier and signified, word and thing, they are between words themselves, within language itself; where similarities in sound between words of seemingly unrelated meaning generate "sense" over and above their ordinary, merely agreed-upon sign value.[183] As Benjamin puts it, "The nexus of meaning (*Sinnzusammenhang*) which resides in the sounds of the sentence is the basis from which something similar can become apparent out of a sound, flashing up in an instant."[184]

We have a fairly straightforward example of this, from *Berlin Childhood*, in Benjamin's reading of the name (and it is significant that it is a name, *onoma*) of his childhood teacher, Helene Pufahl, where the *P* was the *p* of *perseverance*, the *f* of *faithful* and *fruitful*, and so on—taking the connotative over the denotative dimension of names we saw already in Fontane and breaking it down, as in more ancient times, to the level of letters and their acoustic connotations.[185] And we have "distorted" examples of this from the same work, in which the child's mishearing of certain words (*Mark-Thalle, Mummerehlen, Kupferstichen*) leads to connotations, connections, and meaning different from their ordinary denotations, and based instead on the (distorted) similarities of sound.[186] These examples are, however, also somewhat misleading, or distortive, of Benjamin's intent here, insofar as they entail only single words and set "other" meanings, overlooking the syntagmatic, open-ended, and ever-changing dimension of language that also determines its onomatopoetic activity; indeed the same emphasis on movement and temporality—including convoluted temporality—that distinguished Benjamin's model from that of the French and Klages for signs in graphology.[187] Rather, in this model of onomatopoeia, words and letters as sounds become, as it were, their own mimetic subjects and objects, generating and accepting their similarities to all other word- or letter-sounds, and producing through the back-and-forth (the echoing and adumbrating) movement that alone creates the similarities and so, too, the mutually animating signs an attendant, parasitic sense out of those connections, or resemblances, over and above but also in interaction with the ordinary sense and connection of the words—a magical play of similitude quite apart from any magical play of similitude that might directly connect language to the natural world, the world of things. And although it begins to feel like overload, we need to add that this acoustic order of similitude is both apart from and in interaction with the different orders of similitude not only in things themselves and in agreed-upon linguistic meaning but also in the human unconscious: the sympathetic cosmos has not only fallen apart but multiplied, and with it the opportunities for mutual interaction and distortion.

In the case of written language, the magic aspect of language also continues to assert itself, here at the level of the image.[188] Not surprisingly, Benjamin turns to graphology to illustrate this other, visual level of significance, recalling how handwriting generates picture puzzles (*Vexierbilder*) that convey another, unconscious meaning (in)visibly alongside the semantic content of the words themselves—images that "appear" not so much in the form of individual letters or words but rather, as in the sound play of *Sprache*, in the interplay and movement between the various graphemes. However, as in the discussions of graphology proper, and even though the vocabulary is insistently Freudian, Benjamin is again not content simply to stay at the level of the individual or the unconscious in considering what that "something else" is that script might signify. And this is all the more so here, where the object is not an individual's handwriting but writing itself. For this reason, the earlier discussion of children's books (also alluded to here) seems the more revealing reference, where he described how letters were first introduced to children "disguised" (*vermummt*) as image-figures: this would suggest a nonpsychological, sociohistorical training in such "magical" image-reading for the modern-day former child.[189]

But Benjamin's argument again reaches still farther back in time, into primal history (*Urgeschichte*), and, he admits, to more mystical theories of language and ancient orders of magic. That is, he heuristically accepts that originally written letters themselves—quite apart from any individual rendering and long before the comparatively recent tradition of children's literature—were thought to possess mimetic properties, signaling relations and associations independently of the words in which they found themselves (or even more expansively, words independently of their sentences), functioning like hieroglyphs, runes, or the "characters" of the Neoplatonists.[190] It is in this context that he offers the example of

the Hebrew letter beth (ב) as the root of the word for "house"—
a much stronger claim than that letters, too, are things, animate
things, and so connected to the greater world of things. Rather,
letters are posited as originally similar to what they represent, as
directly connected to the thing world not just materially but also as
active and receptive parts of its mimetic network.

Still, as in the case of the onomatopoetic property of spoken language, Benjamin is not claiming that contemporary script retains
those original mimetic relations, the "natural correspondences" to
the signified external, let alone divine, world: this seems all the more
the case as Benjamin's focus is on a historically more recent phonetic alphabet, on script signifying sounds. Rather, his claim is that
like, but also separate from, spoken language and quite apart from
individual unconscious projection or specific sociohistorical training, graphic language retains "magical" mimetic forces embedded
in itself and communicated by suggestive similarities within itself—
even once cut off from outside external reference. The simplest (but
also most static, and also most *unsinnlich*) of these new similarities
is going to be that between the shape of a given letter (*Schriftbild*)
and the sound it is "like," such that the graphic element will participate in the back-and-forth movement of echoes that produces its
acoustically carried ancillary meaning. But there will also be a separate, compounded such play between the graphic elements themselves (the pdbq, the mnuw, etc.) that multiplies the competing or
colluding orders of similitude interacting with and distorting each
other—and this again on top of any imagistic similarities added by
social training, the unconscious, or even the world itself. This seems
to be why Benjamin repeatedly refers to language as an archive of
similarities, a sequestered repository of stored experiences in material form; but also why he says the similarities will be produced
"every time in a new, original, and underivable way"; an interaction
between the sympathetic, associational orders of material language,
both acoustic and visual, and both conscious and unconscious, individual and social, but all also severed from the "natural" correspondence of things, and of the body as directly connected to things.[191]

Even in this cut-off, self-referential, divided, and multiplied condition, then, the magical properties of language and its reading

persist, as does the essential doubleness of the magic reading experience we've observed before—albeit again in somewhat different form. In antiquity, the magical significance of the "stars, entrails, and coincidences" singled out by Benjamin was always attendant or parasitic upon more ordinary systems of signification; similarly, in Keller, the metatextual was attendant upon the realist representation, and in Fontane and Simmel, the same condition held for the sociable significance that emerged spectrally behind the apparent trivialities of small talk. So in Benjamin, this magic side of language is always in complex, interactive, dependent relation to "something alien, precisely the semiotic or communicative aspect of language," on whose basis alone it can appear. But unlike in antiquity, there is no hidden world—either of things or behind things—to which these signs refer; even as unlike in Keller, there seems no metatext behind the text, or unlike in Fontane or Simmel, no sociable community, let alone "life," that the signs connect to. Rather, they seem only to refer back to, to turn back on, the immediate, manifest meaning of language itself. But as a kind of compensation for this delimitation, Benjamin claims that now all reading (*alles Lesen*) is always at once this double reading, bringing the material similarities of sound and image to bear on the semiotic content, producing conjunctions of sound, shape, and sense that first give meaning to the first two (and in this very different from antiquity) and give a second, added meaning to the last, which thus is never "just" itself.

Benjamin describes this double reading as a combination of *Ablesen* (reading off) and *Herauslesen* (reading out from) that responds to and combines the two different aspects of language (semiotic and "magical"). Its designated doubleness is, however, somewhat deceptive: not only because, as we've seen, the nonsemiotic realm of language has multiplied and fractured in ways that can be difficult to reduce to a single unified order, but also because, as we know from earlier in the essay—and know as intended here precisely through those similarities in sound and phrasing being addressed—this double reading is more precisely a triple reading, with the doubleness of its signs only manifest, interpretable, or readable (*herauszulesen*) with the addition of the third term: the occasion of the reader, or reading, itself. It is only in this instance (this *Nu*) of his sympathetic, identificatory participation—in the coincidence of his need, his *Glück*—that the conjunction of the different levels of language can manifest their sudden, fleeting similarity, not just to each other but to him and his moment, triggering the mimetic blending of all three. It is, Benjamin says, out of such a conjunction, such a *Zeitmoment*, that the ancient astrologer reads both fate and future out of the patterns constellated by stars in the sky; and so too the modern reader his meanings out of the (swirling, tinkling) patterns of sound, shape, and sense from words on the page.

As the mention of both fate and the future makes clear, Benjamin regards the double (or triple) reading of the astrologer as a mode of divination. And he just as explicitly regards all reading of the present-day adult as also a form of divination, of clairvoyance (*Hellsicht*), a migration of reading as such out of stars, entrails, and coincidences in mankind's distant past into a new reading (*ein neues Lesen*), based upon the twin relocations of magical logic into the human unconscious, in both its individual and its social forms, and the materiality of language, in both its aural and its visual forms. Even if no longer directly based on the "body reading" of natural life, this new reading is still based on a mimetic chaining of the subject to the similar in what he reads. And whereas what the subject reader mimetically connects to may not directly be the world of things, it is still to language *as* a world of things, perhaps the only world of things still regularly accessible to him. Benjamin underscores this by saying that the reader encounters in language things in their "essences, in their most delicate and transient substances," and as the adjectives indicate, this "essence" of things is not only their isolated materiality but also their reciprocal relationality, their constellating sympathetic force as temporally conditioned mimetic subjects and objects.[192] For this reason, this new reading, too, is still very much a matter of movement, animation, and the coordination of different times, as the future thrust of each series of letters and words inflects and is inflected by its nonlinear, back-and-forth play of sound and image, at once binding and keeping open their past, present, and future sense.

We see, then, that when Benjamin claims the cosmic mimetic force has migrated into language per se and clairvoyance into reading per se, he retains for it many of the key features of magic divination we've found throughout. However, what we do not clearly see retained is perhaps the central component of divination, the one Benjamin himself foregrounds with respect to the ancient tradition but then seemingly does not return to when describing the new reading of modern man: the reading of fate, or rather, of fate and the future (and so, too, *Glück*). The point is a tricky one, but I'm going to suggest that Benjamin does indeed return to this aspect of reading, in fact devotes the concluding paragraph of "Doctrine of the Similar" to it: even that he has been working toward this end throughout.

To some extent, the question of fate has already been adumbrated in what was just said. Insofar as fate is a matter of our connection to things, it seems to have been both lost and recuperated in our present reading practices: lost insofar as the direct connection between the reader's body or natural life and the world of things is imagined to have been severed or forgotten, recuperated insofar as reading retains, even enacts, our now largely unconscious connection to language as its own thing world.[193] Both the connection and the disconnection with the world of fate qua things have, we know, both positive and negative aspects for Benjamin, particularly regarding the subject's need for happiness; and we could sketch out arguments for reading as both the best occasion for happiness in both its connection and its disconnection with the world of fate, and an occasion in which happiness is no longer really possible or at stake—or only falsely at stake, a symptom of modern man's isolated detachment from a broader world, or community, of meaning.[194]

But the question of fate still left open (indeed, left open and residual since our closing section on Fontane) is whether Benjamin believes reading might actually, momentarily and fleetingly, overcome our disconnection with a world beyond language, restore for his modern man the actual magical, natural connection to things themselves: to the broader world or community of meaning beyond our human selves. Benjamin appends to his claim that, in language, the reader encounters things in their most delicate and transient substances, "even in their aromas," hinting at an atavistic, physical level of perception that is even deeper than the human unconscious; and this peculiar, almost Proustian thought might suggest such a restored connection, much as those southern moonlit nights might resurrect the nascent promises that lay in constellations of the stars.[195] But, as the examples of both Proustian smell and the resurrected magic moment also suggest, this is where the matter of fate in connection with things joins most forcibly to the matter of fate in connection with time—and as part of that, fate in its connection not only with the past but with futurity.

We've encountered the question of futurity in its relation to fate and divinatory reading in several different forms over the course of this chapter, beginning with the injunction against raising the question at all: the prohibition against inquiring into the future, or linking *Glück* to the future, that appears from the early "Fate and Character" to the closing sections of the late "On the Concept of History"; an occultation adumbrated in Fontane's late realism and echoed repeatedly in Benjamin's modernist peers. But in our reading of graphology we recovered something of the future in the open temporal line of handwriting, whose movement and future thrust proved essential to the divination of the "other" significance conveyed by its signs. With respect to gambling, we found the crucial factor of acceleration, which allowed for an outpacing of ordinary, conscious time and, again, a kind of future thrust that opened up the gambler qua reader to telepathic contact with the world of (moving) things—the ball—and so, too, to a momentary divination, the happy recognition of what was to come, inflecting the present. And in childhood, or rather, in the memory of childhood, we found how the movement of the reader himself, out of childhood (and its still existent mimetic chains) and into adulthood (where those earlier chains have broken), produced the conditions to divine in childhood another hidden significance, another similarity—the divination of a fate and a future that pertained not only to the child's past life and activity, but to those of the present-day adult as well. We've also just seen how, in the "new reading" of the present essay, time, movement, and the future play a key role in the divination of the "other" significance conveyed by the sequestered sound and image play of all language.

All of these figure in a reading of the last paragraph of "Doctrine of the Similar," which is devoted to the matter of tempo or speed in reading, the speed that Benjamin says is inseparable from clairvoyant reading and our ability to participate in that measure of time "in which similarities flash fleetingly out of the stream of things (*dem Fluß der Dinge*)," and which the reader "must not forget at any cost, lest he go away empty-handed."[196] The language recalls the earlier discussion of the tempo or pace that was a key component of the divination explored in handwriting and gambling; and it echoes as well the earlier discussion of the peculiar temporal dimension to the realm of the similar and the indispensable introduction of the third term, the astrologer qua reader, whose own moving moment, like that of the diary reader or historian (qua back-turned prophet), proved essential to realizing the coordinated *Nu* that revealed fate and future. To this we might add as well one of the leading motifs of Benjamin's writings on hashish, namely, the "heightened velocity of thought" that enables a "quickened empathy with all things," a "tenderness toward all things," connected to the apprehension of an aura that emanates out of them—an experience reproduced, apparently without drugs, in a short passage contemporary with the "Doctrine," entitled "The Tree and Language" (Der Baum und die Sprache). Here Benjamin describes himself climbing a hill, coming under a tree, and

> following its movements with my eyes, I suddenly found that, within me, language was so gripped by it that momentarily the age-old marriage with the tree was suddenly reenacted once again in my presence. . . . A gentle breeze signaled the start of a wedding and soon carried throughout the world the children who had quickly sprung from this bed, like an image-speech (*Bilder-rede*).

> Während ich ins Laubwerk sah und seiner Bewegung folgte, mit einmal [wurde] in mir die Sprache dergestalt von ihm ergriffen, daß sie augenblicklich die uralte Vermählung mit dem Baum in meinem Beisein noch einmal vollzog. . . . Ein leiser Wind spielte zur Hochzeit auf und trug alsbald die schnell entsprossenen Kinder dieses Betts als Bilderrede unter alle Welt.[197]

That is, with this movement, a moment of well-nigh mystical melding is achieved in which language is "once again" joined to things, and the self to both, and in which the "age-old" past, the present, and a "quickly" generated future all seem equally and simultaneously there.[198]

Something very similar seems to be at stake in Benjamin's musings about the speed required for the magic clairvoyance of reading itself, including its production of that rare but blissful, critical moment of magic divination.[199] The rapid pace of reading allows one, even forces one, to outpace strictly rational cognition and its time, and to enter into a different perceptual temporality in which the similarities that sign themselves in moving things—and perhaps especially in the sounds and images, but also in the "aromas" of words as things—themselves magically, suddenly, and fleetingly appear. It is a temporality, a *Zeitmoment* of coordinated lines of movement that Benjamin explicitly suggests achieves a contact with things—of the semiotics of the text with the mimetic thingness of its language and of the mimetic, sympathetic reader with both, but also, it seems, of both language and the reader with the mimetic thingness of the world itself (*der Fluß der Dinge*). And it is a moment, too, in however rich or weak a form, filled with its own futurity, if only we grasp it; a moment of contact with words, both meaning and material, that came before, imbuing them with a future, another meaning, and so too a fate; but a moment, too, in necessary contact with its own future, a future that will show the present its own meaning, its own fate, which the rapidity of reading can make always already present. Realizing this moment, which can happen whenever we read, can bring a special kind of happiness, of *Glück* and "tenderness," that rare moment of "bodily presence of mind" he calls divination.

NOTES

Introduction

1. "How do things link together?" My interrogative version of "Die Dinge verketten sich!"; Conrad Ferdinand Meyer, *Die Hochzeit des Mönchs*, in Meyer, *Sämtliche Werke*, edited by Alfred Zäch and Hans Zeller (Bern: Benteli, 1961), 12:26.

2. Walter Benjamin, "Surrealismus," in Benjamin, *Gesammelte Schriften*, edited by Rolf Tiedemann and Hermann Schweppenhäuser (Frankfurt am Main: Suhrkamp, 1980), 2:307; translation from Walter Benjamin, *Selected Writings*, edited by Marcus Bullock, Howard Eiland, Michael Jennings, et al. (Cambridge, MA: Harvard University Press, 1996–2003), 2:216. These editions will subsequently be referred to in these notes as "GS" and "SW," respectively.

3. See Brooke Holmes, *The Tissue of the World: Sympathy and the Nature of Nature in Greco-Roman Antiquity* (forthcoming), who concentrates on *sympatheia* in ancient medicine; and Alice Kuzniar, *The Birth of Homeopathy out of the Spirit of Romanticism* (Toronto: University of Toronto Press, 2017), who writes on homeopathy and its nineteenth-century aesthetic roots.

4. Michel Foucault, *The Order of Things: An Archaeology of the Human Sciences* (New York: Vintage, 1970), 44.

5. Of course, there is a future dimension to magic as well, one that is understudied and often underappreciated. See Derek Collins, *Magic in the Ancient Greek World* (Malden, MA: Blackwell, 2008), 171n20.

6. Stephen Greenblatt, *Shakespearean Negotiations* (Berkeley: University of California Press, 1988), 1; Peter Brooks, "Freud's Masterplot," *Yale French Studies 55/56* (1977): 283. In this context Greenblatt refers to literature professors as "salaried, middle-class shamans," and except for the professional status, the same would hold for all readers; Brooks also speaks of the "magic" and "demonic" dimensions of reading literary texts (288).

7. The interpreter is not always the same subject as the audience initiating the wish. Rather, the former sometimes serves as the representative agent of the latter, much as the literary critic can act for the general reader.

8. See Lucien Lévy-Bruhl, *How Natives Think* (New York: Washington Square Press, 1966), 61–74; Carl Gustav Jung, *Psychological Types*, edited by R. F. C. Hull (Princeton, NJ: Princeton University Press, 1976), who defines Lévy-Bruhl's mystical participation as denoting "a peculiar kind of psychological connection with objects. It consists in the fact that the subject cannot clearly distinguish himself from the object but is bound to it by a direct relationship which one can describe as a partial identity. This identity is founded upon an *a priori* oneness of object and subject" (456). For the importance of Lévy-Bruhl and his concept of mystical participation to Benjamin's ideas of both magic and reading, see Benjamin, "Probleme der Sprachsoziologie" (Problems in the Sociology of Language), GS 3:455–459; SW 3:70–73; also Anson Rabinbach, "Introduction to Walter Benjamin's 'Doctrine of the Similar'," *New German Critique* 17 (Spring 1979): 63. For Lévy-Bruhl's relevance to contemporary understandings of ancient magic, see Collins, *Magic*, 7.

9. For Benjamin, see chapter 3. For Barthes's theory of reading, see Roland Barthes, *A Lover's Discourse: Fragments*, translated by Richard Howard (New York: Hill and Wang, 1978).

10. There is something of a similar, and similarly significant, overlap in the English between happiness, happenstance, happening, etc. More immediately to the point, in following Benjamin in stressing happiness as both the motive and the goal of reading, I am not so much rephrasing as challenging Barthes's notion of either the pleasure or bliss of reading—for happiness is something quite different from either. See Roland Barthes, *The Pleasure of the Text*, translated by Richard Miller (New York: Hill and Wang, 1975).

11. Edward Burnett Tylor, *The Origins of Culture* (Gloucester, MA: Peter Smith, 1970), 115–119, where contiguity is illustrated by ropes and threads—introducing the idea of chains that will be crucial to our analysis further on—and where imitative is called symbolic or analogic. Sympathy is not an explicit category but is mentioned at 119 (sympathetic ointment) and 130 (the sympathy between the waxing/waning moon and growing/declining nature). James George Frazer, *The Golden Bough: A Study in Magic and Religion*, (New York: Macmillan, 1956), 14; see also Collins, *Magic*, 14f. For the relation to Adam Smith's notion of contagion, see Nancy Armstrong, *How Novels Think: The Limits of Individualism from 1719–1900* (New York: Columbia University Press, 2005), 13–15; for the relation to homeopathy itself, see Kuzniar, *The Birth of Homeopathy*. Michael Taussig, *Mimesis and Alterity: A Particular History of the Senses* (New York: Routledge, 1993), is also interested in the connections between Benjamin's theories of mimesis and similarity and Frazer's categories of sympathetic magic: see esp. Taussig, 44–58. Although by his own admission Taussig's reading

of Benjamin is highly idiosyncratic (23) and certainly differs in its direction from that taken here in connecting Benjamin with magical traditions, I have nonetheless found it deeply suggestive and inspiring for this study as a whole, especially for the chapter on Gottfried Keller.

12. Roman Jakobson, "Two Aspects of Language and Two Types of Aphasic Disturbances," in *Language and Literature*, edited by Krytyna Pomorska and Stephen Rudy (Cambridge, MA: Harvard University Press, 1987), 113. The connection between Frazer's categories for magic and Freud's for dream thought were recognized and discussed by Freud himself in *Totem and Tabu*.

13. Max Horkheimer and Theodor W. Adorno, "The Concept of Enlightenment," in *Dialectic of Enlightenment*, translated by John Cumming (New York: Continuum, 1988), 3–42; Samuel Coleridge, "Science and System of Logic," transcription of Coleridge's lectures of 1822, quoted in Andrea Wulf, *The Invention of Nature: Alexander von Humboldt's New World* (New York: Knopf, 2015), 170.

14. Edward Burnett Tylor, "Magic," in *The Encyclopaedia Britannica: A Dictionary of Arts, Sciences, and General Literature* (New York: Werner, 1896), 15:205.

15. Cf. Benjamin, *Einbahnstrasse*, GS 4:141f.; SW 1:482. Also Peter T. Struck, *Birth of the Symbol: Ancient Readers at the Limits of Their Texts* (Princeton, NJ: Princeton University Press, 2004), a work of seminal importance for the second part of this early history.

16. Aeschylus, *Prometheus Bound* 484–495, in *Aeschyli septem quae supersunt tragoedias*, edited by Denys Page (London: Oxford University Press, 1972).

17. See Derek Collins, "Mapping the Entrails: The Practice of Greek Hepatoscopy," *American Journal of Philology* 129 (2008): 319–345. Derek Collins's work represents the major source for the first part of this early history, and I need to thank him as well for his correspondence and early encouragement of this project.

18. Collins, "Mapping the Entrails," 319–20.

19. Ibid., 328–32, 341–42.

20. Ibid., 330.

21. See A. Magianni, "Qualche osservazione sul fegato di Piacenza," *Studi Etruschi* 50 (1982): 53–88.

22. Collins, "Mapping the Entrails," 326–27.

23. See Derek Collins, "Reading the Birds: Oionomanteia in Early Epic," *Colby Quarterly* 38 (2002): 17–41.

24. See, for example, Homer, *Odyssey* 2.146–180.

25. Collins, "Reading the Birds," 20, 22.

26. Ibid., 24.

27. See Struck, *Birth of the Symbol*, 4.

28. Collins, "Reading the Birds," 22.

29. Ibid., 20. Michael Puri (public lecture) offers a felicitious phrase for this peculiar kind of sign in his analysis of Ravel's musical mnemonics: he speaks of the "premonition of a recollection," a sign we suspect we will have to remember to look back to. I suggest that this might well be an overlooked condition of all signification.

30. Collins, "Reading the Birds," 32–33.

31. Ibid.

32. Ibid.

33. Tylor, *Origins*, refers to these by the technical term *Angang*, "the omens taken from meeting animals and people, especially on first going out in the morning" (120). Although Struck, *Birth of the Symbol*, 90–91, follows Walter Müri in ascribing this use of *symbola* to a secondary meaning of *symballein*, it seems still to resonate with the primary meaning of joined tokens.

34. The "concerned subject" could be a group, not just an individual.

35. Quoted in Struck, *Birth of the Symbol*, 93f.; Homer, *Odyssey* 20.105–121; see also 17.541–547; 18.112–117.

36. See Christopher Wild, "Apertio libri: Codex and Conversion," in *Literary Studies and the Pursuits of Reading*, edited by Eric Downing, Jonathan M. Hess, and Richard Benson (Rochester, NY: Camden House, 2012), 17–39.

37. See Collins, "Homeric Incantations," in *Magic*, 104–131.

38. For a particularly brilliant example of such an associational reading, see Collins, *Magic*, 115–116.

39. Collins, *Magic*, 128.

40. Struck, *Birth of the Symbol*, 231. Brooks, "Freud's Masterplot," refers to something like these chains in Freudian terms as "binding" (289), a word also central to magical practices; see below.

41. Peter Struck, "Microcosm and Macrocosm in Greek Divination" (invited lecture, University Of North Carolina, November 2002).

42. Struck, *Birth of the Symbol*, 227–253.

43. The irony of Plato's dialogue, and the somewhat mocking tone of Socrates's account of the magnetic chain connecting Ion to the divine Homer (and beyond), seem not to have been part of the Neoplatonists' reception.

44. Foucault, *The Order of Things*, 42–44.

45. Ibid., 40–41.

46. Ibid., 42–44.

47. Pierre Hadot, *The Veil of Isis: An Essay on the History of the Idea of Nature* (Cambridge, MA: Harvard University Press, 2006), 247–282. See also Hans-Joachim Mähl, "Novalis und Plotin: Untersuchungen zu einer neuen Edition und Interpretation des 'Allgemeinen Brouillon'," *Jahrbuch des Freien Deutschen Hochstifts*, 1963, 139–250; M. H. Abrams, *Natural Supernaturalism* (New York: Norton, 1971), 146–151; Struck, *Birth of the Symbol*, 272–275.

48. The objects and their magic at stake in this study are not those of the commodity. As Elaine Freedgood, *The Ideas in Things: Fugitive Meaning in the Victorian Novel* (Chicago: University of Chicago Press, 2006), elegantly declares in relation to the British nineteenth century, "mid-Victorians, and the objects in their novels, were not fully in the grip of the kind of fetishism Marx and Marxists have ascribed to industrial culture. The abstraction of the commodity into a money value, the spectacularization of the consumer good, the alienation of things from their human and geographical origins—these were not the only ways of imagining the things in that crowded world. A host of ideas resided in Victorian things: abstraction, alienation, and spectacularization had to compete with other kinds of object relations—ones that we have perhaps yet to appreciate" (7–8). This is also true of the German novels here engaged, and of those objects and object relations in Benjamin that I am interested in: there are other kinds of magic to be appreciated, not least through an inclusion of the more-than-human world.

49. Roland Barthes, "The Photographic Message," in *Image/Music/Text*, translated by Stephen Heath (New York: Noonday, 1977), 22–23 (Barthes's italics).

50. Armstrong, *How Novels Think.*

51. For Benjamin on the novel, see esp. "Der Erzähler" (The Storyteller), GS 2:438–465; SW 3:143–166; and "Zum Bilde Prousts" (On the Image of Proust), GS 2:310–324; SW 2:237–247.

52. Roman Jakobson, "Linguistics and Poetics," in *Language in Literature*, edited by Krytyna Pomorska and Stephen Rudy (Cambridge MA: Harvard University Press, 1987), 82–85.

53. Barthes, "The Photographic Message," 23.

54. Armstrong, *How Novels Think*, 17: the reference is to Adam Smith, *Theory of Moral Sentiments*, 219. For Benjamin on mimetic blending, see Miriam Bratu Hansen, "Benjamin, Cinema, and Experience: 'The Blue Flower in the Land of Technology'," *New German Critique* 40 (Winter 1987): 179–224. Armstrong is ready to associate this effect with "gothic" novels as opposed to realist ones: at least in the German tradition, the distinction doesn't quite hold.

55. Collins, *Magic*, 16; see too Tylor, *Origins*, 116f.

56. Think of Risach in Adalbert Stifter's *Der Nachsommer* and his collection of things, but always things as signs of himself and of nature. And as Eva Geulen notes, "For Stifter, the goal of literature was not the poetic transfiguration of the world but the gathering up of its things, convinced, as he was, that any rock is already precious and valuable or will reveal itself as such one day. Banal objects are thus regularly endowed with the allure of future significance." Geulen, "Tales of a Collector," in *A New History of German Literature*, edited by David Wellbery et al. (Cambridge, MA: Harvard University Press, 2004), 588. I'm reminded, too, of Jean-Jacques Rousseau, *Emile or On Education*, translated by Alan Bloom (New York: Basic Books, 1979): "Our individual persons are now the least part of ourselves. Each man extends himself, so to speak, over the whole earth and becomes sensitive over this entire large surface. Is it surprising that our ills are multiplied by all the points where we can be wounded? . . . We no longer exist where we are: we only exist where we are not" (83).

57. This is part of both Horkheimer and Adorno's and Taussig's reading of the shamanistic dimension to mimesis, a dimension I extend to reading.

58. Brooks, "Freud's Masterplot," 288.

59. Ibid.

60. See Barthes, *A Lover's Discourse.*

61. D. A. Miller, *The Novel and the Police* (Berkeley: University of California Press, 1988), 81–83.

62. Benjamin, GS 4:432–433; SW 2:726–727.

63. Leo Spitzer, *Classical and Christian Ideas of World Harmony: Prolegomena to an Interpretation of the Word "Stimmung,"* edited by Anna Granville Hatcher (Baltimore: Johns Hopkins University Press, 1963), 3, 9–10.

64. Carl Gustav Carus, *Neun Briefe über Landschaftsmalerei* (Dresden: Wolfgang Jess Verlag, 1950), 38.

65. Ibid., 42.

66. Ute Frevert, *Emotions in History—Lost and Found* (Budapest: Central European University Press, 2011).

67. Ibid., 175–76.

68. David Wellbery, "Stimmung," in *Ästhetische Grundbegriffe: Historisches Wörterbuch in sieben Bänden*, edited by Karlheinz Barck et al. (Stuttgart: Metzler Verlag, 2010), 703–733.
69. Barbara Maria Stafford, *Visual Analogy: Consciousness as the Art of Connecting* (Cambridge, MA: MIT Press, 1999), 8–54.
70. Benjamin, "Paris, die Hauptstadt des XIX Jahrhunderts," GS 5:55; SW 3:40.
71. Benjamin, "Der Erzähler," GS 2:460, 462–463; SW 3:159, 160–161.
72. Benjamin, "Surrealismus," GS 2:300; SW 2:210.
73. The English translation of the penultimate sentence of "The Storyteller" in *Selected Writings* actually translates Benjamin's *Stimmung* as "aura." As the editors explain in a note, this equation is supported by a reference to the French version of the essay that Benjamin himself prepared and that includes an added sentence just after this one that refers to the aura [*ce halo*] of the storyteller. See SW 3:166n28.
74. Benjamin, "Kleine Geschichte der Photographie," GS 2:378; SW 2:518–519.
75. "Breath of prehistory" (Hauch von Vorgeschichte): "Über einige Motive bei Baudelaire," GS 1:643; SW 4:336; *stimmungslos*: "Kleine Geschichte der Photographie," GS 2:379; SW 2:519.
76. Hansen, "Benjamin, Cinema, and Experience," 357.
77. Miriam Bratu Hansen, "Benjamin's Aura," *Critical Inquiry* 34, no. 2 (2008): 346; Benjamin, "Über einige Motive bei Baudelaire" (On Some Motifs in Baudelaire), GS 1:646–647; SW 4:338.

1. Painting Magic in Keller's *Green Henry*

1. Gottfried Keller, *Der Grüne Heinrich* (1854/55), in Keller, *Sämtliche Werke: Historisch-kritische Ausgabe*, edited by Walter Morgenthaler et al. (Basel/Zurich: Stroemfeld Verlag/Verlag Neue Zürcher Zeitung, 2005), 11:331. All references to the text of this work will be to this edition. For the translations, I have consulted and at times adapted A. M. Holt's translation, *Green Henry* (Woodstock, NY: Overlook Press, 1960).
2. My thanks to Rory Bradley for conversations helping to formulate this point.
3. It does seem worth stressing that whereas the superceded "magical" sensibility is often equated by critics with romanticism, for Keller, Storm, Raabe, and other central representatives of German realism, the early modern is more accurate: Foucault is helpful in suggesting this. See Andrew Webber, "The Afterlife of Romanticism," in *German Literature of the Nineteenth Century: 1832–1899*, edited by Clayton Koelb and Eric Downing, vol. 9 of *Camden House History of German Literature* (Rochester, NY: Camden House, 2005), 23–43; Michel Foucault, *The Order of Things: An Archaeology of the Human Sciences* (New York: Random House, 1970), 17–45.
4. Nancy Armstrong, *How Novels Think: The Limits of Individualism from 1719–1900* (New York: Columbia University Press, 2005).
5. E.g., the seminal study by Gerhard Kaiser, *Gottfried Keller: Das Gedichtete Leben* (Frankfurt am Main: Insel, 1981).
6. One important facet effaced by this approach is the difference between a Freudian notion of the unconscious and that of, e.g., Keller's contemporary Carl

Gustav Carus, a noted early nineteenth-century theorist of landscape painting (see the introduction). For Carus, *das Unbewußte* is not limited to the human psyche but rather encompasses our relation to the natural world—even as for Ludwig Feuerbach, a noted influence on Keller, our relation to the natural world encompasses our unconscious. See Carl Gustav Carus, *Über Lebensmagnetismus und über die magischen Wirkungen überhaupt* (Leipzig: F. A. Brockhaus, 1857), xx; Ludwig Feuerbach, *Lectures on the Essence of Religion*, translated by Ralph Manheim (New York: Harper & Row, 1967), 91.

7. David Wellbery, "Stimmung," in *Ästhetische Grundbegriffe: Historisches Wörterbuch in sieben Bänden*, edited by Karlheinz Barck et al. (Stuttgart: Metzler Verlag, 2010): 703–733; Ulrich Gumbrecht, *Atmosphere, Mood, Stimmung: On a Hidden Potential of Literature*, translated by Erick Butler (Stanford, CA: Stanford University Press, 2012); Thomas Pfau, *Romantic Moods: Paranoia, Trauma, and Melancholy, 1790–1840* (Baltimore: Johns Hopkins University Press, 2005); Pfau, "The Appearance of *Stimmung*: Play as Virtual Rationality," in *Stimmung: Zur Wiederkehr einer ästhetischen Kategorie*, edited by Anna-Katharina Gisbertz (Munich: Fink Verlag, 2011), 95–111. Other contributors to Gisbertz's volume who will be discussed include Jochen Hörisch, Hermann Schmitz, Caroline Welsh, and David Wellbery. Wellbery's original essay is seminal to most of the contributions to Gisbertz's volume; because it has so far appeared only in German, its impact in the United States has been more limited. I hope by presenting a sketch of its main points here in English that its essential argument might reach a wider audience. Needless to say, the *Stimmung* at stake in all these studies, including the present one, differs considerably from its rather worn usage in much earlier criticsm.

8. Leo Spitzer, *Classical and Christian Ideas of World Harmony: Prolegomena to an Interpretation of the Word "Stimmung"* (Baltimore: Johns Hopkins University Press, 1963).

9. For Storm, see Elisabeth Strowick and Ulrike Vedder, eds., *Wirklichkeit und Wahrnehmung: Neue Perspektiven auf Theodor Storm* (Bern: Peter Lang, 2013). Storm is also an important figure in so-called *Stimmungslyrik*, a tradition that also includes Rilke; for the latter, see David Wellbery, "Der gestimmte Raum," in Gisbertz, *Stimmung*, 157–176.

10. E.g., Keller, 12:73: "Ich fühlte mich gebannt in einer jener dunklen Stimmungen" (I felt myself under the spell of one of those dark *Stimmungen*), where *Stimmung* is presented as a charm or spell, and a dark one at that; 11:297, 301: where *Stimmung* is associated with death, and with a produced effect; 11:269: where *Stimmung* is linked to music; and 11:309: where Heinrich speaks of an *innere Sympathie* when viewing landscape paintings.

11. Caroline Welsh, "Zur psychologischen Traditionslinie ästhetischer Stimmung zwischen Aufklärung und Moderne," in Gisberzt, *Stimmung*, 138–141, is particularly eloquent in describing *Stimmung* in late eighteenth-century theory as connected with the "dark" forces of the mind—drawing on Wolf's distinction (of "dunkle Vorstellungen"): she quotes Carus as defining it as "the first becoming conscious of what until then had been unconscious" (*erstes Bewußtewerden des bis dahin Unbewußten*) in his *Psyche* (Welsh, 140), and sees it as a rarely fully recognized force emanating out of the unconscious, often overriding rationality, and so as possessing all the shaping powers of Freud's unconscious. She doesn't,

as Carus himself does (and others before and after him), also see it as a capacity to sense something outside of itself, part of the external world, and so something more than just the Freudian unconscious: but this would seem also to be intrinsic to its psychological profile; see below.

12. See Eric Downing, "Magic Reading," in *Literary Studies and the Pursuits of Reading*, edited by Eric Downing, Jonathan M. Hess, and Richard Benson (Rochester, NY: Camden House, 2005), 189–215; Burkhard Meyer-Sickendiek, "Über das Gespür: Neuphänomenologische Überlegungen zum Begriff der 'Stimmungslyrik'," in Gisbertz, *Stimmung*, 45–62.

13. The insistence on the nonpsychological, external nature of *Stimmung* is central to Hermann Schmitz, "Die Stimmung einer Stadt," in Gisbertz, *Stimmung*, 63–74; and Meyer-Sickendiek, "Über das Gespür." For the persistence of the vocabulary and conceptual framework of sympathetic magic in the popular literature of Keller's day, see, e.g., Carus, *Über Lebensmagnetismus*. For atmosphere, see Timothy Attanucci, "Atmosphärische Stimmungen: Landschaft und Meteorologie bei Carus, Goethe, und Stifter," *Zeitschrift für Germanistik*, n.s. 24, no. 2 (2014): 282–295.

14. The relation of parts of the observing subject to each other is crucial to Kant's notion of *Stimmung*.

15. This is key to the conception of *Stimmung* in Carus; see Carl Gustav Carus, *Neun Briefe über Landschaftsmalerei* (Dresden: Wolfgang Jess Verlag, 195–?), 39–47.

16. This vocabulary, in good part because influenced by Schelling's *Naturphilosophie* (itself influenced by Neoplatonism: see M. H. Abrams, *Natural Supernaturalism* [New York: Norton, 1971], 146–51; Peter Struck, *Birth of the Symbol: Ancient Readers at the Limits of Their Texts* [Princeton, NJ: Princeton University Press, 2004], 256, 275; John H. Smith, "Religion and Early German Romanticism: The Finite and the Infinite" [forthcoming]), is still part of the nineteenth-century aesthetic discourse of landscape painting: see Gustav Theodor Fechner (quoted in Oskar Bätschmann, "Carl Gustav Carus [1789–1869]: Physician, Naturalist, Painter, and Theoretician of Landscape Painting," in Carl Gustav Carus, *Nine Letters on Landscape Painting*, translated by David Britt [Los Angeles: Getty Research Institute, 2002], 47), Carus (ibid., 91); Charles Blanc (ibid., 50), in the latter case in almost overly literal form.

17. Indeed, *Stimmung* is a field in which the subject-object distinction does not hold, nor the inner-outer. For this reason, it is a field in which the psychological has some place, but only some place. For Lévy-Bruhl's concept of "mystical participation" and its relation to magic, see Derek Collins, *Magic in the Ancient Greek World* (Malden, MA: Blackwell, 2008), 7; also Downing, "Magic Reading," 191.

18. Carus, *Neun Briefe*, following Humboldt, calls it a Cosmos: the term is also central to Spitzer, *Classical and Christian Ideas*.

19. Perhaps worth emphasizing that difference—contrast—is part of this, even as antipathy is, as Foucault argues, part of sympathy. Also mentioned in Carus, *Über Lebensmagnetismus*.

20. For the Neoplatonists, see Struck, *Birth of the Symbol*; also Downing, "Magic Reading."

21. See Spitzer, *Classical and Christian Ideas*, 22.

22. The notions of susceptibility and contagion are of paramount importance for linking the spheres of aesthetics and illness in *Der Grüne Heinrich*, especially in regard to Anna as viewer of Heinrich's artwork; see below.

23. For Friedrich Scheiermacher on divination, see Thomas Pfau, "Immediacy and the Text: Friedrich Schleiermacher's Theory of Style and Interpretation," *Journal of the History of Ideas* 51, no. 1 (1990): 51–73. For Carus, *Neun Briefe*, letter 5.

24. Spitzer, *Classical and Christian Ideas*, who focuses on music and the more ancient roots of the concept (especially in Augustine), has more to say about the intrinsic temporality of *Stimmung* (28ff.).

25. See also Friedrich Nietzsche, *Morgenröte: Gedanken über die moralischen Vorurteile* (Munich: Goldmann Verlag, 1980), 31f.: aphorism 28, "Die Stimmung als Argument."

26. In his subsequent essay, "Der gestimmte Raum," Wellbery more explicitly declares that *Stimmung* is future related (*zukunftsbezogen*). See below, note 32.

27. See Jochen Hörisch, "Sich in Stimmmung bringen: Über poetisches und mediales Mood-and-Mind-Management," in Gisbertz, *Stimmung*, 40. Similarly, Meyer-Sickendiek, "Über das Gespür," uses as his example of *Stimmungslyrik* a Hoffmannsthal poem, "Vorgefühl" (ibid., 50).

28. It is perhaps worth noting how these two passages from Wellbery also suggest a temporal structure and future force similar to that which Freud will associate with anxiety—although of course anxiety is only one possible *Stimmung*, and this model allows for more. Still, anxiety is one of the many forms in which divinatory experience reappears at the center of nineteenth- and early twentieth-century discourse and sensibility; see Johannes Türk, *Die Immunität der Literatur* (Frankfurt am Main: Fischer, 2011). It might also be mentioned that the temporal dimension to *Stimmung* will emerge, in the form of rhythm, as a major theoretical point at the end of the nineteenth century in vitalist philosophy as one of the key elements connecting the human aesthetic subject to natural life, in ways that will become of particular importance also to early film theory. See Michael Cowan, "The Heart Machine: 'Rhythm' and Body in Weimar Film and Fritz Lang's Metropolis," *Modernism/modernity* 14, no. 2 (2007): 225–248; Oliver Gaycken, *Devices of Curiosity: Early Cinema and Popular Science* (Oxford: Oxford University Press, 2015); Inga Pollmann, "Zum Fühlen gezwungen: Mechanismus und Vitalismus in Hans Richters Neuerfindung des Kinos," in *Mies van der Rohe, Richter, Graeff & Co: Alltag und Design in der Avantgardezeitschrift G*, edited by Karin Fest et al. (Vienna/Berlin: Turia + Kant, 2014), 169–176.

29. W. J. T. Mitchell, *Landscape and Power* (Chicago: University of Chicago Press, 2002), would disagree and see the lack of distinction as a problem ("The invitation to look at a view is thus a suggestion to look at nothing," viii). Carus, *Neun Briefe*, also at times insists on the distinction.

30. This latter point seems implicit in Kerstin Thomas, "Der Stimmungsbegriff und seine Bedeutung für die Kunst des 19. Jahrhunderts," in Gisbertz, *Stimmung*, 211–234.

31. For the distinction, see Foucault, *The Order of Things*, 43.

32. This registers both my agreement and my disagreement with an argument Wellbery makes in "Der gestimmte Raum." He claims that while the *Dispositionen*

that are the bases for *Stimmungen* are both future and action oriented (*zukunfts-und handlungsbezogen*), *Stimmung* itself is only ever a potentiality, and never amounts to an actual activity (*Tätigkeit*). In a deliberately pointed formulation, he states: "Um Stimmungsevokation kann es sich nicht handeln, wo die Darstellung in einen narrativen Handlungsgang eingebunden ist und diesem als übergreifendem Zweck dient" (It can't be about the evocation of *Stimmung* where the representation is bound to a narrative plot element and has this as its overarching purpose, 159). While I accept that *Stimmung* does not, even cannot, entail direct action, I still argue that it does entail a kind of activity, an activity that avails itself of the same invisible connections that sympathetic magic depends on; it's a matter not of denying *Tätigkeit*, but of specifying the kind of *Tätigkeit* at stake.

33. See Caroline Domenghino, "Artist as Seer: The *Ahndung* of *Tatkraft* in Moritz's 'Über die bildende Nachahmung des Schönen'" (PhD diss., Johns Hopkins University, 2011); also Pfau, "The Appearance of Stimmung."

34. For more on *actio in distans*, see Hans Blumenberg, *Theorie der Unbegrifflichkeit* (Frankfurt am Main: Suhrkamp, 2007), 10–13.

35. Carus, *Neun Briefe*, 42, uses precisely this same image to describe the *Stimmung* effect of landscape. In a closely related context in *Über Lebensmagnetismus*, he also quotes Cicero and discusses *actio in distans* and *Sympathie*. Another related image is of the piece of paper held high over a candle that suddenly bursts into flame; and of course the image of the magnetic stone as well. See also Pierre Hadot, *The Veil of Isis: An Essay on the History of the Idea of Nature*, translated by Michael Chase (Cambridge MA: Harvard University Press, 2006), 110—along with Spitzer's book one of the most significant "prolegomena" to the present study. It goes without saying that the nineteenth-century fascination with electricity and magnetism greatly increased rather than lessened the speculation about nature's invisible force-fields, speculation that continues even today (think of Einstein's *spukhafte Fernwirkung*, spooky effects at a distance).

36. Nietzsche, *Morgenröte*, aphorism 28, makes the connection between *Stimmung* and divination, and sees in both a mode of action-determining logic (and potential) that nonetheless does not proceed according to rationality.

37. The story is told in Keller, 11:96–106; most of my analysis focuses on its first paragraph, 96–98.

38. As readers of Keller know, witching—whether practiced by men or women—is found throughout his works (the same is true of Storm and Fontane), and never simply as a proxy category for erotic affects or residual cultural beliefs. Rather, it makes a constellation of concerns appear that goes well beyond just these two points, a constellation that proves central to his realism in general and to *Der Grüne Heinrich* in particular.

39. For the theme of *Befangenheit* in Keller in general, see Kaspar T. Locher, *Gottfried Keller: Welterfahrung, Wertstruktur und Stil* (Bern: Franke Verlag, 1985), 51–78. Each of these key words has connotations difficult to convey in English but crucial to the analysis: *Verstocktheit* has the same root as *Stockung*, "stoppage"; *Verstummtheit* suggests clamming up; *Befangenheit*, being caught and held; and *Halsstarrigkeit*, literally, stiff-neckedness, being immovably locked in a static state.

40. Winfried Menninghaus, *Artistische Schrift: Studien zur Kompositionskunst Gottfried Kellers* (Frankfurt am Main: Suhrkamp, 1982), 61–90, would say

Meretlein functions as an analogue for all the women in Heinrich's *Bildungsgeschichte*, but the truth of this claim obscures the more important truth of its particular application to Anna.

41. One of the few works to pay attention to music in this novel is Franziska Ehringer, *Gesang und Stimme im Erzählwerk von Gottfried Keller, Eduard von Keyserling und Thomas Mann* (Würzburg: Königshausen & Neumann, 2004), 38–48.

42. We see something of this reversal suggested in the story itself in the otherwise odd aside made by the pastor (as writer) that he would have had the painter produce a "Counterfey" of himself rather than Meretlein—which in a way, at a different level of the real, he does.

43. This omen-esque quality of metatextual representations— and especially of paintings—is a crucial aspect of their function in many of Keller's works, perhaps most notably in *Die drei gerechten Kammmacher* and *Dietegen*; and as we'll see here, the way the Meretlein story functions has important consequences for and parallels with the way the Heathen Chamber painting mentioned at the outset will function as well.

44. The use of antiquated German for the pastor's inculcated diary entries reinforces this impression of the long-ago.

45. This paradox is thematized in Storm's *Aquis submersus*, analyzed by Robert C. Holub, *Reflections of Realism: Paradox, Norm, and Ideology in Nineteenth-Century German Prose* (Detroit: Wayne State University Press, 1991), 132–151; also Storm's *Viola tricolor*, analyzed by Eric Downing, *Double Exposures: Repetition and Realism in Nineteenth-Century German Fiction* (Stanford, CA: Stanford University Press, 2000), 129–169; more generally, Elisabeth Bronfen, *Over Her Dead Body: Death, Femininity, and the Aesthetic* (New York: Routledge, 1992).

46. This is implicit in Wellbery's masterful analysis of Rilke's lyric in "Der gestimmte Raum."

47. In a wordplay to be repeated later on in regard to the *Buch-baum*, Buchberg can be translated as either Beech or Book Hill.

48. These children are, as it were, the latter-day equivalents of those who follow Meretlein after her death up the Buch-berg.

49. Armstrong, *How Novels Think*, 1–3.

50. See Stephen Greenblatt, "Fiction and Friction," in *Shakespearean Negotiations: The Circulation of Social Energy in Renaissance England* (Berkeley: University of California Press, 1988), 66–93; Daniel Purdy, *The Tyranny of Elegance: Consumer Cosmopolitanism in the Age of Goethe* (Baltimore: Johns Hopkins University Press, 1998).

51. Keller, 11:97.

52. Collins, *Magic*, has a particularly felicitous term for this phenomenon, calling it "fractal personhood" (16); see the introduction.

53. As stated in the introduction (see note 48), the objects in nineteenth-century novels are not solely to be understood as commodities, as the association here with objects from the early modern world—and soon, from the natural world—would seem to underscore: the object relations, and the subject-object relations, in Keller's novel belong far more to these worlds than to one of industrial culture. See Elaine Freedgood, *The Ideas in Things: Fugitive Meaning in the Victorian Novel* (Chicago: University of Chicago Press, 2006), 7–8.

54. See Randall Styers, *Making Magic: Religion, Magic, and Science in the Modern World* (Oxford: Oxford University Press, 2004), 170–175, 223–224: the very discourse that explains the ineliminability of the magic forces also eliminates them.

55. Similar to the crown about her head are the garlands (*Scherpen*) about her body: as Benjamin might put it, she is chained to the world of things, and that's a good thing. The second point here, how the natural world is also consistently half-revealed as a book world, might be referred to the argument of Simon During, *Modern Enchantments: The Cultural Power of Secular Magic* (Cambridge, MA: Harvard University Press, 2002), that magic in the modern/nineteenth-century world involves a hesitation between promoting the illusion of a traditional natural/occult magic and exposing the mechanics of its artifice, the artifice that winkingly assures the audience that there is no real magic but only mystifying magic tricks. But I hesitate fully to embrace this argument for two reasons: first, because the natural magic in this novel does not merely function as an illusion, and in the Meretlein story in particular, written as it is not by Heinrich Lee but by the pastor, it cannot easily be reduced to the machinations of the narrator; and second, because the metatextual itself does not function simply as artifice or trick, but as its own potent source for occulted magic. Both points will become clearer in what follows. A third reason that could be advanced—that realism depends upon *not* exposing the mechanics of its artifice—I would not argue.

56. This is not to say that death does not remain part of the natural life signaled by the white rose: indeed, the first time it appears with Anna it is linked to death: the kiss in the graveyard after the grandmother's funeral (11:304). But unlike with the skull, death is not the whole of it.

57. The word *Vor-bild* included in the section heading is a crucial concept for this analysis, and difficult to translate into English. *Vor-* literally means "before," and *Bild* "picture" or "image"; *Vorbild* is sometimes rendered as "model," "exemplar," and so on, but the reader needs to keep in mind the literal idea of a "fore-image" or a "before-the-image."

58. Keller, 11:230.

59. One of the hardest motifs in the novel to convey in English is that attached to this notion of *altertümlich*, which carries a primary connotation of death—and especially the death of the art world and outdated convention—and a secondary one of the archaic, the primeval that seeps its way into the world via those same conventions and art. It would be too awkward to try to draw this out each time the word occurs; the reader must imagine the force of what is sometimes simply translated as "antiquated."

60. In joining his *Tätigkeit* to that of nature, Heinrich also intends to draw on its power, its *Energie*, for his own ends (11:241).

61. Keller, 11:193. It is unclear whether the *Bild* here is the original or Heinrich's copy; and significantly, it doesn't really matter.

62. Keller, 11:194. The way that forces of the natural world can be summoned into and then redirected out from a mimetic representation, no matter how crude or conventionalized the depiction, is a central concern of Michael Taussig, *Mimesis and Alterity: A Particular History of the Senses* (New York: Routledge, 1993). He provides a deep understanding of how, in primitive cultures, mimesis serves as a form of sympathetic magic, and suggests how this persists even in the most

contemporary instances of representation. As will become clear, I find his model exemplary for an understanding of realism as well.

63. Keller, 11:220f. The motif of the painted oven also occurs in suggestive fashion in Keller's *Dietegen*.

64. In psychoanalytical terms, this would be the move from primary to secondary socialization (Freud); or from the Imaginary to the Symbolic (Lacan).

65. These texts and images are from books and sketches by fictional figures such as Junker Felix, but also by historical figures such as Anthonie Waterloo, Johann Reinhardt, Johann Sulzer, and Salomon Geßner. Sulzer (along with Carus) is mentioned frequently in the Gisbertz volume as advocating and theorizing *Stimmung*, especially by Caroline Welsh. Heinrich Lee reads extensively in Sulzer (11:250); Ruysdael is the subject of Alois Riegl's analysis of *Stimmung* and landscape painting.

66. Recalling also Meretlein, with whom painting was also associated with both *Bildung* and death.

67. Keller, 11:233.

68. A disaster to be repeated with some regularity: e.g., 11:323f. The episode of the painting of the two trees is narrated at 11:251–254.

69. See Mitchell, *Landscape and Power*, 1, which sees all landscape painting as an essentially allegorical mode (as I claim more particularly for *Stimmung*).

70. That one can't paint nature directly is evident when comparing 11:214f. and 11:217; see the point made below, that Anna can't be directly embraced: both are crucial to understanding the realism (and the magic to the realism) instantiated by the novel.

71. I want to say, in the space of the *Vorbild*.

72. Keller, 11:252.

73. For Goethe as "the great shade" (*der große Schatten*), see Keller, 12:15.

74. Keller, 12:15. Heinrich's encounter with Goethe comes relatively late in the "Story of My Youth" (*Jugendgeschichte*), when he engages in the quintessential *Bildung* experience of reading the works of this quintessential *Vorbild* for the *Bildung* tradition itself, and the effect on his own *Bildungsgeschichte* is decisive. Goethe's collected works—Goethe in his unity and totality—simply appear one day in the room Heinrich shares with his mother, where we remember his landscape painting also began: "It seemed to me as if the great shade himself had stepped over my threshold; for, though few years had passed since his death, his image had already assumed a demonic-divine character in the imagination of the most recent generation, such that, when it appeared as a figure in a dream to someone with an unfettered fantasy, it could fill him with a portentous shudder" (Es war mir zu Mute, als ob der große Schatten selbst über meine Schwelle getreten wäre; denn so wenige Jahre seit seinem Tode verfloßen, so hatte sein Bild in der Vorstellung des jüngsten Geschlechtes bereits etwas Dämonisch-Göttliches angenommen, das, wenn es als eine Gestaltung der entfesselten Phantasie Einem im Traume erschien, mit ahnungsvollem Schauer erfüllen konnte, 12:15).

Heinrich reads through all the volumes of the unknown dead man (*dem unbekannten Toten*) without pause, and they inspire in him both a new subject-ive sense of joy and consciousness and a new object-ive sense of the nature of things: "I began to see and to love not only the form, but also the content, the essence and history of things" (Ich begann, nicht nur die Form, sondern auch den Inhalt, das Wesen und die Geschichte der Dinge zu sehen und zu lieben, 12:16f.)—much as in his first encounter with the books on landscape painting, but now no longer limited to mere appearances but extended behind them to the "essence" of things.

In an unusual and highly signaled move, after Heinrich finishes reading Goethe the text suddenly shifts to a different temporality, from the retrospective imperfect to a present tense, to represent the Goethean *Weltbild*—a *Bild*, moreover, in which the name of Goethe drops out and its ruling features are simply presented as those of the world. The implication of this is that, for Heinrich as narrator (as himself behind the text world), Goethe is "the great shade" behind the natural world, the reality principle, as it were, that animates the novel and that Heinrich as character is set amidst.

75. This conforms to the general identification in many German realist works of Goethe as the embodiment not only of *Bildung* and art but of Nature and life, something we see in literature from Büchner through Stifter (and in painting, in Carus). But it is also based on quite particular aspects of *Der Grüne Heinrich*.

76. For derision (*Spott*) as the proper attitude of a father, see Keller, 11:258.

77. To a remarkable degree, the Goethe at the center of Heinrich's account is the same Goethe who is at the center of Wellbery's essay on *Stimmung* (and in both cases, the absence of the word detracts not at all from the presence of the concept). In describing his preconception of Goethe (that is, even before reading him), Heinrich says, "The unknown dead man strode through almost all activities and interests and everywhere drew to himself binding threads, whose ends only disappeared in his invisible hand" (Der unbekannte Tote schritt fast durch alle Beschäftigungen und Anregungen und überall zog er angeknüpfte Fäden an sich, deren Enden nur in seiner unsichtbaren Hand verschwanden, 12:15). The weaving image is joined to a musical one when Heinrich actually reads Goethe's books, which he describes as "a host of shining and singing spirits" (*eine Schar glänzender und singender Geister*, 12:16—see, too, the earlier linkage of these two metaphors at the beginning of Heinrich's exposure to nature). And as mentioned, his first response to his reading is to discover the importance in the external world of the relation of objects in and of themselves (even if also behind themselves), "the right and the significance of every thing . . . and the connectedness and depth of the world" (*das Recht und die Bedeutung jeglichen Dinges . . . und den Zusammenhang und die Tiefe der Welt*), quite apart from both the individual subject and his self-centered (*eigennützige[n]*) moods or fantasies and from the cultural conventions of any aesthetic school (*künstlichen Schule*, 12:16f.). Rather, upon discovering nature's connectedness (*Zusammenhang*), the subject is to experience his own sympathetic relation to its order—and as artist, to reproduce it for others to also experience. As Heinrich says of both the visual and the textual artist, "All proper endeavor aims to lead back and join the apparently separate and different to *one* life-ground" (Alles richtige Bestreben [geht] auf . . . Zurückführung und Vereinigung des scheinbar Getrennten und Verschiedenen auf *einen* Lebensgrund, 12:18, Keller's italics) that is at once nature and, spectrally behind it, Goethe, the unifying force acting on and behind all seemingly separate things: it is the ground of *Stimmung* and its sympathetic magic, and it is the artist's task to engage it. And it is important to see how the arts called upon to capture this *Lebensgrund* cannot, almost by definition, be merely surface ones, that is, cannot ever be an inert mimetic realism; insofar as

their quarry is a spectral one, they must be ghost catchers; insofar as their quarry is binding powers, they must themselves be binding powers. In order to capture the real, the arts *must* be magical.

78. Keller, 12:17.

79. Which at one level is to say, to enter as narrator, and painter, the metatextual space occupied already by Goethe and, in a slightly different way, by the reader. The central idea of mimesis as protection, redirection, and turn-about is elaborated by Taussig in his chapter "In Some Way or Another One Can Protect Oneself from Evil Spirits by Portraying Them," in *Mimesis and Alterity*, 1–18.

80. See the famous last line of Goethe's *Faust*, "Das Ewig Weibliche zieht uns hinan" (The Eternal Feminine draws us on). It seems fitting that the Goethe volumes Heinrich reads on his resting-bed (*Ruhebett*) are soon to be replaced by Anna, who next appears, ailing, on the same bed: such is the way out from under the threat to his own person Heinrich has embraced.

81. More fully, the parallel is secured with the shift from the failed painting of the male beech-tree to that here of the female ash.

82. Keller, 11:253f.

83. Keller, 11:269.

84. A motif of mimesis as stealing we see repeated, e.g., 11:305, also with Anna (see below).

85. Keller, 11:255. Compare the tree in the background of Friedrich Overbeck's "Maria und Elisabeth mit Jesus und Johannes" in the Neue Pinakothek, Munich.

86. Keller, 11:260.

87. To repeat, sympathy also encompasses contrast or antipathy.

88. The allegorical is perhaps already implicit in the wine and schoolhouse, but here extended to the nonhuman.

89. See Carus, "Von dem Entsprechen zwischen Gemütsstimmungen und Naturzuständen," in *Neun Briefe*, letter 3, for the close relation of color and *Stimmung*.

90. Anna's hair is regularly described as braided, which reinforces the relation with the cornrows and also more generally the theme of her binding.

91. Keller, 11:282.

92. Keller, 11:260. See also 11: 283f. for Anna's *Glockenstimme*. The German *verhallen* (to fade or die away) has as its root *hallen*, "to echo."

93. Keller, 11:268.

94. For more on Echo (versus Narcissus), see Bettina Menke, "Rhetorik der Echo: Echo-Trope, Figur des Nachlebens," in *Weibliche Rhetorik—Rhetorik der Weiblichkeit*, edited by Dörte Bischof and Martina Wagner-Egelhaff (Freiburg: Rombach, 2003), 135–159.

95. Keller, 11:358.

96. Keller, 11:359f.

97. Keller, 11:350, see also 11:297. This is exactly what we see with Clarissa in Stifter's *Der Hochwald*: see Downing, *Double Exposures*, 285–286n37.

98. Keller, 11:305.

99. Keller, 11:307. For more on the "magnetic" as erotic, spectral, and magical, see Keller, 12:79–82, esp. 81; also Carus, *Über Lebensmagnetismus*. This same

shared identity between Anna and nature is also expressed in more audial terms when Heinrich reports how when Anna seems absent to him, "the air was empty of any memory of Anna, the grass seemed to know nothing of her, the flowers did not whisper her name, mountain and valley were silent about her, only my heart cried aloud her name into the thankless stillness"; soon countered by "Now the entire land was again eloquent and full of praise of her. Every blade of grass and every leaf spoke to me of her. . . . The blue mountain ranges and the white clouds drew toward her, and from the west, where Anna was, it seemed to sound, lightly but blissfully, over the mountain ridges to me" (11:330).

Keller also employs audial terms in similar if more tragic fashion to describe the *Stimmung* effect near the end of *Romeo und Julia auf dem Dorfe*, where he writes: "The stillness of the world sang and made music in their souls. . . . 'Don't you hear something sounding, like a beautiful song or a ringing of bells?' 'It's the water that sounds.' 'No, there is something else, it's sounding here, and there, everywhere!' 'I believe we hear our own blood sounding in our ears'," and so on; all described as "magic effects" (*magische Wirkungen*, 4:155).

100. Keller, 11:284. The following was edited out of this quotation: "and I danced in [the shawl] like one possessed over the nighttime mountain" (und [ich] tanzte darin wie ein Besessener über den nächtlichen Berg)—reflecting the way the dance of Meretlein and, in the "bean night," of Anna, can be metonymically, infectiously passed back to Heinrich through contact with her "things."

101. Keller, 11:265f.

102. See Holub, *Reflections of Realism*, 48–53, on Büchner; Downing, *Double Exposures*, 29–31, on Stifter; Carus, *Neun Briefe*, 24–25, on landscape, not only for *Stimmung* and the transformation of the landscape into an expression of the human soul, but more generally the distinction between imitation and invention. In the particular case of Heinrich, the move from the one to the other might also reflect something of the Oedipal fantasy we see elsewhere, and so, too, something of the self-projecting magical powers and thinking that are inseparable from that fantasy.

103. Keller, 11:266.

104. Heinrich gives fullest expression to this a bit later (11:367f.): the passage includes consideration of the spirit (*Geist*) behind the natural world as imbued with "pro-vidence" (*Vorsehung*) and as "foresightful" (*voraussehend*). The place of God in a realist poetics, and especially in a novel that from the first seems to aim for a loss of religious belief as part of its realism and *Bildung*, might seem both surprising and paradoxical. But the apparent paradox is hardly unique to Keller and is evident in realist authors as different as Büchner and Stifter; and it is without a doubt the paradoxical legitimating ground for landscape painting throughout the realist period. It is important here because it identifies a space of activity and agency that persists within and behind the realist world even once a transcendental God has disappeared. It is a space accepted by Ludwig Feuerbach, a known influence on Keller, as proper to natural religion; and it remains a space, at once divine and natural, intrinsic to Keller's realism and, in the absence of a transcendent God, one that can be occupied by a figure such as (the quasi-divine force of nature) Goethe—or, as Keller puts it elsewhere, by "Poesie und . . . Stimmung" (quoted by Gerd Sautermeister in his "Nachwort," in Gottfried Keller, *Der Grüne Heinrich* [Munich: Goldmann Klassiker, 1980], 917).

The Feuerbach work that seems most relevant to the novel is not, as sometimes assumed, *The Essence of Christianity* and its one-sided argument for religion as mere human projection (the position of Sautermeister), but *The Essence of Religion* (and its companion *Lectures*) and its more sophisticated representation of religion as grounded in man's complex relation with an external natural world of which he is an inextricable part, in all his unconscious impulses and fantasies. This latter work, not the former, is the basis for the lectures Keller would have heard in Munich: Ludwig Feuerbach, *Lectures on the Essence of Religion*, translated by Ralph Manheim (New York: Harper & Row, 1967). Here Feuerbach writes, "I openly profess religion in the sense just mentioned, that is nature religion. I hate the idealism that wrenches man out of nature; . . . I openly confess that the workings of nature affect not only my surface, my skin, my body, but also my core, my innermost being, that the air I breathe in bright weather has a salutary effect not only on my lungs but also on my mind, that the light of the sun illumines not only my eyes but also my spirit and my heart" (Fifth Lecture, 35f.); and says later, "Nature is light, electricity, magnetism," etc. (Eleventh Lecture, 91), insisting that the invisible is part of nature (Thirteenth Lecture, 113); also that "nature is man, insofar as he acts instinctively and unconsciously" (91). Feuerbach's often missed point is not to deny the divine, but to deny it as "*distinct from things*" (117, Feuerbach's italics): this is, I'd say, also the point or ground of Heinrich's pantheism (see below). The relationship becomes, as it were, functionally equivalent to what we've posited for the metatextual as neither separate nor absent from the text world.

It is worth noting that the Neoplatonists championed a similar distinction, one that posited the difference between a transcendental divine and a divine that dwelt entirely in things; as Iamblichus (*On the Mysteries of the Egyptians, Chaldeans, and Assyrians*) argues, it is the latter that is the proper basis for natural magic, including the divination (the futural power) that dwells in things, a form of magic and divination that is entirely based on what we might call the object-ively real. Along with Hadot, *The Veil of Isis*, I see strong residues of this in the "Orphic" traditions of nature in Germany's nineteenth century.

105. Keller, 11:370.

106. See Collins, *Magic*, 64.

107. The painting episode is described at 11:286–288.

108. The particular form of metonymy here is synecdochy: although here applied to nature, it is closely related to the idea of fractal personhood described by Collins and central to what James Frazer, *The Golden Bough: A Study in Magic and Religion* (New York: Macmillan, 1956), calls contagious magic (see the introduction).

109. To spell it out more fully, the beans are to Meretlein as the flowers are to landscape, and so too as both Meretlein and landscape are to Anna. For the "Du Hexe!" during the *Bohnenabend*, see Keller, 11:290.

110. *Schwanz* is a common word for "penis"; *Schwänzchen* is the diminutive form. Although this interpretation might seem only there for a post-Freudian reader, Holub, *Reflections of Realism*, 124–126, illustrates in his reading of *Romeo und Julia auf dem Dorfe* that this type of imagery is not beyond Keller.

111. Collins, *Magic*, 117, reminds us that it is precisely through such secondary meanings that words come to exercise their contiguous magic.

112. Keller, 11:291. This will be further tied together and connected to the Meretlein episode when the kiss to which Anna is bound during the "bean night" is fulfilled in the graveyard with a new bouquet, this time of roses, including white ones (11:304).

113. Frazer, *The Golden Bough*, 14; Roman Jakobson, "Two Aspects of Language and Two Types of Aphasic Disturbances," in *Language and Literature* (Cambridge, MA: Harvard University Press, 1987), 95–120.

114. Keller, 11:287.

115. In channeling his unwanted emotion or mood into the painting and so, too, eventually onto Anna, Heinrich is engaging in a form of displaced projection or abjection of the kind central to subject formation in *Bildung*. It is one of the reasons he can say, "I now once again felt myself content" (11:287).

116. Keller, 11:288.

117. The "rosy radiance" (*Rosenglut*) will reappear at Anna's death metonymically transferred to the coffin (12:93); see below. *Nachglanz*, here translated "afterglow," has a reflective quality in *Glanz* not captured in "glow."

118. Keller, 11:291f.; for Meretlein burying the skull, 11:103.

119. It should be stressed that this dedication speech is itself performative, summoning and producing the effect with which the framed painting is charged; it is an example of the incantatory magic that normally accompanies such binding charms, every bit as much as Heinrich's *fecit*.

120. Keller, 11:291.

121. The *Heidenstube* episode is narrated at 11:292–294.

122. The link to Meretlein might also be seen in the detail "Her face was framed (*eingefaßt*) by a white ruffle (*Krause*) of her own design" (11:292): although not mentioned in the text, the *Ur-bild* of the Meretlein figure features such a *Krause*, prominently. In any case, the *eingefaßt* bespeaks framing.

123. Keller, 11:293.

124. That the world of the *grüne* Heinrich is a painterly one is conveyed once again by the emphatic coloring of the natural description in the scene: e.g., "the half-dark (*Helldunkel*), through which the furtively shining waves rippled over the rose-red, white, and blue stones"; also Anna's red and white face.

125. For light and dark imagery in Keller's work, see Lucie Karcic, *Light and Darkness in Gottfried Keller's "Der Grüne Heinrich"* (Bonn: Bouvier, 1976).

126. See Keller, 11:268.

127. It is worth noting that, characteristically, their appearance makes Heinrich happy.

128. We know that it is the spectral version of the Heathen Chamber that Heinrich draws because he specifically mentions "that apparition" (*jene Erscheinung*, 11:331) as part of it. The spectral nature of the Heathen Chamber is also evident in the Judith scenes that take place there, discussed below.

129. For the trap, *die gestellte Falle*, 11:413; *die Schlinge*, 11:443.

130. As outlined by Alois Riegl, "Die Stimmung als Inhalt der modernen Kunst" (1899), in Riegl, *Gesammelte Aufsätze*, edited by K. M. Swoboda (Augsburg/ Vienna: Filser, 1929) 31, and mentioned at the outset of this chapter (as quoted by Wellbery, "Stimmung," 718).

131. Keller, 11:444.

132. Ibid., with the crown echoing the earlier, original nature magic of Meretlein, who is also evoked through the white flower Anna subsequently picks, echoing the white rose in the painting, etc. The *Krönchen* is even more heavily emphasized throughout the scene in the later, revised version of the novel published in 1879/80.

133. This is where *Stimmung* and Walter Benjamin's *aura* come most closely together. In "On Some Motifs in Baudelaire," Benjamin writes, "Experience of the aura rests on the transposition of a response common in human relationships to the relationship between an inanimate or natural object and man" and stresses "a concept of the aura that comprises the 'unique manifestation of a distance'" (GS 1:646f.; SW 3:338). Elsewhere he stresses that aura is always a matter of *Gespinst*, of the object perceived set in the nexus of the connections that cluster around it; he also is most likely to define aura originally in terms of the experience of landscape. See the introduction; more in chapter 3.

134. Keller, 11:446.

135. In the 1879/80 version of the novel, Keller adds to the line describing Heinrich's turn to the water, "From its bottom (*Grund*) I saw her mirror image (*Spiegelbild*) with the little crown shining up, as if out of another world" (1:395).

136. Bill Brown, "Thing Theory," *Critical Inquiry* 28, no. 1 (2001): 1–22. See also Peter Schwenger, *The Tears of Things: Melancholy and Physical Objects* (Minneapolis: University of Minnesota Press, 2006); Barbara Johnson, *Persons and Things* (Cambridge, MA: Harvard University Press, 2008); Martin Heidegger, "The Thing," in *Poetry, Language, and Thought*, translated by Albert Hofstadter (New York: Harper & Row, 1971), 161–184. Unlike the object, the thing stands outside any relation to the subject: it eludes human connection or involvement, even connection or involvement with other objects. It is, as it were, unmoored from the sympathetic order: a real in tension with the realist, indeed all but outside the realist, it stands at the very edge of the topos of this inquiry. In somewhat different form, it will appear again as an empty silence behind language in Fontane (chapter 2), and as a disenchanted, aura-less experience in Benjamin (chapter 3); see below.

137. Riegl, quoted in Wellbery, "Stimmung," 718f.; Wellbery, "Der gestimmte Raum"; Freud, passim; Max Horkheimer and Theodor Adorno, "The Concept of Enlightenment," in *Dialectics of Enlightenment*, translated by John Cummin (New York: Continuum, 1988), 3–42.

138. J. P. Stern, *On Realism* (London: Routledge & Kegan Paul, 1973), 113–128, makes a similar claim about realism as a (middle) distance. This might seem to be in tension with Roland Barthes's famous notion, formulated in "The Reality Effect," in *French Literary Theory*, edited by Tzevtan Todorov, translated by R. Carter (Cambridge: Cambridge University Press, 1982), that realist objects are those that don't signify, that have no second order of signification. But overreliance on this one essay needlessly simplifies our understanding of Barthes's position. In other works, notably "The Photographic Message" and *The Fashion System*, he draws on Neoplatonic and vitalist models to elaborate how realist objects come to signify in ways fully resonant with the present argument, and that will be touched on more directly in the following two chapters (and are already cited in the introduction).

139. Keller, 11:371. The description of the painting of the portrait, right up to the accompanying flute-playing, is narrated at 11:371–372.

140. Keller, 11:372.

141. Keller, 11:347.

142. Keller, 11:374. When Heinrich is asked, "What do you have against Anna, so that you behave like this toward (*gegen*) her?" the idea of death slips almost imperceptively into the question and answer: "What reason do you have, not to say to her one single word [*Sterbenswörtchen*, literally, 'a little dead word']?" "I explained that the parchment was my property and I didn't owe any mortal soul (*sterblichen Seele*) an account of it."

143. It is a rare moment of candor in the text, and it calls forth an equally rare moment of near sympathy in Heinrich for what he (with her father) is doing to Anna: "Seeing that in my egotism I thought her inescapably trapped, I almost felt sorry for her in her fineness, and had a kind of pity for her. Still . . ." (11:377).

144. Keller, 11:378f. It is worth noting how the inquisition that precedes the furnishing of the frame echoes key elements of the portrait itself in both the setting and the accompanying activity: it takes place in a garden arbor (*Gartenlaube*), under a roof of vines (*Rebendache*), with all the cousins working on a canvas (*Leinenzeug/Leinwand*). This replication helps motivate their giving of the frame.

145. Keller, 11:379. He also mentioned her white neck ruffle (*Halskrause*); see note 122 above for its connection to both Meretlein and framing.

146. Keller, 11:379. Interestingly, Heinrich describes the portrait he carries away here as like a *Palladium*—which is to say, a supernaturally charged object whose theft brings doom to its original possessors. For other Homeric motifs in the novel casting Heinrich as Odysseus (who steals the Palladium), see Holub, *Reflections of Realism*, 62–100.

147. Certainly one thing to keep in mind is how her death is, apparently, by tuberculosis, a contagious disease (caught by no one else): Anna's susceptibility to the contagious forces of sympathetic nature, the very susceptibility that marks her as aesthetic subject open to the effects of *Stimmung*, also determines her (infected) death. See Carus on sympathy, *actio in distans*, and contagious disease in *Über Lebensmagnetismus*. Beate Allert, "J. W. Goethe and C. G. Carus: On the Representation of Nature in Science and Art," *Goethe Yearbook* 23 (2016): 195–219, emphasizes the therapeutic dimension Carus also ascribes to *Stimmung* and to aesthetic practices; this is not applicable to Anna, though possibly to Heinrich through his practices of immunizing displacement.

148. References for the last two sections of this chapter are to Keller, vol. 12; here, 12:43.

149. Katherine's report includes a new account of Anna's childhood that makes her entire life into a resurrection, securing even more firmly (as if it were needed) Anna's identity with Meretlein. Heinrich listens closely to the story of Anna's childhood illness, "so that I now envisioned a small, snow-white corpse lying prone, with a patient, wise, and always smiling countenance. But the sickly shoot recovered, and the wondrous expression of early wisdom, brought forth by suffering, vanished again into its unknown home" (12:42f.).

150. Keller, 12:46.

151. For Judith as the embodiment of the *sinnlich*, see 12:50.

152. Keller, 12:47f.

153. Keller, 12:47, 49. See also 12:70.

154. The novella "The Ghostseer" (Der Geisterseher) in *Das Sinngedicht* might seem evidence that Keller rejects such an occult realm in his realism. But do note that the man in that story who fails the test because he believes in the spirit world is the guardian of the girl and of the aesthetic sensibility that the protagonist Reinhart's journey is designed to win for him, to educate him. Reinhart's father, who "wins" the contest with his empiricism, is decidedly not the representative of the really important realm, but of that left behind. That Reinhart is first seen isolated in an indoor room dividing up light by means of a prism marks him as what Hadot, *The Veil of Isis*, would call a "Promethean" scientist who needs to be converted to a more "Orphic" (and Goethean) worldview (91–232).

155. A similar parallel might be drawn with the afterlife of Meretlein in her portrait and in the fantastic stories told of her: in both cases, the witchery doesn't disappear but simply reappears at another level.

156. Keller, 12:52f.

157. Keller, 12:52, 33, 52.

158. The seeming identity of Römer with Goethe would seem to reinforce that expectation. For Römer as a parody of Goethe, see also 12:55. Römer believes "that all the threads of European politics ran into his hand . . . he, the hidden center of every worldly government (daß alle Fäden der europäischen Politik in seine Hand zusammenliefen . . . er, der verborgene Mittelpunkt aller Weltregierung)." For the nineteenth-century distinction between (and debate about) imitation versus invention, see Carus, *Neun Briefe*, 24–25.

159. Keller, 12:52.

160. For Heinrich as right in his opposition to Römer (and not only, but also the rebellious Oedipal child), see Keller's letter to Wilhelm Petersen, April 21, 1881, quoted in Martin Müller, *Gottfried Keller: Personenlexikon zu seinem Leben und Werk* (Zurich: Chronos Verlag, 2007), 204. Heinrich's position is clearly indicative of a survival of Schelling-esque *Naturphilosophie*, or what Hadot would call the Orphic tradition as opposed to the Promethean conception of man and nature—an Orphic tradition Hadot links to both the Neoplatonists and, especially, Goethe. Note, too, how Heinrich's position is close to that formulated years ago for realism by Richard Brinkmann, *Wirklichkeit und Illusion: Studien über Gehalt und Grenzen des Begriffs Realismus für die erzählende Dichtung des neunzehnten Jahrhunderts* (Tübingen: Niemeyer, 1966). And finally, note how the fact that Römer is soon seen to be mad adds another critique of his realist doctrine, much as we see in Büchner's *Lenz*.

Admittedly, at a later point in the novel—once Heinrich arrives in Munich—the spiritualism, symbolism, and ghostly quality of his paintings come in for intense criticism, but this only because, in Munich, his paintings have become completely estranged from contact with the natural world. The ideal is still for the two to be one.

161. Keller, 12:42, 44f.

162. That Heinrich the narrator's descriptions should be seen as evidence for Heinrich the painter's poetics is signaled by Römer's equation of *Malerei* and *Gedichte* in critiquing them (12:52).

163. Keller, 12:51. For the relevance of Feuerbach to the interpretation of *pantheistisch* here, see above, note 104.

164. Keller, 12:50, 79.

165. This scene is narrated at 12:80–82.

166. Keller, 12:88.

167. Keller, 12:89.

168. Keller, 12:90.

169. The motif is not restricted to Keller: we see it too in Büchner's *Lenz* and Lenz's attempted resurrection of the dead girl, and in the "Rise, Lazarus" motif in Storm's *Aquis submersus*, both analyzed by Holub, *Reflections of Realism*, 50, 143.

170. The echo of the scene in the Heathen Chamber where Anna becomes a *wesenloser Gegenstand*, a "thing," emphasizes once again how the "real" is the uncanny and opposed to the "realist." We might mark the distinction as one between *Ton* (clay) and *Tönen* (musical notes) here.

171. Keller, 12:91, 96.

172. Keller, 12:91.

173. In the Meretlein episode, the coffin is referred to as "the little death-tree" (*das Todtenbäumlein/Todtenbaum*), 11:105.

174. Keller, 12:93.

175. Keller, 12:94.

176. Keller, 12:95; for the carrying of the portrait, 11:379; for the Meretlein episode, 11:105.

177. Keller, 12:96f.

178. Ibid.

179. Ibid.

180. Keller, 12:97.

2. Speaking Magic in Fontane's *The Stechlin*

1. See M. M. Bakhtin, "Forms of Time and of the Chronotope in the Novel," in *The Dialogic Imagination: Four Essays*, edited by Michael Holquist, translated by Caryl Emerson and Michael Holquist (Austin: University of Texas Press, 1981), 84–258; Lilian R. Furst, *All Is True: The Claims and Strategies of Realist Fiction* (Durham, NC: Duke University Press, 1995), 73–94. The German word *Umwelt*, which suggests more than simply setting but rather the surrounding, encompassing world as it interacts with the given subject, will be used regularly to reflect affinities with the idea of the sympathetic cosmos. See Thomas Sebeok, *Contributions to the Doctrine of Signs* (Bloomington: Indiana University Press, 1976); and Giorgio Agamben on Jakob Uexküll, in Agamben, *The Open: Man and Animal*, translated by Kevin Atell (Stanford, CA: Stanford University Press, 2003), 39–44.

2. For the *Umwelt* as foreground rather than background, and as formative force rather than mere setting, see Helmut Müller-Sievers, *The Cylinder: Kinematics of the Nineteenth Century* (Stanford, CA: Stanford University Press, 2012), 131–138.

3. See R. J. Hollingdale, "Introduction," in *Theodor Fontane: Before the Storm*, trans. Hollingdale (Oxford: Oxford University Press, 1985), vii–xxi.

4. See Peter Demetz, *Formen des Realismus: Theodor Fontane, Kritische Untersuchungen* (Munich: Carl Hanser Verlag, 1964), 36–41, 61–65. See also Gertrude Michielsen, *The Preparation of the Future: Techniques of Anticipation in the Novels of Theodor Fontane and Thomas Mann* (Bern: Peter Lang, 1978); Helen Elizabeth Chambers, *Supernatural and Irrational Elements in the Works of Theodor Fontane* (Stuttgart: Hans-Dieter Heinz, 1980).

5. Theodor Fontane, *Vor dem Sturm*, in Fontane, *Sämtliche Werke*, vol. 3, edited by Walter Keitel (Munich: Carl Hanser Verlag, 1962). All references to Fontane's works will be to this edition; here 3:13. For the translations, I have consulted and adapted those of Hollingdale (see above, note 3).

6. See Michielsen, *The Preparation of the Future*, 11. Fontane refers to this added dimension as "art," associating the divinatory (supernatural and futural) with the metatextual, much as in Keller.

7. *Vor dem Sturm*, 3:50. For anecdotes in Fontane (especially in *Der Stechlin*), see Wolfgang Preisendanz, *Theodor Fontane* (Darmstadt: Wissenschaftliche Buchgesellschaft, 1973), 286–328; Derek Barlow, "Symbolism in Fontane's *Der Stechlin*," *German Life and Letters* 12 (1958/59): 282–286; Martin Beckmann, "Theodor Fontane's Roman 'Der Stechlin' als ästhetisches Formgefüge," *Wirkendes Wort* 39 (1989): 218–239; Andrea MhicFhionnbhairr, *Anekdoten aus fünf Weltteilen: The Anecdote in Fontane's Fiction and Autobiography* (Bern: Lang, 1985); Peter Hasubek, ". . . wer am meisten red't ist der reinste Mensch": *Das Gespräch in Theodor Fontanes Roman "Der Stechlin"* (Berlin: Erich Schmidt Verlag, 1998), 43–50. All focus more on thematic content than formal function.

8. Paul Fleming, "The Perfect Story: Anecdote and Exemplarity in Linnaeus and Blumenberg," *Thesis 11* 104, no. 1 (2011): 72–86. See also Fleming, "On the Edge of Non-Contingency: Lifeworld and Ancedotes," *Telos* 158 (Spring 2012): 21–35; Joel Fineman, "The History of the Anecdote: Fiction and Fiction," in *The New Historicism*, edited by H. Aram Veeser (New York: Routledge, 1989), 49–76; Stephen Greenblatt, *Learning to Curse: Essays on Early Modern Culture* (New York: Routledge, 1990), 6–12; Peter Fenves, *Arresting Language: From Leibniz to Benjamin* (Stanford, CA: Stanford University Press, 2001), 152–173.

9. Joel Fineman, quoted in Greenblatt, *Learning to Curse*, 6f.

10. *Vor dem Sturm*, 3:49. See also 3:51, "the more mysterious, the more stimulating for the fantasy" (*je geheimnisvoller, desto anregender für die Phantasie*). The German original of this first quotation is "Ihr seid Springer," which Keitel glosses as "wie die entsprechende Figur im Schachspiel" (3:721).

11. Fleming, "The Perfect Story." See, too, Stephen Greenblatt, *Marvelous Possessions: The Wonder of the New World* (Chicago: University of Chicago Press, 1991), 3.

12. *Vor dem Sturm*, 3:51.

13. The fire imagery that is inherent even if unstressed in Lewin's anecdotes links up with a sustained motif-chain that threads portentously throughout the novel.

14. Fleming, "The Perfect Story," 78.

15. The way this openness to the possibility of a spectral realm in Fontane itself produces a spectral realm can be glimpsed in Lewin's statement "I have neither the right nor the courage to deny the possibility of such apparitions (*Erscheinungen*)"

(3:52). I believe this is an especially important point to make regarding the spectral in Fontane's realism, but also an especially difficult one to hold on to.

16. See Michael Taussig, *Mimesis and Alterity: A Particular History of the Senses* (New York: Routledge, 1993), speaking of the parallel between the sympathetic magic in "primitive" figurines and that in the ethnographic mode of anecdotal representation that reports on them: "Can't we say that *to give an example, to instantiate, to be concrete*, are all examples of the magic of mimesis wherein the replication, the copy, acquires the power of the represented? And does not the magic power of this embodying inhere in the fact that reading such examples we are lifted out of ourselves into those images?" (16). I.e., anecdotes can be considered as embodied, mimetic "things," imbued with sympathetic power.

17. For the connection between foreign bodies or *Fremdkörper* and archaeological items, consider the *Findlingen* (geologically errant boulders) at the entrance to the Stechlin manor.

18. Among the many such ominous, serial anecdotes are those of the Woman in White and the Woman in Black. It should be noted that it makes little difference whether the events anticipated by the omens are desired or feared.

19. For "nomen et omen," see, e.g., *Vor dem Sturm*, 3:112; 602; *Schach von Wuthenow*, 1:557; *Frau Jenny Treibel*, 6:325; *Die Wanderungen*; and the fragment *Oceane von Parceval*. For the latter, see Bettine Menke, "The Figure of Melusine in Fontane's Texts: Images, Digressions, and Lacunae," *Germanic Review* 79, no. 1 (2004): 41–67. For dreams, it is worth mentioning that the divinatory reading of these is usually reserved for the reader rather than the characters themselves; in antiquity, a distinction was made between omens whose source was divine (or demonic) and those that arose from the natural world: dreams were classified under the former. See Cicero, *De divinatione* I, xviii.34.

20. For the poetry snatches, see *Vor dem Sturm*, 3:431 ("And superstitious, as he was, he saw therein a sign (*Zeichen*) foreboding little good"); see also 3:402. This mode of divinatory reading is a secular version of the type of *biblicae sortes* that are best known as part of Augustine's conversion experience.

21. Playing forfeits (3:105), casting lead (3:300) or gambling (3:635f.). War, too, the central historical background of the text, is presented as a form of gambling in the novel. All such games and matters of fortune play into and color Fontane's perennial theme of *Glück* as fortune/chance/and happiness: indeed, *Glück* is a major motivator for divinatory readings as well as "realist" plots throughout his work. For games as modern avatars of ancient divination, see Edward Burnett Tylor, *The Origins of Culture* (Gloucester, MA: Peter Smith, 1970), 70–112.

22. *Vor dem Sturm*, 3:107.

23. The appearance of reapers in a field (3:60, "And everyone of you knows what that signifies"); northern lights in the sky (3:61, "The heavens send their signs [*Zeichen*]"); crows in a tree (3:632, 636); the chance name of an inn or street (3:601f.). Again, it is important how these signs overlap with or resonate with the overarching imagery systems maintained by the narrator that the reader uses to divine their force.

24. *Vor dem Sturm*, 3:362.

25. At one point a character asserts this claim about *Stimmung* and landscape: "What we call the *Stimmung* of the landscape is, as a rule, our own" (Was wir die

Stimmung der Landschaft nennen, ist in der Regel unsere eigene, 3:417); for *Stimmung* and omens and interpretation, see 3:478f.: "There is also a Lehnin Prophecy . . . which foretells destruction . . . but it is all very obscure and uncertain, so that, as is so often the case, one could in all good faith read out of it the exactly opposite interpretation"; see, too, 3:467f.

26. Compare the discussion in chapter 1 of Römer versus Heinrich: the former is a realist denying the symbolic/spiritual/supernatural dimension, the latter more "realist" in acknowledging it.

27. *Vor dem Sturm*, 3:113.

28. *Vor dem Sturm*, 3:273.

29. *Vor dem Sturm*, 3:673. For magical thinking and superstition, embedded in an enchanted world of natural magic and *not* naïve credulity, Mary Floyd-Wilson, *Occult Knowledge, Science, and Gender in Shakespeare's Plays* (Cambridge: Cambridge University Press, 2013), 2–3, 113–114. Although clearly Floyd-Wilson focuses on a different time period, her point still holds.

30. Consider *Unwiederbringlich*: "That is something women have by nature: women are born prophets" (Das haben die Frauen von Natur, die Frauen sind geborene Seher, 2:589).

31. *Vor dem Sturm*, 3:405. The opening or hinge point in the architecture of the house ("where the old annex met our house at a right angle") as the site for magic entering the novel can be connected to the openings in the teleological fabric of history and the narrative made by anecdotes; and the crookedness of the stick (*Hakenstock*) with the knight's move.

32. *Feenkind*, 3:77; *Nicht von den Menschen, wohl aber von der Natur*, 3:81; discovered asleep in the corn, poppies in her hand, a little bird at her feet, 3:77; the prophecy that she will bring blessings, 3:76.

33. For stars as fate and/or the site of divinatory reading in Fontane, see, e.g., *Der Stechlin*; *Schach von Wuthenow*, *Cécile*.

34. *Vor dem Sturm*, 3:107, 679.

35. *Vor dem Sturm*, 3:629.

36. E.g., her critique of the poet mentioned above.

37. *Vor dem Sturm*, 363.

38. Subplots and minor character relations running parallel to the primary ones function in this regard much like added anecdotes, producing chains of similitude and attesting to a logic of similarity, a *logos* or force that governs the novel via principles of similarity.

39. To overstate the case in Freudian terms, we might say that realist "factuality" serves simply as manifest material and its "objective" historical récit as mere secondary revision, screening the actual magical, literary logic governing the unfolding of events. To read realism "realistically" is to misread.

40. Indeed, the apparent hiddenness of its (authorial) governance (in its third-person presentation), coupled with the supposed transparency of its (narrative) representation—the fiction that it is not a fiction, that there is but one world at stake, one set of forces shaping events—involves the realist text all the more intimately in magical reading of that one world.

41. See the discussion in chapter 1 of Roman Jakobson on realist metonymy: both magic and realism follow the same metonymical logic in generating significance.

42. Christine declares, "I believe in premonitions (*Ahnungen*)" (2:569); we're told, "Women are born prophets" (2:589); and in the event both signs prove fatefully fulfilled. Examples of such ominous openings abound, from *Schach von Wuthenow* to *Effi Briest*.

43. Rose petals fall upon her, and she declares this an omen (2:193, "Das ist mir eine gute Vorbedeutung"); butterflies swarm about her and she says that must mean something (2:207, "Sieh nur, das bedeutet etwas"): she is constantly in a state of wishing to guess the significance of such signs (2:143, "als ob sie den Tiefsinn dieser Zeichen erraten wolle").

44. Rose motif: rose petals, dog roses, red flowers in general, including foxglove/digitalis (see below).

45. The effect will be familiar to readers of *Schach von Wuthenow* or *Effi Briest*, and it rather resembles the conditions for Augustine's biblical hermeneutics, where allegorical interpretation becomes extended beyond the work's explicitly figural language to encompass the whole text—not disavowing the Neoplatonists' magic reading practices, but expanding or universalizing them.

46. Consider Fontane's proclivity to include old lady characters of superstitious bent: *Vor dem Sturm*, *Schach von Wuthenow* (Tante Margerite), *Irrungen Wirrungen* (Frau Dorr), *Effi Briest* (Roswitha), etc.

47. The famous *Gesellschafts-Etwas* of *Effi Briest*, 4:236.

48. E.g., the fabulously beautiful weather on the day of Innstetten's duel; or how Fontane's tragic, socially wronged women (Cécile, Lene, Effi) are so often depicted as aligned with nature, often with animals. See Christian Thomas, "Theodor Fontane: Biologism and Fiction," *Monatshefte* 106, no. 3 (2014): 376–401.

49. For more on homeopathy and its roots in a model of *sympatheia* ultimately indebted to the Stoics and Neoplatonists, see Alice Kuzniar, *The Birth of Homeopathy out of the Spirit of Romanticism* (Toronto: University of Toronto Press, 2017). The concept of allopathy also derives from Samuel Hahnemann, the inventor of homeopathy. For Fontane, a trained pharmacist, on homeopathy as a form of medicine rather than as a poetics, see Theodor Fontane und Bernhard von Lepel, *Der Briefwechsel*, Kritische Ausgabe, vol. 1, edited by Gabriele Radecke (Berlin: Walter de Gruyter, 2006), 493 (letter 327, March 2 and 4, 1858). See also Karl Otto Sauerbeck, "Fontane und die Homöopathie," *Allgemeine Homöopathische Zeitung* 6 (2004): 273–279. The passage in *Unwiederbringlich* also includes a brief related mention of so-called allopathy, its complement.

50. *Unwiederbringlich*, 2:576f.

51. For other such mise-en-abîme moments, e.g., *Cécile*, 2:176f., 196; and for a brilliant reading of their place in *Die Poggenpuhls*, see Elisabeth Strowick, "*Die Poggenpuhls*: Fontanes Realismus der Überreste," in *Herausforderungen des Realismus: Theodor Fontanes Gesellschaftsromanen*, edited by Peter Hohendahl and Ulrike Vedder (Breisgau: Rombach, forthcoming).

52. *Unwiederbringlich* 2:577.

53. Demetz, *Formen des Realismus*, 164–177, seems to contest this micro-macro connection, and Georg Lukács, "Der alte Fontane," *Sinn und Form* 2 (1952): 44–93, to insist on it; Sven-Aage Jørgensen, "Nachwort," in *Theodor Fontane: Unwiederbringlich* (Stuttgart: Reclam, 1971), 287–309, seems to have decided the case very much in favor of Lukács.

54. For "similia similibus," see *Unwiederbringlich*, 2:577; *Sympathie*, 2:592. For "similia similibus," see also *Cécile*, 2:285; for *Sympathie* as medicine, see also *Die Poggenpuhls*, 4:494.

55. *Unwiederbringlich*, 2:577.

56. Schwarzkoppen says to Arne, "All that I can manage is a prophylactic procedure. . . . I'll prepare some stories from my earlier life as a pastor . . . and will try to make these stories work on her in secret. Your sister is equally imaginative and reflective: her imagination will vitalize what she hears, and her reflection will force her to occupy herself with the germ (*Kern*) of the story and perhaps lead her to a change of mind and then to a change of heart" (2:598).

57. To be compared with the hothouse scene in *L'Adultera* or the Harz Mountains for Cécile, or Hohen-Cremmen for Effi, the "Naturkind": being in nature activates women.

58. *Irrungen Wirrungen*, 2:379, 454.

59. *L'Adultera*, 2:137. "Elective affinities," wherein "quite simply the weaker element is suppressed by the stronger and therefore also the more legitimate," where nature is the stronger, society the weaker element or force.

60. "Ahnungen" that are "schon geradezu was Prophetisches," 5:126; itching in her little finger that foretells a visitor, 5:227f., a premonitory experience shared by Dubslav, 5:327.

61. Woldemar, 5:51, Barby, 5:123; also, more parodically, in the story of Schickedanz, 5:118–120.

62. Michielsen, *The Preparation of the Future*, 11; cf. Hasubek, ". . . *wer am meisten red't*", 52.

63. More precisely, binding the natural and the paratextual (i.e., the novel's title)—for our purposes, the distinction is unimportant.

64. *Die Poggenpuhls*, 4:552. See Andreas Amberg, "Poetik des Wassers: Theodor Fontanes *Der Stechlin*," *Zeitschrift für deutsche Philologie*, 1996, 541–559.

65. From its very presentation, the word chain invites a special kind of reading, an anticipatory readiness to divine the connections at stake between these contiguous elements, the connections that bind them together with this one polysemous (but also at first empty) word or name.

66. *Weltbeziehungen, geheimnisvolle Beziehungen*, 5:135.

67. *Der Stechlin*, 5:7. For the translations of *Der Stechlin*, I have consulted and adapted the work of William L. Zwiebel, trans., *Theodor Fontane, The Stechlin* (Columbia, SC: Camden House, 1995).

68. See Walter Müller-Seidel, "Theodor Fontane: *Der Stechlin*," in *Der deutsche Roman: Vom Barock bis zur Gegenwart; Struktur und Geschichte*, vol. 2, edited by Benno von Wiese (Düsseldorf: August Bagel, 1963): "It is an image of nature that at the same time serves as an expression of historical change" (170). See Hasubek, ". . . *wer am meisten red't*", 26.

69. E.g., Hugo Aust, "Nachwort," in *Theodor Fontane: Der Stechlin* (Stuttgart: Reclam, 1978), 464f.; Müller-Seidel, "*Der Stechlin*"; Hasubek, ". . . *wer am meisten red't*", 23.

70. For antipathy in the ancient world, see Brooke Holmes, *The Tissue of the World; Sympathy and the Nature of Nature in Greco-Roman Antiquity* (forthcoming); in the early modern, Michel Foucault, *The Order of Things: An Archaeology*

of the Human Sciences (New York: Vintage, 1970), 23f. For allopathy as counterpart to homepathy, *Unwiederbringlich*, 2:577; also note 49 above. Diethelm Brüggeman, "Fontanes Allegorien (I und II)," *Neue Rundschau* 82 (1981): 290–310, 486–505, is one of the few Fontane critics to suggest a connection between the significatory system of the lake and the early modern worldview. However, Max Rychner, "Theodor Fontane: *Der Stechlin*," in *Deutsche Romane von Grimmelshausen bis Musil*, edited by Jost Schillemeit (Frankfurt am Main: Fischer, 1966), speaks of the novel's relational weave of similarities and sympathies (*Beziehungsgeflecht von Ähnlichkeiten und Sympathien*, 221), and on the whole, the language is hard for critics to avoid.

71. For antipathy's role as part of sympathy, see 5:358; for its double nature, see Holmes, *The Tissue of the World*.

72. It is worth noting, too, that the rooster's appearance exists only anecdotally: 5:7.

73. See, too, Demetz, *Formen des Realismus*, who reads the structure of the novel as simply *additiv* (183).

74. E.g., 5:56, the nondescription of the view from the lookout tower (*Aussichtsturm*). In this last respect (and many others), it is very different from the equally non-plot-driven works of the poetic realist Adalbert Stifter, as well as from the richly nature-descriptive works of Gottfried Keller and Theodor Storm. (Wilhelm Raabe, who can also be rather non-plot-oriented, is an altogether different case.)

75. The only other real exception would be *Die Poggenpuhls*, written close in time to *Der Stechlin*, also arguably one of his best novels.

76. Draft of a letter to Adolf Hoffmann, May/June 1897, cited in Hugo Aust, ed., *Erläuterungen und Dokumente: Theodor Fontane, Der Stechlin* (Stuttgart: Reclam, 1978): "At the end an old man dies and two young people get married; that's really all that happens in 500 pages" (85).

77. Walter Benjamin, "Der Erzähler," GS 2:455; SW 3:155. For the temporal structure of plot, see Peter Brooks, *Reading for the Plot: Design and Intention in Narrative* (Cambridge, MA: Harvard University Press, 1984), 3–36.

78. See Michel Foucault, *History of Sexuality, Volume 1: An Introduction* (New York: Vintage, 1978) 59f. The representation of a protagonist's psychic conflicts can be in relation to either its own subjectivity or the external/social world.

79. There are of course exceptions—such as the figure of Gordon in *Cécile*—and many Fontane critics would no doubt contest this characterization more generally: but if psychology is understood in either a Freudian sense, as entailing the eruption of unconscious "other" forces derived from either childhood or more remote sources (there is no childhood in Fontane), or a more Schelling-esque sense of a natural world-force operating in us, such as we see in Keller—if psychology is understood in either of these ways, it is generally not a factor in Fontane. The obviation of psychology per se in *Der Stechlin* will be explored below in terms of Simmel's notion of sociability.

80. This is not to say that single character focalizations are not central to many of Fontane's other novels (we already mentioned the importance of Lewin's perspective for the *Zeichen* at the ball). See Elisabeth Strowick, "'Schließlich ist alles bloß Verdacht': Fontane's Kunst des Findens," in *Realien der Realismus:*

Wissenschaft—Technik—Medien in Theodor Fontanes Erzählprosa, edited by Stephan Braese and Anne-Kathrin Reulecke (Berlin: Vorwerk 8, 2010), 157–181. But focused perspective and psychological perspective are not always the same thing.

81. See 5:301, "It's only the sharp drawing, the one bordering on caricature, that has an effect"; also 5:62, Krippenstapel's "character, which bordered closely on caricature."

82. *Der Stechlin*, 5:56.

83. The only truly significant exception is the conversation late in the novel between Lorenzen and Melusine, one whose exceptionality is marked not least by both its metatextual force and its being *zu zweit*: 5:268–274.

84. See Peter Fenves, *"Chatter": Language and History in Kierkegaard* (Stanford, CA: Stanford University Press, 1993).

85. For the modernist orientation, see chapter 3.

86. For language as the *Lebensform* of all social interaction and all character, see Dubslav's aperçu "Wer am meisten red't, ist der reinste Mensch" (5:23). See Hasubek, *". . . wer am meisten red't"*, passim. Already in 1912 Gottfried Kricker, *Theodor Fontane: Von seiner Art und epischen Technik* (Berlin: Bonner Forschungen, 1912), spoke of *Gespräch* as *die bestimmende Lebensform* of the novel.

87. As we will see, language use here cannot be described in ordinary linguistic terms as constative, indexical, or even really (in Peirce's terms) "symbolic" or (in Austin's) performative; instead we have to reach for some of the same terms we devised for talking about the conditions of magic reading in the introduction and chapter 1. See below, note 126.

88. See Roman Jakobson, "On Realism in Art," in *Readings in Russian Poetics: Formalist and Structuralist Views*, edited by L. Matejka and K. Pomorska (Cambridge, MA: MIT Press, 1971), 39; Robert C. Holub, *Reflections of Realism: Paradox, Norm, and Ideology in Nineteenth-Century German Prose* (Detroit: Wayne State University Press, 1991), 47, 229; Eric Downing, *Double Exposures: Repetition and Realism* (Stanford, CA: Stanford University Press, 2000), 135. For the idea of "natural" signs—an eighteenth-century notion with continued relevance for much of the nineteenth century—see David Wellbery, *Lessing's Laokoon: Semiotics and Aesthetics in the Age of Reason* (Cambridge: Cambridge University Press, 1984).

89. See Wolfgang Preisendanz, "Zur Ästhetizität des Gesprächs bei Fontane," in *Das Gespräch*, edited by Karlheinz Stierle and Rainer Warning (Munich: Fink, 1984), on the representation of speech (*Gesprächsdarstellung*) as the place where sign and referent coincide (*Zeichen und Referent zusammenfallen*, 478), and as such crucial to Fontane's realism. Fontane in both earlier works and *Der Stechlin* is fond of reproducing letters as well as conversations.

90. Regardless, too, of any question as to whether "people really talk like that," which in Fontane they rarely do.

91. For connotation versus denotation in relation to realism, see Roland Barthes, "The Photographic Message," in *Image/Music/Text*, translated by Stephen Heath (New York: Noonday, 1977), 15–31; and Barthes, *The Fashion System*, translated by Mattthew Ward and Richard Howard (Berkeley: University of California Press, 1983), 226–273; see below, note 99.

92. There are some nuanced differences to language use, especially in the use of dialect for some of the minor characters (more anon), but the point of language's adequacy remains firm. Thomas Mann remarks on the shared Fontanesque *Ton* of all his characters, in "Der alte Fontane," in *Gesammelte Werke* (Frankfurt am Main: Fischer, 1990), 9:9–34.

93. By "securely realist," I mean transparent, common, universalized, and so on; see Russell Berman, *The Rise of the Modern Novel: Crisis and Charisma* (Cambridge, MA: Harvard University Press, 1986), 2.

94. The *Sprachkrise* that is often thought of as announced in Hugo von Hofmannsthal's "Ein Brief" is only a few years away (1902), although, to be fair, it is already adumbrated in such works as Stifter's *Granit*.

95. A protovitalism, one grounded in the silent space beyond speech, is clearly evident in Hofmannsthal's "Ein Brief"; for the "primitivism" inseparable from much of modernism, both texts and visual art, and its irruption into the present as one of the defining features of modernism, see chapter 3.

96. *Der Stechlin*, 5:9. An earlier draft of the novel had a pyramid constructed out of *Findlingsblöcken*, echoing those that flank the entrance to the courtyard (see note 17).

97. Its counterpart in the garden of Adelheid, without the underlying, self-reflecting foil (5:84); looked into as if a *Spiegelbild* by Czako and Rex (5:63); "Ach, wenn ich diese Glaskugeln sehe," 5:172.

98. *Ein fremdes Samenkorn*, i.e., a *Findling* of its own, although here the foreign and native are ironically doubled: the *fremd* is actually the local seed, the aloe the exotic stranger.

99. *Der Stechlin*, 5:352. Henry James, "The Lesson of Balzac," in *The Question of Our Speech: The Lesson of Balzac; Two Lectures* (Boston: Riverside Press, 1905), 85–89, notes that Balzac's objects are similarly charged, which I mention to underscore the broader relevance of this crucial point to an understanding of realism per se. And Roland Barthes, often thought of as the proponent of a view of realist objects as nonsignifying, has this to say about the object world of photography, which he sees as a definitively "realist" medium: "The interest lies in the fact that objects are accepted inducers of associations . . . or, in a more obscure way, are veritable symbols. . . . Such objects constitute excellent elements of signification: on the one hand they are discontinuous and complete in themselves, a physical qualification for a sign, while on the other they refer to clear, familiar signifieds. . . . The connotation somehow 'emerges' from all these signifying units [i.e., things] which are nevertheless 'captured' as though the scene were immediate and spontaneous, that is to say, without signfication. . . . Objects no longer perhaps possess a *power*, but they certainly possess meanings" (Barthes, "The Photographic Message," 22f.). My claim is that their meaning is a power (see the introduction), but do note the clear evocation of a sympathetic model for describing realism.

100. *Der Stechlin*, 5:20.

101. More precisely, Czako prompts Krippenstapel to develop the allegory (5:59); eating chicken wings at Adelheid's cloister (5:92f.). Czako does much the same when eating carp at Schloß Stechlin: these too are immediately transformed into "speaking" allegories (5:27).

102. Flowers (5:64), *Goldwasser* (5:41), *Lacrimae Christi* (5:93), *Flaschen* (5:69).
103. *Der Stechlin*, 5:111.
104. The rococo clock in the center of the central staircase, *mit einem Zeitgeist darüber, der eine Hippe führte* (5:19); the museum of *Wetterfahnen* (see also 5:181, "All men are weathervanes" [Alle Menschen sind Wetterfahnen]).
105. Both Czako and Dubslav have a distinct tendency to turn things into allegories or signs of the political, along the lines of what Czako says of bowling alleys in gardens ("They have something symbolic about them, or didactic, or if you will, political," 5:85). Certainly if *Der Stechlin* is to be taken as a "political" novel, this is primarily based on how people read: its political dimension is mostly in its reading of signs, or rather, of things. Melusine's hats are one example of this need for us to read beyond the political; we'll see many more.
106. For the *Poetensteig* and *Aussichtsturm*, see Gotthart Wunberg, "Rondell und Poetensteig: Topographie und implizite Poetik in Fontanes Stechlin," in *Literatur und Geistesgeschichte: Festschrift für Richard Brinkmann*, edited by Jürgen Brummack (Tübingen: M. Niemeyer, 1981), 467–469. This latter description of the courtyard at Wutz is later complemented by one of the elderberry tree on the other side of the courtyard, whose foliage—much like Dubslav's aloe—is entwined with that of another contrasting tree, and the embracing shadow of this living contrast transforms the disorder and decay of the human elements into something pleasingly natural and aesthetic. For the furniture, 5:97; for the two descriptions of the courtyard at Wutz, 5:79f., 95.
107. In the case of Czako and the Stechlins, they start out as things before becoming names and then transform into characters—characters who are then transformed by their names.
108. Quite contrary to Czako's Goethe quotation, "a name is sound and smoke" (Name ist Schall und Rauch, 5:88) or Melusine's "Names mean nothing" (Namen bedeuten nichts, 5:141). Both statements are made in contexts where their validity is more or less openly refuted: as Woldemar replies to Melusine, "Anyone named Melusine should know what names mean " (see below); cf. 5:285.
109. John Stuart Mill, *A System of Logic* 1.ii.5; Simon Goldhill, *Reading Greek Tragedy* (Cambridge: Cambridge University Press, 1986), 216. See also Walter Benjamin, "On Language as Such and on the Language of Man," SW 1:69: "The proper name is the word of God in human sounds: a man's name is his fate"; Hans Blumenberg, *Vor allem Fontane* (Frankfurt am Main: Insel, 1998), 11.
110. Gottlob Frege, "On Sense and Reference," in *Translations from the Philosophical Writings of Gottlob Frege*, edited by P. Geach and M. Black (Oxford: Blackwell, 1952), 56–79. The distinction between denotative and connotative function can be posited as the motivating factor behind Fontane's slight (but significant) revision of the classical phrase "nomen est omen" to "nomen et omen," where the relationship between name and omen in the latter case is based on contiguity or proximity rather than identity. For "nomen et omen" in Fontane in general, see Walter Glausewitz, "Theodor Fontane: Heiteres Darüberstehen? . . ." *Monatshefte* 45, no. 4 (1953): 202–208; Menke, "The Figure of Melusine," 44.
111. *Nebenbedeutung*, 5:22. See also the connotations/associations of Moscheles, 5:321.

112. For Barthes, see above, note 99.

113. *Der Stechlin*, 5:185; see also 5:181, "One shouldn't hold a man's name against him. But Koseleger! I never know if he's more 'Kose' or more 'Leger'": perhaps both equally." (The wordplay doesn't really carry over into English.)

114. *Die grüne Glashütte*, 5:57; or similarly (seemingly) *Eierhäuschen*; but see below. One could connect the disconnection here with that between the (mundane) labor of the producers and the fetishized commodity-magic of the product, but that sort of explanation would have only very local force.

115. "Is named Krippenstapel, which all by itself will say something," 5:54. Blumenberg, *Vor allem Fontane*, 9.

116. Her name evokes for Woldemar the character (*Bühnenfigur*) from Schiller's *Wilhelm Tell* (5:116), a play that also figures prominently at the end of the Egg Cottage episode (5:159): but what to make of this connotation and connection remains obscure.

117. E.g., Rolf Krake, "A man who has such a nickname, he lives, he is in and of himself a story," 5:261.

118. *Der Stechlin*, 5:127, "But Wrschowitz and Niels! I believe he suffers from this contradiction."

119. Dubslav, 5:11; Czako, 5:212, "It's because of my name. Here, too, 'Czako' already has an aftertaste (*Beigeschmack*)."

120. *Der Stechlin*, 5:141, 110.

121. *Der Stechlin*, 5:214; see, too, Aust, *Erläuterungen und Dokumente*, 58. There is one other dimension to the power of names that needs be mentioned, also associated with their temporality—in this case more with family names than personal ones. If first names have retained some active, living, shaping force, even while sacrificing some of the futurity ominously associated with them—a force, moreover, now almost more linked to a character's reading of the name than to the name itself—last names seem only to have retained a deadening, petrifying force, a kind of binding power that is anything but energizing, open, or natural. We can see this in the case of "Stechlin," especially in the hold it has (the spell it casts) on Adelheid, and the hold she would have it keep on Woldemar (this is what renders the novel's final line so problematic). But it is also the case for those aristocrats such as Triglaff who surround her; and even for the Princess Ermyntrud, who despite marrying into the bourgeoisie insists on drawing the names for her many children from the world of her ancestors. All of these characters attribute a certain magical power to their names, a certain *Sympathie* and force that derives from their connection to the world of the dead (much as we saw in the power of painting conventions in *Green Henry*); see too 5:273. But while these names certainly bind them, names are also shown to be losing their power over others, indeed over the world: over life itself. That is, along with the diminution of future force for names qua omens has come a diminution in their staying power, their binding power, per se: names, and with them language as a whole, have taken on a different temporality, one of historicity, loss, breakdown: names die out by losing their sympathetic connections to the world, their ties to life.

122. See Christian Grawe, "Fontanes neues Sprachbewußtsein in *Der Stechlin*," in *Sprache in Prosawerk: Beisp. von Goethe, Fontane, Thomas Mann, Bergengruen, Kleist, und Johnson* (Bonn: Bouvier, 1974): "Die Sprache [ist] nicht nur

Medium, sondern Objekt des Gesprächs," and characters "sprechen nicht nur, sie reflektieren Sprache" (53); also Hasubek, "... *wer am meisten red't*", 43–50.

123. See Grawe, "Fontanes neues Sprachbewußtsein," on the broken relation (*gebrochene Verhältnis*) of characters to the language they use (53).

124. *Nett*, 5:113; *Rechnungen*, 5:87. The distinction between *Dame* and *Madame* is what Walter Benjamin would call *Intention* (see "Die Aufgabe des Übersetzers," GS 4:14; SW 1:257). Again, these instances bespeak at once connections, as characters spin out the connotative extensions of each word, and evidence of the breakdown of connections, as words cease to have stable associations or relations. A particularly telling example of this might be that of the phonically similar but semantically (and connotatively) different *Millet* and *Millais* momentarily confused by Woldemar in his conversation with Cujacius, which opens up a momentary, embarrassing tear in the common fabric of sociability (5:237); see below.

125. Sociabilty has always been an implicit aspect of *sympatheia*: see Barbara Maria Stafford, *Visual Analogy: Consciousness as the Art of Connecting* (Cambridge, MA: MIT Press, 1999), 19. Here it is made explicit and determinative.

126. Both the threatened loss of and the still realized connections on which realism and magic mutually depend are equally evident in the conversational *Gespräch* in this novel. Conversation here does not for the most part seem to have any conventional communicative function. We could not say, in Roman Jakobson's terms, that it is primarily constative or referential, that is, intent on conveying information about the world, either denotatively or connotatively. Nor is it emotive, conveying information about the speaker-subject; or affective, intent on influencing the listener; or even "poetic," in calling attention to itself (although this, almost inadvertently, comes closest). Neither, in Austin's terms, can we say such talk is performative, at least not without severely curtailing and refining what we consider such a "speech act" to entail, since the words themselves do very little. Rather, *Gespräch* here primarily has what Jakobson would call a *phatic* function, the emptiest of all his categories: speech as merely keeping open the possibility of communication, of connection, regardless of content or the particularities of speaker, listener, or language.

This is most crassly represented in the novel by characters such as Frau Gundermann, about whom we are told, "Actually, she wasn't interested in anything at all; but, proper Berliner that she was, she just needed to be able to talk" (5:39; also her husband's empty phrases [*öde Redensarten*], 5:71), and more genially by figures such as Graf Barby: "Everything that came up in conversation had more or less the same value for the old Count" (5:229). And it is of a piece with the thematization of communication in the novel in terms of telephone and telegraph lines, mere media lines of connection without specified speakers, listeners, or messages; see Christian Thomas, *Theodor Fontane: Autonomie und Telegraphie in den Gesellschaftsromanen* (Berlin: Logos Verlag, 2015). This phatic function includes an important if paradoxically static temporal dimension, captured in the oft-repeated phrase "So the conversation went" (So ging das Gespräch, 5:70, 77; see also 219, 254, 263): in the absence of any forward, futural thrust to either the action or conversation, it answers to the need to maintain the flow, but the flow—the pace or rhythm of exchange, of the unfurling of conversation threads—is something in itself empty, weightless, a foundation without content, what Walter Benjamin might call "empty time." This crucial if immaterial, indeed vacuous dimension is perhaps most notable at moments of its disruption, moments that usually prove embarrassing, sometimes maliciously pleasurable (5:62), and often even uncanny, the opening up of a momentary, for some almost panic-inducing gap in the temporal fabric of their world. But if on the one hand *Gespräch* seems to bespeak a loss of ground in the novel, a threatened vacuity of its significant reality, on the other it is also the very medium for establishing sympathetic, social connections between its participants, the very realm for the promised realization of meaningful connectedness; and the concomitant sense of fullness or presence to the experience of *Gespräch* is the undeniable counterpart to its sense of emptiness and absence, a paradox commented on by the characters themselves; see, e.g., 5:206, 230.

127. Sociology—as the study of communal experience— itself emerged as a field at this time, at the same time as *sympatheia* (and its close relation, *Stimmung*) was being similarly reconceived in other fields as more or less restricted to the human world, as could also be said of language, with the similar emergence of linguistics. For *sympatheia* blending into "sympathy" (*Mitleid*) or "empathy" (*Mitempfindung*), see Ute Frevert, *Emotions in History—Lost and Found* (Budapest: Central European University Press, 2011), 149–204; for *Stimmung* blending into *Laune*, see David Wellbery, "Stimmung," in *Ästhetische Grundbegriffe: Historisches Wörterbuch in sieben Bänden*, edited by Karlheinz Barck et al. (Stuttgart: Metzler Verlag, 2010), 703–733; for both, see the introduction. But sociology also and at the same time emerged as something of an alternative to yet another coeval field, namely, psychology, and as such represented a rather different relocation of *sympatheia* from that offered by the individual interiorized subject; again, see the introduction.

128. Willi Goetschel, "Causerie: Zur Funktion des Gesprächs in Fontanes *Der Stechlin*," *Germanic Review* 70 (1995): 116–122; Thomas Pfau, "Epochenwandel mit metaphysischen Anklängen: Metasprache und Bilderfahrung in *Der Stechlin*," *German Quarterly* 86, no. 4 (2013): 420–442; Husabek, ". . . *wer am meisten red't*", 122–137. Goetschel is the first to look at an extended comparison, but his evaluation of the relation is mainly geared toward foregrounding the vacuousness of *Gespräch* in Fontane's novel, not its fullness or its magic. And it also needs be said that Simmel is not alone among the founders of sociology to be relocating magic into the sociable experience (or put differently, to be pointing out the continued magical forces at work in sociability): Max Weber's "charisma" and Émile Durkheim's "effervesence" work to similar ends, just not quite so tantalizingly proximate to Fontane's novel.

129. Georg Simmel, "Die Geselligkeit (Beispiel der Reinen oder Formalen Soziologie)," in *Grundfragen der Soziologie (Individuum und Gesellschaft)*, 3rd ed. (Berlin: De Gruyter, 1970), 48–68. Translations based on Kurt H. Wolff, trans. and ed., *The Sociology of Georg Simmel* (Glencoe, IL: Free Press, 1923), 40–57. Fontane and Simmel shared a publisher/editor: the evidence for Fontane knowing of Simmel is murky; see Elizabeth Goodstein, *Georg Simmel and the Disciplinary Imaginary* (Stanford, CA: Stanford University Press, 2017).

130. Simmel, "Die Geselligkeit," 48.

131. Ibid., 49.

132. See Stafford, *Visual Analogy*, 19. Interestingly for Fontane, Simmel's sympathy includes antipathy: interesting too for *Der Stechlin*, moments of sympathetic divination are always social visits.

133. Simmel, "Die Geselligkeit," 49: *Energien*, 59: *Verflechtung*, 61: *Schattenkörper*; 64: *Schattenreich* (cf. 51).

134. We've seen the hidden connections between sympathetic relations and art qua metatextuality both in *Green Henry* and in Fontane's work, especially in the relation between the binding forces at work in the novel for the characters and those at work as the novel for the readers. What is perhaps more singular to Fontane is how the readerly experience—the reader's participation in the textual world—can itself be conceived in terms of sociability as outlined here: for Fontane's reader is above all a *sociable* reader in ways not quite true of Keller or other poetic realists, nor of Benjamin or other modernists.

135. The addition of play is certainly appropriate for Fontane, who shares with E. B. Tylor et al. an appreciation of play as a modern avatar of magical experience; see the earlier discussion of the game of forfeits in *Vor dem Sturm* and of Lene's and Botho's flower game in *Irrungen Wirrungen*.

136. See Goetschel, "Causerie." Certainly the problem of an emptied world— of language, society, etc.—is central to the thematics of *sympatheia* qua sociability in *Der Stechlin*: for *Spiel* qua *Spielerei*, see *Der Stechlin*, 5:207.

137. Simmel, "Die Geselligkeit," 51.

138. Ibid.: *symbolische Bedeutung*; seen by neither naturalism (56, 57f., 61) nor by rationalism (53).

139. For Simmel and (not) *Lebensphilosophie*, see Goodstein, *Georg Simmel*. While Simmel's focus is going to be primarily on the sociable *an sich*, Fontane's is going to be more broadly on the connections (and lost connections) between the sociable and the life that resides both outside and within it—and that includes the nonhuman life as well.

140. Simmel, "Die Geselligkeit," 52. Sociability is the good feeling of feeling good together.

141. Simmel, "Die Geselligkeit," 55: "In diesem Sinne nun ist auch der Mensch als geselliger ein eigentümliches, in keiner andern Beziehung so vorkommendes Gebilde."

142. Simmel describes this as the experience of being *only* oneself yet not *wholly* oneself, but "only an element in a group that is held together formally" ("Die Geselligkeit," 55). And it is worth stressing how, in order for the reciprocal determination (*gegenseitiges Sich-Bestimmen*) of sociability to emerge, merely personal moods (*bloß persönliche Stimmung und Verstimmung*) must be eliminated: interiorized autonomy gives way to externalized participation—reciprocal participation—as the site and source of *Stimmung*.

143. Simmel, "Die Geselligkeit," 58.

144. Simmel, "Die Geselligkeit," 54. *Taktgefühl* also, of course, implies contiguity.

145. Although games, like literature, are one of the last refuges of magical thinking in the modern world and as such figure prominently in other Fontane works, they have no independent place in our novel; and although coquetry shares

in the quasi-erotic play of attractive forces also proper to the sympathetically magical world, and even has in Melusine—the most sympathetically magical character
in the text—a foothold in *Der Stechlin*, the decisively nonerotic cast of the novel
keeps coquetry mostly peripheral. For games as sites for magical experience, see
Vor dem Sturm, Irrungen Wirrungen; for coquetry, *Cécile, Unwiederbringlich*.

Coquetry is also the focus of another work by Simmel, but there is one aspect
of his discussion of coquetry here that is of a more general interest to us, insofar
as it inflects the model of sociability as a realm of similarity. He describes how
the coquette—who only exists within sociable relations, not outside of them—
"swings back and forth between 'yes' and 'no' without stopping at either . . .
and manages to embody their polar opposites in a perfectly consistent behavior."
That is, the realm of sociability, for all its foundation in similitude, also ideally encompasses reciprocal opposites or contradictions as somehow one, and
in ways that increase rather than diminish the play of attractive forces (*An-
ziehungskräfte*)—as is true, too, of a sympathetically/antipathetically conceived
kosmos, and optimally (but not always) of the sociable and sympathetic world
of Fontane's novel as well.

146. Simmel, "Die Geselligkeit," 62: *Beziehungsspiel*; 64: *Bindung*, within
which and as part of which Simmel also includes loosening, or rather, the ongoing
rhythm of joining, loosening, and rejoining.

147. For the play of relationality or binding existing "beneath" the objective
content, cf. Simmel's wordplay on *sich unter-halten* ("Die Geselligkeit," 62).

148. Simmel, "Die Geselligkeit," 63.

149. Ibid. See Holmes, *The Tissue of the World*, who presents *sympatheia* as
the conceptual habit of reading relation, of seeing the real in the relation.

150. Simmel, "Die Geselligkeit," 63.

151. In terms developed by Paul Fleming, anecdotes obtain the quality of
"exemplarity."

152. Simmel, "Die Geselligkeit," 66.

153. Ibid.

154. Roughly speaking, *Verstimmung* = discord; *Mißstimmung* = discord;
Zustimmung = concord; *Bestimmung* = determination; *Übereinstimmung* =
accordance; *Umstimmung* = conversion; *Stimme* = voice or vote; *Abstimmung* =
attunement or vote. The way these words link up with each other is itself symptomatic of *Stimmung* at work: they "socialize" and *stimmen* with one another.

155. These occasions seem most often to involve Rex or Woldemar: 5:84, 86,
92, 128, 130.

156. *Der Stechlin*, 5:377.

157. *Der Stechlin*, 5:62.

158. *Umstimmung* (5:331) beneath the apparent *Zustimmung* (5:329). Baruch
"felt something like *Verstimmung*. But so did Dubslav" (5:316).

159. This silence would be more or less the functional equivalent in Fontane's
novel to the experience of touch in Keller's, the moment when, for Heinrich, Anna
suddenly moves from "object" to "thing," followed by Heinrich's anxious attempt
to restore the connective sense of *Stimmung*: in both cases, an uncanny reality that
threatens to undo the realist world. See chapter 1, note 136.

160. *Der Stechlin,* 5:132: there are many more such instances.

161. *Der Stechlin,* 5:358, *Friktionen.*

162. "Assemblage" (not a Deleuzean term) is a first attempt at finding a word that conveys the sense of disparate individual characters whose momentary common presence provides the base condition for the formation, in the social sphere, of a sympathetic order of related (and semblanced) elements. Every assembly, gathering, or group offers anew the possibility for the successful formation of such an order, which, when achieved, is achieved because of sociability but also generates the sense of sociability—the sense of a kind of mystical participation in the macrocosmos (or assemblage). Other words that might suggest themselves, such as "association," also need to be wrenched out of their flattened sense and restored to a fuller meaning (e.g., association as that which is or can be sociated) in order to convey what I'm after (*kosmos* outside of Greek seems too grand).

163. Hasubek, *". . . wer am meisten red't",* 114; *Der Stechlin,* 5:25.

164. The novel has an exemplary instance of such a series in its anecdote "Sausage for sausage!" (Wurst wider Wurst!, 5:43).

165. Simmel, "Die Geselligkeit," 53f.; Max Weber, "The Nature of Charismatic Authority and Its Routinization," in *Theory of Social and Economic Organization,* translated by A. R. Anderson and Talcott Parsons (New York: Oxford University Press, 1947), 358–373; Henry James, "Preface to 'What Maisie Knew'," in *The Art of the Novel: Critical Prefaces* (Chicago: University of Chicago Press, 2011), 140–159. James's use of "tone" in this context seems an attempt to render *Stimmung* into English. See, too, James, "The Lesson of Balzac," 80–83, where he expands on "tone," "atmosphere," and "magic" as key to realism.

166. *Verstimmliches,* 5:90.

167. *Verstimmung* arises despite Adelheid's most ob-liging accommodation (*verbindlichste Entgegenkommen*), 5:82. For the collapse into sameness that threatens the sympathetic world when it excludes antipathetic forces, see Foucault, *The Order of Things,* 24–25.

168. *Zustimmung,* 5:84; *volle Zustimmung,* 86; *gute Stimmung,* 93; *Verstimmliches,* 90 (see also 96): silences, 83, 90.

169. *Der Stechlin,* 5:90.

170. *Stimmung,* e.g., 5:178; repeated references to *Zustimmung,* e.g., 28 (twice), 45, 192 (twice), 194; gestures of *Zustimmung,* 31; references to *Verbindlichkeit,* connecting threads or *Fäden,* 29; *Knauel,* 37, *Sympathie,* 43, 44.

171. *Zu knüpfen,* 5:29 (twice); poetic associations of similitude, e.g., 27; "Had I said the opposite, it would have been just as right," 27 (see also 29, 36); boundaries of tact crossed in matters of taste (the rats) or of politics (Gundermann), 38.

172. Dubslav sitting quietly, 32, and silently expressing his *Zustimmung,* 28.

173. As mentioned in the introduction, these chains or threads are what the Neoplatonists would call *seirai.* Frau Gundermann's Berlin is from her early adulthood; Dubslav's Russia from the time of Czar Alexander himself.

174. *Der Stechlin,* 5:137. The next line reinforces the centrality of *Stimmung*: "And already at the steamship station this *Stimmung* proved beneficial."

175. For bells as a figure of *Stimmung,* see also 5:208, where bells produce *Geselligkeit* and bode forth connectivity; also Stifter, "Granit," etc. Here, the fact that

the bells ring both on the boat and in the surrounding city bespeaks micro-macro connections.

176. *Der Stechlin*, 5:138. For *Stimmung* and *Bereitschaft*, see the section "Stimmung" in chapter 1.

177. I leave out for now the sequences looking back at the servant class, which will be mentioned in the next section.

178. *Der Stechlin*, 5:140.

179. Ibid. One of the most difficult things to formulate in this episode, indeed in the novel as a whole, is the spatial directionality of *Stimmung*. There is a sense in which it is reaching both outward and upward at once as part of its connection with the broader natural *Umwelt*. This is captured in part by having nature represented as at once landscape and the (night) sky, and *Stimmung* as both a laterally joining and literally uplifting experience (as part of its abstraction from the everyday, the material). The upward dimension to the natural world—where it becomes the site for *Stimmung*—is decisive for the evocation of nature as vaguely Neoplatonic, where the progression from the material to more immaterial (and divine) levels is also conceived vertically. But it is also decisive for the evocation of nature as the embodiment of the text's metatextuality, where for the characters to connect with the natural world is also to be drawn into the text or author's overarching governing nexus—drawing on the convention that the author, like divinity, hovers "over" his text. This multidirectionality is made even more complicated in Fontane's novel than it is for the Neoplatonists by the dominant imagery system of the lake with its subterranean communicative system, that is at once the site of the natural, the supernatural, and the metatextual, and that, we'll see, figures beneath this episode as well, not least in the waterway on which the trip takes place—here, the author "beneath" his text. *Stimmung* becomes a matter of connecting outward, upward, and downward with the natural world, which is also the metatextual world: at once requiring the vocabulary, and movement, of "beyond," "above," and "beneath." With my primary focus on the temporal dimension of the *Stimmung* here, I'm not sure I always succeed in getting all that spatial complexity across: hence, the need for this note.

180. *Der Stechlin*, 5:140.

181. *Der Stechlin*, 5:141f.

182. *Der Stechlin*, 5:142, "I cannot agree (*zustimmen*) with you, my dear Count." The factory location has the ugly name of Spindlersfelde, which like Rummelsburger also contributes to the prosaic heaviness.

183. *Der Stechlin*, 5:144.

184. I.e., dematerialized into sound (of the bells) and light (of the lamps).

185. The idea that every such associative chain has some anchor in the material world is part of the Neoplatonic model for *seirai*, and, mutatis mutandis, seems central to this novel as well: the *Dingwelt* becomes allegorical, and so begins the associative transformation by which the real becomes magical, because sympathetic.

186. *Der Stechlin*, 5:152.

187. *Der Stechlin*, 5:151f.

188. *Der Stechlin*, 5:152–154. This story, like the two that proceed it, is of course an anecdote, and as such it also leads the assembled group to seek out the connection of its meaning to their present moment and its future.

189. *Der Stechlin*, 5:153f.

190. *Der Stechlin*, 5:154f.

191. Ibid.

192. *Der Stechlin*, 5:155.

193. For water as landscape, see *Die Poggenpuhls*, 4:552; for water landscapes as *stimmungsvoll*, see *Der Stechlin*, 5:335.

194. "Byway" = *Umweg*, 5:157.

195. *Der Stechlin*, 5:156.

196. *Der Stechlin*, 5:158 (Fontane's italics).

197. See Holmes, *The Tissue of the World*, for kinship (*cognatio*) as one of the forms *sympatheia* frequently takes in the conceptual habit of the sympathetic imagination in antiquity.

198. This has significant parallels in its way with the place of Goethe in *Green Henry*; see chapter 1.

199. For Dubslav as a belated *Schweiger*, see below.

200. For name play and even name changes as part of this episode, see 5:140f., 152, 157f.

201. *Der Stechlin*, 5:159.

202. *Der Stechlin*, 5:158 (Fontane's italics).

203. *Der Stechlin*, 5:387 (Fontane's italics).

204. "Compromised" is admittedly an embarrassingly euphemistic description of "raped," but a required one to draw the connections to/similitudes with other, less violent events in the novel that this one points to.

205. *in ausgezeichneter Laune* and *Wetter/Stimmung*, 5:184; *gar nichts von Verstimmung*, 191; *Zustimmung und Heiterkeit*, 190, 194; *allgemein zugestimmt*, 192; nodding *Zustimmung*, 192; shouting *Stimmt, stimmt*, 190; *anstimmen*, 192.

206. *fatale Verstimmungen*, 5:160.

207. *alle Stimmen auf Dubslav zu vereinigen*, 5:165; *wer gegen uns stimmt, stimmt auch gegen den König*, 190; *wie die Stimmung im Kreise wirklich war*, 164; *Stimmen* qua votes, 190; *Abstimmungsmaschine*, 194; *Volksstimme, Gottesstimme*, 223; see also 5:260, "And have you heard her voice (*Stimme*)? And as you know, the voice is the soul."

208. *Der Stechlin*, 5:273.

209. For the loss of the future, think of Dubslav on the walk before their boat trip, speaking of "the outlook(*Auslug*) from this rickety pier (*Wackelstege*) on which we stand," 5:188.

210. *Tatsache*, 5:197; *Märchen*, 198.

211. The few related anecdotes would include that about restorative (and time-defying) plastic surgery, 5:257; also Sponholz's restorative spa treatments and, of course, Lorenzen's *wieder-geben*.

212. *Wiederherstellung*, 5:199; *Reinheitswiederherstellung*, 197; and the catchphrase "*Blut sühnt*," 197 (Fontane's italics).

213. This is a possibility broached later on by Lorenzen, but one whose potential fulfillment lies outside the time frame of the novel, 5:274.

214. "Die Zukunft liegt also bei *dir*," 5:387. See also what, shortly beforehand, Lorenzen says to Dubslav, "At least very soon the desire will come over [Woldemar] more or less to come around again to the old ways" (369).

215. "Everything takes place in silence": *Der Stechlin*, 5:341.

216. Its faith in the Word and everlasting future life, 5:328f. See Paul Irving Anderson, "Der Stechlin," in *Interpretationen: Fontanes Novellen und Romanen*, edited by Christian Grawe (Stuttgart: Reclam, 1991), 243–274, on the turn from Christian belief (and secular skepticism) to superstitious belief in a world of witchcraft at the novel's end (255).

217. *Der Stechlin*, 5:201.

218. That the lower classes and their speech are somehow closer to nature, more naturalistic, is of course a literary convention of the time—but nonetheless one operant in the novel (not unrelated to the similar association of women with nature).

219. *Der Stechlin*, 5:225.

220. E.g., 5:310, 317, 338f.

221. *Der Stechlin*, 5:226.

222. *Der Stechlin*, 5:226, 373. Fontane's female *Naturkinder*: e.g., Marie, Lena, Cécile, Effi, even Ebba.

223. Agnes comes to seem an omen of the future set in counterpoint to Woldemar and Armgard's foreboded child. Agnes, the heir presumptive of Dubslav's *Wetterfahnen*, is viewed as such a sign by Dubslav not for her political character, as Adelheid does, but for her nonpolitical affiliations with the natural, silent world.

224. There is a connection between silence and the animal that is us: Dubslav says, "Keeping silent doesn't suit everyone. And then of course we are also supposed to distinguish ourselves from the animal through speech. Thus, whoever speaks the most is the most purely human" (5:23). Although usually interpreted as celebrating language and the exclusively human, this also points to the connection shared via silence with the animal world: he who is silent is least separated from the natural world. And that illness draws us close to the animal world might be connected with how it exposes the "pathos"—the openness and vulnerabilty—that is at the center of the concept of sym-pathy (see the sympathetic connections between Anna and nature established by illness in *Green Henry*, explored in chapter 1).

225. *Der Stechlin*, 5:312.

226. For the role of *Bild* in the novel, Pfau, "Epochenwandel," 420–442.

227. For Dubslav, 5:326f.; 339, "'A chaffinch (*Buch-fink* [!]) came today. And I'm absolutely certain he'll be followed by others.' Dubslav's presentiments (*Ahnungen*) proved right." For Melusine's connections to the elemental of the lake, 265–267. The reader is invited to infer that this lake will, at Dubslav's death, send its sign, via the smoke signals of Vesuvius, to Woldemar when all other, merely human means of communication fail: this is possible only because of Dubslav's sympathetic relation to the lake—because of the connection of his fatal *Wassersucht* to the lake. The portent of those smoke signals is one of the novel's clearest examples of the *actio in distans* made possible by the sympathetic (*gestimmt*) order.

228. *nicht sehr sympathisch*, 5:323.

229. *Der Stechlin*, 5:313.

230. For *Fingerhut* as the older familiar term, 5:426.

231. *Grete Minde*, 1:65, "The red foxglove stood in tall bushes all around her. The morning wind had shaken down a pair of its blossoms on Grete, and she took one of them and said, 'What does this signify for me? It's a fairy-tale flower

(*Märchenblume*).' 'Yes, that it is. And it means that you are an enchanted princess or a witch.'"

232. *Cécile*, 2:165.

233. The transformation of *Fingerhut* into digitalis also occurs in *Cécile*, with the move from the opening nature setting into the urban setting, where the protagonist Gordon's attraction becomes deadly—to her (2:289).

234. Anderson, "Der Stechlin," connects both the lake and *Fingerhut* to Melusine (261).

235. As noted earlier, micro-macro relationality is overtly thematized throughout the novel, not least through the lake's connections to the broader world.

236. For "similia similibus," see *Unwiederbringlich*; also *Cécile* (see earlier discussion).

237. The contiguous relation to these *Hexenkünste* is one of the ways that *Fingerhut* becomes contagiously linked to magic as well.

238. "Dat Woater nimmt dat Woater" (5:335, 336).

239. For Dubslav's allegorizations, 5:336.

240. *Der Stechlin*, 5:359, 361.

241. Interestingly, Krippenstapel makes his offering of the honeycomb to Dubslav as something positively medieval (5:358f.), which does seem to suggest something of a *Wiederherstellung* of an earlier era in the present one—even as the attempt is being made, through the figure of a "sympathetically" restored Dubslav, to restore an outmoded political order as well.

242. *Der Stechlin*, 5:367.

243. *Der Stechlin*, 5:328f.

244. *Der Stechlin*, 5:388.

245. *Der Stechlin*, 5:352.

246. *Der Stechlin*, 5:353.

247. The color red in the novel is not, I suggest, readable in the novel, because it could mean so many different things. Cf. Eric Miller, "Die roten Fäden des roten Hahns zu einem Motivkomplex im 'Stechlin'." *Fontane Blätter* 67 (1999): 91–105, who draws a somewhat different conclusion from his evidence than I.

248. Melancholically—but still charmingly: this is, after all, Fontane.

249. This relocation of divinatory reading into retrospective inquiry, especially into childhood but also into history, is an aspect of modernism explored in the next chapter.

3. Reading Magic in Walter Benjamin

1. Hermann Hesse, *Der Steppenwolf*, in *Sämtliche Werke*, edited by Volker Michels (Frankfurt am Main: Suhrkamp, 2003), 4:39–41. Translation from Hermann Hesse, *The Steppenwolf*, translated by Basil Creighton, revised by Joseph Mileck and Horst Frenz (New York: Henry Holt, 1990).

2. Hermann Hesse, "Vom Bücherlesen," in *Sämtliche Werke*, 14:367–372; Theodore Ziolkowski, *The Novels of Hermann Hesse: A Study in Theme and Structure* (Princeton, NJ: Princeton University Press, 1965), 195f.

3. As Benjamin says, "Precisely modernity is always citing primal history"; Benjamin, "Paris, die Hauptstadt des XIX Jahrhunderts," GS 5:55; SW 3:40.

4. Freud's essay on telepathy was known to Walter Benjamin; see Anson Rabinbach, "Introduction to Walter Benjamin's 'Doctrine of the Similar'," *New German Critique* 17 (Spring 1979): 64; also Sarah Ley Roff, "Benjamin and Psychoanalysis," in *The Cambridge Companion to Walter Benjamin*, edited by David Ferris (Cambridge: Cambridge University Press, 2004), 115–133.

5. E.g., "Madame Sosostris, famous clairvoyante, / Had a bad cold, nevertheless / Is known to be the wisest woman in Europe, / With a wicked pack of cards. Here, said she / Is your card, the drowned Phoenician Sailor, / (Those are pearls that were his eyes. Look!)". T. S. Eliot, *The Wasteland*, lines 43–48, in *The Complete Poems and Plays, 1909–1950* (New York: Harcourt Brace and World, 1971).

6. T. S. Eliot, "The Dry Salvages," *Four Quartets*, in *The Complete Poems*, 135–136.

7. Ibid, 117.

8. It is worth noting that Mann explicitly mentions Benjamin's *Trauerspiel* book as an influence while writing *Doktor Faustus*. See Thomas Mann, *Die Entstehung des Doktor Faustus*, in Mann, *Gesammelte Werke in dreizehn Bänden* (Frankfurt am Main: Fischer, 1974), vol. 11.

9. Some of the most explicit connections between the sympathetic world order and divination in Benjamin's work—what he calls *natürliche Prophezeiung*—come in sections 12, 18, and 19 of his essay "Der Erzähler," which, however, will not play a central part in what follows; it was discussed in the introduction. See Benjamin, GS 2:438–465; SW 3:153, 159, 160.

10. Howard Eiland and Michael Jennings, *Walter Benjamin: A Critical Life* (Cambridge, MA: Harvard University Press, 2014), and Miriam Bratu Hansen, "Benjamin's Aura," *Critical Inquiry* 34, no. 2 (2008): 336–375, posit changes, the one in response to his time spent in southern Europe, the other to the rise of fascism. Both have validity without negating the claim here.

11. Benjamin, "Erleuchtung durch Dünkelmänner," GS 3:356; SW 2:653.

12. For the magic of blood and glitter, Benjamin, GS 3:358; SW 2:655. We might also add his critique of surrealism: "But I am not pleased to hear it cautiously tapping on the windowpanes to inquire about its future" (GS 2:298; SW 2:209).

13. For barbarism, Benjamin, "Erleuchtung," GS 3:360; SW 2:656; Benjamin, "Erfahrung und Armut," GS 2:215; SW 2:732.

14. Benjamin, GS 1:704; SW 4:397. There was, however, a Jewish tradition of *sortilegia* that partook of divination; see Christopher Wild, "*Apertio libri*: Codex and Conversion," in *Literary Studies and the Pursuits of Reading*, edited by Eric Downing, Jonathan Hess, and Richard Benson (Rochester, NY: Camden House, 2012), 38.

15. Benjamin, "Schicksal und Charakter," GS 2:171–179; SW 1:201–206.

16. Ibid., GS 2:171; SW 1:201.

17. Ibid., GS 2:172; SW 1:201.

18. Ibid., GS 2:172; SW 1:202. For more on this, see Benjamin, "Analogie und Verwandtschaft," GS 6:43; SW 1:207–209.

19. Benjamin, GS 2:172; SW 1:202.

20. For *Schuldzusammenhang*, Benjamin, GS 2:175; SW 1:204. This notion is a complex one, and crucial to our subsequent reading of the relation between

signification and the material world in Benjamin's thought, but attempting fully to explicate it here would be premature. Briefly, man and nature are joined as part of a material community (man by virtue of his material body); both man and nature exist in a "fallen" state; man's "fall" is into a state of (self-)consciousness that renders both his consciousness and his connection to nature as "guilt"; the same consciousness that knows itself as guilt also interferes with man's ability to know nature. Eiland and Jennings, *A Critical Life*, seem to imply that Benjamin's attitude toward nature changes in the late 1920s/early 1930s, when his visits to Capri and Ibiza lead to a more open embrace: this is the same period in which his interests in divination and *sympatheia* and the mimetic faculty are most acute.

21. Benjamin, GS 2:175; SW 1:204.

22. Ibid., GS 2:176; SW 1:204. See Peter Fenves, *The Messianic Reduction: Walter Benjamin and the Shape of Time* (Stanford, CA: Stanford University Press, 2011), 106–112.

23. GS 2:176; SW 1:204.

24. Ibid.

25. For more on the connection between fate and divination in terms of this peculiar temporal structure, see the section "Nähe und Ferne (Fortsetzung)" in "Schemata zum psychophysischen Problem," GS 6:84; SW 1:398.

26. Benjamin, GS 2:174; SW 1:203.

27. Consider, for example, the statement made in "Der Erzähler," where the religious context is not engaged: "The liberating magic which the fairy tale has at its disposal does not bring nature into play in a mythical way, but points to its complicity with liberated man. A mature man feels this complicity only occasionally— that is, when he is happy: but the child first meets it in fairy tales, and it makes him happy" (Der befreiende Zauber, über den das Märchen verfügt, bringt nicht auf mythische Art die Natur ins Spiel, sondern ist die Hindeutung auf ihre Komplizität mit der befreiten Menschen. Diese Komplizität empfindet der reife Mensch nur bisweilen, nämlich im Glück; dem Kind aber tritt sie zuerst im Märchen entgegen und stimmt es glücklich," GS 2:438–465; SW 3:157). For more on the occasionality (*bisweilen, im Glück*) of this complicity in the mature man, see below.

28. "Late" is a relative term here: 1933 for both essays.

29. See H. J. Jacoby, *Analysis of Handwriting: An Introduction into Scientific Graphology*, 2nd ed. [1st ed. 1939] (London: George Allen and Unwin, 1948); Klara G. Roman, *Handwriting: A Key to Personality* (New York: Pantheon, 1952). Ludwig Klages, *Handschrift und Charakter: Gemeinverständlicher Abriß der graphologishen Technik* (1917; reprint, Bonn: Bouvier, 1989).

30. For Benjamin's own forays into practicing graphology, see Gershom Scholem and Theodor W. Adorno, eds., *The Correspondence of Walter Benjamin, 1910–1940*, translated by Manfred R. Jacobson and Evelyn M. Jacobson (Chicago: University of Chicago Press, 1994), 164, 338, 615.

31. Benjamin's texts on graphology are his "Anja und Georg Mendelssohn, *Der Mensch in der Handschrift*," GS 3:135–139; SW 2:131–134; and "Alte und neue Graphologie," GS 4:596–598; SW 2:398–400. The reference to the riddle is from the former, GS 3:136; SW 2:131.

32. For handwriting as hieroglyphs, Benjamin, GS 3:136; SW 2:132.

33. GS 3:136f.; SW 2:132f.

34. Ibid. In at least some schools of graphology, these associational chains were called "constellations," which is quite suggestive for Benjamin, not least in his apparent use of graphological terminology to describe the reading of astrological constellations in "Lehre vom Ähnlichen." See Jacoby, *Analysis of Handwriting*, passim.

35. Benjamin, GS 3:138f; SW 2:133.

36. See Roman, *Handwriting*, 136.

37. Benjamin, GS 3:136; SW 2:132. For the reading of animals as signs, see Derek Collins, "Mapping the Entrails: The Practice of Greek Hepatoscopy," *American Journal of Philology* 129 (2008): 319–345; Collins, "Reading the Birds: Oionomanteia in Early Epic," *Colby Quarterly* 38 (2002): 17–41. For words or even letters, or rather "characters," as animate natural beings, see Derek Collins, *Magic in the Ancient Greek World* (Oxford: Blackwell, 2008), 73, 75–77.

38. Benjamin, GS 4:597; SW 2:399. See also Benjamin, SW 3:137; SW 2:132.

39. Benjamin, GS 2:175, 178f.; SW 1:204, 206.

40. Benjamin, GS 4:598; SW 2:399. Perhaps a difference can be discerned between this and Gestalt-based theories, which suppose an image "in mind" that the writer consciously tries to follow in his writing.

41. Benjamin, "Lehre vom Ähnlichen," GS 2:208; SW 2:697.

42. One of the best places to pinpoint the distinctions between Freud's and Benjamin's positions on this matter comes in a passage where they seem to come closest together. In a letter to Gretel Adorno, Benjamin mentions a passage in one of Freud's essays in which he (Benjamin) finds expressed some of his own ideas. The passage concerns telepathy (and for graphology and gambling as divinatory forms of telepathy, see below): "The telepathic process is supposed to consist in a mental act in one person instigating the same mental act in another person. What lies between these two mental acts may easily be a physical process into which the mental one is transformed at one end and which is transformed back once more into the same mental one at the other end. . . . Only think if one could get hold of this physical equivalent of the psychical act! It would seem to me that psychoanalysis, by inserting the unconscious between what is physical and what was previously called 'psychical', has paved the way for the assumption of such processes as telepathy. . . . It is a familiar fact that we do not know how the common purpose comes about in the great insect communities: possibly it is done by means of a direct psychical transference of this kind. One is led to a suspicion that this is the original, archaic method of communication between individuals and that in the course of phylogenetic evolution it has been replaced by the better method of giving information with the help of signals which are picked up by the sense organs. But the older method might have persisted in the background and still be able to put itself into effect under certain conditions." Sigmund Freud, "Dreams and Occultism," in *The Standard Edition of the Complete Psychological Works*, edited and translated by James Strachey (London: Hogarth Press, 1999), 22:55.

Benjamin calls particular attention to the insect example, which unlike Freud's own insertion of an unconscious between the physical and the psychical, entails a more or less direct corporeal connection, one that, insofar as it does persist in the human case, would subtend both conscious and unconscious communications or contacts. I suspect Benjamin supposes that the unconscious might well be a different, and possibly distorting, medium from that of the body (*ein natürliches*

Leben im Menschen) itself. For Benjamin's letter, see GS 2:952f.; mentioned in Roff, "Benjamin and Psychoanalysis," 126. I should add that Max Pulver seems to have embraced a somewhat similar position regarding the biological focus of graphological analysis.

43. Benjamin, GS 3:138; SW 2:133.

44. See note 39. We might say Benjamin sees graphology as a physiognomy of words, physiognomy as a graphology of the body.

45. Benjamin, GS 3:139; SW 2:134.

46. As described in the introduction, the connections between the microcosmic and macrocosmic realms were thought to be mediated by the force that the Stoics and Neoplatonists called *sympatheia*, a sense of participation in a common *logos* that connects all parts of nature by contact and likeness. The idea is key to the conception of sympathetic magic elaborated by James George Frazer in *The Golden Bough: A Study in Magic and Religion* (New York: Macmillan, 1956) and persists, via the Neoplatonists, as an often undervalued center of the romantic notion of sympathy, not least in the practice of sympathetic reading. For Benjamin's rejection of the graphological doctrines of the *Lebensphilosophien* and occult sciences, see Benjamin, GS 3:137; SW 2:133.

47. The connection of magic reading with telepathy as well as divination is also a concern in the essay on surrealism as well as in the fragments on gambling discussed below. As suggested above (note 42), telepathy is also an ongoing preoccupation of Freud's.

48. Benjamin, GS 3:139; GS 2:137.

49. Ibid.

50. Ibid., GS 3:139; SW 2:133f.

51. Edward Burnett Tylor, *The Origins of Culture* (Gloucester, MA: Peter Smith, 1970), 78–83; he notes, "Arts of divination and games of chance are so similar in principle that the very same instrument passes from one use to the other" (80). Benjamin's other concerns with gambling link it to capitalist thought and particularly modern experience (including time); I do not claim comprehensive coverage of his take on this topic.

52. For card playing, see entry O13a,2 in *Das Passagenwerk*, GS 5:640; English translation: Walter Benjamin, *The Arcades Project*, translated by Howard Eiland and Kevin McLaughlin (Cambridge, MA: Harvard University Press, 1999), 514. For *das Brett lesen*, GS 6:189; SW 2:297. More precisely, Benjamin writes *das Brett umsichtig lesen*. For the importance of the idea of *umsichtig* (circum-spectly) to Benjamin's concept of divinatory reading, including the connection to both fate and the future, see the section "Nähe und Ferne (Fortsetzung)" in "Schemata zum psychophysischen Problem," GS 6:84; SW 1:398. Unfortunately the English translation is more or less useless in this instance. Eiland and Jennings, *A Critical Life*, point out that Benjamin was himself not only an amateur graphologist but also a gambler—sometimes successful, often not.

53. Benjamin, "Notiz zu einer Theorie des Spiels," GS 6:189; SW 2:297. In a different context (to be discussed below), Benjamin refers to the human body as our most ancient and reliable instrument of divination: GS 4:142; SW 1:483.

54. *[Tele]pathie*, in Benjamin, GS 6:188; not included in SW. For Benjamin's notion of innervation, see Miriam Hansen, "Room-for-Play: Benjamin's Gamble

with Cinema," *October* 109 (Summer 2004): 3–45; Hansen, "Benjamin, Cinema, and Experience: 'The Blue Flower in the Land of Technology'," *New German Critique* 40 (Winter 1987): 179–224; Hansen, "Benjamin and Cinema: Not a One-Way Street," *Critical Inquiry* 25, no. 2 (1999): 306–343. See also the section in "Kurze Schatten (II)" on gambling (which in fact does seem to situate innervation more internally), GS 4:425–428; SW 2:700.

55. GS 6:188.

56. For the "hostile suggestions," GS 6:188. For the contact with the realm of fate, Benjamin, GS 6:189; SW 2:297. The description of parrying here adumbrates Benjamin's later accounts of Freud and Baudelaire on trauma, or *Erfahrung*, and consciousness, in "Über einige Motive bei Baudelaire," GS 1:605–653; SW 4:313–355.

57. Benjamin, GS 6:189; SW 2:297f.

58. In extispicy, for example (and as described in the introduction), this is why animal, not human, livers were employed: since animals themselves have no future consciousness—and especially no anticipatory response to impending death or danger—their own conscious expectations would not mark livers in ways that might be mistaken for divine signs. Similarly, birds were used in augury precisely because their animated movements were free of human interference, which made them privileged conduits for the communication of another, invisible realm of divine will and authority—which is also what transformed them into signs. See Collins, "Entrails"; Collins, "Birds." For Benjamin's more generally known positions on consciousness and trauma, and consciousness and *Erfahrung*, see "Über einige Motive bei Baudelaire," GS 1:605–653; SW 4:313–355.

59. Benjamin, GS 6:189; SW 2:298. The implication is that "what it is" at that point is "too late"; compare the brief entry in *Das Passagenwerk*, "Only the future that has not entered as such into his consciousness is parried by the gambler" (O13,2), GS 5:639; *Arcades Project*, 513.

60. Benjamin, GS 4:141; SW 1:483. The passage continues, "Each morning the day lies like a fresh shirt on our bed; this incomparably fine, incomparably tightly woven fabric of pure prediction fits us perfectly. The happiness of the next twenty-four hours depends on our ability, on waking, to pick it up."

61. Interestingly enough, he calls this gap a *Schuldgefühl*, GS 4:141; SW 1:483.

62. Benjamin, GS 6:190; SW 2:298; also GS 4:141–142; SW 1:483, which states, "To turn the threatening future into a fulfilled "now," the only desirable telepathic miracle, is a work of bodily presence of mind" (Die Zukunftsdrohung ins erfüllte Jetzt zu wandeln, dies einzig wünschenswerte telepathische Wunder ist Werk leibhafter Geistesgegenwart). See also *Arcades Project*, O12a,2; also "Der Weg zum Erfolg in dreizehn Thesen," GS 4:252; SW 2:145. For the body as *das verläßlichste Instrument der Divination*, GS 4:142; SW 1:483.

63. Benjamin, GS 4:141; SW 1:482.

64. There is a suggestion here that the fall into rational consciousness, which is in some sense a fall from direct connection to things, is also a fall into sequential time—and perhaps, too, into ordinary language; see Benjamin, GS 4:142; GS 1:483. For the different kind of future from that based on sequential time, see GS 6:84; SW 1:398.

65. Benjamin, GS 6:189; SW 2:297.

66. Ibid., GS 6:190; SW 2:298. For the gambler's *Zeitmoment*, see also Benjamin, *Arcades Project*, O12a,2, which addresses as well the issue of acceleration. See too O2a,5; O4a. For *hazard* (viz. *Hasard*), a term suggestively combining notions of chance, danger, and potential happiness, see *Arcades Project*, O7a,5; O7a,7; O10a,5; O11,2.

67. It is also crucial to his notion of modernity; see Benjamin, *Arcades Project*, "Fashion" (B2,1): the advent of new velocities, which gave life an altered rhythm.

68. Benjamin, GS 6:190: SW 2:298. For the role of acceleration (*Schnelligkeit*) in achieving the clairvoyant divination of *das Lesen schlechthin*, see Benjamin, "Lehre vom Ähnlichen," GS 2:209f.; SW 2:697f.; and "Über das mimetische Vermögen," GS 2:231; SW 2:722. ꜩ

69. Benjamin, GS 6:190; SW 2:298. See too *Arcades Project*, O13, 3, GS 5:639; *Arcades Project*, 513: "The proscription of gambling could have its deepest roots in the fact that a natural gift of humanity, one which, directed toward the highest objects, elevates the human being beyond itself, only drags him down when applied to one of the meanest objects: money. The gift in question is presence of mind. Its highest manifestation is the reading that in each case is divinatory."

70. The importance of such movement to realizing the happy moment of connection is something we saw adumbrated in more modest form in the Egg Cottage episode in *Der Stechlin*.

71. Benjamin, GS 6:190; SW 2:298. Consider again the passage from "Der Erzähler": "The liberating magic which the fairy tale has at its disposal does not bring nature into play in a mythical way, but points to its complicity with liberated man. A mature man feels this complicity only occasionally—that is, when he is happy" (GS 2:438–465; SW 3:157). Magic, complicity with nature, occasionality, and "Glück": all conjoined in a related, if different, description of reading.

72. Benjamin, GS 6:189; SW 2:297.

73. For Hesse's efforts to get Benjamin's *Berliner Kindheit* published, see Eiland and Jennings, *A Critical Life*, 299, 437.

74. This will need qualification: In "Kulturgeschichte des Spielzeugs," Benjamin clearly sees children as historically situated against the nineteenth century (GS 3:117; SW 2:116). But then in "Kinderliteratur" he seems to have the child's relation to primers recapitulate that of history itself (GS 7:250–257; SW 2:250–256); more below.

75. GS 6:127; SW 3:253.

76. For *Stimmung* as one of the group of terms—including *aura*—that Benjamin uses to describe the realm, activity, and effect of *sympatheia*, see below (also the introduction).

77. The phrase is from James Rolleston's translation of Bernd Witte, *Walter Benjamin: An Intellectual Biography* (Detroit: Wayne State University Press, 1991), 11, which is itself paraphrasing both Friedrich Schlegel and Benjamin himself; see GS 1:1237; SW 4:405.

78. GS 2:371; SW 2:510.

79. Roland Barthes, *Camera Lucida: Reflections on Photography*, translated by Richard Howard (New York: Hill and Wang, 1981).

80. As is not unusual for Benjamin, the vignette is repeated in revised form across several works. Here, see also *Berliner Chronik*.

81. GS 4:251f.; SW 3:389f.

82. Or is (potentially) carried over into the future/carries with it a renewed future thrust (see GS 1:1237; SW 4:405).

83. We might compare this to a passage from *Berliner Chronik*: "This dead corner of the Zoological Garden was an image of what was to come, a prophesying place. It must be considered certain that there are such places; indeed, just as there are plants that primitive peoples claim confer the power of clairvoyance, so there are places endowed with such power" (GS 6:484; SW 2:610).

84. Eliot, *Four Quartets*, 133.

85. See Werner Hamacher, "'Jetzt': Benjamin zur historischen Zeit," *Benjamin Studien* 1 (2002):147–183; and Michael G. Levine, *A Weak Redemptive Power: Figures of a Time to Come in Benjamin, Derrida, and Celan* (New York: Fordham University Press, 2014). The aspect is also suggested in the introductory remarks in *Berliner Kindheit* to "The Reading Box," where Benjamin writes, "We can never entirely recover what has been forgotten. And this is perhaps a good thing. The shock of repossession would be so devastating that we would immediately cease to understand our longing. But we do understand it; and the more deeply what has been forgotten lies buried within us, the better we understand this longing" (GS 4:267; SW 3:395). On longing (*Sehnsucht*), see below.

86. Hansen, "Benjamin's Aura," 368.

87. Significantly, the thwarted wish is described with the same word—envy (*Neid*)—that figures so decisively in the second thesis of "Über den Begriff der Geschichte": see Hamacher, "Jetzt." For the importance of the wish, and especially the wish made in childhood, see "Über einige Motive bei Baudelaire" GS 1:634–635; SW 4:331 (where Benjamin also says that the gambler does not wish in this way).

88. GS 4:113; SW 1:263. All references to this vignette are on these pages.

89. For Benjamin's snow imagery, see Werner Hamacher, "The Word *Wolke*—If It Is One," in *Benjamin's Ground: New Readings of Walter Benjamin*, edited by Rainer Nägele (Detroit: Wayne State University Press, 1988), 147–176.

90. This is signaled here by the way the description of the child shifts from the second to the third person at the moment he enters the text.

91. Although here elaborated only in relation to the child, and elsewhere as far less immediately accessible to grown-ups, Benjamin nevertheless will also claim that "something of this perspective is contained in every act of reading," where the text's given meaning becomes "merely the background on which rest the shadows cast" by one's arbitrarily imposed focus or desires, "like figures in relief." See the "Denkbild," "Brezel, Feder, Pause, Klage, Firlefanz," GS 4:432–433; SW 2:726ff. For adult reading, see below.

92. "Zu einer Arbeit über die Schönheit farbiger Bilder in Kinderbüchern," GS 6:123; SW 1:264; "Die Farbe vom Kinde aus Betrachtet," GS 6:111; SW 1:51.

93. See Fenves, *The Messianic Reduction*, 60–66, on children and color.

94. "Die Farbe vom Kinde aus Betrachtet," GS 6:111; SW 1:51. For *anlegen*, see "Aussicht ins Kinderbuch," GS 4:609; SW 1:435.

95. GS 6:110f.; SW 1:50f.

96. GS 6:111; SW 1:51. Although the word *Stimmung* does not, as it did for Keller and Fontane, appear often in Benjamin as a synonym for *sympatheia*, it

does still occur, for example, in his discussion of surrealism, and then elsewhere in his discussion of aura, another of his magical terms related to *sympatheia* and something of a precursor of the mimetic faculty (see the introduction).

97. "Aussicht ins Kinderbuch," GS 4:609; SW 1:435. For fairy tales and their relation to the natural world of sympathetic relations, see "Der Erzähler," GS 2:190; SW 3:157.

98. See too "Alte vergessene Kinderbücher," GS 3:19ff.; SW 1:411.

99. This "porous" realm of colors is also described as this "cloud at the core of things" (*das Stumme, das Lockere, das . . . im Kern der Dinge wölkt*; "Das Mummerehlen," in *Berliner Kindheit*, GS 4:262; SW 3:392).

100. "Alte vergessene Kinderbücher," GS 3:20; SW 1:411.

101. "Aussicht ins Kinderbuch," GS 4:613ff.; SW 1:442.

102. "All form, every outline that man perceives, corresponds to something in him that enables him to reproduce it" (Aller Form nämlich, allem Umriß, den der Mensch wahrnimmt, entspricht er selbst in dem Vermögen, ihn hervorzubringen, GS 4:613ff.; SW 1:442); the body as the organ of active relations (ibid.); as the medium of the child's reading, and reading as a form of enactment (GS 3:19ff.; SW 1:411).

103. See too "Über die Sprache des Menschen und die Sprache überhaupt," discussed below.

104. As he says, the child always ignores the *noli me tangere* and *kritzelt* instead (GS 3:19ff.; SW 1:411). In "Lesendes Kind," he notes that, when reading, "one hand always lies upon the page" (GS 4:113; SW 1:463).

105. "Aussicht ins Kinderbuch," GS 4:613ff.; SW 1:435.

106. "Alte vergessene Kinderbücher," GS 3:20; SW 1:411.

107. For color versus sound rather than equivalent, see "Aussicht ins Kinderbuch," GS 4:613ff.; SW 1:442; for sound as pure nature, see "Die Bedeutung der Sprache in Trauerspiel und Tragödie," GS 2:137f.; SW 1:59f.

108. "Kinderliteratur," GS 7:250; SW 2:250.

109. GS 2:137f.; SW 1:60.

110. The connection to color is conveyed in the description of *tönende* snowflakes, where elsewhere snowflakes are the image of enveloping colors: GS 4:613ff.; SW 1:435.

111. GS 7:250f.; SW 2:251.

112. GS 7:250ff.; SW 2:251; GS 4:611; SW 1:437: "in disguise" = *vermummt*. The relation between *vermummen* (see GS 4:262; SW 3:392), *anlegen*, and *übernennen* would be worth considering.

113. GS 3:15–18; SW 1:407–409. See Comenius's *Orbis sensualium pictus*, whose system, arrangement, and method come "straight out" of Campanella's book of astral magic (1602); see also Frances Yates, *The Art of Memory* (Chicago: University of Chicago Press, 1966), 337f.

114. GS 4:613ff.; SW 1:436.

115. GS 3:18; SW 1:409.

116. GS 4:613ff.; SW 1:437.

117. The *Zauber-bücher* to which Benjamin refers seem to be what in English we call "mix 'n' match" books; the example he gives of the dress-up book is *Isabellas Verwandlungen*, GS 4:613ff.; SW 1:437.

118. GS 4:83; SW 1:463; earlier called *tönende* snowflakes, GS 4:609; SW 1:435.

119. The rebus-like picture books in which "alle Substantiva, die das irgend zulassen, durch schön ausgemalte sachliche oder allegorische Bildchen bedeutet [sind]" (GS 4:611; SW 1:437) also signal the beginning of the tendency "die Anschauung so weit wie nur möglich vom Wort, geschweige vom Buchstaben zu emanzipieren" (GS 7:251; SW 2:251).

120. For the *Sehnsucht*, again, see also "The Reading Box," GS 4:267; SW 3:395: see note 85 above.

121. For the vitalists, theosophy, and anthroposophy, see Hansen, "Benjamin's Aura," 336–339.

122. For the *Dingwelt* of the child's play world as humanly produced, see GS 3:113ff.; SW 2:116, 118.

123. Certainly the distance from a natural world of sympathetic relations is far more the case than with the child Meretlein or Anna in Keller's novel.

124. This is in contradiction to the vitalists. For modernism as a move from a poetics of connection to one of detachment, see Barbara Stafford, *Visual Analogy: Consciousness as the Art of Connecting* (Cambridge, MA: MIT Press, 1999), 8–54.

125. One might speculate that it is due in part, too, to the equally increased antipathy toward the natural world, itself partly a reflexive response to the increased detachment from "nature" on the part of the urbanized, technologized, and intellectualized adult; and partly, too, a reactive, considered response to the perceived dangers of the vitalists.

126. GS 7:792; SW 2:692.

127. The distinction between identity and similarity is a crucial one for Benjamin's thinking about mimesis, which is to say, the mimetic faculty, perhaps nowhere more urgently than here.

128. *Einbahnstraße*, GS 4:116; SW 1:465.

129. "Die Mummerehlen" comes in several versions, most fully in the 1934 version (GS 4:260–263; SW 3:390–393); the quoted sentence actually adumbrates it and is from one of the precursor essays to "Lehre vom Ähnlichen," the "Denkfigur" of 1933, "Die Lampe," GS 7:794; SW 2:693.

130. GS 4:261; SW 3:392.

131. For *Vorwelt*, see Benjamin, "Franz Kafka," GS 2:409–438; SW 2:794–816; for *Urgeschichte*, "Paris, Hauptstadt des XIX. Jahrhunderts"; for *Stimmung*, "Surrealismus," where Benjamin writes: "Surrealism brings the immense forces of 'Stimmung' concealed in past things to the point of explosion"; and insofar as they do so, the surrealists are, he says, "visionaries and augurs" (GS 2:300, 299; SW 2:210). Elsewhere, in "Kleine Geschichte der Photographie," he uses *Stimmung* and *Aura* as synomyms (GS 3:378–379; SW 2:519); and in "Über einige Motive bei Baudelaire," he refers to *Aura* as the breath of prehistory (*Hauch von Vorgeschichte*, GS 1:643; SW 4:336); Miriam Hansen in turn refers to "aura" as an early formulation of the mimetic faculty ("Benjamin, Cinema, and Experience," 357), and has this to say about it: "The reflexivity of [such] a mode of perception, its reciprocity across eons, seems to both hinge upon and bring to fleeting consciousness an archaic element in our present senses, a forgotten trace of our material bond with nonhuman nature" ("Benjamin's Aura," 346).

132. Compare how in "Die Mummerehlen" and elsewhere in *Berliner Kindheit*, the words to which the child yields are first distorted by him (GS 4:260–263; SW 3:390–393).

133. "Kulturgeschichte des Spielzeugs," GS 3:117; SW 2:116 (see too "Spielzeug und Spielen," GS 3:128; SW 2:118); "Alte Vergessene Kinderbücher," GS 3:16f.; SW 1:408. The connotations of *sprunghaft* are similar to those we connected with the knight's move in chapter 2 (in German, the knight in chess is *der Springer*).

134. GS 4:115; SW 1:465.

135. GS 3:113–117; SW 2:115.

136. Ibid.

137. "Verstecktes Kind," GS 4:116; SW 1:465.

138. It is perhaps worth stressing how this model of the child's place in the spectral world of hidden embedded relations matches up with Benjamin's model of aura; see the discussion of aura and *Stimmung* in the introduction.

139. For its typical modernist characteristic, think of Proust, or Eliot—or, of course, Joyce. See Theodore Ziolkowski, "James Joyces Epiphanie und der Überwindung der empirischen Welt in der modernen deutschen Prosa," *Deutsche Vierteljahrsschrift* 35 (1961): 594–616.

140. For a qualification of its value for the adult (similar to the qualification for the child), see GS 3:133, quoted in Eiland and Jennings, *A Critical Life*, 213.

141. GS 7:792–794; SW 2:692; cf. GS 6:192f.; SW 2:685; for the moon, cf. GS 4:300–302; SW 3:405ff.; and Hamacher, "*Wolke*."

142. *seltene Augenblicke*, GS 6:192f.; SW 2:685; *seltenste Augenblicke*, GS 6:190; SW 2:298.

143. Eiland and Jennings, *A Critical Life*, argue for a crucial awakening to the power of nature when Benjamin migrated to Ibiza in Spain, where he wrote many of the essays associated with the mimetic faculty, including that from which this quotation comes: if we follow this, these moonlit moments are crucially "southern," as is this nature.

144. GS 7:792–794; SW 2:692.

145. This suggests how every memory can become a dialectical image, via the similitude of past thing and present memory; and how the "recognizability" that divines the dialectical image is an instance of the mimetic faculty at work.

146. GS 2:99; SW 2:12.

147. GS 2:99f.; SW 2:13. "We, the time of things, know no time" seems to refer to an experience of something like the Bergsonian *durée*, the sense of continuity to our subjective experience that links past, present, and future seamlessly together and so negates the sense of (clock) time itself. Although important in itself, it is not necessarily so to the present analysis, except insofar as it secures one pathway back to childhood, and insofar as its interruption (by the interval) will provide another, based not on continuity but on similitude.

148. GS 2:99; SW 2:12.

149. Ibid.

150. GS 2:102; SW 2:15.

151. For these connective correspondences as themselves magical correspondences, see the essay "Über einige Motive bei Baudelaire," where the significance

of the "yearly" (*jährlich*) time of commemoration (*Eingedenken* and its association with rituals or festivities) in the correspondences is also laid out: GS 1:605–653; SW 4:333f.

152. A comparative thought to close out this section: in Keller, magic is practiced on another, and as a form of *actio in distans*; in Fontane, magic is practiced communally, on the self and others at once (as *Geselligkeit*); in Benjamin, magic is practiced on oneself, especially on one's past self, via memory as its own form of *actio in distans*.

153. "Lehre vom Ähnlichen," GS 2:206; SW 2:695; see also "Zur Astrologie," GS 6:193; SW 2:685; "Lehre vom Ähnlichen," GS 2:209; SW 2:697.

154. GS 2:140–157; SW 1:64. In his "Reflexionen zu Humboldt," this is precisely the aspect/side of language Benjamin says Humboldt overlooks: GS 6:26; SW 1:424. Seminal studies of this essay include Winfried Menninghaus, *Walter Benjamins Theorie der Sprachmagie* (Frankfurt am Main: Suhrkamp, 1980), 9–32; Peter Fenves, *Arresting Language: From Leibniz to Benjamin* (Stanford, CA: Stanford University Press, 2001), 174–248; Fenves, *The Messianic Reduction*, 125–151; Bettine Menke, "'Magie' des Lesens: Der Raum der Schrift; Über Lektüre und Konstellation in Benjamins 'Lehre[n] vom Ähnlichen'," in *Namen, Texte, Stimmen: Walter Benjamins Sprachphilosophie*, edited by Thomas Regehly and Iris Gniosdorsch, Hohenheimer Protokolle (Stuttgart: Akademie der Diözese Rottenburg-Stuttgart, 1994), 107–135.

155. Kathrin Busch, "Dingsprache und Sprachmagie: Zur Idee latenter Wirksamkeit bei Walter Benjamin," in *Politics of Translation*, eipcp Webjournal Translate, www.translate.eipcp.net (2006).

156. Benjamin, GS 2:147; SW 2:67.

157. I am tempted to say that this language of things is a "dark" one, in the Wolfian sense evoked in chapter 1 to describe *Stimmung*: below representation, but striving toward it, and so the aesthetic par excellence—and a variant of *Stimmung* itself.

158. GS 2:147; SW 2, 67. As discussed in the introduction, Benjamin formulates this in terms more clearly approaching Neoplatonism in "Der Erzähler," while still (in the word *kreatürlich*) retaining a Judeo-Christian inflection: GS 2:460–463; SW 3:159–161.

159. And knew it as good: man's subsequent knowledge, or judgment, of "good and evil" is thus fatuous or distorting, since originally and essentially it's all good.

160. Thus, Benjamin writes, "Through the word, man is bound to the language of things. The human word is the name of things"—and so, he adds, "Hence, it is no longer conceivable, as the bourgeois view of language maintains, that the word has an accidental relation to its object" (GS 2:150; SW 1:69).

161. See note 20, our delayed explication of the term *Schuldzusammenhang*. Benjamin is explicitly conflating the Fall in Eden with that of the Tower of Babel: the fall into human "knowledge" is also the fall into human "language." This is also why, Benjamin says, a mystical linguistic theory that contends the word simply is the essence of the thing is as misconceived as the bourgeois theory: it fails to recognize the loss and dislocations occasioned by the Fall.

162. GS 2:155; SW 1:73.

163. GS 2:153; SW 1:71.

164. GS 2:146; SW 1:66. Note how this contrasts with Keller, where God guarantees realism: we might say the "Fall" is one from realism as well. Revelation (*Offenbarung*) is in many ways the opposite of divination; and even in the Neoplatonists, the direct communication or revelation initiated by the divine is contrasted to the residual divine communication that can be ferreted out of the material world by natural magic.

165. This turn to ancient traditions includes, albeit more mutedly, their present forms in both occult science and ethnology.

166. GS 6:192; SW 2:684. Benjamin's reading of Ficino et al. is attested in the "Trauerspiel" book, and seem the likely source of this model. See Jane O. Newman, *Benjamin's Library* (Ithaca, NY: Cornell University Press, 2011), 163, 180.

167. GS 2:205, 206; SW 2:695.

168. As he suggests elsewhere, the first magic knowledge or reading of the world is based on a kind of *ahnen* or presentiment based on a kind of *ahmen* or imitation of the *ähnlich* or similar—a mode of reading derived from our *Ahnen* or ancestors. GS 7:795; SW 2:717: for *Ahnen*, see Hamacher, "*Wolke*."

169. This distinction between modern and ancient physiognomy was mentioned earlier in connection with fate and handwriting; see above.

170. Obviously so in the case of animals, but really no less so in the case of astrology's tracking of the movement of the planets and stars (an animation reinforced by their perceived resemblance to animals).

171. GS 2:206; SW 2:695.

172. GS 2:207; SW 2:696.

173. And not only in Benjamin, but also in Eliot and others.

174. "Die Lampe," GS 7:792; SW 2:691. See also "Der Erzähler": "Consider the story 'The Alexandrite,' which transports the reader into 'that old time when the stones in the womb of the earth and the planets at celestial heights were still concerned with the fate of men—unlike today, when both in the heavens and beneath the earth everything has grown indifferent to the fates of the sons of men, and no voice (*Stimme*) speaks to them from anywhere, let alone does their bidding'" (GS 2:43; SW 3:153). Do note how this passage suggests a link between Benjamin's notion of the "*Stimmung* concealed in [past] things" (GS 2:300; SW 2:210) and *Stimme*.

175. GS 2:205; SW 2:695.

176. Somewhat surprisingly, memory is not one of them, even though as we said earlier, he elsewhere conceives of memory as one of the primary sites for the present operation of the mimetic faculty for modern man/the present-day adult.

177. "Its magic is different . . . but equally magical" (Seine Magie ist eine andere . . . aber gleich sehr Magie, GS 2:153; SW 1:71). There is an inherent ambiguity to the idea of similitude in the mimetic faculty that makes this issue even more fraught, since similarity seemingly hesitates between identity and difference. Benjamin puzzles over some of these difficulties in the fragment "Analogie und Verwandtschaft" (GS 6:43–44; SW 1:207–209), noting in a *Vorbemerkung* how the lack of clarity in his analysis of the title's two terms stems from his failure to distinguish clearly between *Gleichheit* and *Ähnlichkeit*.

178. We might ask, does the child or the ancient diviner have an unconscious for Benjamin? To a decisive degree I would say no; also that, as for Lacan, the unconscious for him is the product of consciousness, rather than, as for the vitalists,

something that precedes it. See the essay "Franz Kafka," on the *Vorwelt* as a product of social organization (where, on the other hand, he implies everything forgotten merges: GS 2:421, 430; SW 2:803, 809f.). Perhaps the best evidence for the distinction is the line in "Zum Bilde Prousts" that states that Proust's finger points, but it cannot touch (GS 2:321; SW 2:245).

179. Sigrid Weigel, *Entstellte Ähnlichkeit: Walter Benjamins theoretischer Stil* (Frankfurt am Main: Fischer, 1997).

180. Or, similarly, how the names of man might differ from the word of God. The magic of language at stake is admittedly quite different in Benjamin from that in Fontane, in once again having no discernible interpersonal, "human" dimension and, too, in playing off not so much the semantic values of language as material ones, as in the ancient or child's world.

181. Foucault, *The Order of Things*, 43.

182. GS 2:207; SW 2:696.

183. Both Hamacher, "*Wolke*," and Linda Rugg, *Picturing Ourselves: Photography and Autobiography* (Chicago: University of Chicago Press, 1997), 133–152, illustrate this in their respective exemplary readings of *Berliner Kindheit*.

184. GS 2:209; SW 2:697.

185. For Benjamin on the special force, and fatefulness, of proper names, see "Über die Sprache" (cited in chapter 2).

186. We can also add those experiences of the child disappointed by the gap between word and thing, such as with *Pfaueninsel*, GS 7:408–409; SW 3:366.

187. Menninghaus, *Sprachmagie*, 66, also stresses the inadequacy of single words and the need for the syntagmatic for understanding Benjamin's point. For the notion of convoluted or intertwined temporality (*verschränkte Zeit*), see "Zum Bilde Prousts," GS 2:320; SW 2:244.

188. See Benjamin, "Surrealismus": "And it is as magical experiments with words, not as artistic dabbling, that we must understand the passionate phonetic and graphic transformational games that have run through the whole literature of the avant-garde for the past fifteen years" (GS 2:295–310; SW 2:212).

189. For the reference to the schoolboy and ABC book here, GS 2:209; SW 2:697.

190. For the "character" (not mentioned by Benjamin), see Collins, *Magic*, 73, 75–77.

191. GS 2:208; SW 2:697.

192. For this understanding of essence, see "Zur Astrologie," GS 6:193; SW 2:685.

193. In "Über das mimetische Vermögen," Benjamin captures both the loss and the recuperation in the word *liquidieren* (GS 2:213), which ends the essay; cf. *ergießen* in "Lehre," GS 2:205.

194. The idea of the false stakes of happiness in modern reading is sketched out in the essays "Der Erzähler" and "Zum Bilde Prousts."

195. For Proust, smell, and recovery beyond even unconscious memory, see "Zum Bilde Prousts," GS 2:323; SW 2:246f.; "Über einige Motive bei Baudelaire," GS 1:641; SW 4:335; also GS 4:115; SW 1:465. For nascent promises, cf. "Zur Astrologie," GS 6:193; SW 2:685.

196. SW 2:698.

197. From "Kurze Schatten (II)," GS 4:425f.; SW 2:699.

198. Described as happening in the ominous fullness of Zarathustra's noon, when things and their shadows are joined: GS 4:428; SW 2:702.

199. I am aware that this is in some ways the reverse or mirror image of the example just quoted.

WORKS CITED

Abennes, J. G. J., S. R. Slings, and I. Sluiter, eds. *Greek Literary Theory after Aristotle*. Amsterdam: Vrije University Press, 1995.

Abram, David. *The Spell of the Sensuous: Perception and Language in a More-Than-Human-World*. New York: Vintage, 1997.

Abrams, M. H. *Natural Supernaturalism*. New York: Norton, 1971.

Aeschylus. *Aeschyli septem quae supersunt tragoedias*. Edited by Denys Page. London: Oxford University Press, 1972.

Agamben, Giorgio. *The Open: Man and Animal*. Translated by Kevin Atell. Stanford, CA: Stanford Uuniversity Press, 2003.

Allert, Beate. "J. W. Goethe and C. G. Carus: On the Representation of Nature in Science and Art." *Goethe Yearbook* 23 (2016): 195–219.

Amberg, Andreas. "Poetik des Wassers: Theodor Fontanes *Der Stechlin*." *Zeitschrift für deutsche Philologie*, 1996, 541–559.

Anderson, Paul Irving. "Der Stechlin." In *Interpretationen: Fontanes Novellen und Romanen*, edited by Christian Grawe, 243–274. Stuttgart: Reclam, 1991.

Armstrong, Nancy. *How Novels Think: The Limits of Individualism from 1719–1900*. New York: Columbia University Press, 2006.

Attanucci, Timothy. "Atmosphärische Stimmungen: Landschaft und Meteorologies bei Carus, Goethe, und Stifter." *Zeitschrift für Germanistik*, n.s., 24, no. 2 (2014): 282–295.

Aust, Hugo, ed. *Erläuterungen und Dokumente: Theodor Fontane, Der Stechlin*. Stuttgart: Reclam, 1978.

———. "Nachwort." In *Theodor Fontane, Der Stechlin*, 459–485. Stuttgart: Reclam, 1978.

Bakhtin, M. M. "Forms of Time and of the Chronotope in the Novel." In *The Dialogic Imagination: Four Essays*, edited by Michael Holquist, translated by Caryl Emerson and Michael Holquist, 84–258. Austin: University of Texas Press, 1981.

Barlow, Derek. "Symbolism in Fontane's *Der Stechlin*." *German Life and Letters* 12 (1958/59): 282–286.

Barthes, Roland. *Camera Lucida: Reflections on Photography*. Translated by Richard Howard. New York: Hill and Wang, 1981.

———. *The Fashion System*. Translated by Matthew Ward and Richard Howard. Berkeley: University of California Press, 1983.

———. *A Lover's Discourse: Fragments*. Translated by Richard Howard. New York: Hill and Wang, 1978.

———. "The Photographic Message." In *Image/Music/Text*, translated by Stephen Heath, 15–31. New York: Noonday, 1977.

———. "The Reality Effect." In *French Literary Theory*, edited by Tzevtan Todorov, translated by R. Carter, 11–17. Cambridge: Cambridge University Press, 1982.

Bätschmann, Oskar. "Carl Gustav Carus (1789–1869): Physician, Naturalist, Painter, and Theoretician of Landscape Painting." In Carl Gustav Carus, *Nine Letters on Landscape Painting*, translated by David Britt, 1–73. Los Angeles: Getty Research Institute, 2002.

Beckmann, Martin. "Theodor Fontane's Roman 'Der Stechlin' als ästhetisches Formgefüge." *Wirkendes Wort* 39 (1989): 218–239.

Benjamin, Walter. *The Arcades Project*. Translated by Howard Eiland and Kevin McLaughlin. Cambridge, MA: Harvard University Press, 1999.

———. *Gesammelte Schriften*. Edited by Rolf Tiedemann and Hermann Schweppenhäuser. 12 vols. Frankfurt am Main: Suhrkamp, 1980.

———. *Selected Writings*. Edited by Marcus Bullock, Howard Eiland, Michael W. Jennings, et al. 4 vols. Cambridge, MA: Harvard University Press, 1996–2003.

Bennett, Jane. *Vibrant Matter: A Political Ecology of Things*. Durham, NC: Duke University Press, 2010.

Berman, Russell. *The Rise of the Modern Novel: Crisis and Charisma*. Cambridge, MA: Harvard University Press, 1986.

Blumenberg, Hans. *Theorie der Unbegrifflichkeit*. Frankfurt am Main: Suhrkamp, 2007.

———. *Vor allem Fontane: Glossen zu einem Klassiker*. Frankfurt am Main: Insel, 1998.

Brinkmann, Richard. *Wirklichkeit und Illusion: Studien über Gehalt und Grenzen des Begriffs Realismus für die erzählende Dichtung des neunzehnten Jahrhunderts*. Tübingen: Niemeyer, 1966.

Bronfen, Elisabeth. *Over Her Dead Body: Death, Femininity, and the Aesthetic*. New York: Routledge, 1992.

Brooks, Peter. "Freud's Masterplot." *Yale French Studies* 55/56 (1977): 280–300.

———. *Reading for the Plot: Design and Intention in Narrative*. Cambridge, MA: Harvard University Press, 1984.

Brown, Bill. "Thing Theory." *Critical Inquiry* 28, no.1 (2001): 1–22.

Brüggeman, Diethelm. "Fontanes Allegorien (I und II)." *Neue Rundschau* 82 (1981): 290–310, 486–505.

Büchner, Georg. *Sämtliche Werke und Briefe*. Edited by Werner R. Lehmann. Hamburg: Christian Wegner, 1967.

Busch, Kathrin. "Dingsprache und Sprachmagie: Zur Idee latenter Wirksamkeit bei Walter Benjamin." In *Politics of Translation*, eipcp Webjournal Translate, translate.eipcp.net (2006).

Carus, Carl Gustav. *Neun Briefe über Landschaftesmalerei*. Dresden: Wolfgang Jess Verlag, 195-?.

———. *Nine Letters on Landscape Painting*. Translated by David Britt. Los Angeles: Getty Research Institute, 2002.

———. *Über Lebensmagnetismus und über die magischen Wirkungen überhaupt*. Leipzig: F. A. Brockhaus, 1857.

———. *Zwölf Briefe über das Erdleben*. Edited by Ekkehart Meffert. Stuttgart: Verlag Freies Geistesleben, 1986.

Chambers, Helen Elizabeth. *Supernatural and Irrational Elements in the Works of Theodor Fontane*. Stuttgart: Hans-Dieter Heinz, 1980.

Cicero. *De divinatione*. In *Cicero, De senectute, De amicitia, De divinatione*, translated by William Armistad Falconer, 222–539. Cambridge, MA: Harvard University Press, 1992.

Coleridge, Samuel. "The Science and System of Logic." *Fraser's Magazine*, 1835, 619–629.

Collins, Derek. *Magic in the Ancient Greek World*. Malden, MA: Blackwell, 2008.

———. "Mapping the Entrails: The Practice of Greek Hepatoscopy." *American Journal of Philology* 129 (2008): 319–345.

———. "Reading the Birds: Oionomanteia in Early Epic." *Colby Quarterly* 38 (2002): 17–41.

Comenius, Johann Amos. *Orbis sensualium pictus: Hoc est omnium principalium in mundo rerum, & in vita actionum, pictura & nomenclatura*. Translated by Charles Hoole. London: S. Leacroft, 1777.

Cowan, Michael. "The Heart Machine: 'Rhythm' and Body in Weimar Film and Fritz Lang's Metropolis." *Modernism/modernity* 14, no. 2 (2007): 225–248.

Demetz, Peter. *Formen des Realismus: Theodor Fontane, Kritische Untersuchungen*. Munich: Carl Hanser Verlag, 1964.

Domenghino, Caroline. "Artist as Seer: The *Ahndung* of *Tatkraft* in Moritz's 'Über die bildende Nachahmung des Schönen'." PhD diss., Johns Hopkins University, 2011.

Downing, Eric. *Double Exposures: Repetition and Realism in Nineteenth-Century German Fiction*. Stanford, CA: Stanford University Press, 2000.

———. "Magic Reading." In *Literary Studies and the Pursuits of Reading*, edited by Eric Downing, Jonathan M. Hess, and Richard Benson, 189–215. Rochester, NY: Camden House, 2012.

Downing, Eric, Jonathan M. Hess, and Richard Benson, eds. *Literary Studies and the Pursuits of Reading*. Rochester, NY: Camden House, 2012.

During, Simon. *Modern Enchantments: The Cultural Power of Secular Magic*. Cambridge, MA: Harvard University Press, 2002.

Ehringer, Franziska. *Gesang und Stimme im Erzählwerk von Gottfried Keller, Eduard von Keyserling und Thomas Mann*. Würzburg: Königshausen & Neumann, 2004.

Eiland, Howard, and Michael Jennings. *Walter Benjamin: A Critical Life*. Cambridge, MA: Harvard University Press, 2014.

Eliot, T. S. *The Complete Poems and Plays, 1909–1950*. New York: Harcourt Brace and World, 1971.

Fenves, Peter. *Arresting Language: From Leibniz to Benjamin*. Stanford, CA: Stanford University Press, 2001.

———. *"Chatter": Language and History in Kierkegaard*. Stanford, CA: Stanford University Press, 1993.

———. *The Messianic Reduction: Walter Benjamin and the Shape of Time*. Stanford, CA: Stanford University Press, 2011.

Ferris, David, ed. *The Cambridge Companion to Walter Benjamin*. Cambridge: Cambridge University Press, 2004.

Feuerbach, Ludwig. *The Essence of Christianity*. Translated by George Eliot. New York: Harper, 1957.

———. *Lectures on the Essence of Religion*. Translated by Ralph Manheim. New York: Harper & Row, 1967.

Fineman, Joel. "The History of the Anecdote: Fiction and Fiction." In *The New Historicism*, edited by H. Aram Veeser, 49–76. New York: Routledge, 1989.

Fleming, Paul. "On the Edge of Non-Contingency: Lifeworld and Anecdotes." *Telos* 158 (Spring 2012): 21–35.

———. "The Perfect Story: Anecdote and Exemplarity in Linnaeus and Blumenberg." *Thesis 11* 104, no. 1 (2011): 72–86.

Floyd-Wilson, Mary. *Occult Knowledge, Science, and Gender in Shakespeare's Plays*. Cambridge: Cambridge University Press, 2013.

Fontane, Theodor. *Sämtliche Werke*. Edited by Walter Keitel. 22 vols. Munich: Carl Hanser Verlag, 1962.

Foucault, Michel. *History of Sexuality, Volume 1: An Introduction*. New York: Vintage, 1978.

———. *The Order of Things: An Archaeology of the Human Sciences*. New York: Vintage, 1970.

Frazer, James George. *The Golden Bough: A Study in Magic and Religion*. New York: Macmillan, 1956.

Freedgood, Elaine. *The Ideas in Things: Fugitive Meaning in the Victorian Novel*. Chicago: University of Chicago Press, 2006.

Frege, Gottlob. "On Sense and Reference." In *Translations from the Philosophical Writings of Gottlob Frege*, edited by P. Geach and M. Black, 56–79. Oxford: Blackwell, 1952.

Freud, Sigmund. "Dreams and Occultism." In *The Standard Edition of the Complete Psychological Works of Sigmund Freud*, edited and translated by James Strachey, 22:31–56. London: Hogarth Press, 1999.

———. *Totem and Tabu*. In *The Standard Edition of the Complete Psychological Works of Sigmund Freud*, edited and translated by James Strachey, 13:1–161. London: Hogarth Press, 1999.

Frevert, Ute. *Emotions in History—Lost and Found*. Budapest: Central European University Press, 2011.

Furst, Lilian R. *All Is True: The Claims and Strategies of Realist Fiction*. Durham, NC: Duke University Press, 1995.

Gaycken, Oliver. *Devices of Curiosity: Early Cinema and Popular Science*. Oxford: Oxford University Press, 2015.

Geulen, Eva. "Tales of a Collector." In *A New History of German Literature*, edited by David Wellbery et al., 587–592. Cambridge, MA: Harvard University Press, 2004.

Gisbertz, Anna-Katharina, ed. *Stimmung: Zur Wiederkehr einer ästhetischen Kategorie*. Munich: Fink Verlag, 2011.

Glausewitz, Walter. "Theodor Fontane: Heiteres Darüberstehen? . . ." *Monatshefte* 45, no. 4 (1953): 202–208.

Goethe, Johann Wolfgang. *Faust*. In *Sämtliche Werke: Briefe, Tagebücher und Gespräche*, edited by Dieter Borchmeyer et al., vol. 7. Frankfurt am Main: Deutscher Klassiker Verlag, 1985–.

Goetschel, Willi. "Causerie: Zur Funktion des Gesprächs in Fontanes *Der Stechlin*." *Germanic Review* 70 (1995): 116–122.

Goldhill, Simon. *Reading Greek Tragedy*. Cambridge: Cambridge University Press, 1986.

Goodstein, Elizabeth. *Georg Simmel and the Disciplinary Imaginary*. Stanford, CA: Stanford University Press, 2017.

Grawe, Christian. "Fontanes neues Sprachbewußtsein in *Der Stechlin*." In *Sprache in Prosawerk: Beisp. von Goethe, Fontane, Thomas Mann, Bergengruen, Kleist, und Johnson*, 38–62. Bonn: Bouvier, 1974.

Greenblatt, Stephen. *Learning to Curse: Essays on Early Modern Culture*. New York: Routledge, 1990.

———. *Marvelous Possessions: The Wonder of the New World*. Chicago: University of Chicago Press, 1991.

———. *Shakespearean Negotiations: The Circulation of Social Energy in Renaissance England*. Berkeley: University of California Press, 1988.

Gumbrecht, Hans Ulrich. *Atmosphere, Mood, Stimmung: On a Hidden Potential of Literature*, translated by Erik Butler. Stanford, CA: Stanford University Press, 2012.

Hadot, Pierre. *The Veil of Isis: An Essay on the History of the Idea of Nature*. Translated by Michael Chase. Cambridge, MA: Harvard University Press, 2006.

Hamacher, Werner. "'Jetzt': Benjamin zur historischen Zeit." *Benjamin Studien* 1 (2002): 147–183.

———. "The Word *Wolke*—If It Is One." In *Benjamin's Ground: New Readings of Walter Benjamin*, edited by Rainer Nägele, 147–176. Detroit: Wayne State University Press, 1988.

Hansen, Miriam Bratu. "Benjamin and Cinema: Not a One-Way Street." *Critical Inquiry* 25, no. 2 (1999): 306–343.

———. "Benjamin, Cinema, and Experience: 'The Blue Flower in the Land of Technology'." *New German Critique* 40 (Winter 1987): 179–224.

———. "Benjamin's Aura." *Critical Inquiry* 34, no. 2 (2008): 336–375.

———. "Room-for-Play: Benjamin's Gamble with Cinema." *October* 109 (Summer 2004): 3–45.

Hasubek, Peter. ". . . *wer am meisten red't ist der reinste Mensch": Das Gespräch in Theodor Fontanes Roman "Der Stechlin."* Berlin: Erich Schmidt Verlag, 1998.

Heidegger, Martin. "The Thing." In *Poetry, Language, and Thought*, translated by Albert Hofstadter, 161–185. New York: Harper & Row, 1971.

Hesse, Hermann. *Der Steppenwolf*. In *Sämtliche Werke*, edited by Volker Michels, 4:5–203. Frankfurt am Main: Suhrkamp, 2003.

———. *Steppenwolf*. Translated by Basil Creighton. Revised by Joseph Mileck and Horst Frenz. New York: Henry Holt, 1990.

———. "Vom Bücherlesen." In *Sämtliche Werke*, edited by Volker Michels, 14:367–372. Frankfurt am Main: Suhrkamp, 2003.

Hofmannsthal, Hugo von. "Ein Brief." In *Sämtliche Werke*, edited by Rudolf Hirsch et al., 31:45–55. Frankfurt am Main: Fischer Verlag, 1975.

———. *Der Tor und der Tod*. In *Sämtliche Werke*, edited by Rudolf Hirsch et al., 3:61–80. Frankfurt am Main: Fischer Verlag, 1975.

Hollingdale, R. J. "Introduction." In *Theodor Fontane: Before the Storm*, translated by R. J. Hollingdale. Oxford: Oxford University Press, 1985.

Holmes, Brooke. *The Tissue of the World: Sympathy and the Nature of Nature in Greco-Roman Antiquity*. Forthcoming.

Holub, Robert C. *Reflections of Realism: Paradox, Norm, and Ideology in Nineteenth-Century German Prose*. Detroit: Wayne State University Press, 1991.

Homer. *Homeri opera*. Edited by Thomas W. Allen. Oxford: Oxford University Press, 1908.

Hörisch, Jochen. "Sich in Stimmmung bringen." In *Stimmung: Zur Wiederkehr einer ästhetischen Kategorie*, edited by Anna-Katharina Gisbertz, 33–44. Munich: Fink Verlag, 2011.

Horkheimer, Max, and Theodor W. Adorno. "The Concept of Enlightenment." In *Dialectic of Enlightenment*, translated by John Cumming, 3–42. New York: Continuum, 1988.

Iamblichus. *On the Mysteries of the Egyptians, Chaldeans, and Assyrians.* Translated by Thomas Taylor. Cambridge: Cambridge University Press, 2011.

Jacoby, H. J. *Analysis of Handwriting: An Introduction into Scientific Graphology.* 2nd ed. London: George Allen and Unwin, 1948.

Jakobson, Roman. "Linguistics and Poetics." In *Literature in Language,* edited by Krytyna Pomorska and Stephen Rudy, 62–94. Cambridge, MA: Harvard University Press, 1987.

———. "On Realism in Art." In *Readings in Russian Poetics: Formalist and Structuralist Views,* edited by L. Matejka and K. Pomorska, 38–46. Cambridge, MA: MIT Press, 1971.

———. "Two Aspects of Language and Two Types of Aphasic Disturbances." In *Language and Literature,* edited by Krytyna Pomorska and Stephen Rudy, 95–119. Cambridge, MA: Harvard University Press, 1987.

James, Henry. "The Lesson of Balzac." In *The Question of Our Speech: The Lesson of Balzac; Two Lectures,* 55–116. Boston: Riverside Press, 1905.

———. "Preface to 'What Maisie Knew'." In *The Art of the Novel: Critical Prefaces,* 140–159. Chicago: University of Chicago Press, 2011.

Johnson, Barbara. *Persons and Things.* Cambridge, MA: Harvard University Press, 2008.

Jørgensen, Sven-Aage. "Nachwort." In *Theodor Fontane: Unwiederbringlich,* 287–309. Stuttgart: Reclam, 1971.

Jung, Carl G. *Psychological Types.* Edited by R. F. C. Hull. Princeton, NJ: Princeton University Press, 1971.

Kaiser, Gerhard. *Gottfried Keller: Das Gedichtete Leben.* Frankfurt am Main: Insel, 1981.

Karcic, Lucie. *Light and Darkness in Gottfried Keller's "Der Grüne Heinrich."* Bonn: Bouvier, 1976.

Keller, Gottfried. *Green Henry.* Translated by A. M. Holt. Woodstock, NY: Overlook Press, 1960.

———. *Sämtliche Werke: Historisch-kritische Ausgabe.* Edited by Walter Morgenthaler et al. 33 vols. Basel/Zurich: Stroemfeld Verlag/Verlag Neue Zürcher Zeitung, 2005.

Klages, Ludwig. *Handschrift und Charakter: Gemeinverständlicher Abriß der graphologischen Technik.* Bonn: Bouvier, 1989.

Koelb, Clayton, and Eric Downing, eds. *German Literature of the Nineteenth Century: 1832–1899.* Vol. 9 of *Camden House History of German Literature.* Rochester, NY: Camden House, 2005.

Kricker, Gottfried. *Theodor Fontane: Von seiner Art und epischen Technik.* Berlin: Bonner Forschungen, 1912.

Kuzniar, Alice. *The Birth of Homeopathy out of the Spirit of Romanticism.* Toronto: University of Toronto Press, 2017.

Levine, Michael G. *A Weak Redemptive Power: Figures of a Time to Come in Benjamin, Derrida, and Celan.* New York: Fordham University Press, 2014.

Lévy-Bruhl, Lucien. *How Natives Think.* New York: Washington Square Press, 1966.

Locher, Kaspar T. *Gottfried Keller: Welterfahrung, Wertstruktur und Stil.* Bern: Franke Verlag, 1985.

Lukács, Georg. "Der alte Fontane." *Sinn und Form* 2 (1952): 44–93.

Magianni, A. "Qualche osservazione sul fegato di Piacenza." *Studi Etruschi* 50 (1982): 53–88.

Mähl, Hans-Joachim. "Novalis und Plotin: Untersuchungen zu einer neuen Edition und Interpretation des 'Allgemeinen Brouillon'." *Jahrbuch des Freien Deutschen Hochstifts,* 1963, 139–250.

Mann, Thomas. "Der alte Fontane." In *Gesammelte Werke in Dreizehn Bänden,* 9:9–34. Frankfurt am Main: Fischer, 1990.

————. *Die Entstehung des Doktor Faustus.* In *Gesammelte Werke in Dreizehn Bänden,* 11:145–301. Frankfurt am Main: Fischer, 1990.

Menke, Bettine. "The Figure of Melusine in Fontane's Texts: Images, Digressions, and Lacunae." *Germanic Review* 79, no. 1 (2004): 41–67.

————. "'Magie' des Lesens: Der Raum der Schrift; Über Lektüre und Konstellation in Benjamins 'Lehre[n] vom Ähnlichen'." In *Namen, Texte, Stimmen: Walter Benjamins Sprachphilosophie,* edited by Thomas Regehly and Iris Gniosdorsch, 107–135. Hohenheimer Protokolle. Stuttgart: Akademie der Diözese Rottenburg-Stuttgart, 1994.

————. "Rhetorik der Echo: Echo-Trope, Figur des Nachlebens." In *Weibliche Rhetorik—Rhetorik der Weiblichkeit,* edited by Dörte Bischof and Martina Wagner-Egelhaff, 135–159. Freiburg: Rombach, 2003.

Menninghaus, Winfried. *Artistische Schrift: Studien zur Kompositionskunst Gottfried Kellers.* Frankfurt am Main: Suhrkamp, 1982.

————. *Walter Benjamins Theorie der Sprachmagie.* Frankfurt am Main: Suhrkamp, 1980.

Meyer, Conrad Ferdinand. *Sämtliche Werke.* Edited by Alfred Zach and Hans Zeller. Bern: Benteli, 1961.

Meyer-Sickendiek, Burkhard. "Über das Gespür: Neuphänomenologische Überlegungen zum Begriff der 'Stimmungslyrik'." In *Stimmung: Zur Wiederkehr einer ästhetischen Kategorie,* edited by Anna-Katharina Gisbertz, 45–62. Munich: Fink Verlag, 2011.

MhicFhionnbhairr, Andrea. *Anekdoten aus fünf Weltteilen: The Anecdote in Fontane's Fiction and Autobiography.* Bern: Lang, 1985.

Michielsen, Gertrude. *The Preparation of the Future: Techniques of Anticipation in the Novels of Theodor Fontane and Thomas Mann.* Bern: Peter Lang, 1978.

Mill, John Stuart. *A System of Logic Ratiocinative and Inductive, Being a Connected View of the Principles of Evidence and the Methods of Scientific Investigation.* In *The Collected Works of John Stuart Mill,* edited by John M. Robson, vol. 7. Toronto: University of Toronto Press, 1974.

Miller, D. A. *The Novel and the Police.* Berkeley: University of California Press, 1988.

Miller, Eric. "Die roten Fäden des roten Hahns zu einem Motivkomplex im 'Stechlin'." *Fontane Blätter* 67 (1999): 91–105.

Mitchell, W. J. T. *Landscape and Power*. Chicago: University of Chicago Press, 2002.

Müller, Martin. *Gottfried Keller: Personenlexikon zu seinem Leben und Werk*. Zurich: Chronos Verlag, 2007.

Müller-Seidel, Walter. "Theodor Fontane: *Der Stechlin*." In *Der deutsche Roman: Vom Barock bis zur Gegenwart; Struktur und Geschichte*, vol. 2, edited by Benno von Wiese. Düsseldorf: August Bagel, 1963.

Müller-Sievers, Helmut. *The Cylinder: Kinematics of the Nineteenth Century*. Stanford, CA: Stanford University Press, 2012.

Newman, Jane O. *Benjamin's Library: Modernity, Nation, and the Baroque*. Ithaca, NY: Cornell University Press, 2011.

Nietzsche, Friedrich. *Morgenröte: Gedanken über die moralischen Vorurteile*. Munich: Goldmann Verlag, 1980.

Pfau, Thomas. "The Appearance of *Stimmung*: Play as Virtual Rationality." In *Stimmung: Zur Wiederkehr einer ästhetischen Kategorie*, edited by Anna-Katharina Gisbertz, 95–111. Munich: Fink Verlag, 2011.

———. "Epochenwandel mit metaphysischen Anklängen: Metasprache und Bilderfahrung in *Der Stechlin*." *German Quarterly* 86, no. 4 (2013): 420–442.

———. "Immediacy and the Text: Friedrich Schleiermacher's Theory of Style and Interpretation." *Journal of the History of Ideas* 51, no. 1 (1990): 51–73.

———. *Romantic Moods: Paranoia, Trauma, and Melancholy, 1790–1840*. Baltimore: Johns Hopkins University Press, 2005.

Plato. *Platonis opera*. Edited by John Burnet. Oxford: Oxford University Press, 1903.

Pollmann, Inga. "Zum Fühlen gezwungen: Mechanismus und Vitalismus in Hans Richters Neuerfindung des Kinos." In *Mies van der Rohe, Richter, Graeff & Co: Alltag und Design in der Avantgardezeitschrift G*, edited by Karin Fest et al., 169–76. Vienna/Berlin: Turia + Kant, 2014.

Preisendanz, Wolfgang. *Theodor Fontane*. Darmstadt: Wissenschaftliche Buchgesellschaft, 1973.

———. "Zur Ästhetizität des Gesprächs bei Fontane." In *Das Gespräch*, edited by Karlheinz Stierle and Rainer Warning, 473–487. Munich: Fink, 1984.

Purdy, Daniel. *The Tyranny of Elegance: Consumer Cosmopolitanism in the Age of Goethe*. Baltimore: Johns Hopkins University Press, 1998.

Rabinbach, Anson. "Introduction to Walter Benjamin's 'Doctrine of the Similar'." *New German Critique* 17 (Spring 1979): 60–64.

Radecke, Gabriele, ed. *Theodor Fontane und Bernhard von Lepe: Der Briefwechsel*. Kritische Ausgabe, vol. 1. Berlin: Walter de Gruyter, 2006.

Riegl, Alois. "Die Stimmung als Inhalt der modernen Kunst." In *Alois Riegl, Gesammelte Aufsätze*, edited by K. M. Swoboda, 28–39. Augsburg/Vienna: Filser, 1929.

Roff, Sarah Ley. "Benjamin and Psychoanalysis." In *The Cambridge Companion to Walter Benjamin*, edited by David Ferris, 115–133. Cambridge: Cambridge University Press, 2004.

Roman, Klara G. *Handwriting: A Key to Personality.* New York: Pantheon, 1952.

Rousseau, Jean-Jacques. *Emile or On Education.* Translated by Alan Bloom. New York: Basic Books, 1979.

Rugg, Linda. *Picturing Ourselves: Photography and Autobiography.* Chicago: University of Chicago Press, 1997.

Rychner, Max. "Theodor Fontane: *Der Stechlin.*" In *Deutsche Romane von Grimmelshausen bis Musil,* edited by Jost Schillemeit, 218–229. Frankfurt am Main: Fischer, 1966.

Sauerbeck, Karl Otto. "Fontane und die Homöopathie." *Allgemeine Homöopathische Zeitung* 6 (2004): 273–279.

Sautermeister, Gerd. "Nachwort." In Gottfried Keller, *Der Grüne Heinrich,* 892–926. Munich: Goldmann Klassiker, 1980.

Schmitz, Hermann. "Die Stimmung einer Stadt." In *Stimmung: Zur Wiederkehr einer ästhetischen Kategorie,* edited by Anna-Katharina Gisbertz, 63–74. Munich: Fink Verlag, 2011.

Scholem, Gershom, and Theodor W. Adorno, eds. *The Correspondence of Walter Benjamin, 1910–1940.* Translated by Manfred R. Jacobson and Evelyn M. Jacobson. Chicago: University of Chicago Press, 1994.

Schwenger, Peter. *The Tears of Things: Melancholy and Physical Objects.* Minneapolis: University of Minnesota Press, 2006.

Sebeok, Thomas. *Contributions to the Doctrine of Signs.* Lisse, Netherlands: Peter de Ridder Press, 1976.

Simmel, Georg. *Grundfragen der Soziologie.* 3rd ed. Berlin: De Gruyter, 1970.

Smith, John H. "Religion and Early German Romanticism: The Finite and the Infinite." Forthcoming.

Spitzer, Leo. *Classical and Christian Ideas of World Harmony: Prolegomena to an Interpretation of the Word "Stimmung."* Edited by Anna Granville Hatcher. Baltimore: Johns Hopkins University Press, 1963.

Stafford, Barbara Maria. *Visual Analogy: Consciousness as the Art of Connecting.* Cambridge, MA: MIT Press, 1999.

Stern, J. P. *On Realism.* London: Routledge & Kegan Paul, 1973.

Stifter, Adalbert. *Werke und Briefe: Historisch-kritische Gesamtaufgabe.* Edited by Alfred Doppler and and Wolfgang Frühwald. Stuttgart: Kohlhammer, 1982.

Storm, Theodor. *Sämtliche Werke.* Edited by Albert Köster. Leipzig: Insel, 1919.

Strowick, Elisabeth, "*Die Poggenpuhls:* Fontanes Realismus der Überreste." In *Herausforderungen des Realismus: Theodor Fontanes Gesellschaftsromane,* edited by Peter Hohendahl and Ulrike Vedder. Breisgau: Rombach, forthcoming.

———. "'Schließlich ist alles bloß Verdacht': Fontane's Kunst des Findens." In *Realien der Realismus: Wissenschaft—Technik—Medien in Theodor Fontanes Erzählprosa,* edited by Stephan Braese and Anne-Kathrin Reulecke, 157–181. Berlin: Vorwerk 8, 2010.

Strowick, Elisabeth, and Ulrike Vedder, eds. *Wirklichkeit und Wahrnehmung: Neue Perspektiven auf Theodor Storm.* Bern: Peter Lang, 2013.

Struck, Peter. "Allegory, Aenigma, and Anti-Mimesis: A Struggle against Aristotelian Literary Theory." In *Greek Literary Theory after Aristotle*, edited by J. G. J. Abennes et al., 215–234. Amsterdam: Vrije University Press, 1995.

———. *Birth of the Symbol: Ancient Readers at the Limits of Their Texts.* Princeton, NJ: Princeton University Press, 2004.

Styers, Randall. *Making Magic: Religion, Magic, and Science in the Modern World.* Oxford: Oxford University Press, 2004.

Taussig, Michael. *Mimesis and Alterity: A Particular History of the Senses.* New York: Routledge, 1993.

Thomas, Christian. *Theodor Fontane: Autonomie und Telegraphie in den Gesellschaftsromanen.* Berlin: Logos Verlag, 2015.

———. "Theodor Fontane: Biologism and Fiction." *Monatshefte* 106, no. 3 (2014): 376–401.

Thomas, Kerstin. "Der Stimmungsbegriff und seine Bedeutung für die Kunst des 19. Jahrhunderts." In *Stimmung: Zur Wiederkehr einer ästhetischen Kategorie*, edited by Anna-Katharina Gisbertz, 211–234. Munich: Fink Verlag, 2011.

Türk, Johannes. *Die Immunität der Literatur.* Frankfurt am Main: Fischer, 2011.

Tylor, Edward Burnett. "Magic." In *The Encyclopaedia Britannica: A Dictionary Of Arts, Sciences, and General Literature*, 15:200–207. New York: Werner, 1896.

———. *The Origins of Culture.* Gloucester, MA: Peter Smith, 1970.

Webber, Andrew. "The Afterlife of Romanticism." In *German Literature of the Nineteenth Century: 1832–1899*, vol. 9 of *Camden House History of German Literature*, edited by Clayton Koelb and Eric Downing, 23–43. Rochester, NY: Camden House, 2005.

Weber, Maximilian. "The Nature of Charismatic Authority and Its Routinization." In *Theory of Social and Economic Organization*, translated by A. R. Anderson and Talcott Parsons. New York: Oxford University Press, 1947.

Weigel, Sigrid. *Entstellte Ähnlichkeit: Walter Benjamins theoretische Schreibweise.* Frankfurt am Main: Fischer 1997.

Wellbery, David. "Der Gestimmte Raum." In *Stimmung: Zur Wiederkehr einer ästhetischen Kategorie*, edited by Anna-Katharina Gisbertz, 157–176. Munich: Fink Verlag, 2011.

———. *Lessing's Laokoon: Semiotics and Aesthetics in the Age of Reason.* Cambridge: Cambridge University Press, 1984.

———. "Stimmung." In *Ästhetische Grundbegriffe: Historisches Wörterbuch in sieben Bänden*, edited by Karlheinz Barck et al., 703–733. Stuttgart: Metzler Verlag, 2010.

Welsh, Caroline. "Zur psychologischen Traditionslinie ästhetischer Stimmung zwischen Aufklärung und Moderne." In *Stimmung: Zur Wiederkehr einer ästhetischen Kategorie,* edited by Anna-Katharina Gisbertz, 131–156. Munich: Fink Verlag, 2011.

Wild, Christopher. "Apertio libri: Codex and Conversion." In *Literary Studies and the Pursuits of Reading,* edited by Eric Downing, Jonathan M. Hess, and Richard Benson, 17–39. Rochester, NY: Camden House, 2012.

Witte, Bernd. *Walter Benjamin: An Intellectual Biography.* Translated by James Rolleston. Detroit: Wayne State University Press, 1991.

Wolff, Kurt H., trans. and ed. *The Sociology of Georg Simmel.* Glencoe, IL: Free Press, 1923.

Wulf, Andrea. *The Invention of Nature: Alexander von Humboldt's New World.* New York: Knopf, 2015.

Wunberg, Gotthart. "Rondell und Poetensteig: Topographie und implizite Poetik in Fontanes *Stechlin.*" In *Literaturwissenschaft und Geistesgeschichte: Festschrift für Richard Brinkmann,* edited by Jürgen Brummack, 458–473. Tübingen: M. Niemeyer, 1981.

Yates, Frances A. *The Art of Memory.* Chicago: University of Chicago Press, 1966.

Ziolkowski, Theodore. "James Joyces Epiphanie und der Überwindung der empirischen Welt in der modernen deutschen Prosa." *Deutsche Vierteljahrsschrift* 35 (1961): 594–616.

———. *The Novels of Herman Hesse: A Study in Theme and Structure.* Princeton, NJ: Princeton University Press, 1965.

INDEX

Titles of works will be found under the name of the author.

ABC primers, 231, 235–38, 260
actio in distans: Benjamin and, 240,
    322n152; Fontane's *The Stechlin*
    and, 146, 310n227; Keller's *Green
    Henry* and, 38, 46, 74, 87, 91, 118,
    280n35, 290n147, 322n152
Adorno, Gretel, 314n42
Adorno, Theodor, 7, 94, 275n57
Aeschylus: *Agamemnon*, 12;
    Prometheus Bound, 8, 13
allopathy, 145, 296n49, 298n70
altertümlich, 57–58, 282n59
anecdotal narration: in Fontane's
    Before the Storm, 125–28; in
    Fontane's *The Stechlin*, 187–93
animal divination: birds (augury),
    10–12, 17, 18, 33, 215, 316n58;
    entrails (extispicy), 8–10, 11, 17,
    18, 215, 316n58

antipathy, 145, 158, 241, 278n19,
    285n87, 297n70, 298n71, 305n132,
    320n125
anxiety, 279n28
Armstrong, Nancy, *How Novels Think*,
    20–21, 22, 38, 52, 54, 275n54
associational chains. *See* chains,
    associational
augury (divinatory reading of birds),
    10–12, 17, 18, 33, 215, 316n58
Augustine (saint), 14–15, 23, 279n24,
    296n45
aura, Benjamin on, 33–34, 112,
    268, 273n73, 289n133, 319n96,
    320n131, 321n138

Balzac, Honoré de, 300n99
Barthes, Roland, 6, 20, 21, 25, 227,
    272n10, 289n138, 300n99

Baudelaire, Charles, 316n56
Befangenheit, 47, 48, 61, 280n39
Before the Storm. See Fontane,
    Theodor, *Before the Storm*
Benjamin, Walter, 2, 3, 202–69; on
    aura, 33–34, 112, 268, 273n73,
    289n133, 319n96, 320n131,
    321n138; on the baroque, 18;
    chains, associational, and, 207,
    214, 220, 237, 242, 248, 254, 258,
    260, 265, 267, 314n34; on child
    hiding (hide-and-seek), 238–50; on
    child reading, 230–38, 240, 260;
    on childhood, 224–30, 317n74;
    on the diary, 247–49; on double
    (or triple) reading, 264–65; on
    fate, 19, 209–12, 215–18, 224,
    265–67; Fontane's *The Stechlin*
    and, 239, 241, 257, 259, 264, 267,
    303–4n126, 303n124, 317n70,
    322n152, 324n180; Freud and,
    205, 209, 216–17, 225, 258, 262,
    312n4, 314–15n42, 315n47,
    316n56; on futurity, 267–68; on
    gambling, 219–24, 241, 315n52;
    on *Glück* (happiness or fortune),
    211–12, 219–20, 223–24, 229,
    247, 257, 265, 269; on graphology,
    212–19, 253, 261; on happiness and
    reading, 6, 272n10; on identificatory
    participation, 25; Jewish tradition
    against inquiring into future and,
    209, 267–68, 312n14; Keller's
    Green Henry and, 112, 219, 239,
    240–41, 247, 255, 257, 264,
    282n55, 320n123, 322n152,
    323n164; landscape and, 247–49;
    on language, 251–54, 259–64,
    266–69, 322nn160–61, 324n180;
    Lebensphilosophie and, 32, 208,
    212, 315n46; magic, preoccupation
    with, 208–9; on "meaning of life"
    (*Sinn des Lebens*) in realist works,
    147; on memory, 225–26, 229,
    241, 247, 249–50, 267, 321n145,
    322n152, 323n176; on micro/
    macro connections, 217–19, 255,

257, 315n46; D. A. Miller's revision
    of, 25; mimesis and, 6, 22, 212,
    230, 240, 244–47, 266, 320n127,
    323n177; modernist preoccupation
    with magic reading and, 202–8;
    natural world and, 313n20,
    320n125, 321n143; Neoplatonists
    and, 19, 217, 251, 254, 259, 262,
    322n158; on reading as such,
    250–69, 318n91; realism, defining,
    20; romantic influences on, 19; on
    Schuldzusammenhang (connection
    between man and nature),
    211–12, 312–13n20, 322n161; on
    Stimmung, 32–35, 225, 233–36,
    239, 241, 243, 245–47, 251,
    252, 255, 257, 289n133, 317n76,
    318–19n96, 321n138, 322n157,
    323n174; on surrealism, 1, 33,
    312n12, 315n17, 319n96, 320n131,
    324n188; *sympatheia* and, 216, 225,
    239, 241, 246–49, 254, 317n76,
    318–19n96; Taussig's reading
    of, 272–73n11; on telepathic
    phenomena, 1, 220, 312n4,
    314–15n42, 315n47, 316n62;
    on tempo and speed in reading,
    268–69; temporal involution in,
    201; on the unconscious, 258–59,
    314–15n42, 323–24n178
Benjamin, Walter, works: *Arcades
    Project (Passagen-Werk)*, 220,
    316n59, 317n69; *Berlin Childhood
    around 1900 (Berliner Kindheit um
    Neunzehnhundert)*, 227–28, 229,
    233–34, 242, 261, 318n85; *Berlin
    Chronicle (Berliner Chronik)*, 229,
    317n80, 318n83; "Child Hiding,"
    from *One-Way Street*, 238–50;
    "Child Reading," from *One-Way
    Street*, 230–38, 240; "Disorderly
    Child," from *One-Way Street*,
    244; "The Doctrine of the Similar"
    (Lehre vom Ähnlichen), 212,
    250, 253–54, 268; "Experience
    and Poverty" (Erfahrung und
    Armut), 208; "Fate and Character"

(Schicksal und Charakter), 208, 209–10, 215, 216, 217, 218, 219, 222, 223, 241, 267; "Light from Obscurantists" (Erleuchtung durch Dünkelmänner), 208; "Little History of Photography" (Kleine Geschichte der Photographie), 33–34, 226–27; "The Metaphysics of Youth" (Metaphysik der Jugend), 247; "The Mimetic Faculty" (Über das mimetische Vermögen), 212, 250; "On Astrology" (fragment), 254–56; "On the Concept of History" (Über den Begriff der Geschichte), 208, 209, 222, 229, 267; "On Language as Such and on the Language of Man" (Über die Sprache überhaupt und die Sprache des Menschen), 251–53, 254, 259, 260; *One-Way Street* (*Einbahnstraße*), 221, 229; *The Origin of German Tragic Drama* (*Ursprung des deutschen Trauerspiel*), 217, 260, 312n8, 323n166; "Pretzel, Feather, Pause, Lament, Clowning" (*Breze, Feder, Pause, Klage, Firlefanz*), 25–26; "The Storyteller" (Der Erzähler), 22–23, 24, 33, 276n73, 312n9, 313n27, 317n71, 323n174; "The Tree and Language," 268

Bergson, Henri, 239, 321n147
biblicae sortes, 14–15, 23, 230
Bildungsroman tradition: Fontane's *The Stechlin* and, 123, 148; Keller's *Green Henry* as, 3, 36, 47, 108
binding: Benjamin and, 211, 216, 225, 240–43, 245, 246, 248, 250, 255, 265; in divinatory magic and reading generally, 6, 12, 21, 23–24, 31, 32, 274n40; in Fontane's *The Stechlin*, 142–45, 147, 162, 163, 166, 169, 170, 173–78, 182, 184–88, 193, 302n121, 305n134, 306nn146–47; in Fontane's works generally, 130, 131, 137, 139, 141–42, 297n63, 297n65; Hesse

and, 203, 204; in Keller's *Green Henry*, 37, 42, 47–49, 51–55, 61–62, 64, 66–72, 74, 76, 77, 79–86, 91, 92, 94–100, 104, 108, 111, 113, 116, 284–85n77, 285n90, 288n119; *Verbindlichkeit* (sense of obligation), 160, 169–71, 173, 175, 188, 307n167, 307n170
birds, divinatory reading of (augury), 10–12, 17, 18, 33, 215, 316n58
Blumenberg, Hans, 125, 157, 158
Brooks, Peter, 6, 23–24, 272n6, 274n40
Brown, Bill, 94, 112
Brüggeman, Diethelm, 298n70
Büchner, Georg, 284n75, 286n104; *Lenz*, 292n169

Campanella, Tommaso, 236–37, 319n113
Carus, Carl Gustav, 276–77n6, 277n11, 279n29, 280n35; *Nine Letters on Landscape Painting* and *Twelve Letters on Earth-Life*, 27–28
chains, associational: Benjamin and, 207, 214, 220, 237, 242, 248, 254, 258, 260, 265, 267, 314n34; in divinatory magic and reading, 10, 16–19, 21–23, 25, 272n11, 274n40, 274n43; in Fontane's works, 124, 126, 130, 136, 144–46, 167, 177–85, 187, 188, 190, 192, 199, 293n13, 295n38, 297n65, 307n173, 308n185; in graphology, 214, 314n34; in Keller's *Green Henry*, 43, 53, 55, 72, 77, 83, 94, 99–100, 282n55; *seirai*, 16, 18, 23, 237, 307n173, 308n185
child hiding (hide-and-seek), Benjamin on, 238–50
childhood, Benjamin on, 224–30, 317n74
child reading, Benjamin on, 230–38, 240, 260
Cicero, *De divinatione*, 12, 27, 46, 280n35
Coleridge, Samuel, 7

Collins, Derek, 3, 8, 10, 15, 22, 273n17. *See also* animal divination; distributed or fractal personhood

Comenius, Johann Amos, *Orbis sensualium pictus*, 236–37, 319n113

contagion/contiguity: Benjamin on, 242; concept of, 7, 23, 272n11; in Fontane's *The Stechlin*, 164, 167, 173, 174, 177, 189, 299n147, 311n237; in Keller's *Green Henry*, 43, 74, 81, 82, 84, 112, 117, 279n22, 287n108, 290n147; of *Stimmung*, 43–45

coquetry, 165, 305–6n145

Crépieux-Jamin, Jules, 212

Dauthendey, Karl, 226–27

death of Anna in Keller's *Green Henry*, 37–38; Anna paintings and, 71, 79, 87, 91; burial, 118–20; coffin, 114–18, 288n117; contagion and, 290n147; final illness and death, 101–9; laying-out of Anna, 110–14; white rose and, 56, 71, 118, 282n56, 289n132

Demetz, Peter, 123

distributed or fractal personhood, 22, 100, 281n52, 287n108

divinatory magic and reading, 1–35; in ancient world, 8–18; binding in, 6, 12, 21, 23–24, 31, 32 (*see also* binding); distinction between, 7–8; in early modern period, 18–19; emergence of poetic realism out of romanticism, 2, 3, 29; futurity and, 2, 271n5; in German realist and modernist literature, 1–2, 19–26 (*see also* Benjamin, Walter; Fontane, Theodor; *specific entries at* Keller, Gottfried); hidden nature of, 4–5, 6, 10; shared features of, 4–7; social realism, 2, 3; sympathetic world order and concept of *Stimmung*, 2, 26–35 (see also *Stimmung*); transformation of *Naturphilosophie* into *Lebensphilosophie* and, 3, 19, 26, 27, 32; transition from realism to modernism, 2, 25–26, 32

divine providence *(Vor-sehung)*, 28–29, 78, 286n104

double (or triple) reading, Benjamin on, 264–65

During, Simon, 282n55

Echo and Narcissus in Keller's *Green Henry*, 68, 71–75, 94, 101, 112

Eiland, Howard, 313n20, 321n143

Einstein, Albert, 280n35

Eliot, T. S., 205–6, 209, 211, 226, 228; *Four Quartets*, 206; *The Wasteland*, 205, 312n5

entrail reading (extispicy), 8–10, 11, 17, 18, 215, 316n58

fate, Benjamin on, 19, 209–12, 215–18, 224, 265–67

Fenves, Peter, 125

fetishes and fetishism, 112, 274n48, 302n114

Feuerbach, Ludwig, 277n6, 286–87n104, 292n163

Fichte, Johann Gottlieb, 42

Fineman, Joel, 125

Fleming, Paul, 125, 126

Fontane, Theodor: binding in works of, 130, 131, 137, 139, 141–42, 297n63, 297n65; *Cécile*, 137–38, 296n48, 297n57, 298n79, 306n145, 311n233, 311n236; chains, associational, and, 124, 126, 130, 136, 144–46, 167, 177–85, 187, 188, 190, 192, 199, 293n13, 295n38, 297n65, 307n173, 308n185; *Delusions, Confusions (Irrungen Wirrungen)*, 137, 138, 141–42, 296n46, 305n135, 306n145; *Effi Briest*, 137, 138, 139, 296n42, 296nn45–48, 297n57; *Grete Minde*, 137, 310–11n231; *Irretrievable (Unwiederbringlich)*, 137, 139–41, 143, 295n30, 296n49, 298n70, 306n145, 311n236; Keller compared, 123, 137, 139, 143, 145, 151, 156, 157, 193,

293n6, 298n74, 298n79, 305n134, 306n159, 309n198; *L'Adultera,* 137, 139, 297n57, 297n59; opening presentation of ominous signs in works of, 124, 143; play and games in works of, 220, 305–6n145, 305n135; *Die Poggenpuhls,* 298n75; *Schach von Wuthenow,* 137, 138, 296n42, 296nn45–46; *Wanderings through the March of Brandenburg,* 122, 143. See also *Stimmung* in Fontane's works

Fontane, Theodor, *Before the Storm* (*Vor dem Sturm*), 122–36; anecdotal presentation of omens in, 125–28; characters and their reading abilities, 130–33, 140, 150–51, 296n46; metatextuality and, 133–34, 139–41, 143, 163, 177, 184, 189, 190, 193, 197, 264, 293n6, 299n83, 308n179; "nature women" in, 193; opening presentation of ominous signs in, 124, 143; play and games in, 305n135, 306n145; potential absence of supernatural world in, 159; realism and divinatory reading practices in, 135–36; role of omens, prophecies, and signs in, 123–25; trivial moments, divinatory readings of, 128–30; *Umwelt* in, 122, 129, 131, 136

Fontane, Theodor, *The Stechlin,* 2, 3, 142–201; absence of plot in, 146–48; anecdotal narration in lost election episode, 187–93; assemblage of characters in, 173, 307n162; Benjamin compared, 239, 241, 257, 259, 264, 267, 303n124, 303–4n126, 317n70, 322n152, 324n180; binding in, 142–45, 147, 162, 163, 166, 169, 170, 173–78, 182, 184–88, 193, 302n121, 305n134, 306nn146–47; centrality of witching to works of Fontane, 280n38; character psychology, description, and conversation, diminution of, 148–50; everything

as signs in, 152–61, 199–200; Freud and, 295n39, 298n79; language, central role of, 149–52, 174, 300n92, 303–4n126; micro/macro connections in, 133, 134, 140, 141, 144, 146, 172, 179, 184, 186, 189, 196, 308n175, 311n235; mimesis and, 151; opening presentation of ominous lake in, 143–46; silent restorative communion with nature in, 193–202, 310n224; small talk in, 149–50, 161, 166, 169–71, 173, 176, 177, 187, 259, 264; *Stimmung* (space) in, 168–76, 308n179; *Stimmung* (time) in Egg Cottage episode, 176–87, 3317n70; *sympatheia* and sociability in, 161–69, 239, 241, 246, 304n127, 305n132, 305n134, 305n136, 305n139, 305n142, 309n197, 318n96; *Sympathie* and *Stimmung* in, 30, 31; *Umwelt* in, 142, 144–46, 149, 160, 163, 167, 169–72, 174, 178, 179, 185, 292n2, 308n179; *Verbindlichkeit* (sense of obligation) in, 160, 169–71, 173, 175, 188, 307n167, 307n170. *See also* sociability

fortune or happiness (*Glück*), Benjamin on, 211–12, 219–20, 223–24, 229, 247, 257, 265, 269

Foucault, Michel: on antipathy and sympathy, 278n19; Benjamin and, 220, 260; Fontane's *The Stechlin* and, 200; Keller's *Green Henry* and, 38–41, 47, 54, 56, 276n3, 278n19; on language and world of things, 260; on magic and literature, 5, 18–25, 30, 276n3; *The Order of Things,* 18–19, 307n167

fractal or distributed personhood, 22, 100, 281n52, 287n108

Frazer, James G., *The Golden Bough,* 7, 9, 205, 258, 273n12, 287n108, 315n46

Freedgood, Elaine, 274n48

Frege, Gottlob, 157

Freud, Sigmund: on anxiety, 279n28; Benjamin and, 209, 216–17, 225, 258, 262, 312n4, 314–15n42, 315n47, 316n56; Brooks and, 274n40; on condensation and displacement, 7; on fetishism, 112; Fontane's work and, 95n39, 298n79; Frazer and, 273n12; Hesse influenced by, 205; Keller's *Green Henry* and, 38, 39, 41, 44, 47, 54, 56, 82, 94, 112, 283n64; magic, preoccupation with, 205; on the unconscious, 276–77n6, 277–78n11, 314–15n42

Frevert, Ute, *Emotions in History—Lost and Found*, 29, 30, 31

gambling, Benjamin on, 219–24, 241, 315n52

games and play, 219–20, 305–6n145, 305n135

Geselligkeit. See sociability

Geulen, Eva, 275n56

Glück (happiness or fortune), Benjamin on, 211–12, 219–20, 223–24, 229, 247, 257, 265, 269

Goethe, Johann Wolfgang von: Carus influenced by, 27; *Faust*, 109, 285n80; Fontane's *The Stechlin* and, 121, 301n108, 309n198; Hesse and, 203, 204; Keller's *Green Henry* and, 63–64, 67, 78, 87, 94, 101, 107, 109, 283–84nn73–75, 284–85n77, 285nn79–80, 286n104, 291n154, 291n158, 291n160, 309n198

Goetschel, Willi, 161

graphology, Benjamin on, 212–19, 253, 261

Greenblatt, Stephen, 5, 125, 272n6

Gumbrecht, Hans Ulrich, 40

Hadot, Pierre, 19, 280n35, 287n104, 291n160

Hahnemann, Samuel, 296n49

Halsstarrigkeit, 47, 51, 280n39

Hansen, Miriam, 34, 230

happiness and reading, 6, 272n10

happiness or fortune (*Glück*), Benjamin on, 211–12, 219–20, 223–24, 229, 247, 257, 265, 269

Heathen Chamber/picture of Heathen Chamber in Keller's *Green Henry*, 37, 58, 77, 79, 88–94, 96, 100, 109–11, 114, 281n43, 288n128, 292n170

hermeneutic dimension of divinatory magic and reading, 6

Hesiod, 10

Hesse, Hermann, 202–7, 211, 224–25, 230, 231, 317n73; *Glass Bead Game*, 207; "On Reading Books" (Vom Bücherlesen), 203–4; *The Steppenwolf*, 202–3, 204, 206

hide-and-seek (child hiding), Benjamin on, 238–50

Hofmannsthal, Hugo von, "Ein Brief," vii, 300nn94–95

Hölderlin, Friedrich, 241, 245

homeopathy, 5, 7, 139–41, 144–45, 196–98, 296n49

Homer, *Iliad* and *Odyssey*, 12, 14–16, 18, 25, 259, 274n43, 290n146

Horkheimer, Max, 7, 94, 275n57

Humboldt, Alexander von, 27, 278n18, 322n154

Iamblichus, 16, 287n104

Jakobson, Roman, 7, 21, 157, 295n41, 303n126

James, Henry, 174, 300n99, 307n165

Jennings, Michael W., 313n20, 321n143

Jewish tradition against inquiring into future, 209, 267–68, 312n14

Jung, C. G., 6, 205, 272n8

Kafka, Franz, 209

Keller, Gottfried: Fontane compared, 123, 137, 139, 143, 145, 151, 156, 157, 193, 293n6, 298n74, 298n79, 305n134, 306n159, 309n198; "The Ghostseer" (Der Geisterseher),

291n154; *Romeo und Julia auf dem Dorfe*, 286n99, 287n110

Keller, Gottfried, *Green Henry*, 2–3, 36–120; Anna's father in, 37, 48, 65, 68, 70, 71, 75–80, 84, 86–88, 90, 98–100, 103, 110–12, 114; Benjamin and, 112, 219, 239, 240–41, 247, 255, 257, 264, 282n55, 320n123, 322n152, 323n164; as *Bildungsroman*, 3, 36, 47, 108; binding in, 37, 42, 47–49, 51–55, 61–62, 64, 66–72, 74, 76, 77, 79–86, 91, 92, 94–100, 104, 108, 111, 113, 116, 284–85n77, 285n90, 288n119; centrality of witching to works of Keller, 280n38; chains, associational, 43, 53, 55, 72, 77, 83, 94, 99–100, 282n55; contagion/contiguity in, 43, 74, 81, 82, 84, 112, 117, 279n22, 287n108, 290n147; dead father of Heinrich Lee in, 59, 60, 61, 64, 65; disenchantment in, 36–37, 101–2; figure of Anna in, 67–76; flower-bouquet painting, 79–88, 90, 94, 98, 99; Foucauldian approach to, 38–41, 47, 54, 56, 276n3, 278n19; Freudian approach to, 38, 39, 41, 44, 47, 54, 56, 82, 94, 112, 276–77n6, 277–78n11, 279n28, 283n64; Goethe and, 63–64, 67, 78, 87, 94, 101, 107, 109, 283–84nn73–75, 284–85n77, 285nn79–80, 286n104, 291n158, 291n160, 309n198; Heathen Chamber/picture of Heathen Chamber, 37, 58, 77, 79, 88–94, 96, 100, 109–11, 114, 281n43, 288n128, 292n170; landscape and landscape painting in, 29, 36, 37–38, 40, 45–46, 56–67, 68, 78, 91–93, 97, 105, 107; magical realism in, 76–79; on memory, 42, 95, 96, 110, 286n99; metatextuality and, 48, 49, 54, 56, 64, 70, 72, 73, 88, 90, 91, 95, 104, 264, 282n55, 285n79; micro/macro connections in, 41–42, 72, 92, 97, 105, 114, 116; music in, 40, 43, 48, 57, 59, 73, 75, 97–98, 107, 113–14, 117, 118, 284n77, 286n99, 292n170; Narcissus and Echo in, 68, 71–75, 94, 101, 112; objects, objectivity, and Anna, 110–20, 281n53, 289n136, 289n138; portrait of Anna in, 94–101; Römer and Judith in, 101–9, 291n158, 291n160; "Story of My Youth" (*Jugendgeschichte*), focus on, 37–38; *sympatheia* and *Stimmung* in, 239, 241, 318n96. *See also* death of Anna in Keller's *Green Henry*; Meretlein in Keller's *Green Henry*, painting and story of; *Stimmung* in Keller's *Green Henry*

Kierkegaard, Søren, 149

Klages, Ludwig, 212, 213, 215, 216, 239, 261

kledonomancy (divinatory reading of chance works and coincidences), 8, 13–16, 27, 356

Lacan, Jacques, 6, 283n64, 323–24n178

landscape and landscape painting: Benjamin and, 247–49; in Keller's *Green Henry*, 29, 36, 37–38, 40, 45–46, 56–67, 68, 78, 91–93, 97, 105, 107; music and, 73, 97–98, 107; *Stimmung*, concept of, 27–29, 45–46, 58, 59, 60, 62–64, 91–94, 294–95n25

language: Benjamin, "On Language as Such and on the Language of Man" (*Über die Sprache überhaupt und die Sprache des Menschen*), 251–53, 254, 259, 260; Benjamin on, 251–54, 259–64, 266–69, 322nn160–61, 324n180; centrality of, in Fontane's *The Stechlin*, 149–52, 174, 300n92, 303–4n126; character psychology, description, and conversation, diminution of, in Fontane's *The Stechlin*, 148–50; Foucault on language and world of

language *(continued)*
  things, 260; small talk in Fontane's
    The Stechlin, 149–50, 161, 166,
    169–71, 173, 176, 177, 187,
    259, 264
Lebensphilosophie, 3, 32, 164, 201,
    208, 212, 218, 315n46
Leskov, Nikolai, 33
Lévy-Bruhl, Lucien, 6, 22, 272n8
Liebenstoeckl, Hans, *The Occult
    Sciences in the Light of Our
    Age*, 208
liver, divinatory reading of, 8–10, 11
locus amoenus, 37
Lotze, Hermann, *Mikrokosmos*, 144

magic, divinatory. *See* divinatory magic
    and reading
magic idealism, 19
Mann, Thomas, 121, 206–7, 300n92;
    Doktor Faustus, 207, 312n8; *The
    Magic Mountain*, 206–7; *Mario and
    the Magician*, 207
Marx, Karl, and Marxism, 112, 209,
    274n48
memory: Benjamin on, 225–26, 229,
    241, 247, 249–50, 267, 321n145,
    322n152, 323n176; Keller's *Green
    Henry* on, 42, 95, 96, 110, 286n99
Mendelssohn, Anja and Georg,
    215–16
Menninghaus, Winfried, 324n187
Meretlein in Keller's *Green Henry*,
    painting and story of: afterlife of,
    291n155; as analogue for all women
    in novel, 280–81n40; analysis of,
    46–56; Anna paintings and, 80–83,
    85–88, 90, 91, 93, 97, 100, 101;
    Benjamin and, 241, 243, 245, 255,
    320n123; coffin in, 292n173; figure
    of Anna and, 68, 71, 73, 287n109,
    288n112, 289n132, 290n149;
    framing of, 288n112, 290n145;
    illness and death of Anna and,
    104, 108; landscape painting in
    Green Henry and, 56–58, 64–67;
    latter-day equivalents of children

following, 281n48; magic realism
    and, 77; natural/artificial qualities
    of magic and, 282n55; objects,
    objectivity, and Anna, 113, 114,
    118, 119; omen-esque quality of,
    281n43; painting associated with
    Bildung and death by, 283n66;
    pastor's aside on, 281n42
metatextuality: Benjamin and, 264;
    of divinatory magic and reading
    generally, 5, 29–30; Fontane's *The
    Stechlin* and, 133–34, 139–41, 143,
    163, 177, 184, 189, 190, 193, 197,
    264, 293n6, 299n83, 308n179;
    Hesse and, 203; Keller's *Green
    Henry* and, 48, 49, 54, 56, 64, 70,
    72, 73, 88, 90, 91, 95, 104, 264,
    282n55, 285n79
Meyer-Sickendiek, Burkhard, 41
Michon, Jean-Hippolyte, 212
micro/macro connections: Benjamin
    and, 217–19, 255, 257, 315n46;
    in divinatory magic and reading,
    9–10, 17, 19, 25, 27, 30, 31; in
    Fontane's *The Stechlin*, 133, 134,
    140, 141, 144, 146, 172, 179, 184,
    186, 189, 196, 308n175, 311n235;
    in Keller's *Green Henry*, 41–42, 72,
    92, 97, 105, 114, 116; *sympatheia*
    as mediating, 315n46
Mill, John Stuart, 157
Miller, D. A., 25
mimesis: Benjamin and, 6, 22, 212,
    230, 240, 244–47, 266, 320n127,
    323n177; Fontane's *The Stechlin*
    and, 151; Taussig on, 282–83n62,
    285n79
Mitchell, W. J. T., 279n29
modernism, 1–4, 202–8, 276n3. *See
    also* Benjamin, Walter; divinatory
    magic and reading
music: in Keller's *Green Henry*, 40,
    43, 48, 57, 59, 73, 75, 97–98, 107,
    113–14, 117, 118, 284n77, 286n99,
    292n170; in Keller's *Romeo und
    Julia auf dem Dorfe*, 286n99;
    landscape painting and, 73, 97–98,

107; Ravel's musical mnemonics, 273n29; *Stimmung* and, 27, 40, 46, 277n10, 279n24, 286n99
mystical participation, 6, 28, 31, 45, 230, 272n8, 278n17, 307n162

names, connotations of, 158–59, 261, 302n121, 324n180, 324n185
Narcissus and Echo in Keller's *Green Henry,* 68, 71–75, 94, 101, 112
Naturphilosophie, 3, 19, 26, 27, 32, 139, 278n16, 291n160
Neoplatonists and Neoplatonism: Barthes and, 289n138; Benjamin and, 217, 251, 254, 259, 262, 322n158; magic reading practices of, 16–18, 296n45; natural magic and, 287n104; Orphic tradition and, 291n160; Plato's irony and, 274n43; revelation for, 323n164; romantics influenced by, 19, 26; Schelling's *Naturphilosophie* and, 278n16; on *seirai,* 16, 18, 307n173, 308n185; *Stimmung* and, 43, 308n179; on *sympatheia,* 9, 32, 165, 296n49, 315n46
Nietzsche, Friedrich, 280n36
Novalis, 19

objects and object relations, 110–20, 274n48, 281n53, 289n136, 289n138, 300n99
occasionality of magic reading, 24
Oedipal fantasy, 13, 286n102, 291n160
onomatopoeia, 263
Orphic tradition, 287n104, 291n154, 291n160
Overbeck, Friedrich, 285n85

Pfau, Thomas, 40
photography, 33–34, 226–27, 242, 300n99
Piacenza model liver, 9–10
Plato, *Ion,* 18, 274n43
play and games, 219–20, 305–6n145, 305n135

practice, reading as, 25
Proclus, 16
Proust, Marcel, 201, 207, 225, 267, 321n139, 324n178, 324n195
Pseudo-Plutarch, *Life of Homer,* 14
Pulver, Max, 315n42
punctum, 227
Puri, Michael, 273n29

Raabe, Wilhelm, 276n3, 298n74
Ravel's musical mnemonics, 273n29
reading and magic. *See* divinatory magic and reading
realism, 1–4. *See also* divinatory magic and reading; Fontane, Theodor; Keller, Gottfried
retrospection, 23–24
Reynolds, Joshua, 52
Riegl, Alois, 45, 93, 94, 283n65, 288n130
Rilke, Rainer Maria, 277n9, 281n46
romanticism: emergence of poetic realism out of, 2, 3, 29; magical sensibility and, 276n3; Neoplatonism and, 19, 315n46; on sympathy, 315n46
Rousseau, *Emile or On Education,* 275n56
Ruhe in Bewegung (stillness in motion), 63–65

Saudek, Robert, 214
Schelling, Friedrich, and *Naturphilosophie,* 19, 27, 278n16, 291n160
Schiller, *William Tell,* 91, 93
Schlegel, Friedrich, 317n77
Schmitz, Hermann, 278n13
Schuldzusammenhang (connection between man and nature), Benjamin on, 211–12, 312–13n20, 322n161
seirai, 16, 18, 23, 237, 307n173, 308n185
silence in Fontane's *The Stechlin,* 193–202, 310n224
Simmel, Georg: Benjamin and, 234, 254, 255, 264; on coquetry,

Simmel, Georg *(continued)*
306n145; Fontane's *The Stechlin*
and, 161–70, 172–74, 176, 177,
180, 186, 187, 200, 304n129;
on sociability and *sympatheia*,
31, 161–70, 298n79, 304n128,
305n132, 305n139, 305n142,
306n146
small talk in Fontane's *The Stechlin*,
149–50, 161, 166, 169–71, 173,
176, 177, 187, 259, 264
Smith, Adam, 22
sociability (*Geselligkeit*): anecdotal
narration in Fontane's *The Stechlin*
and, 187–88; coquetry and,
306n145; as magic, in Fontane's
The Stechlin, 322n152; Simmel's
concept of, 31, 161–68; small talk
in Fontane's *The Stechlin* and,
149–50, 161, 166, 169–71, 173,
176, 177, 187, 259, 264; *Stimmung*
(space) in Fontane's *The Stechlin*
and, 176–87, 3317n70; *Stimmung*
(time) in Fontane's *The Stechlin* and,
176–87; *sympatheia* in Fontane's
The Stechlin and, 161–69, 239, 241,
246, 304n127, 305n132, 305n134,
305n136, 305n139, 305n142,
309n197
Sophocles, *Elektra* and *Oedipus
Tyrannos*, 13
sortes, 25
Spitzer, Leo, 26, 40, 279n24, 280n35
Stafford, Barbara, 32
Stechlin, The. See Fontane, Theodor,
The Stechlin
Stifter, Adalbert, 284n75, 286n104,
298n74; *Granit*, 300n94, 307n175;
Der Hochwald, 285n97; *Der
Nachsommer (Indian Summer)*, 36,
275n56
stillness in motion *(Ruhe in
Bewegung)*, 63–65
Stimmung, 26–35; as activity,
279–80n32; anxiety and, 279n28;
aura as, 33–34, 112, 268, 273n73,
289n133, 319n96, 320n131,
321n138; Benjamin and, 32–35,

225, 233–36, 239, 241, 243,
245–47, 251, 252, 255, 257,
289n133, 317n76, 318–19n96,
321n138, 322n157, 323n174;
contagion/contiguity of, 43–45; as
energeia or *Tatkraft*, 46; *Geselligkeit*
(sociability) and, 31, 161, 162,
168, 176, 241, 307n175, 322n152;
hidden quality of magic and, 28–29,
31, 33, 44; landscape/landscape
painting and, 27–29, 45–46, 58,
59, 60, 62–64, 91–94, 294–95n25;
in late eighteenth-century
theory, 277–78n11; music and,
27, 40, 46, 277n10, 279n24,
286n99; Neoplatonists and, 43,
308n179; no subject-object or
inner-outer distinction in, 278n17;
nonpsychological, external nature
of, 278n13; preconceptual nature
of, 41; relational nature of, 41–43;
temporality and, 44–45; Wellbery
on, 40–46
Stimmung in Fontane's works,
192–94; anecdotal narration in lost
election episode of *The Stechlin*
and, 187–89; Keller's *Green Henry*
compared, 122, 139, 145; in
opening of *The Stechlin*, 145–46;
role of language in *The Stechlin*
and, 151; *Stimmung* (space) in
The Stechlin, 168–76, 308n179;
Stimmung (time) in *The Stechlin*,
176–87; *sympatheia* and sociability
in *The Stechlin*, 164, 165, 239,
318n96; *Sympathie* and *Stimmung*,
30, 31
Stimmung in Keller's *Green Henry*:
Anna paintings and, 84, 85, 91–94,
97; associations of, 277n10; concept
of, 29, 40–46; figure of Anna
and, 72–75, 78; Fontane's works
compared, 122, 139, 145; as goal,
241; landscape painting and, 45–46,
58, 59, 60, 62–64, 107; Meretlein,
painting and story of, 46–50, 55,
56; objects, objectivity, and Anna,
110, 112–16, 118, 120, 289n136,

289n138; *sympatheia* and, 239, 241, 318n96

Stimmungslyrik, 277n9

Stoics, 9, 17, 315n46, 496n49

Storm, Theodor, 40, 276n3, 277n9, 280n38, 298n74; *Aquis submersus*, 281n45, 292n169

Struck, Peter, 3, 16, 274n33. *See also* Neoplatonists and Neoplatonism, *subhead* magic reading practices of; *symbola*

Sulzer, Johann, 283n65

surrealism, 1, 26, 33, 207, 312n12, 315n17, 319n96, 320n131, 324n188

symbola, 14, 16–18, 274n33

sympatheia: Benjamin and, 216, 225, 239, 241, 246–49, 254, 317n76, 318–19n96; in divinatory magic and reading, 9, 16, 17, 26–28, 31–35; Neoplatonists on, 9, 32, 165, 296n49, 315n46; sociability and, in Fontane's *The Stechlin*, 161–69, 239, 241, 304n127, 305n132, 305n134, 305n136, 305n139, 305n142, 309n197, 318n96; *Stimmung* and, in Keller's *Green Henry*, 239, 241, 318n96

sympathetic magic, concept of, 7, 315n46

sympathetic world order, 2, 4, 26–35, 208, 225, 312n9

Sympathie, 26, 29–32, 141, 175, 277n10, 280n35, 302n121

sympathy, romantic notion of, 315n46

Taussig, Michael, 272–73n11, 275n57, 282–83n62, 285n79, 294n16

telepathic phenomena, Benjamin and Freud on, 1, 220, 312n4, 314–15n42, 315n47, 316n62

temporality: Fontane's *The Stechlin*, *Stimmung* (time) in, 176–87; in realist literature, 22–24; *Stimmung* and, 44–45

thing versus object, 289n136

Tylor, E. B., *The Origins of Culture*, 7, 128, 205, 274n33, 305n135, 315n51

Umwelt: Benjamin and, 240, 242, 246; defined, 122, 292n1; in Fontane's *Before the Storm*, 122, 129, 131, 136; in Fontane's *The Stechlin*, 137, 138, 142, 144–46, 149, 160, 163, 167, 169–72, 174, 178, 179, 185, 308n179; as foreground versus background, 292n2; Hesse and, 204; importance in Fontane's novels, 122

unconscious, the, 258–59, 276–77n6, 277–78n11, 314–15n42, 323–24n178

Verbindlichkeit (sense of obligation), in Fontane's *The Stechlin*, 160, 169–71, 173, 175, 188, 307n167, 307n170

Verstocktheit, 47, 280n39

Virgil, *Aeneid*, 12–13

vitalism, 32, 164, 201, 205, 213, 230nn124–25, 239, 259, 279n28, 289n138, 300n95, 320n121, 323–24n178

Vorbild, 60, 68, 87–88, 282n57, 283n71, 283n74

Vorbilder. *See* landscape painting

Vor-sehung (divine providence), 28–29, 78, 286n104

Weber, Max, 174, 304n128

Weigel, Sigrid, 259

Wellbery, David: on divinatory magic and reading, 29, 30, 31; Fontane's *The Stechlin* and, 177; Goethe and, 284n77; Keller's *Green Henry* and, 40–45, 94, 107, 277n7, 279–80n32, 279n26, 279n28, 284n77; on Rilke, 281n46; on *Stimmung*, 40–46

Welsh, Caroline, 277–78n11

Wundt, Wilhelm, 213

Ziolkowski, Theodore, 203

CPSIA information can be obtained
at www.ICGtesting.com
Printed in the USA
FFOW02n0326050318
45383598-46067FF